MANAGING PENSION PLANS

Financial Management Association Survey and Synthesis Series

MANAGING PENSION PLANS

A Comprehensive Guide to Improving Plan Performance

Dennis E. Logue
Jack S. Rader

Harvard Business School Press
Boston, Massachusetts

01 00 99 98 97   5 4 3 2 1

Logue, Dennis E.
    Managing pension plans : a comprehensive guide to improving plan
performance / Dennis E. Logue, Jack S. Rader
        p.   cm. -- (Financial Management Association survey and
synthesis series)
    Includes index.
    ISBN 0-87584-791-9 (alk. paper)
    1. Pension trusts--United States--Management. 2. Pension trusts-
-United States--Investments.   I. Rader, Jack S., 1949-
II. Title.   III. Series.
HD7105.45.U6L633 1997
332.67'254--dc21   97-25803
                                                                                        CIP

The paper used in this publication meets the requirements of the
American National Standard for Permanence of Paper for Printed Library
Materials Z39.49-1984

Contents

Introduction

The Context of Pension Plan Management

The U.S. population is getting older. The number of people aged 60 and over, though currently below 20% of the total population, will rise to 30% by 2030, barring any radical change in immigration policy. The ratio of people of working age to those who are retired is currently 5 to 1 but will be closer to 3 to 1 in 50 years, as reported by Beck. According to a 1994 survey reported in *The Economist* (1996, S8), "80% of Americans of working age felt 'not too confident' or 'not at all confident' that Social Security would provide them with the same benefits as today's pensioners."

The nature of work in the United States also is changing. Manufacturing has become less important and the service and technology sectors have increased greatly in importance. At the same time, private- and public-sector pension funds have grown rapidly in terms of assets, ownership of capital stock, and importance in the financial markets. It is to these pension schemes that American workers will be looking to supplement or provide the bulk of their retirement assets and incomes for the 20 to 30 years a retiree at the age of 65 normally might expect to live. These changes are fundamental. They have important implications for the nature of and preferences of the workforce and, as a result, for pension plan desirability and design and pension asset management.

What parties are affected by pension funds and the demographics of an aging population? A partial list would include employees and their families who are receiving or will be receiving retirement benefits. The employers in both the private sector and public sector who are the sponsors of these plans are affected, because the plans they offer and the manner in which they manage these plans will bear directly on the success of the organization. Further, employer stakeholders—shareholders for private companies and taxpayers for public plans—have an interest in pension funds and their management, as do the unions that represent employees. Finally, the nation's policymakers—corporate senior managements and boards of directors, public-sector officials and public pension boards, and lawmakers—are all involved either as plan sponsors, employees who will benefit, and/or policymakers who can affect the shape and health of the American pension system in the years to come.

Pension plan management is viewed by some merely as investment management. If only the world were this simple! Although investment principles and decision-making tenets are certainly important, there are numerous other factors that are just as important or that shape the nature of the pension investment process. This book offers a comprehensive framework within which the factors that are unique to pension management can be combined with sound investment management. We hope to accomplish two goals: to demonstrate how important it is to manage a pension plan with regard to the special relationship between the plan and the sponsoring organization, whether public or private; and to show that the complexities unique to pension fund decision making must be addressed in their entirety rather than as isolated elements of a whole never quite seen.

U.S. pension funds come in a variety of forms. The basic dichotomy is that of defined benefit plans and defined contribution plans. These necessarily form the basis for much of the discussion in this book, but by no means exhaust the potential types of plans that are available. Combined "floor" plans, cash balance plans, and other hybrid structures offer important alternatives. Thus, to understand the various structures available to sponsors, the first chapter of this book asks why pension plans are desirable at all. The discussion examines the basic functions of pension plans: providing retirement assets and/or income by sharing tax, insurance, and investment efficiencies; attracting competent employees and motivating desirable employee behavior; and serving as a more or less desirable form of compensation. Chapter 2 extends this discussion by showing how different plan structures may prove superior for different organizations and explaining how organizations should choose the structure that is best for them.

Pension plan management is legally and perhaps morally unique in that it is a relationship of trust that carries with it a fiduciary responsibility to use care, be diligent, and be loyal to plan beneficiaries (who are generally the employees of the sponsor). Although the statutory standards for public and private pensions often differ substantially, the special relationship of trust is both instructive and constraining in determining what is good pension management. These issues are raised for the first time in Chapter 3 and are woven throughout the remainder of the book.

Every pension plan should have in place well thought-out, comprehensive policies that govern the management of the plan and guide decision making. Pension plans do not exist in a vacuum. The pension plan itself is inexorably linked to the sponsoring organization. It is the sponsor that determines the nature of the pension liability to be funded and how the pension scheme fits within the overall compensation structure of the organization. Sponsors do not operate as they please, however. Plan structures and the contracts that create plan liabilities are subject to the forces that govern the labor market and the nature of the contracting between employers and employees. The specific structure chosen for the plan and the contracts that define the nature of the plan liability in turn affect the economics of pension asset management. With this as the foundation, Chapter 4 explains the central elements of pension investment policy and shows how policy statements should be structured to provide sufficient coverage of key issues as well as the flexibility to adapt to dynamic change.

One of the core competencies of a pension fund, whether it is a defined benefit plan managing a large pool of assets or an employee-directed defined contribution plan with a large number of small asset pools, is the fund's investment activities. Of all the investment questions that should be asked, the most important question is: What is the most appropriate long-term asset allocation? This question leads to several others: What assets are appropriate investments? How should the asset allocation be set? How should the allocation be changed in response to changes in the financial markets, if indeed it should be changed at all? Chapter 5 answers these questions by drawing on the insights offered by modern investment theory and practice. Additionally, the chapter describes alternative asset allocation strategies of value in managing plan assets. Chapter 6 focuses on how the strategic asset allocation should be made and what issues must be resolved before a decision is reached. Because of the complexity of this decision, an analytical approach to setting the strategic asset allocation is presented.

Chapters 7 and 8 extend the discussion in the previous chapters by examining the evidence available on actual pension plan investment performance and the factors that contribute to many pension funds' historically poor performance. Chapter 7 explains how pension plan performance should be measured and discusses the questions that must be answered if the analyst is to gain useful insights into how a pension's asset pool has performed. Chapter 8 explains the uses and limitations of performance evaluation and offers several suggestions for improving future investment performance.

Risk and risk management are the focus of Chapters 9 and 10. Managing investment risk is difficult for any organization. Pension funds, however, face a number of risks that are not addressed by the traditional approaches to controlling risk. Rather, those who are involved in pension risk management must understand a number of complex factors, including the impact of surplus volatility on plan health, the difference between hedging and return enhancement strategies, the emerging measurement technologies of value at risk and stress analysis, and the prudent use of derivatives.

An important aspect of pension plan policy is how the managers of investment portfolios should be managed. Should the plan use internal managers or look outside for investment expertise? What pitfalls exist in managing managers? What is the best way to monitor the plan's managers and to ensure that the costs of investment management are reasonable? Chapter 11 discusses the parameters of the manager selection decision and offers insight into the nature of investment costs and the impact of the use of soft dollars and directed commissions by the plan sponsor.

Accounting for pensions is not strictly a management issue, but its role in informing decision makers and the potential it creates for harmful consequences when the users of this data do not understand the differences between accounting data and the underlying economic reality of the plan are of critical importance. Those who manage pension plans must understand the complexity of accounting rules for pension reporting and must also realize that pension accounting relies on subjective judgment. This latter aspect often leads to some rather perverse consequences. Chapter 12 describes the fundamental accounting issues that everyone involved in pension management should understand, and shows how misunderstanding the accounting data may lead to suboptimal decisions.

Chapter 13 explains how pension funds can and should act as shareholders and the role pension plans should take in corporate governance activities. These are difficult issues in that these activities have avid proponents and equally avid opponents. They are not unimportant, however, to completing the pension management paradigm in that they have the potential to shape significantly the future of both plan performance and corporate management in the twenty-first century.

The final chapter presents a summary of the material in the main body of the book. It serves to clarify and put into context the points of view endorsed by the authors on the issues addressed. After Chapter

14 are appendixes that extend the discussion of various issues raised in the main text.

This book will be of interest to all who come in close contact with public and private pension plans. Chief financial officers, of course, should find it of interest. Pension plan administrators, investment managers, consultants, and members of corporate boards of directors and public pension trustees will also find much of value here, as will pension actuaries, accountants, and even those who comment on the pension scene for one reason or another. Some of the material may seem a bit challenging for those who are not trained in economics or finance. Nonetheless, pension fund management is challenging, but we hope the analysis is not excessively daunting. Where we have had to assume a level of technical expertise that some readers may not have (for example, in discussing risk management and the proper use of derivatives) in order to put the germane issues on the table, we did so knowing that there are other resources available to the interested reader. We ask your understanding: pension management is not easy, so the topics do not always lend themselves to simple assertions or rules of thumb.

This book, then, hopes to be instructive for the reader by identifying the issues that are central to successful pension plan management and suggesting ways to improve pension performance, however defined. We hope you will find it of interest; more importantly, we hope you will find it of use.

We are grateful to the many readers who offered helpful and constructive criticism on the early drafts of this book. These include Rebecca Warren of Cambridge Associates, Roger Murray of Columbia University (Emeritus), Charles Elson of Stetson University Law School, and several others who remain anonymous. Thanks also to Marjorie Williams and Kirsten Sandberg of Harvard Business School Press for all their assistance and support. And not least of all to Marcella Logue and Mary Rader for their patience and tolerance.

MANAGING PENSION PLANS

Chapter **1**

Why Have Pension Plans at All?

Pension Plans for Organizations and Employees: Basics

Pension plans are employee benefit plans established to provide retirement benefits to employees. There are three kinds of plan sponsors: (1) employers, such as a business or government; (2) employee organizations, such as a union; and (3) a combination of two or more employers, and one or more employee organizations. Because plan sponsors are a heterogeneous group with different interests and needs, they structure and manage their plans differently.

Plans can be public (generally taken to represent federal, state, and local government employees) or private (generally businesses). This is an important distinction because there are two significant differences between public and private plans. First, sponsors of public plans receive no tax deduction since they pay no taxes (although participants in public plans receive favorable tax treatment on their pension savings and investment). Second, public plans are not covered under the Employee Retirement Income Security Act (ERISA). Thus, unlike private plans, they have no mandated funding standards or explicitly stated fiduciary responsibilities. Also, their beneficiaries are not protected by the Pension Benefits Guaranty Corporation (PBGC).

Single-employer plans may be public or private. Their assets may be managed by the sponsor or the employee beneficiary. Multi-employer plans, however, are administered by unions. These plans collect contributions from many employers (e.g., trucking employers contributing to the Teamsters Benefit Fund). Multiemployer plans are sponsored and regulated under the Taft-Hartley Act. Among the more important characteristics of these plans are the requirement that unions share control with management, and that such plans frequently make lump-sum payouts to beneficiaries at retirement. This latter characteristic is becoming increasingly important as growing numbers of people reach retirement age.

Pension plans in the United States have a long history. In 1636, the Plymouth Colony settlers' military retirement plan was established; in 1797, Gallatin Glassworks established a profit-sharing plan, according to the *Employee Benefits Research Institute Databook on Employee Benefits*. The first fully documented pension plan was established in 1859 by the Corporation for the Relief of Poor and Distressed Presbyterian Ministers and for the Poor and Distressed Widows and Children of Presbyterian Ministers. In 1875, the American Express Company set up the first employer-sponsored plan in the United States; benefits were to equal 50% of the average pay over the final ten years of employment, but not more than $500 annually (Hewitt Associates, 1976).

Pension plans have grown immensely from these humble beginnings. According to a report by the Employee Benefit Research Institute (EBRI), at the end of 1993 nearly 51 million public and private sector employees were covered by pension plans. Total private pension fund assets stood at roughly $2.5 trillion and public plan assets stood at $1.4 trillion; union plan assets, which are included in private pension assets, totaled roughly $300 billion. If present trends continue, total pension plan assets could easily reach $7 trillion by the turn of the century.

Not only is the total dollar value of assets huge, but every year more contributions are added to the pool. In 1993, for instance, total contributions to both public and private pension plans approximated $155 billion, or roughly 4% of total payroll costs. Private employer contributions in 1993 have been estimated at 2.9% of payroll; the contributions from public plan sponsors have been estimated at 16.1%. Employer contributions in 1993 exceeded more than $100 billion. Total benefits paid by private and public plans in 1993 totaled $319 billion, according to the *EBRI Databook on Employee Benefits*.

Public plans, although not subject to ERISA and the full-funding rules that private sponsors are, typically offer higher benefits. Part of the reason is that because nearly 30% of state and local government employees are not covered by Social Security, these employees receive the bulk of their retirement benefits from their pension plans. Thus, government entities need to compensate for the difference to remain competitive in the employment marketplace.

Pension plans come in several forms and have a variety of features. From the employer's perspective, however, it is not always obvious why pension plans are desirable. Why should employers offer pensions? Do employees value pensions? Do employees behave differently in organizations that offer pension plans? If so, what types of plans are most likely to achieve the sponsor's behavior goals? These are not easy questions to answer, but they are important to consider before any meaningful paradigm of pension plan management can be developed. Similarly, since the structure of any particular pension plan should ideally meet the needs of both the sponsoring organization and its employees, it is necessary that those individuals involved in decision making understand the alternatives available—the types of plans and the features of each—and the way different pension schemes may accomplish different objectives.

Motivations for Pension Plans

Pension plan management begins by asking why pension plans are desirable. After all, many people are covered by Social Security and anyone may save and invest independently to meet the need for post-retirement income.

Some authorities, such as Mark Roe writing in 1995, have suggested that the prominence of today's pension funds is partially due to increasing wealth, life spans, and preference for early retirement coupled with a reduced willingness of the currently employed generation to care for the previous generation. This perspective, although of interest in terms of economic policy, gives little guidance to prospective plan sponsors or to those organizations that already have pension plans.

Zvi Bodie's 1990 analysis offers sponsors and potential sponsors a useful way to think about the desirability of pensions in the aggregate by suggesting that pensions are a convenient way to provide insurance to individuals who are concerned about the uncertainty of retirement income. He identifies five sources of retirement income risk:

- The risk of the rate of wage replacement
- Longevity risk
- The risk that Social Security will be cut

- The risk that investment returns on savings will not be adequate
- Inflation risk

If employers can provide retirement insurance in a profitable manner through pension schemes, a motivation to sponsor a pension emerges.

There are two other factors that make pension plans desirable. First, pension plans are attractive as a tax-efficient way to provide for retirement. Second, employers have found that pension plans can motivate employees; a properly designed pension plan as part of a total compensation package can encourage employee productivity and loyalty.

Pension Plans as Tax-Efficient Means of Savings

Government policy makes pension funds attractive to both sponsors and employees by providing favorable tax treatment of pension plans. This helps reduce the political pressure on the government to provide all retirement income, and it tends to encourage sufficient saving so that older workers can leave the workforce and free up opportunities for younger employees.

The government offers two tax incentives to encourage pension growth. First, pension fund contributions are tax deductible. This is true for tax-paying employers who make contributions on behalf of their employees and for individuals who contribute to a plan whether or not the plan sponsor is a taxable entity. (Employees covered under public defined benefit plans normally contribute to the plan while employees covered by private defined benefit plans normally do not [see the *EBRI Databook on Employee Benefits*].)

Second, investment earnings—both income and capital appreciation—are treated favorably for tax purposes. This incentive is attractive to employees of both private and public plans because it allows greater and more rapid accumulation of retirement assets than can be obtained through an equivalent amount of taxable investments.

Note that although plan beneficiaries do not pay tax until funds are paid out at retirement, pension withdrawals are taxed at ordinary income tax rates regardless of whether the distribution is attributable to contributions, interest, dividends, or capital gains. The advantages of early deductions and tax-deferred accumulations over long periods of time, however, make the subsequent taxation at income tax rates of little importance.

Consider an individual who for each of thirty years contributes $8,000 per year that is treated as a tax-deductible expenditure to a pension fund and who expects the investment fund to earn 10% per year. At the end of thirty years the fund will have grown to $1,315,920, which translates to $921,144 after taxes if withdrawn in one lump sum. If, however, the investments are not tax deductible and the investment income is not tax deferred, the result is quite different. Given a 30% tax rate, $5,600—the after-tax equivalent of $8,000—per year would be invested. Similarly, the after-tax return might be around 7% (the after-tax equivalent of the pre-tax 10%). In thirty years the amount invested would grow to $528,982 after tax. This is only 57% of the after-tax pension accrual accumulation achieved with the tax-deferral option.*

This illustration shows how potent the tax effect can be. Until the tax reform of 1986, the United States had a highly progressive income tax structure. Under the old multitiered system, many employees were in a much higher tax-rate bracket during their working years than during their retirement years. These employees would thus have gained an even greater benefit from the tax deferral on pension plans because lower tax rates would be applied to pension funds withdrawn during retirement years than would have been applied when the income was originally earned. Although the later 1986 tax reform and subsequent tax reform acts mitigate this second-order effect, it is still important.

The idea that the tax system has played a significant role in establishing the desirability and, hence, the growth of pension plans suggests the beginning of a theory of pensions that goes to the heart of the question "why have pensions?" If tax considerations encourage pension plans, then pensions may be viewed, at least in part, simply as deferred wages. As such, pension plans offer an efficient way for both employers and employees to defer taxes or even permanently reduce taxes (which is the case if tax rates are lower in retirement than during employment). The employer and employee jointly conspire to exploit the U.S. tax code (which, as we have noted, was intentionally set up to

---

*One estimate in the *EBRI Databook on Employee Benefits* is that retirement plans lower tax collections by roughly $60 billion. Many economists (e.g., Venti and Wise) suggest that the existence of pension plans adds to the aggregate accumulation of savings. With greater savings, there can be greater investment, hence more rapid economic growth. The higher rate of growth may expand the tax base sufficiently to offset the taxes not collected because of favorable tax treatment for pensions. However, there is not universal agreement on this point. Some work in progress suggests that once income and educational levels are held constant, the existence of pension plans seems not to affect savings behavior.

encourage the formation and use of pension plans). This "conspiracy" takes the form of employees accepting lower taxable wages in return for higher pension contributions. This "splitting of pie," as it were, through pension plans is desirable for employers because they can pay less in total compensation by offering pensions than the equivalent in fully taxed compensation.

This view of pensions is not complete by itself. For instance, if pension benefits were pure deferred wages set up only as a way to save on taxes, then we would not expect to see vesting requirements or any other conditions imposed on collection by recipients. Since pension plans do offer these features, employers and employees must be entering into these sorts of contracts for reasons besides tax advantages.

Pension Plans as Motivating Contracts

The pension plan is a contract between the employer and the employee. It is not highly rigid; often the employer can change the arrangement unilaterally. Nonetheless, there is a strong understanding between the parties.

As we know, different sorts of contractual provisions can induce different kinds of employee behavior. The government-mandated wage and price controls during World War II and the Korean War taught employers and employees about the incentives that pension plans can provide. Under wage controls, employers still needed employees, but they could not attract them by offering higher wages in the form of current income. Accordingly, many employers raised the total compensation by adding pension plans to the compensation package since pensions did not count as wages under the wage-price control laws. (The offering of pension plans was, of course, further motivated by the tremendous advantage of tax deferral during a period when top personal tax rates exceeded 80%.)

Employers soon found that pension plan contracts could be structured to produce employee work incentives that differed from those produced by an equivalent dollar amount put directly into the cash portion of the total compensation package. Specifically, employers learned that pension plans helped to bind employees to their organizations, to provide incentives for employees to leave their organizations at the right time, and to improve productivity. Fundamental to why this is so is the issue of whether pensions are simply deferred wages or are made-up compensation for underpayments of wages in the early years of multiyear employment relationships.

Pension Plans as Compensation: Two Views

As we saw earlier, if tax considerations alone were able to account for the appeal of pension plans, there would be grounds for contending that pensions are nothing but deferred wages. In turn, this would suggest that the labor market could be characterized as a spot market, to use Jeremy Bulow's term.

In a spot market, labor's compensation through wages, pension benefits, and health benefits in any period is equal to the market value of the employee's production in each and every period; the employee is paid exactly what he or she is worth, and nothing is "carried over" from the end of one period to the next. The structure of compensation does not itself contribute to a longer relationship between the employer and employee since, at the end of the day, nothing is carried over.

A different view has been offered by Logue, Lazear, and others. In this view, employees get less than the true value of their contributions to their employers in total compensation during the early portion of their careers, but their total compensation is more than their contributions are worth later in their careers (technically, their later career compensation is greater than the current value of the work provided to the employer).

According to this view, labor markets are not spot markets, but rather are multiperiod, contractual markets in which relationships are formed. The connection between the employer and employee is more than just a transaction for a day's labor. Instead, there is an implicit contract between the employer and employee that so long as employee performance remains satisfactory, the employee will be kept on the payroll—until that time when the portion of total compensation attributable to the pension plan is high enough to make up for the low total compensation received earlier in the career. Bear in mind, however, that recent corporate "re-engineering" with downsizing, shutdowns, asset sales, and so forth may have done much to dispel the notion that there is an implicit contract between a company and its workers. There will not be sound evidence on this point, however, for a few years.

The dispute between these two views is not concerned with whether pension plans can be used to develop implicit contracts or whether employees subsequently will be fully rewarded for the early career shortfalls in total compensation. Rather, the issues are whether pension plans have actually been designed to provide these components and whether they have been successful in doing so. Though the issue is unresolved, the weight of the evidence favors the notion that the labor market has many implicit contractual elements.

There are many instances of the operation and enforcement of the implicit contract in labor markets. For example, in the early 1970s many employers had pension plans that multiplied a workers' average salary over his or her entire career by the number of years worked, times some set percentage—say 1.5%. During the inflation of the 1970s, however, workers' salaries grew very quickly to keep pace with rising prices. Thus early-career salaries began to bear almost no relation to late-career salaries, even in the absence of promotions. For instance, someone earning $10,000 per year in the early 1960s would have to be earning about $30,000 per year in the mid-1970s just to have kept pace with inflation. In response to this, employers quickly adjusted pension-benefit formulas so that pension payments would compensate employees for inflation by using the final-year (or a final three- to five-year average) salary, rather than the full-career average, to multiply by the years of service and the pension percentage. This kept the pension payments where employers wanted them to be: in real—that is, inflation-adjusted—terms. (Of course, sponsors could index the percentage term, which is used to multiply the years worked, to accommodate inflation in order to achieve the same pension effect. However, this would break the link between the current value of an employee's effort as reflected in his or her salary and the pension.)

Although this adjustment accommodates workers who are just about to retire, it does not explicitly help retired workers. Many employers, without admitting a legal obligation to do so, voluntarily stepped up payments in the 1970s to those already retired in order to offset the financial harm they suffered from inflation. Employers continue to do this. Here is where the nature of the implicit contract really comes to light. With no legal obligation—and perhaps not even a moral obligation—to adjust pension payments, did employers boost benefits for the sake of the retirees exclusively? Of course not! Although there was undoubtedly an element of compassion, the employer's underlying motive was to demonstrate to current employees that they too would be protected from inflation if the employer/sponsors had the financial resources to do so. Presumably, if the current employees did not recognize the gesture as an implicit guarantee about their future, they would have insisted on higher current wages, explicit contractual remedies, and the like. Some employee groups did indeed do this. But many, perhaps most, interpreted their employees' actions toward existing retirees as implicit contracts providing that they too would be cared for should inflation again become problematic. In other words, many employees embrace the idea that their pensions will be more or less fixed in real terms as part of an implicit understanding with their employers, even though this may not actually be the case.

Pension Plans as Motivation

With this background on pension contracting, we now examine the idea that pension plans can motivate employees to behave in certain ways. Specifically, we look at how pension plan features can affect employee longevity, severance, and productivity.

Longevity. Many economists (e.g., Kotlikoff and Wise) have demonstrated how pension plans can be used to retain employees for long periods. This is accomplished by explicitly rewarding longevity through vesting and backloading.

For example, suppose an employer determines that employee turnover at the mid-level of management is, by its standards, excessive and too costly. A pension plan provision could, in principle, be introduced so that mid-level managers would be penalized financially through a disproportionate loss of pension benefits for leaving the employer too soon. One way to do this is offering a pension plan that places a disproportionately heavy weight on employment earnings at the end of a career. Thus, middle-aged (and younger) employees considering a job switch would have to factor into their decisions a very large loss of pension benefits, a built-in penalty for those who leave early and a reward for employees who stay a long time. When setting up such plan provisions, however, private plans must take care to avoid the nondiscrimination rules set up and administered by the Internal Revenue Service.

Severance. Pensions also can provide powerful incentives for workers to leave their jobs at the normal retirement age rather than staying on longer than the sponsor might wish (anti-age discrimination laws allow many employees this option). For example, many employers do not increase pension benefits after an employee has worked a specified maximum number of years—that is, some employers stop counting after 30 years on the job. Accordingly, someone who works, say, 45 years may get no more annual pension benefit than someone who has worked far fewer years. Moreover, since the long-working recipient is likely to be older, and hence likely to die sooner, he or she has fewer years to collect the same annual benefit. Thus, in many plans, working after the normal retirement age reduces both total pension receipts and the incentive to continue working.

Pensions can also be used as severance pay, as pointed out by Lazear and others, and to encourage early retirements. Early retirement may replace older, less productive, more highly paid employees with more efficient, less highly paid employees. Pensions may accomplish this by replacing enough of the employee's salary to motivate the employee to retire. This is discussed in more depth in the section "Defined Benefit Plans" in Chapter 2.

Productivity. The idea that pension plans can play a significant role in enhancing corporate productivity is an inviting one. Financial theory holds that owners perform better than nonowners. For this reason, special pension arrangements such as Employee Stock Ownership Plans (ESOPs) (see Appendix A) have been established in part to tie workers' motivation and productivity to the performance of the employer's common stock. By making employees into owners through an ESOP, the employer aligns the interests of employees with those of other owners, thus, theoretically, achieving higher productivity.

Of course, ESOPs are not available to public plans in which the sponsor is a government or other non-profit organization. However, in both public and private plans employers may use backloading to ensure an orderly and somewhat efficient transfer of organization-specific knowledge from older, more experienced workers to younger, less experienced workers. This is consistent with the view that older workers have accumulated the equivalent of equity in the organization by virtue of their highly specialized knowledge of the way the organization conducts its business (see the article by Bulow). As the older workers train younger workers, they are in essence selling their equity or organization-specific human capital to those who follow. This accumulation/decumulation of "equity" ties employees to the interests of other stakeholders and thus raises productivity.

Encouraging Trustworthy Behavior and Improving Employee Selection

Employers have two other problems that may be partially resolved by offering properly structured pension plans. First, many employers must be concerned with providing the proper incentives for employees to act in a trustworthy manner. This is especially important to public employers who are entrusted with public safety and the stewardship of the public's tax dollars but are not subject to the discipline of the financial markets. Second, all employers are concerned with how to go about selecting the types of employees they want.

Pensions and Trustworthy Behavior

Consider the example of police officers. It is generally accepted that to do their jobs, police officers must behave in a trustworthy fashion, enforcing the law in an evenhanded manner and refraining from corrupt or illegal acts. How can their employers encourage this without incurring excessive monitoring costs?

One way for an employer to encourage trustworthy behavior is by offering a substantial financial reward if the desired behavior is exhibited over the course of the police officer's employment. For example, the employer could post a bond payable upon retirement as long as the performance on the job meets some predetermined standard (e.g., no dishonest behavior). However, the full amount would be forfeited if the officer were convicted of a crime or found guilty of unbecoming behavior of some type. This, of course, is much like a defined benefit pension where all benefits are forfeited if certain events transpire, a not uncommon arrangement for employees in the armed services and in public safety positions. Even private-sector employees may face some after-the-fact "settling up." Indeed, some executives at Texaco saw their pension benefits reduced retroactively as a consequence of alleged wrongdoing while employed by Texaco.

Interestingly, there are data consistent with the view that public employers, on average, may prefer a different total compensation mix of wages and pensions than private employers do. Zorn has shown that while employees of private employers receive more of their compensation from wages, salaries, and supplemental pay (74.2% of total compensation) than do public employees (who receive 70.7%), public employees receive proportionately more in the form of retirement benefits (12.4% of total compensation) than do private employees (8.9%). There doubtless are other factors at play, such as the political incentive of public sponsors to disguise pay raises by increasing pension benefits. However, since the vesting schedules of public funds are not subject to ERISA and are on average longer than they are for private plans, the data are consistent with the notion of a scheme that rewards trustworthy behavior with substantial future payments in the form of pension rights. This approach is of more limited value for private employers who are subject to ERISA vesting requirements.

Pension Plans as an Aid in Employee Selection

Ippolito has developed a theory that pension funds are a mechanism by which workers may be sorted according to the value of the work they provide to a sponsor. To see how this might work, consider a world in which there are two kinds of people. People in group A assign a high value to the future consequences of the actions they currently take. They are less likely to skip work on the pretext that they are sick because they value their reputation as reliable. They want to be seen as "low cost," so they take care of the equipment they use. They work hard so they will get promoted. People in group B, on the other hand, are the opposite of group A people. They call in sick without reason. They do not take care of the equipment they use, nor do they work especially hard.

Group A people exhibit qualities that identify them as high-quality, productive people. Consistent with the way they assign a high value to the future consequences of the actions they currently take, they place a high value on savings relative to current consumption (i.e., they have low discount rates). They are desirable workers, and they are likely to see pension benefits as valuable.

Group B people exhibit qualities that identify them as low-quality workers or workers who are more likely to take inappropriate risks. In particular, they may not be desirable workers where productivity and reliability are important. Consistent with the way they assign a low value to the future consequences of the actions they currently take, they place a low value on savings relative to current consumption (i.e., they have high discount rates). They are not likely to see future pension benefits as valuable.

Now consider two employers, Employer X and Employer Y. Employer X offers a pension plan that is quite generous, while Employer Y offers somewhat higher wages but no pension plan. Ippolito's theory suggests that type A people will assign a high present value to the pension benefits offered by Employer X and thus may find X's total compensation more attractive than Y's. Type B people will see little value in the future pension benefits and thus will be attracted to the higher current wages at Y.

In a world with competition, type A people will receive the value of their higher marginal work product. This is what employers will have to pay to attract and retain them. According to Ippolito, employers that want high-quality type A employees have two options. They will either (1) have to search for these "low discounters" (a potentially costly process) and monitor the workers they have and attempt to pay more to the more productive workers (also incurring potentially high costs); or (2) use a pension plan as a low-cost sorting device to attract and keep high-quality, low-discount workers.

Is this "natural selection" a sensible theory to explain why employers have pensions and why employees want pensions? There are certainly other factors—tax efficiencies, rewarding longevity, and so forth—but to view differences in personal discount rates as attributable to differences in the way people assign value to the future consequences of their actions is somewhat appealing. All that is needed is that there be a high correlation between personal discount rates and the types of behaviors that are characteristic of high-quality workers.

Conclusion

Collectively, the incentives and potential benefits described in this chapter, coupled with the desire of employees to have secure retirements, suggest that pensions are a sensible form of compensation.

First, pension plans are a tax-efficient means of compensation, broadly defined. Employers and employees may jointly exploit the tax code to make each better off. For employees this translates to a higher total compensation than they might otherwise get, and yet for the employer this translates to paying lower total compensation than it might otherwise pay. (As we will see in Chapter 2 and other chapters, the potential for good investment performance can lower employer costs further still.)

Second, pension plans can be used as a multiperiod contracting device to motivate desirable behavior in employees. Properly structured pension plans are an efficient way to manage the organization's human resources, giving employers numerous options (e.g., the option to manage turnover) that contribute to the organization's ability to plan and to adapt change.

Third, pension plans are useful devices in solving special problems. Pensions can provide incentives for trustworthy behavior on the part of employees; they also can reduce monitoring costs where trust is important. In addition, they are potential tools for attracting and retaining high-quality employees.

Overall, there is no question that pension plans are useful to many employers and valuable to most employees. There are sound economic grounds supporting the continued existence of pension plans. At issue is what type of pension plan is best suited for a given employer or is most attractive to a given employee.

Chapter **2**

Choosing the Best Pension Plan

An important aspect of the decision to offer a pension plan is determining what plan structure is best. There is a fundamental choice to be made: will the plan offer defined benefits or defined contributions, or will it be a hybrid plan that exhibits characteristics of both defined benefit and defined contribution plans? (The Employee Stock Ownership Plan [ESOP] is a very special type of defined contribution plan; it will be treated separately in Appendix A.) To make the right choice, sponsors and the other parties involved in the decision-making process must understand the differences in the attributes of these structures regarding funding, sponsor liability, benefit assurance, and the differences in who bears the risks and rewards of investment performance.

Defined Benefit Plans

Defined benefit plans (DBPs) promise the employee a specific dollar payment per period in retirement. Because the benefit normally is paid for the beneficiaries' lifetime (and possibly beyond if there are survivorship rights), the DBP plan sponsor bears mortality risk—that is, some beneficiaries could receive benefits for a very long time. Structurally, the most important features of DBPs are the benefit formula, the replacement rate, and funding.

Benefit Formulas

As noted in Chapter 1, through the early 1970s, the benefit formula typically used the average pay a worker earned over his or her entire career with that specific employer. This average dollar amount was multiplied by the number of years of service; the resulting quantity was multiplied by a fractional pension benefit. For example, a worker who earned a career average of $25,000 per year, who worked for the same employer for thirty years, and whose employer's pension fraction was 1.5%, would have a pension benefit equal to $11,250 per year. (This assumes the plan was not integrated with the employee's Social Security receipts as will be discussed later.) In the late 1970s and early 1980s, many employers switched from using a career-average to using final-pay benefit formulas. In final-pay plans, the employer uses either the last year's salary or an average of the final three or five years' salaries to determine pension benefits. Inflation prompted this change; averaging wages over thirty years came to make little sense.

A common modern benefit formula is the number of years of service times average salary over final three years times 1.5%. Thus, an employee with thirty years on the job and an average final three-year salary of $40,000 would get an annual pension benefit of $18,000. This formula rewards longevity; it rewards more highly paid people more generously, and it aims, generally, at producing a retirement benefit that is high enough to induce people to retire. These benefits are not costless to the sponsor, however. The career-end formula greatly increases the exposure of the plan and hence of the sponsor to the inflation component of wages. It also raises the specter of contributions that are higher than anticipated if inflation is unexpectedly high—or even if there is a modest amount of inflation (though more than anticipated) over a long period. Perhaps the investment returns on the assets set aside to fund the plan will offset the effects of inflation; there is a risk, however, that they will not.

There are other types of defined benefit payment formulas. The type just described is generally used for nonunion employees. For union employees or multi-employer plans, the formula is generally a flat dollar amount times years worked. Of course, this formula could produce the same results relative to final salary as the formula above; it all depends on the flat dollar amount. The flat dollar amount is the result of negotiations between employer and unions.

Replacement Rates

In determining target benefit levels, employers generally work backward from a target replacement rate. The *replacement rate* is the rate at which salary is "replaced" by the pension benefit and/or Social Security; it is the annual pension payment as a percent of final pay. Its economic importance is tied to inducing employees to retire when the sponsor desires them to and to employees' compensation requirements. (Sponsors are also providing insurance against Social Security payment cuts to those employees who are covered by Social Security.)

In determining replacement rates, it generally is assumed that career employees retire at the normal retirement date and careers are customarily assumed to span thirty to forty years. Thus, if an employee's projected pension benefit is $20,000 and the final year's salary of that employee is expected to be $40,000, the proposed pension replacement rate would be 50%; that is, the benefit will replace 50% of the employee's current salary.

To determine an appropriate replacement rate, first the employer asks whether this will be enough to induce retirement when best for the employer. Second, the employer asks whether the prospect of a 50% pension replacement rate is enough to compensate current employees later for present cash compensation that is less than the value of their contribution to the employer. In cases where Social Security payments are not included in the 50% pension replacement rate, the employee will have a retirement income of greater than 50% of the final year's salary—the 50% replacement rate plus Social Security. This provides a greater inducement to retire and provides an even larger amount of deferred compensation. To answer these questions, sponsors generally hire consultants who, among other things, offer a database that enables them to tell their clients what other sponsors are doing. Comparisons can be helpful in revealing what employees are willing to accept in return for the work and skills they provide. This helps the employer understand the trade-off between cash wages and pensions.

Some employers consider Social Security payments to be part of the pension plan. Hence they establish a replacement rate target that includes Social Security payments. These integrated plans will be discussed later in this chapter.

Funding

Pension plans may be funded on a pay-as-you-go basis or by setting aside an asset pool that, in combination with future contributions from the sponsor, will be sufficient to pay promised benefits. DBPs may be overfunded (in which case they have more assets than are needed to pay all future benefits), adequately funded, or underfunded. Over time, unfunded benefits must be funded either through additional contributions from the sponsor or through investment returns. Thus, the funding status of a pension plan partially describes, at a specific point in time, the financial health of the plan as well as the ability of the plan to bear risk.

Once the target replacement rate for a plan is known and usable estimates have been made regarding future salaries and life expectancies, the sponsor, assisted by actuaries and financial experts, must develop expectations for alternative asset allocations and investment rates of return. These financial advisors and the sponsor then can work backward to determine how the sponsor must invest money contributed to the pension plan now and money contributed over time to provide the promised benefit. If the amount already invested together with the income projected on these funds exceeds the amount necessary to deliver the promised retirement benefit, the employer can reduce or eliminate future contributions. If the investment results on the invested funds fall below expectations, then the employer is supposed to make up the difference. For private plans, this is a legal obligation under ERISA. For public plans, there is no comprehensive funding requirement.

Note that for DBPs, the pension recipient is entitled to the promised pension even though the asset pool and future investment returns may be insufficient to pay it. The plan sponsor earns the reward of exceptionally good investment performance, but also bears the risk of poor planning and poor investment results.

Defined Contribution Plans

In a defined contribution plan (DCP), employers and/or employees contribute a specified percentage of wages or a dollar amount to a pension plan. Upon retirement, the employee receives either a lump-sum distribution or an annuity purchased with however much has accumulated in the plan. Thus, in contrast with DBPs, DCPs have no benefit formula, the replacement rate is at best a target, and funding is not directly influenced by factors such as investment performance or actuarial estimates of life expectancies. Also, in contrast with DBPs, DCP beneficiaries bear mortality risk—that is, they may outlive their retirement assets.

The 401(k) plan has become the most popular type of DCP for private plans. A 401(k) may be funded by the sponsor, the employee, or both. The 403(b) and 457 plans are the public sector's versions of the 401(k). There are numerous other DCP plans—among them profit-sharing plans, money purchase plans, and so forth.

In theory, the employer offering a DCP can go through an analysis similar to the analysis necessary for a defined benefit plan. That is, the employer may target a replacement rate; form some estimates about final salary, career length, and investment returns; and then, working backward, deduce what percentage of salary or dollar amount ought to be put aside each year to produce the intended results. Should the investment performance exceed expectations, the employee can, in principle if not always in practice, take a lump sum and convert this to an annuity that produces a far higher replacement rate than originally envisioned. Of course, should the investment performance of the fund fall below expectations, the ultimate replacement rate and hence the retirement benefits provided can be far lower than anticipated.

In some DCPs, the employer allocates assets for employees. This requires a definition or profile of a *representative employee*—a composite of all the plan's beneficiaries. Legal and regulatory forces are making this approach much less attractive as sponsors fear they may be held liable for poor investment performance.

In many DCPs, the beneficiary participates in the investment decision by choosing to allocate money to asset classes such as equities or fixed-income investments, and sometimes by choosing the specific investment fund or funds within each asset class. Thus, the beneficiary plays a role in determining the risk profile of the investment fund. This is attractive, as it allows employees to meet their own unique needs and preferences, but it can also be risky, as good asset allocation requires knowledge.

Defining the Benefit, the Contribution, or Both

Whether a DBP is more attractive than a DCP is not a straightforward issue. Although the tax incentives of DCPs and DBPs are pretty much the same, DCPs differ from DBPs in important respects.

Specifically, the ability to structure contracts that motivate desirable behavior, such as longevity and loyalty, is much weaker for DCPs because they cannot easily be backloaded and they typically are portable. However, employees who want to obtain retirement income insurance will not find DCPs attractive unless funding is quite high. Employees who value portability and the option of changing employers without incurring high costs in forfeited pension benefits will find DCPs attractive. In general, attractive aspects of each type of plan from the sponsor's perspective may not be attractive to employees, and vice versa. Thus, sponsors and employees may not always agree that one form is more suitable than the other.

In recent years there has been a sharp increase in the number of defined contribution plans and very little growth in defined benefit plans. One possible reason is the administrative burdens of ERISA, which diminish greatly with defined contribution plans; there is no robust empirical support for this view, however. An alternative reason is that the shift toward defined contribution plans is motivated by other factors. Indeed, the data show that a large part of the growth of defined contribution plans is attributable to companies adopting plans that are supplementary to their defined benefit plans and the adoption of DCPs by smaller employers. Finally, note that since government policy is not neutral with respect to worker mobility—more mobility is preferred under current policy—DBPs have lost some of their previous advantages of binding employees to the organization.

So which scheme is better for a sponsor? It depends on what the sponsor wants to accomplish and is permitted to do by regulatory and labor market forces. From the viewpoint of an employee, the optimal plan is a function of the employee's attitude toward risk.

Empirical Evidence on Plan Choice

Supporting the view that there is a trend toward installing defined contribution plans in place of defined benefit plans are data in the 1995 *Employee Benefit Research Institute Databook on Employee Benefits* showing that by 1990 defined contribution plans had more than 50% of total pension plan participants (as opposed to 27% in 1975) and represented over 80% of the total number of plans. In 1975, 28% of private pension plan assets were in defined contribution plans; by 1993 more than 45% of private pension assets were in defined contribution plans.

However, other data are worth pondering (see the article by Rohrer). For example:

- Employees are no more mobile today than they were 15 years ago.
- For the year ending September 30, 1995, the IRS approved four times as many defined benefit plans as defined contribution plans.
- As of mid-1996, defined benefit assets for public and private plans combined are around $4 trillion. Defined contribution assets are $1.2 trillion, including $675 billion in 401(k) plans.

These data suggest that the popularity of defined contribution plans posited by various commentators during the 1980s and early 1990s may be waning, at least for private plans. Reversions of excess assets now are more difficult and less attractive due to the imposition of a tax surcharge; thus, a major motivation for converting DBPs to DCPs no longer exists. Additionally, sponsors are more aware of the "hidden" liabilities of defined contribution plans now: there is a possibility that the sponsor may have to make up the shortfall if employee expectations for asset accumulations are not met. Finally, the advantages of defined benefit plans for some employers in some circumstances are coming to be better understood. That said, some large public funds are evaluating the advantages and disadvantages of DCPs. Thus, a whole new wave of plan restructuring could be coming.

Regardless of trends per se, individual organizations must choose the pension scheme that makes the most economic sense for their particular goals and circumstances. The interaction between funding and investment performance, the desired level of employee mobility, the value of organization-specific knowledge, plan costs, and the variability of the sponsor's cash flows are all important factors in making this decision.

Funding and Investment Performance

A significant difference between the two plans is funding. A defined contribution plan (DCP) is, by definition, always fully funded if promised contributions have been made. The asset value equals the liability. A defined benefit plan (DBP) may or may not be fully funded. An employer must make contributions to a defined contribution plan as it has promised. An employer may, however, make less than actuarially adequate contributions to a defined benefit plan in the early years and then either hope for exceptional investment performance or plan on heavier contributions in later years.

For private single-employer and multiemployer DBP plans, both the level of funding and the source of funding are guided by legislation that is technically consistent. It is, however, philosophically separate. ERISA legislation, originally designed to strengthen private pension plans, encourages more funding rather than less to make plans safe. For private pensions, IRS legislation—the intent of which is raising revenues—tends to hold funding down to enhance tax collections, because pension contributions are tax deductible. In recent years, the band of permissible funding has grown fairly small. For public pensions, there is no equivalent to ERISA and thus no blanket mandate forcing adequate funding. There is, however, a plethora of state rules and regulations and union contracts governing funding for public pensions.

The level of funding for DBPs is also affected by the investment performance of the pool of assets owned by the plan. Thus, a key difference between the two types of plans has to do with who bears the risk of, and stands to benefit from, investment performance. Given that the sponsor of a DBP must increase funding if investments do not perform as expected, why not shift to a DCP? One reason is that DBPs are more efficient than individuals in risk bearing and insurance. Thus, there is a surplus to be divided. Another reason to stay with a DBP is that DCPs carry an implied obligation to educate employees about investing. The risk of not doing so is that the courts may shift the investment risk back to the sponsor.

The tradeoff, then, is between funding costs on one hand and investment performance on the other. Some sponsors may believe they can reduce the total contributions made to employee pensions by offering DBPs in an attempt to profit from investment performance. Other sponsors may be willing to make higher funding payments over time in order to shift the risks and benefits of investment performance to employees by offering DCPs. Regardless of which view they take, however, sponsors must remember that employees also have preferences. There is no reason to believe that employees will be indifferent between one dollar of DBP funding and one dollar of DCP funding. Some employees may find the burden of investment risk (and mortality risk) unattractive if a sponsor shifts from a DBP to a DCP. In return for bearing the risk of adverse investment performance on their retirement security, they may demand higher levels of funding for DCPs.

Employee Mobility

Defined benefit plans, as earlier noted, are currently heavily backloaded as a result of the strong tendency among employers to offer final pay plans. That is, the benefit levels have virtually nothing to do with early-career salary experience and much to do with late-career salary experience. Of course, this discourages employee mobility and provides an incentive to work hard and long for a single employer because by achieving a high ending salary, the employee is rewarded twice: first by the salary and second by the pension benefit based on the high salary. However, such backloading can reduce the attractiveness of the plan to new employees by raising the cost of leaving the organization.

Consider an employee who switches jobs in mid-career and anticipates getting identical 10% annual pay increases in the old and new jobs, and who anticipates the application of the same pension formula. Taking into account the advantage of the higher salary, Gustman and Steinmeier suggest that a 3% higher starting wage in the new job followed by identical percentage wage increases will leave the employee with about the same current value of benefits—that is, a 3% higher starting wage will offset over time the loss of the backloading portion of pension benefits from the first job. (This does not take into consideration the net non-pecuniary benefits of a new job.)

Vesting requirements are another aspect of mobility. Vesting means that a worker must remain with a sponsor for a specific number of years before becoming entitled to full pension benefits. Before 1975, some companies had vesting periods of twenty-five years or longer. ERISA initially required that every full-time eligible worker must become fully vested after fifteen years. Subsequent adjustment to the law now requires five-year cliff (all at once) vesting or seven-year graded (incremental) vesting. This rule applies to both private defined benefit and defined contribution plans. Public plan vesting is not covered under national legislation, so vesting requirements can be quite different and may depend on state legislation and union agreements.

Under DBPs, workers lose all or part of their pension benefits if they take a job with a different employer before they are fully vested. Thus, vesting requirements also tend to discourage workers from changing jobs during the vesting period. From the sponsor's perspective, vesting requirements may be beneficial because they may keep turnover and associated replacement hiring and training costs low, and because they allow employers to recapture the implied pension contribution should employees leave sooner than an employer would like. Additionally, vesting requirements allow employers to fire unsatisfactory short-term workers without having to make long-term commitments to them. Thus, from an employer's perspective, vesting helps to retain employees that the employer wants to keep and provides strong incentives to get rid of low-productivity employees quickly before they vest.

Defined contribution plans frequently, though not always, vest immediately (although contributions may not be made for the first 3 years of employment) and are frequently independent of the number of years of service to an employer and of employee age. This is a disadvantage to employers since a DCP does nothing to discourage valuable employees from leaving; however, this portability feature is attractive to employees.

Employer-Specific Knowledge

Although there is no definitive theory or robust empirical studies that indicate why one type of plan is favored over the other, one school of thought suggests that the choice has to do with the amount of employer-specific human capital that a plan sponsor determines is optimal or, more generally, acceptable. Consider, for instance, university professors, most of whom have defined contribution plans. What professors do requires very little employer-specific human capital. Intricate knowledge of the university's organization or technological base is not necessary to perform the jobs of teaching and research. Rather, the professor's set of skills—those necessary in teaching and research—are presumably valuable at virtually any university. Therefore, there is no general reason for a university to set up a pension plan that rewards length of service or a large investment in organization-specific skills.

Many public and private organizations, however, really do need employees to possess a great deal of employer-specific knowledge for decisions to be made correctly. Such organizations can reward long-time employees, those who have invested in building a lot of employer-specific human capital, through back-end loaded defined benefit pension plans. In this context, back-end loading of pension plans is a reward for not contributing to turnover and for enabling an employer to economize on the searching and training costs of replacement employees, rather than a penalty for job hopping.

According to Gustman and Steinmeier, there is evidence that the shifting job mix of our economy in recent years accounts for a good portion of the trend to DCPs. This evidence is consistent with the view that as manufacturing growth declines, the need for pension plans that reward employees for building employer-specific human capital diminishes.

Plan Costs

Another important factor in the choice of plan type is the financial and other costs the employer will bear in providing the pension benefit. In general, the marginal costs of the plan chosen should be equal to or less than the marginal benefits to the sponsor and ultimately the shareholders/taxpayers in whose interest the sponsor is presumably acting.

Administrative Costs

According to a study by Hay/Huggins, an actuarial consulting firm, the cost of administering a defined benefit plan for a large firm (with over 500 employees) was about one-third greater than the cost of administering a defined contribution plan. Moreover, this cost differential widened substantially as the number of participants decreased. With 15 participants, the administrative costs of a defined contribution plan were half the cost of administering a defined benefit plan. This appears to explain a large part of the appeal of defined contribution plans to small and new firms that chose to offer pensions. There is no reason to believe that relative costs have changed since 1990.

Funding Costs

Another perspective on cost comes from investment theory. Accepted theory tells us, and practice confirms, that people have different discount rates for investments that are more or less risky. On average, people will have higher discount rates for investments they view as very risky than they have for investments they view as not very risky. Consider, from the employee's perspective, pension plans as investments. A basic difference between a DCP and a DBP is who bears the risk of adverse investment performance and inadequate accumulation of future wealth. Faced with the choice of either a DBP or a DCP, employees should view the DBP as less risky, all else the same, and hence use a lower discount rate when evaluating its worth. This suggests that if sponsors can deliver good investment management at relatively low cost—due to economies of scale not available to employees and to accumulated knowledge likely to be seen as costly to acquire by employees—DBPs may have a cost advantage over DCPs. In other words, employers offering DCPs may have to make higher contributions to offset the risk premium demanded by employees because of the added risk. (Note that for defined benefits to have a high present value, the sponsor and workers must agree that the sponsor has a long time horizon [that is, the sponsor is a good credit risk] and that employee turnover will be low [see the 1995 article by Ippolito].)

The Options in Defined Benefit Plans

Total costs must be evaluated within the context of the benefits gained as a result of the course of action that gives rise to the costs. Although they may have higher administrative costs, defined benefit plans offer the sponsor many valuable options. For example, DBPs offer the sponsor the latitude to manage the demographics of its workforce. Frequently, sponsors can adjust benefit formulas on an ad hoc basis to encourage early retirement (e.g., increase benefits ex post to offset unanticipated inflation) or some other behavior it deems necessary. Sponsors also may use pension schemes to reward high-quality or "fast track" workers. If these workers are low discounters (see Chapter 1), they are likely to see back-end loaded defined benefit plans as economic reward for their superior performance. Employers may also be able to use DBPs to fund post-retirement benefits if the investment performance of the underlying asset pool is good enough. These types of options may be sufficiently valuable to offset the more obvious pension costs.

Variability of Sponsor Cash Flows

One last insight into plan choice is offered by Petersen. He has demonstrated that companies with highly variable cash flows may be able to reduce their operating leverage (the variability in operating cash flow that comes about due to variable revenues and the mix of variable costs and fixed costs) by opting for DCPs that are related to profit, not wages. For this to work, the plan must be structured as a profit-sharing plan. In a profit-sharing plan, contributions are a percentage of profits. If there are no profits, there are no contributions. Thus, contributions can be adjusted to compensate for variations in cash flow. When profits are high, dollar contributions would be high; similarly, when profits are low, contributions would be low.

Choosing the Basic Plan

Defined benefit plans are not necessarily as unattractive as some authorities have argued. This form of pension offers employers and employees numerous benefits as well as costs.

Organizations that value longevity, firm-specific knowledge, the option of restructuring the workforce, the opportunity to motivate certain types of behavior, and the potential to lower total funding by capturing the results of favorable investment performance should give careful consideration to DBPs. Organizations that do not value these things, that can not afford to pay for them, or that have highly variable cash flows should consider DCPs. Organizations that find elements of both attractive and unattractive may want to consider the hybrid plans that have evolved in recent years.

Hybrid Pension Schemes

The choice of defined contribution or defined benefit plan is not easy. In many situations, the choice is impeded by the dilemma of having to give up something one party really wants for something the other party really wants. These are not good choices to make if they can be avoided. To address these dilemmas, some alternative structures to the traditional defined benefit/defined contribution plan structures have emerged. These include combined plans (combinations of the two basic forms), cash balance plans, pension equity plans, and target benefit plans. (An example of a hybrid plan is given in Appendix B.)

Combined Plans

Following an in-depth analysis of DBPs and DCPs, Bodie, Marcus, and Merton do not find either to be clearly preferable. They suggest that a hybrid *floor plan* could come to dominate either type in terms of employee/employer preference. This plan consists of a minimum guarantee of retirement income (the floor) based on a defined benefit formula. The floor is then supplemented with a defined contribution plan. Many employers already have such plans, with the defined contribution plan being a 401(k) type of plan. The DBP portion offers the employer the opportunity partially to create desirable incentives (e.g., raise the cost of leaving through backloading) and offers employees the benefits of risk-sharing insurance. The supplement (the DCP portion) offers reduced investment risk for the employer and has desirable customization and portability attributes for the employee. Both, of course, are attractive due to their tax-advantaged status.

Recall the importance of organization-specific knowledge discussed earlier. Most organizations are somewhere between the two extremes—those that favor DCPs (for professors) or those that favor DBPs (for organizations that require employer-specific skills). Thus a combined plan offering attributes of both will make sense for many sponsors. The issue to resolve will be the relative importance of organization-specific capital. The rule of thumb is that if organization-specific capital is important, make the DBP relatively important. If an employer does not require much organization-specific capital in its employees, make the DCP relatively important.

Cash Balance Plans

The first *cash balance pension plan* (CBP) was established in 1984 for BankAmerica Corporation. Only in recent years, however, have cash balance plans started to become a significant alternative for pension sponsors to consider. Approximately 200 defined benefit plans have been converted to cash balance plans. Thus, although the collective size of these plans is not significant right now, they do seem to offer some features that are attracting attention.

For private employers, CBPs are subject to ERISA funding regulations and are covered under Pension Benefit Guarantee Corporation (PBGC) insurance. CPBs are technically defined benefit plans, but they also have some of the features that make defined contribution plans attractive. Benefits accrue in a manner consistent with DCPs, the plan payout is normally in the form of a lump sum, and benefit values are defined in terms of account balances. On the other hand, assets are pooled, and the employer bears the investment risk. Additionally, like DBPs, CBPs can be structured to induce early retirement. Like DCPs, the risk of outliving plan assets is borne by the employee (unless the plan is annuitized by the employer on retirement or the employee uses the proceeds to purchase an annuity). The employee also bears the risk of inflation after retiring. Cash balance plans are portable, allowing vested employees to take accrued benefits with them upon leaving the organization. They also are easier for employees to understand since plan accounts accumulate pay and interest credits that are tied directly to benefits to be paid.

To see how a cash balance plan works, consider an employee who has been with a sponsor for ten years and earns $40,000 a year. The sponsor credits participant accounts based on a percent of salary schedule, which may vary by number of years worked. In this example, let us assume that someone who has worked for ten years receives a credit of 5% of his or her salary each year. The account also may receive interest credits based on some observable market index or interest rate. Thus, if the index is the long Treasury bond rate, and Treasury bonds in the previous year provided a 7% return, the interest credit on the account balance would be 7%. In our example, further assume the employee has an account balance at the beginning of the eleventh year of $8,000. At the end of this year, assuming the above treasury bond rate and pay credit, the employee's account will increase by $2,560 ($2,000 due to the 5% pay credit [0.05 × $40,000] and $560 [0.07 × $8,000] due to the 7% interest credit). At the end of the eleventh year, the employee's account has a cash value of $10,560. Should the employee then leave the organization, this balance is paid out.

Cash balance plans cannot be easily backloaded (unlike traditional defined benefit plans), and the interest credit component may perversely result in rewarding poor workers more highly than they should be rewarded. Additionally, there is an investment risk because the assets invested in support of a plan may earn less than the value of the pay and interest credits. This risk, however, may be beneficial in that the sponsor can keep any excess above the total credit amount. Cash balance plans can be coupled with minimum-benefit levels, 401(k) plans, matching plans, and profit-sharing plans. Additionally, credits can be tied to a final-average-pay/years-of-service formula, thus offering the sponsor some of the advantages of backloading. Termination benefits for CBPs, when paid, tend to be higher than for traditional defined benefit plans. Thus, these plans will be costlier than traditional DBPs to organizations with a high employee turnover rate. This is at least partially offset, however, by lower future retirement benefits. According to Brenner, the importance of lowering future retirement benefits can be particularly appropriate for organizations that have large numbers of retirees relative to the number of active employees.

Cash balance plans affect other aspects of plan management as well. For example, the additional liquidity needs brought about by lump-sum payouts may result in holding larger percentages of plan funds in short-term money market investments and income-producing securities such as bonds. This increased emphasis toward lower total return asset classes could increase future contributions. Cash balance plans can be less costly to administer than defined contribution plans, since they do not have loans, self-directed investment options, and the like.

Pension Equity Plans

An alternative hybrid to the cash balance plan is the *pension equity plan (PEP)* described by Wyatt. First used by RJR Nabisco in 1993, PEPs are designed to factor in age and final average pay in determining benefits. In so doing, they address some of the benefit accrual disadvantages of CBPs.

To see how this works, consider the PEP adopted by IBM in 1995. Benefits accrue on a point basis that varies by age. Employees who are 29 years old or younger earn 7 points a year, while those who are 45 years old or older earn 16 points a year. Upon retirement, the total number of points accumulated (there is a cap) is multiplied by the average of the final five years' pay and then converted to an annuity. The joint effect of the age and final salary weightings make the plan more attractive to mid-career hires and more effective than a CBP in rewarding fast-track employees.

Target Benefit Plans

A *target benefit plan (TBP)* is a defined contribution plan that is structured to replicate the payout structure of a defined benefit plan (see Matthews and Thomas). The targeted benefit can be a specified dollar amount or a percentage of pay. Thus, in appearance, the TBP seems to be a DBP while legally, it is subject to defined contribution rules. Sponsors gain some of the flexibility associated with DCPs while plan participants have a pension plan that conceptually mimics DBPs by directly targeting a specific payout to beneficiaries.

Contributions are not age related, and benefit accrual is similar to that of DBPs. Annual contributions are based on actuarial cost methods as well as interest and mortality actuarial assumptions. Plan participants have separate accounts to which contributions and investment earnings are credited. The actual benefit received will be determined by the actual amount of the plan participant's account on retirement. Because actual investment returns may be more or less than the interest assumptions used to calculate the annual contribution, the benefit actually received by plan participants may be higher or lower than the targeted benefit. Additionally, as is the case for DCPs in general, beneficiaries bear the mortality risk of outliving their retirement assets unless they use the proceeds to purchase an annuity.

These plans may be especially attractive to small businesses that want to offer pension benefits that favor highly paid employees and yet keep the administrative costs of the pension plan low. TBPs also may be attractive to businesses in which employees who are more valuable to the organization tend to be older on average than employees who add less value. Thus, TBPs are useful in attracting mid-career employees. A disadvantage of TBPs is that the nondiscrimination rules are complex. Thus, although there are safe harbor rules available to sponsors, the design of a TBP's plan documents can be challenging.

Pension Scheme Choice in Context

Pension schemes do not exist in a vacuum; they are part of the organization's total compensation package. Thus, they do have to cover every possible employee behavior that a sponsor may wish to influence. Other forms of contracting may be more efficient or effective. Regardless of sponsor preferences, the labor market will constrain sponsor choice of pension scheme.

When evaluating alternative plan structures, it is worth thinking about the issue of "fairness." Some writers have argued that DCPs promote fairness primarily because they do not penalize workers for moving from one firm to another. Whereas these plans allow for greater labor mobility, it is far from obvious that greater labor mobility is fair to all concerned. This preference for a specific element of social policy obscures an important issue in thinking about pension plans and their role in serving both employers and employees with the nature of the contracting between employees and employers. Employees trade their human capital for wages and retirement benefits paid by employers who desire the skills and knowledge that employees possess. In a market-driven economy, fairness is determined by the contracting that takes place between the two parties. Is it fair to shift mortality and investment risk to employees? Is it fair to take valuable options away from employers without giving anything in return? We caution sponsors against getting caught up in a simplistic notion of naive fairness; the process of attracting, motivating, and rewarding competent employees is quite complex. Indeed, it is sufficiently complex that rules that limit the range of mutually agreeable choices available to employees and employers are as likely to reduce fairness as to increase it.

Determining Pension Plan Features

Once the choice of what type of pension plan to establish has been made—whether the plan is to be a defined benefit plan, a defined contribution plan, or a hybrid—attention must be turned to designing plan features. A discussion of the role of management in making these decisions, and of the key design features follows.

The Role of Management

To begin, the design and funding of a pension plan are sufficiently complex and important to merit the attention of the top decision makers in an organization. Thus, boards of directors or government officials as well as senior management and the finance and human resources teams must accept a leadership role in forming and structuring pension plans.

The level of benefits, the nature of the implicit contracts, and likely employee responses to pension parameters demand careful analysis because of the impact—desirable or otherwise—that pensions have on employee incentives and behavior. Review by tax experts is also necessary to ensure that none of the plan's provisions results in the loss of tax advantages for the sponsor or the employee. Finally, board-level approval and, ultimately, oversight is necessary so that the pension plan and all its features can be reconciled at the highest levels with the means and willingness to finance the plan. Without the involvement of the organization's leaders, it becomes all too easy to make seemingly innocuous adjustments in plan provisions that have significant and unfortunate financial implications.

Key Features

Benefit levels, integration with Social Security, vesting, and other features warrant careful attention.

Benefit Levels

The first important feature to be determined is the benefit level or the target replacement rate. This is the proportion of wages an employee's pension benefits are intended to provide or "replace" upon retirement.

The optimal replacement rate must be based in part on the rates of competing employers. This rate may also be computed by estimating what fraction of pre-retirement income would be necessary for the employee to continue to enjoy the same lifestyle in retirement, allowing for reduced expenditures on items such as clothing, entertainment, commuting, and taxes. Finally, this rate may be determined in an acceptable funding/investment framework.

For a defined benefit plan (or the floor of a combined plan), the replacement rate becomes operational through the benefit formula to which the sponsor and employees agree. The number of years worked, the percentage multiplier (or flat dollar amount), explicit inflation indexing, and related factors are all components that must, in total, be consistent with the target replacement rate. Backloading via a heavy weighting on the final years of service may or may not be desirable. For defined contribution plans, the concept of replacement rates is nebulous, at best. Targets may be set, but since the assets in these plans tend to be managed by the beneficiaries, and since the sponsor is not willing to guarantee the amount of the benefit, alternative replacement rates are virtually impossible to evaluate.

Though many considerations go into its computation after counting Social Security, defined benefit plans seem to have target total replacement rates in the vicinity of 50 to 70% for long-term private-sector employees. The targets are higher—70 to 90% for public-sector retirees, according to the 1997 edition of the *EBRI Databook on Employee Benefits*. The following data from the *Databook* are useful in seeing how these replacement rates come about:

- 58% of private plans (medium and large employers) base benefits on terminal earnings.
- 43% of private plans use a flat percentage per year of service (the most common rate lies between 1.50 and 1.74%).
- 62% of private plans vary the percentage earned per year of service.

- State and local government plans virtually all use terminal-earnings formulas.
- 78% of public plans use a flat percentage per year of service (the most common rate is 2.00 to 2.24%).

Social Security Integration

Sponsors must decide whether the target replacement rate will take into account or exclude Social Security payments. Essentially, *integration* means that the pension plan payments move inversely to Social Security payments. Sponsors that integrate argue that their contribution to the Social Security system on their employees' behalf should be taken into account when deciding how large their direct pension obligation should be.

Private pension plan integration with Social Security is a very complex area, as Allen, Melone, Rosenblum, and Van Derhei show. All else remaining the same, however, an integrated plan requires less funding and is thus less costly at a given replacement rate than a plan that excludes Social Security. Employees may, of course, find the plan less attractive and raise other compensation demands—or find it less costly to leave.

For defined contribution plans, the only way to integrate potential Social Security payments is to allow for Social Security contribution percentages in the defined contribution arrangements. For instance, a nonintegrated defined contribution percentage may be stated as 12% of salary per year. An integrated contribution, however, could be 12% of salary in excess of the Social Security wage base that goes into the defined contribution plan, along with the difference between 12% and the Social Security tax rate on wages up to the Social Security wage base. For example, if the Social Security wage base was $65,000, the plan would contribute 12% of salary in excess of $65,000 and the difference between 12% and the Social Security tax rate on the first $65,000 of income. So if the salary was $100,000, and the Social Security tax rate was 8% of the $12,000 in employer contributions, $5,200 would go to the Social Security system and $6,800 would go to the pension fund. Arrangements such as this are not uncommon.

Social Security payments can be integrated directly into defined benefit plans; integration does not have to be done at the early, contributory stage. There are two methods: the *offset* approach and the *excess* approach (see Logue or Merton, Bodie, and Marcus).

In *offset* plans, the computed pension payment can be reduced under current law by up to 37.5% of the Social Security payment. Thus, if an employee had a final three-year average pay of $40,000, with forty years on the job, and the employer offered 1.5% times the above, the computed annual pension benefit would be $24,000. The replacement rate would be 60%. If Social Security payments were to be $10,000 per year, the sponsor's pension payment would be $24,000 less 37.5% of $10,000, or $20,250. Note that the recipient would get $20,250 from the sponsor's pension payment plus the $10,000 Social Security payment, or $30,250. Everything considered, the replacement rate would be 75.6%. Of course, the employer would factor into the decision on the benefit percent that is originally chosen the fact that the entire Social Security payment cannot be deducted from the computed pension benefit.

Excess plans produce benefits only above a specified amount. The pension benefit is computed only on excess income, the amount by which income exceeds the Social Security wage base or some fraction thereof. A variant of the excess plan is the *step-rate* excess plan. In the step-rate plan, full benefits are paid on excess income as well, but benefits might still be paid on the base income, though at a lower rate.

The choice of whether to integrate or not can be very significant in terms of sponsor costs and in terms of the replacement rates realized by retirees. Concerning the latter, a nonintegrated plan tends to provide more protection against inflation to workers than an integrated plan because pension benefits are not reduced as Social Security benefits rise. Of course, many sponsors with integrated plans as well as those with nonintegrated plans have voluntarily made upward adjustments on an ad hoc basis in the past to compensate for inflation. Whether they will do so in the future is anyone's guess. However, because Social Security payments themselves are indexed (adjusted for inflation), those employers who do not integrate at least put themselves in a position where they cannot cut their own benefits in an inflationary environment. It should also be noted that such employers need not increase their benefits in the event that Social Security benefits are reduced.

Roughly 50% of private defined benefit plan participants participate in integrated plans, according to the 1995 *EBRI Databook on Employee Benefits*. In contrast, only about 10% of public-sector employees who participate in defined benefit plans participate in integrated plans.

Vesting

The number of years a worker must work before gaining "ownership" of a pension is an important factor in plan design, and hence in the sort of incentives generated. Legislation limits the range of possibilities for private pension plans. Nonetheless, even the narrow range of choices left could still have some impact on employee incentives, labor mobility, and sponsor cost. With most private defined benefit pension plans, employees are fully vested after five to seven years with the sponsor. Public pension plans, as would be expected in the absence of ERISA-like legislation, have a wider variety of vesting schedules. Ten-year cliff vesting is as common as five-year vesting (except for some federal employees); twenty-year vesting is used by the military. With most defined contribution plans, vesting occurs when funding occurs.

Qualifying Requirements

Pension plan sponsors generally specify age and service requirements before an employee can qualify for a pension fund. Typically, these might be twenty-one years old and two years on the job. These sorts of requirements simply allow sponsors to avoid setting up administrative accounts and putting money aside for very short-term employees. These requirements are highly regulated for private plans.

Retirement Provisions

Retirement provisions include early retirement options, normal retirement age, spousal death benefits, and a host of other features that individually may not seem financially substantial. In terms of attracting and keeping good employees and motivating desired behavior, however, they may be both useful and costly. They are thus worth careful scrutiny when designing pension plans.

Funding Status

Funding status is not a question for DCPs since they are, by definition, fully funded. However, funding status is an important element of plan operation for DBPs. For private plans, ERISA and the PBGC provide rules governing acceptable levels of underfunding, and the IRS provides rules that discourage excessive overfunding. Public pensions have no comparable set of rules within which to determine what the sponsor finds to be acceptable.

Funding status is a policy parameter. Nonetheless, it may be thought of as a plan feature in some regards. In general, underfunding may be a desirable feature from the employer's perspective because it may keep wages lower than they might otherwise be. With an underfunded plan, employees may be reluctant to press for wage increases that would further weaken the sponsor's financial health. Additionally, an underfunded plan may bond workers to organizations since the value of the pension benefit is more directly tied to the success of the firm. Of course, if the underfunding is severe, younger workers may find the cost of leaving the organization lower than it might otherwise be because future pensions are risky and thus have a lower present value.

Advisory Services

To advise and assist the plan sponsor in structuring plans with the right features and in making other pension decisions, there exist a plethora of consultants. Benefits consultants help sponsors determine the proper replacement rate and the appropriate plan design for particular employers. They advise with respect to compliance with pension law, and they also help set up various plans for different sectors of the sponsor's business.

Tax lawyers advise regarding the plan's compliance with IRS rules and regulations. Similarly, actuaries tell the defined benefit sponsor how much it needs to set aside each period to comply with the law and to have enough money to pay retirees.

There are consultants who help plan sponsors find and monitor the performance of external money managers and the dealer/brokers who provide research and execute investment trades. These consultants further assist in developing investment strategies for both internally and externally managed funds.

Thus, the pension plan supports and has access to advice, counsel, and service from six different service industries. Pension plans are "big business," and they create other big businesses that work on their behalf.

Public Policy and Pension Fund Attractiveness

A problem with determining what form of pension plan is best and how a chosen plan should be structured is that the rules and tax rates keep changing. In recent years, the tax code and both federal and local regulations have been rewritten numerous times.

Some examples will illustrate this. In 1974, ERISA profoundly changed the private defined benefit sector as it codified various issues regarding retirement security. In 1986, the Single Employer Pension Plan Amendments Act reduced the attractiveness of private plan terminations and, arguably, the attractiveness of defined contribution plans where the sole motivation was to capture excess assets. The Omnibus Budget Reconciliation Act of 1993 set compensation limits for qualified plans at $150,000. Furthermore, distributions from pension plans have been affected by NAFTA and GATT treaties and various IRS notices (e.g., the January 19, 1996, Notice 96-8 concerning distributions from cash balance plans, according to Wyatt). And throughout the last several years, tax rates have decreased and increased and state and local regulations governing public pension funds have changed. These changes invariably affect the tax and regulatory incentives associated with pension plans.

Scholes has pointed out that changes in tax rates and regulations have numerous, sometimes unintended effects. For example:

- Lower tax rates make funding less attractive for taxable sponsors and employees.
- Higher taxes reduce the demand for pensions as employees have less income with which to maintain their standard of living.
- Antidiscrimination rules reduce pension growth as those who benefit from this presumed "equity" are those least likely to value pensions; the limits on compensation to lower-paid, newer workers (especially for defined benefit plans) make defined contribution plans relatively more attractive than defined benefit plans.
- Limits on reversions reduce the attractiveness of defined benefit plans.

Continuing change and unintended consequences make pension planning a challenge. Nevertheless, good planning is the precursor to good management. We do not pretend to know the future direction of public policy nor the incentives and disincentives that may exist two years from now or twenty years from now. What we do know is that the desirability of alternative pension fund schemes and structures is likely to change over time on both an absolute and a relative basis. Sponsors and employees will have to adapt, perhaps through the design of new structures, perhaps by shifting the mix of current to future compensation, or perhaps in other ways.

Conclusion

Pension schemes make sense for many organizations. The U.S. pension system has worked well as an employee motivator and as a provider of a special form of social insurance for employees. Many decisions about pension plans have significant workforce and financial implications. Because pensions are part of the total compensation package, they are useful in attracting and selecting employees and may motivate what the sponsor believes to be desirable behavior. To be useful, however, they also must be desirable from the employee's perspective. Addressing these issues requires close collaboration among treasury managers under the careful supervision of top management and the employees for whom the plan is designed. Optimal pension plan design will have to meet the needs—conflicting at times—of employers and employees. Optimal design also is—and will continue to be—affected by the forces that shape the labor markets and by public policy.

Defined contribution plans, defined benefit plans, and the hybrid variations all offer economies of scale with regard to information and management. All are efficient means of saving for retirement. All have subtle and not so subtle advantages and disadvantages with respect to financial implications and employee incentives.

Sponsors who wish to encourage longevity and retirement when it is most convenient for them may find DBPs attractive. Employees, however, may find the immediate vesting and mobility of DCPs attractive. Similarly, although sponsors may desire to shift investment risk to beneficiaries by offering DCPs, employees may have a preference for a known benefit stream and the possible protection DBPs may offer against inflation and the failure of Social Security to keep pace. For private plans, the risk of an unsatisfactory pension is less because of funding standards and, as a last resort, because of the PBGC. DBPs cannot be customized to meet individual employee needs, however. DCPs are easy to understand and value, while DBPs are more complex. Investment expertise is required for both, but may be more efficiently delivered through a DBP.

Finally, in evaluating the advantages and disadvantages of DCPs and DBPs, remember that the U.S. equity markets were unusually robust from 1982 to 1996. Would DCPs be as appealing following the 1973 to 1974 period when, in a period of roughly one and a half years, the equity market fell by over 40%? If U.S. equity returns are less spectacular in the future than they have been in the recent past, how will employee morale be affected in organizations that offer only DCPs?

With all of these sometimes conflicting factors, a multidimensional plan (for example, a defined benefit plan coupled with a defined contribution plan) has a certain appeal in allowing employers to structure appropriate incentives while accepting the preferences of those in the labor force. Ultimately, choice of pension plan structure depends jointly on the nature of the industry/organization and the preferences of employees in that industry.

Chapter 3

The Prudent Pension Fiduciary: A Pragmatic View

A fiduciary is a juridical person—that is, a real person or legal "person" such as a bank or insurance company—who manages business affairs on behalf of another. As such, a fiduciary is an agent who enjoys a special relationship of trust and responsibility with the principal (either a person or an organization) that entrusted assets to the control of the fiduciary. Conflicts of interest must be resolved in favor of the principal or beneficiary; only when all other things are the same can a fiduciary act on self-interest.

Fiduciary Responsibility Defined

Fiduciaries are charged with the duties of care and loyalty. *Care* in this context means that fiduciaries must give extensive consideration, using generally available and widely used methods of analysis and modes of behavior, before committing the principal's resources to a particular course of action. With respect to pension plans, this aspect of fiduciary duty deals in large part with prudent investment decision making. *Loyalty* in this context means that the fiduciary must act in the best interest of the principal who assigned the fiduciary responsibility, even if this is not the best course of action for the fiduciary. This aspect of fiduciary

Rebecca Warren of Cambridge Associates contributed much to the development of this chapter.

standards is concerned with conflicts of interest that may arise between the financial beneficiary of the investment fund and the fiduciary. Appendix I provides a quick guide to responsible fiduciary behavior.

For someone who manages funds for private pension plans, there is an even more stringent standard of care. Under ERISA, that person must be a *prudent expert*. This means, in general, that there is an affirmative obligation to use those methods of analysis and modes of behavior that other experts employ to manage the funds with which the fiduciary has been entrusted. The managers of public pension plans are also fiduciaries. The explicit obligations of these fiduciaries differ from state to state because public plans are not covered by ERISA; rather, they are subject in general to state trust law. Standards of behavior are generally less stringent than those under ERISA. However, at present (in 1997), an increasing number of states are legislating standards similar to those of ERISA.

The broad requirements of fiduciary responsibility apply more or less to plan trustees, corporate boards, chief investment officers, plan administrators, and internal money managers. They also apply to outside money managers and any others who render advice for a fee. Moreover, the requirements for being prudent apply not only to the governance, oversight, and investment aspects of a pension plan, but they apply to the everyday management aspects of a plan as well. For example, all of the actuarial and accounting work must meet the standards of prudence.

In this chapter we first offer an overview of the obligations that must be satisfied by a prudent fiduciary. This is the legal aspect of prudence. Next, we discuss what this means from a practical perspective: What sorts of analysis and behavior are most likely to pass the test of prudence? What must a person who is a fiduciary do to remain within the limits of prudence? We begin with ERISA and what ERISA means for private pension plan fiduciaries and for fiduciaries of public plans subject to ERISA-like legislation. After this, we turn to the fiduciary issues that are unique to public plans.

Although private plans are governed by ERISA while public plans are governed by state trust laws, the responsibilities of those charged with administering them are quite similar. Thus, we shall not draw any fine distinctions between those who are agents of shareholders and those who are agents of taxpayers. This chapter constitutes the organizing principle for the rest of the book. It tells the reader why the material in the following chapters is important and how each aspect of pension plan management fits with the others. As we will see, the prudent fiduciary develops overall investment policy, selects managers, monitors performance, keeps the books straight, and does what is possible to enhance investment performance and the likelihood that promised or expected benefits will materialize. The challenge the prudent fiduciary must heed is that these tasks require a delicate balancing act among competing interests.

The Prudent Investor

In 1830, the case of *Harvard v. Amory** set the precedent for what is now commonly known as the *Prudent Investor law* (originally termed the "Prudent Man law"). The decision stated that:

> All that can be required of a trustee to invest is that he shall conduct himself faithfully and exercise sound discretion. He is to observe how men of prudence, discretion, and intelligence manage their own affairs, not in regard to speculation, but in regard to the permanent disposition of their funds, considering the probable income, as well as the probable safety of the capital to be invested.

More than a century later this broad statement was modified, but not much. In 1940, the Trust Division of the American Bankers Association adopted a slightly modified version of this language to establish the Model Prudent Man Investment Act. It reads:

> In acquiring, investing, reinvesting, exchanging, retaining, selling, and managing the property for the benefit of another, a fiduciary shall exercise the judgment and care, under the circumstances then prevailing, which men of prudence, discretion, and intelligence exercise in the management of their own funds, considering the probable outcome, as well as the probable safety of their capital.

ERISA Rules

The Employee Retirement Income Security Act (ERISA), which strengthened considerably employees' claims on promised pension benefits, was passed in 1974 to stop perceived abuses of private pensions by sponsors and others involved in managing plans and plan assets. It specifically stated that a private pension fund manager has fiduciary responsibilities to the pension fund and is therefore required to use the prudent investor standard in making investment decisions.

Although public pension plans are not governed by ERISA, their managers must comply with the fiduciary standards established by the

---

*126 Moss (9 pick) 446 (1830).

applicable state statutes and legal precedents. Some states roughly follow federal standards, sometimes adding "legal lists" and other restrictions; others apply standards that seem more relevant to the nineteenth than the late twentieth century because they have apparently ignored virtually every advance in investment theory and practice. In our discussion we generally consider ERISA to be a higher standard against which specific actions may be evaluated. In situations where public plans face unique, non-ERISA constraints, of course, some of our conclusions may be inappropriate. Many state and local regulations, however, are moving toward ERISA standards, so there is clearly some commonality in attitudes among state and local governments, and thus a reasonable basis for taking ERISA as a reasonable standard.

The fiduciary obligations specified in ERISA cover six areas of pension fund management and administration.* The fiduciary duty of care entails four of these. The first obligation of the duty of care is the prudent expert requirement, which is a bit more stringent than the prudent investor standard. In the language of ERISA this means the fiduciary must exercise the "care, skill, prudence and diligence under the circumstances then prevailing that a prudent man acting in a like capacity and familiar with such matters would use in the conduct of an enterprise of a like character with like aims."†

Second, ERISA requires that plan assets be diversified. This rule is bent a great deal in Employee Stock Ownership Plans (ESOPs), in stock bonus plans, and sometimes in 401(k) plans that invest heavily in the stock of the sponsoring employer. Apart from these general situations, the requirement means that the plan must hold a variety of securities and may hold a variety of asset classes, including real estate and even collectibles. Importantly, ERISA standards allow individual assets to be viewed as a part of a diversified portfolio. That is, a particular investment may be allowable no matter how risky so long as it adds little to total portfolio risk. In contrast, many states still require that each asset be able to stand alone as a prudent investment; thus for these states there is no meaningful diversification standard. An unintended consequence of setting standards on an asset-by-asset basis is that it is possible to end up with a portfolio that is poorly diversified, taking too much risk for too little expected return.

---

*This section relies heavily on the article by William G. Drums (see bibliography).
†ERISA, §404 (a)(1)(B).

The third ERISA requirement of the duty of care is the documents rule, which states that a plan must be administered in accordance with its governing documents—for example, the plan sponsor's investment guidelines—so long as those documents do not conflict with other ERISA rules. (Consider, for instance, investment guidelines issued by a plan sponsor stating that plan assets should be held entirely in, say, modern art—these would not provide safety to the pension manager from ERISA's prudence and diversification requirements.) As long as the investment guidelines themselves are financially sensible, they must be followed. Among other things, this requirement strongly suggests that a plan sponsor have a set of written investment guidelines.

The fourth obligation of the duty of care is an indicia of ownership rule that states that, with few exceptions, documents relating to asset ownership must be within the jurisdiction of U.S. courts. Basically, this means that U.S.-based trustees must be used by U.S. pension plans.

The fiduciary duty of loyalty has two aspects. The first is that a pension plan must be administered solely in the interest of the beneficiaries. This means that when there is a conflict between the welfare of the fiduciary and the welfare of the pension plan, the choice that is made must not be disadvantageous to the plan or its beneficiaries. Second, the plan must be administered for the exclusive purpose of providing benefits to participants and beneficiaries and defraying reasonable administrative expenses. This means, for example, that a plan must not buy stock in a company so that the chairman of the stock-purchasing firm can get a seat on the board of directors of the portfolio company.

The Prudent Investor Law

Since ERISA was drafted, the vagueness of the prudence language has led to confusion and concern about making appropriate investment decisions and proper decisions regarding other aspects of fund management. The practical, economic definition of *prudence* has evolved with changes in both financial theory and the capital markets. Court opinions also have contributed to an environment in which prudence is not fixed but evolves. The result is that the interpretation of the Prudent Investor laws changes over time, and it is the responsibility of the fiduciary to update his or her knowledge continuously regarding these changes.

Recently, The American Law Institute drafted a new standard Prudent Investor law that, as of the end of 1995, sixteen states, including the states with the largest public pension plans—California and New York—had already adopted for the trust funds administered in those states as well as state and local pension plans. The new "Prudent Investor Rule" urges courts to adopt a flexible standard of review in the context of modern financial theory. It provides the following specific standards:

- Any and all investments must be considered as part of the portfolio and not be judged on an individual basis.
- No investment should be considered inherently prudent or imprudent.
- In the majority of cases, trust assets must be diversified.
- Inflationary effects must be given consideration in investment decisions. That is, the focus must be upon real values. (This is a significant departure from the original notion that the primary risk to protect against was the erosion of nominal principal.)
- Investment skill must be demonstrated by the fiduciaries, or else the investment management should be delegated to a qualified party; this is the "prudent expert" position.

Although the restatement of the Prudent Investor law helps to clarify some of the vagaries in many states (with many more soon expected to adopt similar legislation), the dynamic nature of financial markets and investing theory presents a challenge to fiduciaries to stay current with both as well as with current legal theory. Furthermore, although the requirements for behaving as a prudent fiduciary may appear to be benign, they are not. Taken as a whole, they can be hard to follow and may create situations in which the law and economic rationality are, or at least seem to be, at odds. Resolving such conflicts in a prudent manner can pose a difficult challenge for even an experienced fiduciary.

Prudence and Financial Theory

For over one hundred years after the *Harvard v. Amory* decision, stocks were considered too risky an investment to be made by any prudent trustee. Today, modern portfolio theory and the accumulated experience of most investors across many countries would suggest that failing to invest in stocks is imprudent. The rates of return on stocks have been very high relative to those on bonds, and stocks have provided better long-run inflation protection.

Indeed, even as we write, finance theory is altering the concept of prudent behavior. For instance, despite the general public's view that the use of derivative securities (such as puts, calls, futures, and swaps) is very risky, a case can be made that not using derivatives is riskier still in some instances. For example, in light of the widespread use of derivatives as a means of reducing risk and achieving cost-effective diversification, fiduciaries may now be required to "understand and use derivatives in certain circumstances while avoiding derivatives in circumstances where they are not suitable," according to George Crawford. Of course, many derivatives are primarily speculative in nature and as such should clearly be avoided by fiduciaries unless the advantages of their use are substantial. At the same time, some derivative instruments are prudent investments within the context of a specific investment strategy, providing definable costs or risk-reducing benefits to a portfolio. As a result, a fiduciary may be liable to the beneficiaries for not taking advantage of all that the financial markets offer. These and other dramatic changes and innovations in financial theory are constantly changing the definition of the role of a trustee.

The Role of Theory: An Illustration

To further illustrate the point that innovation in financial theory affects the role of a fiduciary, consider the impact that the introduction of the capital asset pricing model (CAPM) and the efficient market hypothesis (EMH) have had. Together they suggest that passive investing through market indexing (i.e., buying a portfolio that mimics a broad index, such as Standard & Poor's 500 Index) provides an efficient means of portfolio investing and diversification. The CAPM allegedly showed that to achieve higher expected returns, greater market risk had to be borne. The semi-strong form of the EMH argued that current security prices already reflect all available public information, so there is no information an investor can obtain from public sources that is not already incorporated in a security's price. That is, all securities are priced correctly conditional upon publicly available information. Thus, if the market cannot be beaten, why spend time and money trying to beat it? In light of the theory and empirical work, many academics and practitioners argue that no security could ever be objectively viewed as under- or overvalued. In short, many argue passive investing via indexing is the most cost-effective way to manage an investment portfolio.

More recent studies, however, have cast doubt on both the CAPM and the EMH models, suggesting that some active security selection and tactical asset allocation may in fact be prudent and provide beneficiaries with a better risk/reward tradeoff than simple indexing. It is this continual change in the accumulating body of knowledge that makes it imperative for fiduciaries to stay current on changes in investment theory and practice and observe how these changes are being exploited by other (presumably expert) managers.

Prudence and the Courts

Prudent expert behavior on the part of a fiduciary mandates that the fiduciary be up-to-date on mainstream innovations in investment and financial theory and associated empirical findings. It does not require a manager to believe and embrace these innovations: it simply requires that the manager know about them and have good reason for incorporating them or ignoring them in making investment decisions. From an economic perspective, it means that a fiduciary should have some view regarding how asset prices are determined and how and why they move, and should understand clearly how to exploit that view for the investment benefit of the pension plan. Given current widespread use of derivatives such as futures and options to help implement various investment strategies and hedges, and given also the perpetual evolution of financial products, the educational implications for fiduciaries can be substantial. They must invest much time in training and education.

Despite the fast pace of new financial developments that pension fiduciaries must understand, they cannot ignore historical context and precedent, as these can provide the basis for allegations of imprudent behavior. In other words, the manager must be forward looking, but must not ignore prior legal and economic views. To help demonstrate the slow evolution of legal action on as mundane a topic as what constitutes a prudent investment, note that almost twenty years ago, in 1979 the Department of Labor (DOL) took specific steps to try to clarify the debate about whether or not investments should be judged individually or within the context of the entire portfolio. The DOL clarified this issue by stating that "the prudence of an investment decision should not be judged without regard to the role that the proposed investment or investment course of action plays within the overall plan portfolio" (see the article by Droms). Despite this, litigation still commonly arises from losses suffered as a result of individual investments. Prudence, an *ex ante* concept, is often challenged by after-the-fact results. Although prudence is not intended to be determined on the basis of realized performance, the poor performance of any individual investment or set of investments ultimately may provoke litigation. So, despite what the Department of Labor, ERISA's monitor, wrote in the 1970s, the single investment view is still alive in the 1990s.

A good example is the 1992 case of the *State of West Virginia v. Morgan Stanley*. (Morgan Stanley is a firm that offers a number of financial products, including investment management.) The case involved West Virginia's $4 billion public pension fund. The state sued Morgan Stanley because of its use of bond options and futures in managing the portfolio. Because of some losses, the state made an *ex post* case that the investments were imprudent. The state court initially decided the case without considering the context of these investments, with regard to the rest of the portfolio investments, and found for plaintiff. This sort of chilling court decision lead fiduciaries to make investment decisions on the basis of an assessment of whether a particular investment is likely to result in litigation or not, not whether a particular investment makes sense in the context of the total portfolio.

Furthermore, this case and others like it have effectively made fiduciaries into guarantors against losses; in *State of West Virginia v. Morgan Stanley*, the lower court initially did not allow the gains from successful iterations of the proscribed activity to offset actual losses from these investments in calculating damages. The financial damage to the pension plan was the gross loss, not the net loss, said the court. If this were to become a general rule, fiduciaries would be expected to cover the losses of a particular investment without considering any offsetting gains. The implications are that a portfolio manager is expected to invest in a manner consistent with modern portfolio theory, recognizing the benefits of diversification, but also must justify each individual investment on its own merit.[*]

Regulation and legal precedent can have perverse consequences. Empirical evidence suggests that enforcement of the single security version of the prudent investor law in fiduciary situations has resulted in a tilting of the affected portfolios toward the "high-quality, prudent sector of the equity market," according to Del Guercio. However, since returns are generally linked with risk, too little risk typically leads to low relative returns. Thus, holding portfolios that are heavily weighted toward "prudent" stocks may be inadvertently taking too little risk and thus inadvertently getting too little return. Low relative returns will require higher contributions and may, ironically, reduce the security of plan ben-

---

*Note that the State Supreme Court reversed the lower court ruling and a new trial was set.

efits. Nonetheless, many fiduciaries may fear being found "imprudent" if they invest or authorize investment in "imprudent" securities with promising returns.

Prudent Investment Strategies

What fiduciaries believe about asset pricing is important because these beliefs will determine the investment strategies they pursue or approve. Thus, there are implications of various asset pricing theories for prudent investment management. There are two main kinds of investment strategies: passive and active. Each is based on a specific belief about how assets are priced. We consider each from the perspective of prudence in the following sections. (In Chapter 4, we consider this issue from the perspective of asset pricing.)

Is Passive Investing Prudent?

Passive investment strategies include the use of index funds that are designed to provide the investor with the return of a financial market or sector without the expense of holding the entire market; they offer a cost-effective means of portfolio management and are the appropriate choice for any investor who is firmly convinced asset prices reflect currently available information as postulated by the EMH. A passive fund may also be appropriate for an investor who believes that there are small pockets of market-pricing inefficiency, but does not want to base an entire investment strategy on this belief. Accordingly, such investors may invest in an indexed *core* portfolio and actively manage the remainder.

For private pension managers, debate has arisen about the amount of monitoring that the Prudent Investor law requires when the manager employs a passive investment strategy. Passive investing is cost-effective in part because it does not require the investment manager to monitor the performance of the individual companies included in the portfolio. However, this lack of monitoring means that eventually a company that goes bankrupt may be included in the portfolio. There are many who believe bankruptcy is a forecastable event using available data. Further, they believe the market does not always correctly assess this prospect (see, for instance, Edward Altman's book, *Corporate Financial Distress*). As a consequence, an item-by-item scrutiny of the holdings of a passive portfolio could result in problems for the fiduciary, as principals are able to identify specific stocks that are excessively risky—poor or imprudent investments.

The benefits of passive investing are applauded only within the context of the EMH. Passive investing will fall under increased scrutiny as attacks on the EMH intensify. Since its 1976 preamble on prudent asset management, the DOL assumes that a pension trustee generally screens an index fund for poor performers. The DOL may at some point reconsider its 1976 screening assumption in a more inflexible format. Thus, managers who rely entirely on passive investing could have an increasingly difficult time explaining why they do what they do.

Specific questions for fiduciaries surrounding the use of passive investment strategies using index funds include:

1. Should pension plans be invested in index funds, and if so what percentage of the portfolio should be invested in indexes?

2. In the event that pension fund managers choose to use index funds, how can they prudently choose from the array of different index funds available? What is the relevant market portfolio? For instance, should the index used be the Standard & Poor's 500 or some broader index?

3. Should the component securities in index funds be monitored or screened by pension managers to ensure that the fund is likely to track the broad index chosen, and if so, how often?

4. Does the use of index funds limit the pension manager's liability for the investment?

5. Does the use of index funds have any implications for pension managers regarding the extent to which they should be active in corporate governance, encouraging companies included in the index portfolio to improve their financial performance?

The answers to these questions are the subject of academic and legal debate, so no absolutes can be given. However, we do briefly summarize the issues involved with each question and offer guidance in how to make the right decision.

Investing in Index Funds

Recent criticism of the CAPM and efficient market theory suggests that active management may be an effective means of adding value and that indexing may not be the "answer" for prudent stock investing that it was once thought to be. As a result of this debate, "trustees should be counseled to consider active investment strategies as an adjunct to indexing," according to Koppes and Reilly. Indexing may provide important cost benefits, however, particularly for those who do not wholeheartedly believe either view the efficient or imperfect markets view of the world. Institutional index funds typically cost around 2 to 15 basis points as a percentage of average assets per year. Additionally, the limited trading activity that occurs will result in a small amount of transaction costs. Overall, passive funds are very low cost and thus have only a low hurdle to clear in providing returns. Indexing probably should not be considered superior to all active management strategies because it is unlikely all markets or sectors are equally and completely efficient in pricing assets. For example, the stocks of smaller companies may not be priced as efficiently as those of larger companies. The exact percentage of the portfolio to be indexed should ultimately be determined by the overall portfolio strategy of the plan, especially with respect to what markets are deemed to be appropriate for investment. It is decided the plan should have exposures to markets that are not likely to be very efficient, the plan should at least consider active management in these markets. Thus, decision makers must decide what they believe about asset pricing on a market-by-market basis and translate these beliefs into percent allocations of actively managed assets.

Choosing the Right Index

The choice of an index fund requires the same care and diligence that an active fund choice requires. The prudent choice should focus on three issues:

1. What is the correct risk/return mix for the fund?

2. What are the costs of maintaining an index fund?

3. How effectively does the index fund meet its objective? How much tracking error exists?

There are now a very large number of investment managers offering a wide array of index products. Some index products essentially are indexes of a particular strategy—for example, a value stock index fund may be useful to an indexer who believes markets overreact but not to an investor who believes there is no predictable overreaction.

Other products faithfully try to construct a portfolio in which returns will mimic most of or all of the companies in the relevant security market. If a fund manager believes the EMH, then a broad market index is appropriate.

If an index fund is meeting its objective, its tracking error should be small. The tracking error indicates how the price movement of an index fund is different from the price movement of its benchmark. One would normally expect some tracking error, resulting from the effect of cash flows into and out of the index fund due to withdrawals and contributions. Dividend receipts and transaction costs—the costs of buying and selling the index stocks—also contribute to tracking error. Tracking error also arises because many index funds do not actually buy the entire group of companies included in the index, but rather a representative subset of the index. In this case, an investor could inadvertently be buying a "semi-active" index fund, because the managers are actively working to maintain a sample or subset of securities that behaves as the entire population does.

Bear in mind, finally, that indexes are themselves managed. When companies leave an index because of failure or merger or changed industry focus and they are replaced, the stocks selected by those who determine the index for replacements are not selected randomly or chosen by a fixed formula. So, to the extent that those who construct indexes select companies that they believe will remain in the index for a long time and will produce high investment returns, the index itself is managed.

Monitoring Component Securities in Index Funds

Choosing passive management instead of active management also heightens the debate over the level of monitoring and screening that should be required for a passive portfolio strategy. Even though a fund is indexed, a manager should periodically examine the components of the index fund to make sure that the index portfolio really replicates the broad index, and to eliminate obviously failing companies—an action that appears at least partially active in nature. Index fund screening is sometimes criticized for the following reasons:

1. Accurate screening incurs potential added costs.

2. Screening causes management inefficiency.

3. The typical focus of screening is on past investment performance, which is often regarded as reactive rather than proactive.

Nonetheless, the DOL considers screens, at least initially, to be a measure of prudence for investing in an index fund. The investment community, however, is divided as to whether screening is a useful and necessary tool. It is important to note that in some instances the duties of *screening* are considered to require the removal of inappropriate investments, while the duty of *monitoring* excludes the removal obligation and focuses mainly on the collection and appraisal of investment performance and information. For a private pension fund manager, however, they both potentially lead to significant increases in cost. This increase in cost may significantly reduce the cost advantage of indexing, especially in markets where the likelihood of company failure is relatively high.

Index Funds and Fiduciary Liability

The anti-delegation doctrine is pervasive in common law and was reaffirmed for private pension funds in ERISA. This doctrine dictates that trustees may not delegate decision making to escape liability. The problem that arises is that, in some ways, this doctrine directly conflicts with the efficient market formulation on which indexing was based. The anti-delegation doctrine requires that fiduciaries take responsibility for specific decisions. They are allowed to defer to consultants and advisors only as part of that decision-making process. One result of this is that a fiduciary's "duty to monitor" must still be considered with passive strategies.

Although the courts are clear that the choice of managers or consultants must be made with care, they are less clear about how passive strategies are to be monitored, especially over time. Although the first ten years under ERISA produced little judicial elaboration on the Prudent Expert law, the focus of the courts generally is shifting away from the performance of individual assets and toward the performance of the portfolio as a whole. This makes the world a bit safer for indexing. Additionally, as individual states begin to accept the view that no single investment should be judged prudent or imprudent on a stand-alone basis, passive strategies become more acceptable for public pension plans.

Unfortunately, the nature of ERISA and ERISA-based legislation discourages managers from undertaking "untested" investments or strategies. ERISA encourages managers to imitate the behavior of others. Overall, then, it is evident that fiduciaries should not expect that the choice of a passive portfolio strategy can be made without any liability.

Index Funds and Corporate Governance

Once a passive investment strategy has been chosen for all or even a portion of the pension fund, the manager is expressing the view that there are substantial limitations to choosing undervalued stocks or moving funds from overvalued to undervalued investment sectors. In other words, the underpinning of the passive strategy is there is no or at best only a small way to add value through security selection or market timing. Better absolute performance could be achieved, however, if the companies in which the portfolio owns shares performed better. Therefore, it is reasonable to ask whether the pension manager has an affirmative obligation to get companies in which the portfolio has a stake to perform as well as possible.

Some pension managers believe they must play an active role in corporate governance to get better share performance; others believe they should not. However, both face the same constraint: it is costly to sell their shares in the very largest companies; if they do, it is difficult to remain fully invested in equities. Since, in effect, they cannot exit, they may find that expressing their concerns about performance to boards and top company managers is a viable way to meet their fiduciary duties to the plan participants better. Accordingly, corporate intervention may be one route to better investment performance even for those who do believe in the EMH. (See Chapter 13 for an extended discussion of being a more effective shareholder.)

Is Active Investing Prudent?

Active stock and bond investment strategies assume that the capital markets are not highly efficient. They assume that specific choices regarding either individual securities or asset mix can affect investment returns. Under ERISA, the increased legal risks involved when managers take active positions somewhat discourage active management. However, as the efficient market theory comes under increasing academic attack, active management is regaining its status as an important alternative for managing pension assets.

When markets are viewed as inefficient or at least pockmarked by minor, though exploitable, imperfections, active security selection or active asset allocation would be expected to enhance investment performance. That is, returns above those justified by the level of risk borne are believed to be achievable with astute investment decision making in the face of a market that does not quickly incorporate new information on security prices.

There is mounting evidence that markets are not as informationally efficient as many financial economists once believed them to be. Many academics and practitioners are finding that not all known information is reflected in an asset's price. Further, sometimes asset prices are slow to respond to new information. Sometimes asset prices overreact to good or bad news. Sometimes it seems possible to predict future price movements based on past price movements. And sometimes the relative performance of equity and fixed-income markets produces predictions concerning the future of each market.

The prudent fiduciary who supports active investment management should have a credible basis for action regarding security selection or asset allocation, or both. At a minimum, active investors who wish to demonstrate prudence are better off legally if they have some empirical evidence that supports their beliefs and justifies their decisions. Thus, as a practical matter, any fiduciary who advocates active management ought to document the analytical or empirical basis for the trading strategies actually used.

Every active decision should be motivated by some set of basic beliefs in order to be viewed as prudent. This means there should be an implicit theory of asset price behavior in mind whenever an active investment strategy is selected and implemented. A theory does not have to be written down or supported by exotic mathematic formulae or statistics. However, without theory, one is merely throwing darts, and in a world in which asset markets are considered to be inefficient, random selection is imprudent.

Fiduciaries should have a reasoned framework for deciding that an asset is under- or overvalued, or for deciding that one asset class is more likely to produce excess returns than another. Prudent fiduciaries should articulate these asset valuation theories so that there can be no mistaking the motivation for any particular transaction. Indeed, some pension fund advisors are given a written statement regarding asset valuation. This will reduce the likelihood of adverse legal consequences and, more importantly, will impose an investment discipline upon managers that may prevent substantial losses due to unauthorized departures from policy. It also forces the prudent fiduciary to ask whether he or she really understands the strategy, its theoretical support, its trading rules, and how it can be expected to perform in various types of markets.

The theory behind investment decision making need not be uni-dimensional—that is, there need not be a single unified theory. For instance, although it may be quite acceptable for a prudent fiduciary to adopt and act upon, say, a contrarian view that holds that the best buys are the stocks that have the lowest price-earnings multiples or the lowest market-to-book ratios, it is not necessary that a prudent fiduciary always behave in the same way. The prudent fiduciary may look at growth forecasts, interest rates, or any other indicator and decide that, in the foreseeable future, the market itself may not reward a contrarian investment theme more than the alternative stock picking methods.

Prudent fiduciaries can be opportunistic. That is, they may accept the view that the securities markets go through various stages and that specific investment strategies may work only cyclically. In this case, the prudent fiduciary should have a theory that is as explicitly stated as possible about the seasonality, cyclicality, or life cycle of different investment strategies. Such a "theory of investment themes" would have its roots in the emerging field of behavioral finance, and, as such, would be grounded in (possibly implicit) theories regarding systematic and hence predictable investor behavior under certain conditions (see, for instance, the article by Tversky).

Due Diligence

Under the Prudent Investor law, the fiduciary must meet certain standards of due diligence. Although what constitutes sufficient due diligence is not always completely obvious, there are particular steps that fiduciaries can take to ensure that they are reasonably protected from serious litigation risk as well as from poor financial results.

The Department of Labor has made it clear that a written investment policy on the part of a plan sponsor helps to ensure that a rational and prudent investment strategy is carried out. The written investment policy also provides the fiduciaries with a written document that can support an individual investment in the context of a broader strategy. Such a policy should be given to any money managers and pension consultants the plan sponsor employs.

A fiduciary is responsible for answering the following questions when considering a particular investment:

1. Does it meet the diversification and minimum quality standards, if there are any, set forth in the overall plan?

2. Does it assist the plan in meeting its overall investment strategy objective? How does it expect to do this?

3. Is the investment cost-effective, and are the costs of implementing the investment reasonable?

4. Does it offer an appropriate expected reward-to-risk ratio within the context of the overall portfolio?

It is essential to note that these standards also apply when choosing an investment manager: fiduciary responsibility cannot be avoided by delegation. The decision to use an outside manager to carry out either an active or a passive strategy does not reduce the need for care, skill, and caution in the selection process. A manager should be evaluated on his or her administrative costs, transaction fees, overall performance in the context of his or her chosen investment strategy, and willingness to conform to the specified investment policy. When choosing an investment manager, a benchmark should be selected to assist in the ongoing assessment of performance. Benchmarks are discussed in detail in Chapter 7, but suffice it to say that an appropriate benchmark is the standard against which various actions may be deemed to be prudent—or not prudent.

Documentation and monitoring are both critical to prudent decision making and to due diligence. For example, fiduciaries should both evaluate investment strategies and managers regularly and document the analysis and the decision to retain or terminate either. This activity forms the basis for a formal ongoing program analysis that, if properly established and executed, ensures prudent monitoring and provides evidence that monitoring is ongoing.

The monitoring process is described in detail in Chapter 11.

Exclusive Benefit Rule

Apart from the prudent investor aspect of pension management, there are other rules that are vague and challenging that sponsors must obey. One such rule is the exclusive benefit rule. (For an excellent discussion of problems with this requirement, see the article by Fischel and Langbein.)

ERISA requires that fiduciaries carry out their duties for the exclusive benefit of participants and beneficiaries. This means they are restricted from doing anything that is in conflict with the interests of the beneficiaries. However, numerous conflicts arise in managing pension plans. An obvious conflict is posed by the relationship between the implicit consolidation of a plan and sponsor liablities. Economically targeted investments, socially responsible investing (investing in socially desirable activities or avoiding investing in tobacco or gambling stocks, for example), asset reversions from plan terminations, and directed commissions are also situations in which those who manage the plan or its assets may have interests that diverge from those of regular plan beneficiaries. Resolving these conflicts in the interest of beneficiaries, noble as it sounds, is, however, an elusive concept.

Consolidation of Liabilities

The intent of the exclusive benefit rule is to ensure that companies that provide private pension plans for their employees manage those plans in the employees' best interest. (It is not clear, however, who wins if there is a conflict between retired and present employees.) At the same time, ERISA established that pension fund liabilities are the most senior debt obligation of the firm, ranking immediately behind tax obligations. As a result, despite the accounting separation of the pension fund liabilities, the "economic model of the firm" considers the total liabilities and assets of the firm to include the assets and the liabilities of the pension plan itself. These two issues—the exclusive benefit rule and the consolidation of liabilities—lead to inherent conflicts of interest.

A case cited by Copeland clearly demonstrates the sort of conflict of interest that can arise in private pension fund management. In 1982 International Harvester switched $250 million, out of a total of $1.35 billion in pension assets, from stocks to bonds. The intent of this switch was to diminish the volatility of future pension contribution requirements on the part of the company. Such moves may make the pension plan seem safer, but can also lead to the need for larger contributions in the future, because stocks are likely to produce higher returns than bonds. What may appear to be in the best interest of the plan beneficiaries may be negatively affecting the future wealth of the firm. This may eventually cause problems for the beneficiaries of the plan because lower future profits may hamper future investment and the firm's long-run ability to compete and provide employment.

It is worth noting that although private fund managers have a strict primary obligation to the beneficiaries, they also have implicit obligations to their managers (bosses), which can be directly or indirectly enforced by the threat of job loss. Thus, those who manage pension plans may face pension regulations that run counter to what is best for their careers.

Under state law similar conflicts may arise. One case noted by Fischel and Langbein dealt with the New York City Municipal Unions

Pension Plans during New York City's fiscal crisis in the early 1970s. The pension plans bought very risky municipal debt to help the city stave off insolvency. Not only can one question the wisdom of a tax-exempt fund buying tax exempt bonds, but the bonds were so risky that the pension plans' safety was compromised. Older workers sued the pension plans, contending that the investment helped the city, not them. In fact, the investment hurt them because of the increase in risk and the increased chance of the pension plans going bust while benefits were still owed. The court found that younger workers benefited from the investment because it increased the city's chances of long-run solvency. The courts allowed the investment, but the argument for exclusive benefit to beneficiaries was stretched. The court, in effect, sided with current employees and went against retired and soon-to-be retired employees. "Exclusive benefit" remains an elusive concept.

Economically Targeted Investments

Further complexity in the exclusive benefit issue is illustrated in the debate over economically targeted investments (ETIs). ETIs are "capital projects that are designed to provide economic benefit to the economies of the geographic regions in which they occur," according to Ronald Watson. This suggests that a pension plan investment designed to benefit a certain geographic region or type of worker would be "prudent," so long as no direct economic benefits to the plan were sacrificed. However, though slim and relatively anecdotal, the evidence points to the fact that ETIs generally have performed less well than investments of similar risk using traditional rate-of-return measurements. As a result, there is considerable debate as to their prudence.

Because ERISA governs the action only of privately managed pension funds and not of publicly managed funds, and because the Department of Labor has not required (though it does encourage) private plans to make ETIs, the effects of ETIs on fiduciary prudence might be best illustrated by comparing the differences between publicly and privately managed pensions. Public pension plans have invested in ETIs for years. In many cases, they are required to do so. Although investment in ETIs by public plans may be more appropriate due to the more probable overlap between plan beneficiaries and ETI beneficiaries (as, for example, a teacher pension plan investing in real estate development in communities where more schools will be needed), it is also true that their use is more accepted because the exclusive benefit rule and the prudent investor rule do not play as large a role in public plan decision making as they do in private plan decision making.

Socially Responsible Investing

Another investment issue that arises periodically is the idea of socially responsible investing. *Socially responsible investing* involves constructing portfolios that may include specific companies because of special criteria in addition to projected investment returns, and may exclude companies that make or produce things that some portion of the investing public views as morally wrong.

For example, when apartheid was still the law of the land in South Africa, many portfolios, particularly the endowment funds of colleges and universities and public employee pension plans, eliminated the stocks of companies doing business in South Africa. There also are institutional investors that exclude gambling, tobacco, and alcoholic beverage companies from their portfolios; some that exclude weapons producers and nuclear power suppliers; and some that exclude companies with poor labor relations or that are not family friendly.

The issue for pension plan managers is whether, under existing law, pension portfolios that consist of only "socially responsible" companies, however defined, are acceptable within the law. By definition, because of their refusal to consider the entire universe of common stock investment opportunities, such portfolios are not as well diversified as they might otherwise be. Further, sponsors of such portfolios have goals other than the exclusive benefit of the pension plan beneficiaries. On these grounds, one could also argue that the prudent fiduciary of a defined benefit pension plan should not use social criteria to select securities.

The evidence, although not extensive, does not show that socially responsible mutual funds have produced lower risk-adjusted returns than conventional mutual funds. In other words, these portfolios have not been punished for systematically narrowing their investment universes, though the time period during which performance has been scrutinized is short. Admittedly, this tells us little directly about the investment performance of public or private pension plans that employ social criteria relative to those eschewing such criteria, but the evidence we have at least suggests that it may be possible to run a socially responsible portfolio without financial sacrifice. Thus, although there may be legal problems connected to socially responsible pension funds, so long as there are no deleterious financial consequences, a limited amount of such behavior is likely to be tolerated because it incurs no significant financial damage.

Plan Terminations

There are other examples where prudence and the exclusive benefit rule can produce unexpected conflict. In the mid-1980s, many corporations found themselves with heavily overfunded pension plans as a result of the sharp rise in stock prices that occurred after 1982. Under ERISA rules, they could not simply withdraw the amount by which the plans were overfunded; however, they could reduce or eliminate future contributions until the surplus was exhausted. In order to capture this overfunding, corporations had to terminate their existing pension plans. Thus, many companies terminated plans to capture the excess assets and used a portion of the total assets from the terminated pension plan to buy annuities from insurance companies that would give workers the pensions they had been promised. A number of companies that chose to recapture the pension plan overfunding in this way conducted bid processes amongst annuity providers to select the insurance company that would handle the terminations.

Many companies chose Executive Life Insurance Company, the insurance subsidiary of First Executive Corporation, because it was the lowest cost provider. It also had, through 1987 at least, a top credit rating from A.M. Best, an insurance company credit-rating agency, and from Standard & Poor's, as well as a very good rating from Moody's. Unfortunately, Executive Life Insurance Company was seized by the California Insurance Commission in 1991, and for a variety of reasons was unable to meet 100% of its pension plan annuity obligations. Lawsuits flew. They were filed by aggrieved former workers, unions, and the Department of Labor.* These suits alleged that the companies that purchased Executive Life Insurance Company pension termination annuities had behaved imprudently and ignored the exclusive benefit rule. They behaved imprudently, the suits alleged, because although Executive Life had top ratings, its investment portfolio contained "too many" junk bonds. Moreover, the suits alleged that these companies violated the exclusive benefit rule because they chose the low bidder, Executive Life, and passed the savings from choosing

---

*See, for example, *Crystal Calobrace et al. v. American National Can Company et al.* Civil Action No. 93 CO999. There are many other such cases, most of which have now been settled.

Executive Life instead of a higher bidding, allegedly safer (though not more highly rated) insurance company, along to their shareholders. Although most of these suits have been settled on reasonably favorable terms for the companies that terminated their pension plans, the story shows how ambiguous the interpretation of prudence and the exclusive benefit rule can be.

Directed Commissions

One last issue deserves mention in connection with the exclusive benefit rule. This is the issue of "soft dollars." *Soft dollars* arise in connection with directed commissions. Soft dollars are credits granted to a money management firm or other service provider from a broker in return for trades that are directed to the broker. Soft dollars can be used to pay for a particular investment service such as research.

The pitfall for fiduciaries with soft dollars is that the soft dollar credits may not be used for the benefit of the plan, and even when they are, the practice reduces accountability and disguises transfers of value between parties. As a result, directed commissions make it possible for some money management firms or pension plan sponsors to use the soft-dollar credits to obtain some service that is not useful for the pension plan. For example, a manager might rationalize thusly: since the security trading commissions are being spent anyway, why not get a product or service for them that could be useful in some other area of the pension plan's sponsor's organization, or buy some research that the investment manager wants even though the research may not apply to the plan?

Although this rationale might seem reasonable, it ignores the economic reality that the benefits that are generated from directing trades to one broker or another are rightfully an asset of the fund and hence belong to the fund's beneficiaries. Further, it may result in commissions and other trading costs being higher than they should be, to the detriment of the fund. Finally, it may be unlawful. All things considered, the misuse of soft dollars that arise from directed commissions violates the exclusive benefit rule and should be avoided. Thus, if soft-dollar arrangements are used, policy should specify that the benefits arising from these arrangements must go directly to the pension plan to be used for the benefit of plan beneficiaries. Further, the decision to direct or allow directed commissions should be documented in internal memos and through explicit written instructions and limitations on investment managers' behavior.

Concerns for Public Pension Plans

As we have noted, the rules governing public pension plans regarding prudence and other aspects of the fiduciary relationship are set in the states, not by the Department of Labor through ERISA. Generally, state courts have been more tolerant of ETIs, more tolerant of social investing, and more tolerant of low levels of diversification than federal regulators. Moreover, until quite recently, state courts have generally considered the prudence (or riskiness) of individual securities to be germane, and have not given much weight to the fact that a very risky individual security can actually reduce the risk of the entire portfolio.

All of these considerations, however, seem poised for change as states increasingly adopt rules that conform more or less to those laid out by ERISA. Accordingly, over time we expect a greater convergence between state and federal rules regarding the behavior of the prudent fiduciary. Within this framework we offer the following thoughts on public plans and prudent management.

Regulation, Politics, and Newspapers

As a result of the rapid growth in plan assets and the total number of plan participants throughout the United States, the issues that define exactly what prudent behavior is for public pension fiduciaries have become more important in recent years. With the advances in investment theory and the changes in the regulatory landscape, these issues also are much more complex.

For public pension sponsors, as for private pension ones, prudent behavior is defined in part by legislation and what the courts say it is, and in part by informed management practice. Conceptually, it seems reasonable that public pension sponsors and plan administrators can and probably should mimic some of the economically sensible legal constraints imposed or suggested by ERISA—such as diversification and the need to view investments in a portfolio context, and so forth. However, there is no universally agreed-to definition of prudent behavior within the context of the public pension, as the rules and regulations with which public pensions must comply vary from place to place. Additionally, public pensions face a number of unique constraints that private pensions generally do not have to consider.

Public pensions have to exist within the fabric of the political process and respond to the use of undue influence to accomplish political rather than economic or plan goals. Inappropriate political influ-

ence can create problems or incentives that may be counter to the interests of plan beneficiaries. In particular, this can lead to imprudent
results—such as hiring the wrong managers or too many managers or
appropriation of fund assets for general spending. Additionally, the
financial health of the plan may be threatened as politicians approve
popular increases in post-retirement benefits (hidden pay raises) without considering their impact on the funding status and health of the
plan. Finally, the pay-as-you-go mentality that is so politically popular
is counter to what many consider rational economic funding of plan
obligations.

Public pensions are also subject to uneven but occasionally intense
(sometimes naive) public scrutiny. This is the "How would I feel if I read
about it in the paper" issue. Public pensions are in the public eye, and
as such the decisions they make—and the consequences of those decisions—are fair game for newspaper reporters and politicians. This
would not be especially troubling if the information presented were fair
and balanced and the people who receive the information were knowledgeable about investing (even good stocks do go down). However, this
is not typically the case. To the contrary, misinformed public opinion
can lead to harmful legislation, such as legal lists of suitable investments and other restrictions that may reduce portfolio diversification.

Being a Prudent (Public) Fiduciary

The central concern for sponsors for public pension plan fiduciaries, then, is to develop effective ways of encouraging and delivering
prudent plan governance and administration despite the factors at
work in politics and newspapers. One "higher standard" that the public pension fiduciary must accept is the burden of educating the parties
involved in decisions that will affect the fund—legislators, trustees,
employers, union representatives, and so forth—as well as potential
critics of the fund and its management.

There is more that can be done, however. In its 1994 report on the
Virginia Retirement System, the Joint Legislative Audit and Review
Commission made several recommendations that are consistent with
better fiduciary practice. We have drawn from this report in providing
the following suggestions for the constituencies who collectively are
responsible for the public pension plans and their management:

1. Appoint qualified trustees who have an appropriate level of
   investment knowledge and judgment (rather than simply seeking representatives of various constituencies).

2. Provide sufficient statutory authority and responsibility (as opposed to implied authority) to manage the plan.

3. Select a qualified chief investment officer.

4. Make a commitment to sound actuarial funding with special attention to:

   • the impact of cost of living adjustments (COLAs),
   • sound economics and accounting assumptions, and
   • openness and full disclosure.

5. Discourage the use of extensive "legal lists."

6. Develop written policy statements, with special attention to asset allocation policies.

7. Anticipate and reduce the potential for adverse political influence.

If these recommendations are followed, the issues of prudent fiduciary management that still face public pension plans are not very different from those facing private plans. For example, it is prudent to apply current investment theory and follow sound practice in such areas as diversification, using stocks to offset inflation, managing risk in a cost-efficient manner, and so forth. It is prudent to attend to the interests of employees as well as to those of the employer even if there is an absence of ERISA-like legislation. It is prudent to evaluate carefully the value of the services or performance that the fund is getting from its managers, consultants, and others in light of their costs. It is certainly not prudent to follow investment strategies that are poorly understood or that have no theoretical support.

Defined Contribution Plans

Most of the rules governing the behavior of pension plan sponsors and managers were written with the defined benefit plan in mind. Superficially, at least, this seems to make sense, since the assets and liabilities of defined contribution plans always match, and since in increasingly popular self-directed plans beneficiaries select their own investment vehicles from a menu of selections offered by employers. However, the plan sponsor is not completely free of responsibility. Although not responsible for actual investment decisions, the plan's sponsor, as a fiduciary, still has the responsibility to ensure that

- the beneficiaries have the ability to invest in the appropriate asset classes;
- the investment managers who are available to beneficiaries are themselves chosen prudently;
- there is a routine level of monitoring and evaluating of investment performance, with investment-manager changes made when appropriate; and
- the costs are reasonable and controlled, since most investment expenses are the direct expense of the beneficiary. (See, for instance, the article by Dyer.)

Thus, although defined contribution plans reduce the risks the organization bears in providing beneficiaries with a "guaranteed" level of retirement income, they do not eliminate the fiduciary responsibilities that plan managers and trustees incur.

Recently there has been a great deal of debate about the level of guidance that the sponsor of a defined contribution plan should provide the beneficiaries on issues such as asset allocation and general investing principles. If private plans comply with 404(c) regulations written by the DOL (which are voluntary), then the sponsor of the plan has a safe haven from the liability resulting from an individual beneficiary's decision. The regulations of 404(c) require that a sponsor structure the product offering to supply an appropriate offering of asset classes along with a myriad of other administrative disclosures. If a sponsor complies, that sponsor theoretically is protected from an individual who suffers losses due to poor individual decisions about what proportion of each of the funds to invest in. However, these regulations are not intended to protect a sponsor that includes a high-cost, poorly performing fund or one that defrauds its investors.

Among other things, the 404(c) regulations establish the need for and limit the amount of education that a sponsor should provide in order to limit its fiduciary liability. The intent of 404(c) regulations is to discourage sponsors from acting as investment advisors while encouraging them to provide broad-based guidelines for making informed investment decisions. As an example, if a sponsor educates its beneficiaries on the benefits of diversification, it should be careful not to dictate directly how best to effect a diversification strategy. If the DOL determines that the education provided constitutes an investment advisory role, then companies will be held to the full fiduciary requirements and 404(c) has not limited any of their liability. Once again, there are many unresolved vagaries, and this type of regulation can be expected to evolve further in the future.

There is no unified body of regulation similar to 404(c) for public pension plans. As with much of ERISA, however, there are aspects of the motivation for the 404(c) safe harbor—education and choice—that are essential if plan sponsors want beneficiaries to be successful in managing their retirement assets.

Over the last decade the number of defined contribution plans has exploded, and the issues surrounding the responsibilities of the sponsor have come under increased scrutiny. The fiduciary requirements of due diligence and monitoring are mandated for sponsors of both defined contribution plans as well as defined benefit plans. It is not enough that defined contribution plan sponsors offer numerous investment choices—they must also monitor the ongoing suitability of these choices and make changes when the existing money managers falter (see the article by Ochs). Further, plan costs imply a fiduciary duty. In regard to the philosophy of what being prudent means, defined contribution plans and defined benefit plans are most similar. In neither case can a sponsor avoid fiduciary responsibilities.

Employee Stock Ownership Plan and Prudence

Employee stock ownership plans (ESOPs) are a special form of defined contribution plan available to private pension sponsors. (ESOPs are dicussed in Appendix A.) The responsibilities of fiduciaries with regard to ESOPs are similar to those of private sponsors in general, with some important exceptions (see Hartzell). Ordinarily, ESOPs and those who are considered fiduciaries for ESOPs are exempt from the ERISA requirement of diversification. However, recent decisions by U.S. courts of appeals raise the specter of potential liability. In one case, the issue of liability became germane as ESOP trustees continued to use employee funds to purchase company stock for the ESOP even though they had knowledge of the sponsor's deteriorating financial condition. In another case, a trust-to-trust transfer of assets triggered by an agreement to sell a division of the sponsoring company took eighteen months to complete. During this time, the sponsor's stock lost about 80% of its value—and again the issue of liability surfaced.

Neither of these cases resulted in unambiguous rulings or guidelines that ESOP fiduciaries can follow to avoid liability. They do suggest, however, that good record keeping, documenting the decision-making process followed and the data considered, is essential. More important, they suggest that a fiduciaries' risk of liability is a direct consequence of the amount of attention fiduciaries give to prudent and loyal actions.

Conclusion

Pension plan fiduciaries have a clear obligation to invest prudently and for the exclusive benefit of the beneficiaries of the plan. Moreover, they must administer the plan in an economically sensible fashion, not spending excessively on activities that bring only relatively small benefit to the plan. However, both the definition of what is or is not prudent and the measurement of "exclusive benefit" are the source of considerable legal and regulatory debate and uncertainties. At this time, it appears that this means fiduciaries are required first and foremost to be familiar with the issues surrounding their investment strategies and their specific implementation. These issues and implementations include but are certainly not limited to

- the specifics of any investment, including reading the prospectus for new securities, and the recent financial experience of portfolio companies;
- the current financial theory supporting the application of a particular investment strategy;
- the behavior and attitude of peer pension investors, and how they operate regarding particular investment strategies;
- the possible legal ramifications surrounding the use of certain types of financial instruments and the implications of these ramifications for pension management;
- the estimated risk-to-reward ratios for any given total portfolio composition;
- the need for careful monitoring of any activity that is delegated outside the immediate authority of the fiduciary; and
- careful documentation of the decision-making process, the data used, the philosophies followed, the competence of involved parties, and the policies used to reduce conflicts of interest.

ERISA for private plans and new rules for state and local plans have placed ever-increasing responsibilities on fiduciaries to gain greater depth of expertise regarding financial market behavior, to become much more careful in the monitoring of organizations providing advice or discretionary authority over plan assets, and to be much more aware about who the true beneficiaries of any decision are.

In general, private pension fund managers should expect that the debate surrounding the use of index funds and other passive investment strategies will continue to evolve. To be safe, the use of indexing strategies should include the same level of care as that used for active strategies, and thus should warrant some degree of monitoring. Ironically, this may negate some of the cost benefits that indexing offers.

Although this chapter may not help pension plan sponsors entirely avoid poor results or even lawsuits, we believe the probability of making poor investment and policy decisions as well as the prospect of suffering serious legal damages can be reduced if the suggestions presented here are heeded.

Chapter 4

Establishing Pension Investment Policy

The stakes of pension investment policy—employee security and incentives, the consequences of adverse investment performance, the rights to surplus assets, and so forth—are too high to delegate entirely to lower-level managers or to external consultants and money managers. Trustees, pension boards, top management, and those who represent the interests of shareholders, taxpayers, and employees must play a role in setting, monitoring compliance with, and reviewing pension investment policy.

Sound policy means providing written guidelines for all important decisions concerning the plan, its assets, and its management over time and in different financial markets. Policy should communicate the scope and objectives of the plan unequivocally to all stakeholders, plan managers, consultants, and others.

This chapter has four sections. The first examines the policy implications of whether a defined benefit plan should be managed as a separate entity or integrated into the overall financial management of the sponsoring organization. We then show how the pension liability affects investment policy choices for both defined benefit and defined contribution plans, and how differing views on the nature of the labor market lead to different policies for defined benefit plans. The third section reviews the key elements of investment policy as they relate to the goals of accumulation of wealth and providing retirement income in general. The final section discusses the policy parameters that are unique to defined contribution plans.

Pension Plans and their Sponsors: Separate or Integrated?

Setting investment policy begins by determining the extent to which the management of the pension plan should be integrated with the management of the sponsoring organization. Some pension funds are run as entities completely separate from the sponsoring organization; others are managed as if an integral part of the sponsor. The implications of this choice are significant.

In defined benefit plans, beneficiaries expect that plan sponsors will make up any shortfalls if pension assets are not sufficient to pay promised benefits. If assets are less than liabilities, over time the sponsor is expected to contribute enough cash to the plan (by diverting cash from the acquisition of operating assets, increasing tax collections, or reducing the payment of dividends) to eliminate the gap. One could therefore argue that the pension plan and the operating aspects of the sponsor should be viewed as integrated and should be managed that way. This point of view is not without its critics, however. Some analysts argue that the economic exposures of a sponsoring organization ought not be considered when deciding on the appropriate asset structure of the pension fund; to use a balance sheet analogy, they argue that the balance sheet of the plan and that of the sponsor should be completely separate. Not uncommonly, the proponents of a separate balance-sheet approach to pension asset management worry that there may be a misappropriation of pension assets or similar breach of fiduciary duty if the two are not separated.

Evidence on Integrating the Management of Pension Plans with Sponsors

The interaction between the operations (income statement) and asset/liability structure (balance sheet) of the sponsor and the financial health of the pension plan can most easily be seen by examining private plans. Prior to ERISA, private pension funds and their sponsoring corporations were much more separate than they now seem. A firm could terminate its pension plan, and it was just "too bad" if the pension assets were insufficient to meet the benefit payments that employees expected. What prevented most firms from behaving in this manner—that is, promising benefits and then not delivering them—was the fact that sooner or later potential employees would insist on compensation that would offset the anticipated losses from the future recontracting between the employee and employer that led to lower than expected benefits. In short, plan sponsors could recontract with employees only once, then employees would catch on and not let them get away with it again. The future incremental costs of continuing in business could have a current value much greater than the amount saved by reneging on the original pension promise. Accordingly, very few firms abused employees in this way.

Several firms did, however—notably the old Studebaker Corporation, which left thousands of retirees high and dry. This instance was such a major abuse, that, coupled with much union pressure, it led to the passage of the Employee Retirement Income Security Act (ERISA) and the establishment of the Pension Benefits Guarantee Corporation (PBGC). Under ERISA, unfunded pension claims have a status in bankruptcy equal to that of tax liens. Although this claim on sponsor assets is limited to a portion of net worth, what is relevant here is not the specific magnitude of the claim. Rather, the fact that the assets supporting pension liabilities are no longer merely pension assets means the pension plan can lay claim to other assets of the corporation. If pension plans have this claim in bankruptcy, it is not difficult to make the case that, conceptually at least, there is a claim on or interaction with the sponsor's assets on an ongoing basis. Further, in the absence of ERISA, formal and informal contracting and employee welfare concerns can at least partially extend this concept of a claim on the sponsor's assets to public funds. (See the 1977 article by Treynor for the first elaboration of the integration notion.)

There is strong evidence that private pension plan sponsors behave as if the pension plan is part of the overall corporation. This has important implications for policies governing pension fund asset management and decisions regarding the sponsor's contributions to the pension plan. For instance, Bodie, Morck, and Taggart found that the actual allocation of pension plan assets between stocks and bonds was related to the riskiness of the sponsoring corporation and the corporation's own tax status. They also found that the level of funding of the plan was connected to the financial strength of the firm: the stronger the firm, the greater the degree of funding. No doubt this was in part due to the tax deductibility of pension contributions: because the pension fund would have to be funded sooner or later, strong corporations chose to do it earlier so as to capture the tax deduction associated with pension contributions. Their findings suggest that corporate managers tend to make decisions regarding their pension plans within the broader context of the financial position and policies of the entire corporation; that is, the operating aspects of the business influence decisions such as how high the funding ought to be. One can infer, then, that other decisions—for example, the type and amount of assets to hold in the pension fund's asset pool—also are likely to be made in this integrated manner.

Evidence also supports the view that investors see the pension plan as an integral part of the corporation For instance, studies by Feldstein and Morck and by Ambachtscheer have demonstrated that the total market value of a corporation—its bonds and stocks—is diminished when it has unfunded pension obligations. Another study by Bulow, Morck, and Summers has shown that the value of common stock of a firm reflects the firm's unfunded pension obligation and is lower than it would be if the firm had no unfunded pension obligation.

Finally, the experience of pension plan terminations provides evidence supporting the notion of integration. If the defined benefit pension plan was intended by law to be separate from the corporation, then upon the termination of a plan that had assets in excess of termination or windup estimates of its liabilities, the pension plan itself would retain these (see Bulow and Scholes for further discussion). However, in all but one case—the A&P Company pension termination—the excess of assets over liabilities has been returned to the pension-sponsoring organization. (In the A&P pension plan termination, the court ordered a portion of the excess assets be retained in the plan to enhance employee benefits.) This evidence also ratifies the idea that the pension plan is part of the sponsoring organization, not separate, and the excess assets really belong to shareholders (or to taxpayers), not to the pension beneficiaries.

There is no evidence for or against the integrated income statement/balance sheet view for public plans. However, the pay-as-you-go approach to funding common in the public sector suggests that sponsors see the cash flows needed to service pension liabilities as akin to debt service or operating cash flows. Additionally, public plans are more likely to engage in economically targeted investing as a way to increase the local tax base or provide jobs for plan participants. These actions are consistent with an integrated approach.

Ownership of Excess Assets

Retention of excess pension plan assets by the sponsor upon plan termination is one way to think about the issue of who can claim "ownership" to the excess of assets over the liabilities of the plan. Ownership rights can be claimed in other ways as well. If the sponsor "owns" excess assets, this supports an integrated approach to pension management.

Economic theory generally argues that the risk taker should receive the rewards of taking risk. In a defined benefit plan (DBP), beneficiaries have a fixed claim. They do not gain from strong investment performance except to the extent that a large surplus makes their claim less risky. On the other hand, a large surplus could lead to much lower sponsor contributions; in this case, however, the surplus is likely to be reduced over time, increasing the plan's risk. Thus, for both public and private plans, the economic link between excess assets and contributions is compelling and implies that the better claim to assets beyond those needed to meet the pension benefit requirements of the plan is that of the sponsor.

By similar reasoning, an organization's investment policy governing pension fund diversification might consider the pension plan plus the claim the plan holds on the sponsor's cash flows and assets. The combined exposure could be viewed as a well-diversified portfolio, even if the pension portfolio, when considered alone, is not. Pursuing such ideas on asset choice might, in extreme cases, actually lead a sponsor to hold all bonds in its pension portfolio or all stock, depending on the riskiness of the plan sponsor itself. These extreme prescriptions for portfolios could leave very risky sponsors holding a portfolio of risky pension plan assets, say all stocks, and leave safe sponsors holding very safe pension plan assets, such as bonds.

According to the view that excess assets belong to the sponsor rather than to the beneficiaries, the sponsor's attitude toward the surplus will, to a very large extent, determine the plan's risk tolerance and, hence, guide its selection of return targets. For example, if plan sponsors decide to behave as if their shareholders or taxpayers own excess plan assets, they may be willing to assume more risk in the pension plan than they would otherwise to pursue a higher return and subsequently lower future contributions.

On the other hand, if plan sponsors believe the plan ought to be managed solely for the welfare of the participants (as ERISA seemingly mandates), and if it is possible to determine who the representative beneficiaries are—and what their risk/return preferences are—sponsors might adopt investment policies and practices that are similar, perhaps identical, to those of defined contribution plans. In this case, shortfalls in pension assets relative to liabilities would be made up by higher sponsor contributions.

Similarly, sponsors that believe the pension plan ought to be managed solely for the welfare of the participants may try to minimize the chance that the promised benefits will not materialize. Or, they may aggressively pursue return in the hopes of being able to give higher benefits to beneficiaries.

Setting pension plan policy with respect to the categoration of the sponsor and the plan and which has the better claim to excess assets is challenging. The nature of the regulations to which pension plans are subject is different from that to which the sponsor may be subject. Further, the economic interests of the sponsor and plan beneficiaries are not likely to be the same. Sponsors want lower and predictable funding costs and beneficiaries want higher benefits and a high likelihood of those benefits materializing, according to a 1995 article by Ambachtscheer. Resolution of this conflict can be achieved only through informed mutual agreement or, more appropriately, through contracting a pension deal that addresses these issues. To resolve these issues, it is necessary to understand the nature of the pension liability and something of the interaction between plan liabilities and assets. This in turn helps define the appropriate relationship between the sponsor's financial well-being and the financial health of the pension plan.

Pension Liabilities and Investment Policy

The term *funding adequacy* refers to the extent to which pension assets are sufficient to cover or offset pension liabilities. If, as noted earlier, the market value of plan assets is less than the present value of plan liabilities, the plan is said to be *underfunded*; if the market value exceeds the present value of plan liabilities, the plan is said to be *overfunded*. The adequacy of funding is affected by two broad sets of policy-level decisions made by plan sponsors: the policies governing contributions to the pool of assets from the sponsor (subject to regulatory and contractual constraints) and the policies that govern the investment of plan assets. The latter is addressed in detail later in this chapter. The former is addressed here.

In defined contribution plans, the value of the pension liability always equals the value of the pension plan assets. That is the nature of the defined contribution plan. The rewards of superior investment results and the risks of inferior results theoretically are borne entirely by the plan beneficiary. Moreover, because pension assets accumulate as money is contributed to the plan, and they rise or fall as the value of pension assets rise or fall, the assets may or may not be sufficient to cover planned retirement expenditure. If plan accumulations are not sufficient, individuals must adjust their retirement plans—their liabilities—without recourse to the sponsor (at least conceptually). Accordingly, there is no mystery about the measurement of the pension liability in a defined contribution plan.

Understanding and measuring pension liability for a defined benefit plan, in contrast, poses several conceptual as well as many practical problems. These problems must be understood to set sensible policy.

Funding Adequacy

A central element of investment policy is the adequacy of plan funding—the degree to which pension assets are sufficient to meet plan liabilities. How well funded are pension plans in general?

Using the accumulated benefit obligation (ABO) as the liability (the present value of pension benefits earned to date, assuming no salary increases), Buck Consultants reported that, for 489 of the *Fortune 1000* companies it examined, 75% were fully funded at the end of 1994. This was the first increase of the ratio of pension assets to liabilities since 1988. The Segal Company reported that for the 475 multi-employer plans it examined, 65% were fully funded with respect to their vested benefits (see the article by Schanes). Zorn reports that the average projected benefit funding (PBF) ratio for public pension plans increased from 82.7% in 1992 to 85% in 1994, continuing a long-term trend in improvement.

From the above, it is clear that there are several measures of a pension plan's liability and thus several ways to measure funding adequacy. Pension liabilities may be alternatively measured as

- the percent value of vested benefits (those earned by employees who will retain them even if they leave the organization);
- the present value of earned benefits vested and not vested; or
- the present value of all future benefits, including benefits likely to be earned (see Copeland and Weston).

The third way to measure the pension plan's liability requires estimates of employee turnover, salary increases, return rates, life expectancies, growth in the number and demographics of the pool of eligible employees, and so forth. It can be thought of as the true or economic value of the liability. The ABO accounting measure is analogous to the second method above; the PBO is similar conceptually to the third but, because it ignores important factors such as additional years of work, it typically understates the actual liability.

The analyst must be careful to know which limit is being used or should be used. In general, the best or most appropriate measure depends on what the analyst believes about the labor markets, the subject of the next section.

In setting investment policy, it is necessary to understand how regulation affects funding adequacy. Public defined benefit plans (DBPs) are not required to have a large pool of assets supporting their defined benefit pension obligations. They are not bound by ERISA to protect their pension obligations with a reservoir of capital. They can make payments on a pay-as-you-go basis, unless, of course, some state or local statute or union contract precludes such behavior. State or local statutes requiring a specific level of funding are rare, however, because it is in the interest of mobile taxpayers who can move from state to state to avoid advance-funding pension plans in order to keep current taxes low. If anything, a contractual or legal requirement that there be a reservoir of assets out of which pension obligations may be paid would arise most likely either as a consequence of collective bargaining arrangements between government entities and the relevant public employee unions, or from politically motivated concerns having to do with the welfare of public employees.

Because corporate pension plans and multiemployer plans that are governed by the Taft-Hartley Act are subject to the ERISA statutes, they are not permitted to run their pension plans on a pay-as-you-go basis. That is, they cannot rely on their current pension contributions to meet current obligations. Rather, there must be a pool of assets to which contributions are made and from which obligations are drawn. For this pool to be sufficient to fund the total pension liability, it should, under most circumstances, be many times the size of the current obligation. For any obligation, the larger the asset pool, the safer the pension plan.

To determine whether the asset pool is sufficient to assure the safety and the security of timely pension payments now and in the future, the size of the asset reservoir should, of course, be measured so that it can be compared to the present value of the liability. Fortunately, the value of most pension assets can easily be measured, and the measured values should be fairly close to true values—even for assets the values of which can be hard to measure. Differences between measured values and true values could arise only because of the difficulty of estimating the value of illiquid pension assets, such as real estate or complex derivatives. But even here, the gap between true and estimated value should never be too great. Further, it is clear that the financial health of a pension plan is jointly affected by the amount of assets owned by the plan relative to the magnitude of the plan's liability—whatever that is.

Plan Liabilities and Labor Contracts

Plan liabilities are related to the nature of the employment contract between the plan sponsor and the employee. Recall from Chapter 1 that labor contracts may be considered within the context of either spot or multiperiod, implicit contractual markets. If sponsor and employee agree that their relationship can best be viewed as a spot contract, then the true pension liability should equal only the present value of vested, accrued pension payments as of the date of the valuation. The pension liability is that which must be paid to the employee when he or she retires, if the employee immediately leaves for other employment. On the other hand, if the unspoken or implicit contract between the sponsor and the employee is mutually understood to be long term in nature, then the appropriate measure of the pension liability is the current value of accrued benefits plus those that will be accrued in the future as the employee continues to work for the sponsor, and as the sponsor continues to raise the employee's salary by giving promotions, merit raises, and cost-of-living adjustments. Similarly, if the sponsor sees itself as a going concern and has no agreement with employees that would allow it to alter its previous plan without making other arrangements with its employees, then a liability measure reflecting this is justified. Again, this is not a straightforward issue, nor is its resolution devoid of profound implications for pension plan sponsors.

If an employee receives total compensation in every period equal to the exact marginal value of his or her effort over the period—that is, if wages plus pension accrual equal marginal value product—this arrangement is consistent with a spot labor market. After each period, neither the worker nor the firm owes the other anything. Bulow and then Bulow and Scholes argue that, because the firm can terminate the pension plan at nearly any time, its pension liabilities are really only those that have already been accrued. This is certainly the case when employees have defined contribution pension plans, and it is also consistent with cash balance plans, in which wages plus the amount contributed to the plan equal the value delivered by the employee. In these plans, there is no trace of an implicit contract in the employment arrangement.

In a multiperiod labor market, the books are not cleared after each period. There is a carryover from period to period, and both employee and employer trust each other to "make good" later on today's under- or overcompensation. As the relationship goes forward, one or the other party may owe the other something at the close of each period. Even when there is no *explicit* contract extending over several periods, there is nonetheless an *implicit* one. Both worker and employer implicitly understand that in any period the books may not balance, but over the course of a career they will, much as over a long enough time period, accrual accounting and cash accounting tend to converge.

If the implicit contract theory is valid, one would expect to see salary plus accrued pension benefits that are less than the marginal value of employees' services early in their careers, with a reversal later in their careers. In other words, the combined cash wage plus pension accrual in the early years of a career are less than the value of the employee's labor, but in the later years of a career, total compensation exceeds the value of the period's labor.

Support for the validity of the implicit contract theory for labor markets and thus as a useful guide for measuring pension liabilities comes from several sources. First, most defined benefit plans provide benefits that are tied to final wages and number of years of employment. Expected pension benefits rise much more rapidly later in a career than earlier—they are back-end loaded. This means that expected pension benefits will rise with wage increases due to promotion, merit, and, importantly, inflation. Accordingly, pensions at the start of the retirement period tend to become fixed in real terms, though legally they are fixed only in nominal terms. Only implicit contract theory can explain why plan sponsors would be so generous as to promise the kind of automatic inflation protection that arises from final-pay plans. Moreover, only this theory explains why plan sponsors often voluntarily enhance the benefit payment of those who have already retired. At the same time, the theory also suggests that employees "lend" the sponsor money early in their careers; they take less than their marginal product early on with the expectation of recouping, with interest, their "banked" effort. In effect employees become unsecured bondholders of the sponsor; thus not only are they hesitant to quit but they are also hesitant to shirk on the job for fear of getting fired and losing some portion of the bond's value.

A second source of support for the validity of the implicit contract theory is offered by a 1985 study by Ippolito that found wages were not significantly inversely related to pension size. That is, higher wages did not lead to lower pension accruals and vice versa, when other elements of the labor contract were the same. In the spot contract theory, wages would be strongly negatively related, because given productivity implies a specific level of total compensation; higher cash wages would require lower pension accruals.

In addition to providing guidance in determining exactly what the liability to be funded is, there are also structural implications for the spot and implicit contracting theories. If the nature of the labor market—employer demand and employee supply—is such that long-term relationships are not valued or anticipated, defined contribution plans are likely to be appropriate. If long-term relationships are valued, defined benefit plans (DBPs) (and hybrids with distinct DBP tilts) will be appropriate.

Funding Policies and the Value of the Pension Liability

As a policy parameter, the value of the liability matters because it affects the nature of the pension plan's portfolio and the timing of and optimal level of funding. The funding status of the pension plan is an important variable in setting policy because it provides information on the financial health of the plan and insights into the plan's ability to bear risk and into future contributions the sponsor must make. As noted, determining the funding status of a plan, however, is subject to a number of choices the analyst may make with regard to what will be determined to be its liability and how it should be measured.

The weight of the evidence suggests that the correct liability measure for DBPs is that of implicit contract theory—that is, the correct liability to use in setting long-term policy should be the present value of all future benefits. This measure of the liability assumes the pension fund is a going concern, whereas a measure such as ABD assumes the pension fund should be concerned with the liability it would incur if it terminated today. One 1986 study by Ippolito has shown the implicit contract-based liability is much greater, obviously, than the spot contract liability; indeed, it could be as much as three times the measure of pension liabilities that has been explicitly sanctioned by the accounting profession, the projected benefit obligation (see Chapter 13). (The same study also shows that if the implicit contract theory is correct, pension plan underfunding is quite substantial and widespread. Another study by Ippolito from 1989 demonstrated that although the average ratio of assets to liabilities for all pension plans was 126% in 1986 using the termination [spot contract] measure of liability, the average funding ratio was only 87.5% using the liability measure implied by implicit contract theory.)

Computing the Liability of a Defined Benefit Plan

The total liability in a defined benefit plan can be computed only after assumptions regarding the following items can be made:

1. At what rate will a worker's salary grow?

2. For how many years beyond the present will the worker work?

3. How long will the worker live after retirement?

4. What discount rate ought to be used to bring these projected payments back to the present?

An example will make this clear.

Example

Ms. Landers is 50 years old, has been on the job for 10 years, and now earns $50,000 per year. She expects to work for the same employer until the age of 70, a total of 30 years. At that time, her life expectancy will be 15 years. She further expects her actual salary to increase by 5% per year. Her company provides a pension benefit equal to 2% of her final salary multiplied by the number of years of service, and makes no adjustment for the Social Security payments received. Finally, the discount rate that will be used in estimating the present value of the pension liability is the current long-term corporate bond rate, 10%. (Of course, as in all other aspects of the application of financial theory, the discount rate should reflect the riskiness of the projected stream of payments. In this case, the discount rate would be the corporate bond rate—there is a contractual obligation—but should the liability become safer still through, say, government guarantees, then the Treasury bond rate might be appropriate.)

The Spot Contract Liability. Using the spot contract theory, the pension liability would be the present value of an annuity that begins in 20 years and will last for 15 years after that. The size of the future annuity would be 0.02 × $50,000 × 10 years, or $10,000 per year. This takes no account of Ms. Landers's likely future efforts on behalf of the plan sponsor or of future raises.

The present value (PV) is

$$PV = (1/1.1)^{20} \sum_{t=1}^{15} \frac{10,000}{1.1^t} = \$11,333$$

If spot contract view of the world is correct, one way to compute unfunded pension obligation would be to subtract this amount from

Ms. Landers's pro rata share of the total pension plan's assets measured at current values. Alternatively, one could assume that the value of the assets would grow at more than 10% per year. In this case, the asset values would be projected for 20 years, and from this the liability that would exist in 20 years would be deducted. The difference between the two would then be discounted to the present. For real organizations, actuaries would actually aggregate over all vested employees to compute the liability, then compare this to the market value of assets.

The Implicit Contract Liability. If the implicit contract view of the obligation is valid, however, the spot contract theory does not reflect the true obligation accurately. The analyst must assess the future salary and the future employment profile of the employee to get a true measure of the plan's liability.

Table 4-1 shows future salary projections and the estimated present values of pension benefits as of the date of retirement and as of the present date. It also shows how annual pension cost might be computed. The "normal cost" is simply the amount by which present value of benefits increases from year to year. The benefit increase reflects the fact that salary is rising, one more year has been worked, and Ms. Landers is one year closer to retirement.

Under the implicit contract theory, the expected pension liability as of the present time, year 0, seen in the "Current Year" column, is $90,199. It increases each year as the employee becomes one year closer to pension time, so the reverse telescope of present value computation gets shorter. The expected pension liability does not rise due to expected future salary increases or longevity because these expectations are already built into the computation.

Sponsor Contributions and the Unfunded Liability. Unfunded liabilities will persist unless there is market action (net of interest rate effects that affect liabilities) that increases the value of plan assets, or the sponsor increases funding, or both. For starters, note that one of the truly strange things about computing unfunded liabilities is that, as Ezra so aptly pointed out in 1980, the magnitude of the unfunded pension liability will change depending on the method a plan sponsor has adopted to fund the plan. The various methods each have a different profile regarding when cash gets injected into the fund.

What becomes truly complicated is computing the unfunded pension liability. At year 0, let us assume that $11,333 is Ms. Landers's pro

Table 4-1. Pension Liability

Current Year	Length of Service (yrs)	% Multiplier	Salary	Accrued Annual Retirement Benefits	Total Value of Benefits at Retirement[a]	Present Value of Accrued Benefits to be Received at Retirement[a]	Normal Cost[b]	Pension Liability[c]
0	10	2%	$50,000	$10,000	$76,061	$11,306	0	$89,994
1	11	2%	52,500	11,550	87,850	14,364	$3,058	98,994
2	12	2%	55,125	13,230	100,628	18,099	3,735	108,893
3	13	2%	57,881	15,049	114,465	22,646	4,547	119,782
4	14	2%	60,775	17,017	129,433	28,168	5,522	131,760
5	15	2%	63,814	19,144	145,612	34,858	6,690	144,937
6	16	2%	67,005	21,442	163,086	42,946	8,087	159,430
7	17	2%	70,355	23,921	181,943	52,702	9,757	175,373
8	18	2%	73,873	26,594	202,278	64,452	11,750	192,911
9	19	2%	77,566	29,475	224,191	78,578	14,126	212,202
10	20	2%	81,445	32,578	247,790	95,534	16,956	233,422
11	21	2%	85,517	35,917	273,189	115,859	20,325	256,764
12	22	2%	89,793	39,509	300,507	140,189	24,330	282,440
13	23	2%	94,282	43,370	329,875	169,278	29,089	310,684
14	24	2%	98,997	47,518	361,428	204,017	34,739	341,753
15	25	2%	103,946	51,973	395,312	245,458	41,441	375,928
16	26	2%	109,144	56,755	431,681	294,844	49,386	413,521

17	27	2%	114,601	61,884	470,698	353,643	58,799	454,873
18	28	2%	120,331	67,385	512,538	423,585	69,943	500,360
19	29	2%	126,348	73,282	557,385	506,714	83,129	550,396
20	30	2%	132,665	79,599	605,436	605,436	98,722	605,436

[a]Using the current year's salary to compute the liability at the end of the year. At the end of the current year (0), the $50,000 salary generates a benefit of $10,000 (2% × 10 years × $50,000). The value of 15 years of $10,000 retirement payments is $76,061 at the beginning of the retirement period 20 years hence. The present value of $76,061 is $11,306, the liability roughly analogous to the ABO.

[b]Annual costs to a pension plan for the benefits accrued by employees.

[c]If it is highly likely that the employee will be with the organization for the next 20 years, an alternative liability computation uses the expected salary 20 years hence [$50,000 × (1.05)^{20}] to determine an annual benefit of ($79,599 × 2% × 30 years). The value of this benefit at the end of the current year is $89,994. In future years, as the time to retirement draws closer, the benefit increases as the number of years used to multiply to get the benefit (i.e., the number of years of service) increases and the liability—roughly analogous to the PBO—increases as the time to retirement decreases.

rata portion of the pension plan assets. If that is true, and if it can safely be assumed that the combined increase in the value of the asset and the sponsor's contribution were to equal $3,074 in year 1, $3,706 in year 2, $4,551 in year 3, and so forth, the computed unfunded pension obligation will be zero. The true pension assets in this case are considered to be the actual pension plan assets, plus the expected changes in value, plus the amount the sponsor has committed to put into the plan.

Now let us suppose that instead the sponsor adopts the following funding schedule: the sponsor will contribute nothing in year 1 but will contribute $6,780 (the sum of the normal costs for the first two years) in year 2, and thereafter what has just been specified. Also, let us assume there will be no asset growth in either year 1 or year 2. In this case, the plan will show an unfunded liability in year 1 of $3,074, even though the funding will take place later, just as the other funding will take place. So an unfunded liability arises when the annual contribution plus appreciation is less than the computed normal cost (the change in the value of the liability). The plan would also show an increase in the unfunded pension liability if promised benefits were enhanced before contributions to cover those benefits were made.

Funding Approaches and Assumptions

Berkowitz and Rowe (1990, pp. 33-7 and 33-8) note there are generally four approaches to funding a pension plan. In all of these, there is a "normal cost" component—the portion of the contribution allocated to the current year and a "past service cost" component—the portion of the contribution allocated to past years that have not yet been funded. Defined benefit plans use a variety of actuarial cost methods, and they differ in their allocation of costs over the worker's service life—level payments or varying amounts—and in the length of time over which costs are allocated. There are two broad classifications of actuarial methods: *accrued benefit* and *projected benefit* cost methods. (Caution should be taken to avoid confusing the concept of accounting costs with the cash needed to fund the plan.)

Generally, actuarial cost methods break down the cost of a plan into the normal cost and the supplemental cost. The *normal cost* is the annual cost attributable to a given year of the plan's operation. The *supplemental cost* arises when there is a liability for past service or for prior underfunding. Thus the total annual cost equals what a sponsor must set aside for the year's work plus what the sponsor must set aside for prior work.

Because each funding method produces different rates of pension plan funding, the magnitude of a measured unfunded pension obligation and hence the appropriate level of the desired contribution will change depending on the method chosen. Sponsors can change methods and assumptions (e.g., discount rates), thus altering the estimate of unfunded liabilities. Note that for private plans the Internal Revenue Service has a strong interest in keeping contributions as low as possible, because the higher the tax-deductible contributions, the less tax is collected. The intent of ERISA is to increase the safety of pension plans, and safety is enhanced by higher levels of funding. This conflict in the goals of the two agencies could ultimately lead to some strange legislative initiatives as Congress tries to walk a fine line between collecting more taxes and making pension plans safe.

The Discount Rate

In addition to funding or contribution schemes, changes in the assumed discount rate (actuaries call this an *interest rate assumption*) also affect measured pension fund obligations. In the example of Ms. Landers's defined benefit plan liability computation, the normal costs would have been much lower had a discount rate of, say, 12% been chosen, because this would have allowed the computed present value of future benefits to be much lower. What should the discount rate be?

For 1996, *Institutional Investor* (July 1996) found that more than 81% of respondents to a survey of corporate (800) and public (250) funds used discount rates between 7 and 8.4%. The previous year, 82% of respondents reported using rates of 8 to 9%. As a result of this change in discount rates, 70% reported that their liabilities had increased 5% or more over the previous year, with nearly 32% reporting an increase of 15% or more.

Most analysts argue that the discount rate should be related to existing capital market rates and should not be arbitrary (see, for example, the 1988 article by Ezra). Of those cited above who changed rates, 77% stated that the reason they had changed was to be in line with market rates. The rates on either long-term government bonds or long-term corporate bonds are reasonable rates to use. The fact that aggregate pension obligations might stretch out for 60 years (the time at which the currently youngest worker or surviving spouse would be expected to die) whereas the customary maturity of long-term bonds is only 20 or 30 years should not be a reason to adapt an arbitrary rather than a market-based number. Indeed, Ezra has shown that what happens after 20 years does not matter very much anyway, because big changes in discount rates more than 20 years out have very little effect on the computed value of the liability today. More to the point, a market rate should be used because this is a rate that investors believe will obtain over the foreseeable future. It is the rate investors use to value bonds. Because pension obligations are, in many ways, similar to bonds held by employees, they should be valued similarly. Should a sponsor wish to be more precise by applying different discount rates to different future periods, a reasonable approach to doing this (demonstrated by Barrett) is to compute forward interest rates.

If a sponsor uses a market rate to discount future obligations, the value of the liability will vary as market interest rates vary. Given that interest rates have been volatile in recent years, this means that liability values will be highly variable, even though this may be untidy. A constant discount rate determined arbitrarily should generally not be used to value liabilities—or to project asset values, for that matter. Such an arbitrary discount rate would divorce estimates of the financial soundness of pension plans from reality. Of course, some pension plan sponsors have chosen assets that will vary in value with the estimates of their pension liabilities. This issue is explored in later chapters.

Liabilities, Contributions, and Investment Policy

Not only is the measurement of unfunded pension liabilities sensitive to the choice of future funding schemes and the rate chosen to discount future obligations, it is also sensitive to the rate of return forecasted to be earned on plan assets. Further, as the estimated rate of return will be a function of how much risk the sponsor wants to bear, assumptions about the risk/return trade-off implicit in various asset allocations must be made and will in turn affect the measurement of the liability.

How much real cash has to be set aside in each period to meet obligated payments depends on the assumptions made about discount rates, forecasted rates of return, and other factors, such as the degree of risk aversion on the part of the decision maker. A formal data analysis can help in informing decisions about how to allocate assets and how to structure the contribution stream (an example is presented in Chapter 6). One thing is clear: there is a trade-off between the investment performance of pension assets and the contributions the company must make. The asset allocations that are most likely to reduce the sponsor's contributions in the long run, however, also have high investment risk. If there is adverse market action, there may be unexpected funding needs and, in especially severe market downturns, the financial health of the plan could be threatened.

A partial solution to the question of what degree of risk is appropriate is to use a hybrid approach which distinguishes between that part of the asset pool that matches relevant liabilities (as defined by the sponsor) and that part that exceeds liabilities. For instance, some employers may consider the relevant "serious" liabilities to be the present value of the actuarially expected amount that must be paid to the current population of retirees; this amount would rise or fall only as the retired population increases or decreases. Against these claims, the sponsor might determine that an appropriate policy is to set up a dedicated bond portfolio— that is, a bond portfolio the value of which would rise or fall with the present value of liabilities and in essence match them in value.* For the nonretired group, the sponsor would hold assets such as stocks that would be most likely to increase in value as the size of the claim rose due to wage increases resulting from promotions, productivity gains, and inflation. Of course, the more the value of the assets rise, other things being equal, the smaller the contributions the equity holders or taxpayers of the sponsoring organization would have to make. This would be the risky portion of the portfolio. Sponsors who establish pension funds in this bifurcated way apparently consider the pension ownership issue to be different for retired and active employees, with the former being treated as owners and the latter being treated as if the equity holders or taxpayers are the owners of the asset pool.† This inconsistency can lead to suboptimal decision making as managers ignore important interactions that affect the financial well-being of the plan, its beneficiaries, and the sponsor. (We return to this issue in Chapter 6.)

Plan sponsors and those who manage pension asset pools must recognize that the questions of joint ownership, integration, and funding affect the pension plan's asset structure and hence its risk/return profile. Further, senior managers, board members, and others who are charged with the responsibility of setting or implementing investment policy must understand that the way the liability is measured will affect their perception of the adequacy of the plan's funding. Finally, managers must understand how the willingness of the sponsor to make contributions is entwined with the demands for investment returns (and risks) that will be placed on the plan's asset pool. These factors have a profound impact on the strategic side of pension investment policy.

---

*One way that matching a bond portfolio to the present value of liabilities can be done is by matching the cash throw-off of the bonds with the obligations that must be paid. There are other more complex ways to achieve bond portfolio dedication, but cash-flow matching is the simplest. Cash-flow matching would ensure that the promised payments—the legal claims—of the plan beneficiaries were safe.

†An alternative hybrid pension fund management strategy might distinguish between the present value of vested liabilities and all other liabilities, and then treat the funding of these two pools differently.

Strategic Parameters of Investment Policy

Whether the plan is a defined benefit or defined contribution plan, a pension plan's investment policy must define what risk the plan can tolerate and what return is necessary to achieve the plan's funding, contribution, and benefit objectives. Additionally, any constraining factors that are relevant should be identified. For defined benefit plans and employer-directed defined contribution plans, the sponsor must take the lead in formulating investment policies. For employee-directed defined contribution plans, the employee has ultimate responsibility for investment policy, although various decisions the sponsor makes will affect the amount of freedom employees have.

The strategic elements of investment policy include diversification, exposure to market risk, procedures for adapting to changing markets or circumstances, preferences for active or passive investment management, what investment styles are appropriate, what levels of management fees are appropriate, and whether the use of derivatives is permitted and if so for what purposes, as well as numerous operational issues including the strategic asset allocation for the plan. We discuss these issues initially in the context of defined benefit plans. However, the fundamental elements of investment policy described in this section form the basis for participant-directed and sponsor-directed defined contribution plans as well.

Risk and Return

A pension plan's tolerance for risk and consequently its ability to choose a realistic return target are affected by several factors. For a defined benefit plan (DBP), the most important of these are the underlying financial strength of the sponsor, the funding status of the plan, and the nature of the plan's liability (e.g., the plan's exposure to inflation through its wage-based benefit formula). For a defined contribution plan (DCP) (we will assume an employee-directed one), the main factors are funding policy, time to retirement, employee income and wealth, access to borrowing, and individual preference.

Risk Tolerance

The importance of specifying the plan's tolerance for risk cannot be overstated; the capital markets allocate return according to risk taken; thus no meaningful return targets can be established until the sponsor (or beneficiary) determines the plan's risk-bearing capacity. In general, a financially strong investor (e.g., a municipality with a significant amount of available taxing power) and a well-funded plan suggest a fairly high tolerance for risk. Similarly, a plan that is exposed to nontrivial inflation due perhaps to its benefit formula or to a long time horizon may have to bear substantial risk in order to earn a real rate of return high enough to offset inflationary pressures. Paradoxically, plans that can bear a lot of risk may not have to, and plans that are at risk may have to bear more— to try to reduce the level of underfunding, for example.

Return volatility and asset volatility are acceptable measures of risk for individual DCP pensions. These measures are not sufficient for DBPs because they ignore the interaction between plan liabilities and assets as well as the interaction between the plan and its sponsor. Thus, in addition to setting acceptable levels of investment risk, DBPs must specify an acceptable level of *surplus volatility* (the volatility of changes in the value of plan assets relative to changes in the value of plan liabilities). Viewing risk as surplus volatility focuses attention on the sensitivity of plan assets and liabilities to factors such as interest rates rather than erroneously assuming that these factors are unrelated to plan risk.

Similarly, policy should recognize the dynamics of plan performance and the sponsor's financial performance as they affect future plan contributions. For example, a sponsor in a highly cyclical industry may not be able to make up funding shortfalls if there is unusually poor investment performance.

Policy, then, with regard to risk is a matter of defining what is at risk, then defining what level of volatility is acceptable. If low investment risk is desired, this should be stated (useful quantitative measures include beta and duration) and acceptable exposures to the various asset classes should be explicitly defined. If very low surplus volatility is desired, this must be stated as policy so that the asset allocation can emphasize duration-matching strategies. If the sponsor's financial health is itself quite cyclical, this must be translated in a policy that prohibits further exposure to the same cyclical factors and directs investments into assets that are likely to perform well when the sponsor is likely to do poorly.

Return

A plan's return target follows naturally from policies defining acceptable risk exposures for the plan. Return targets, in essence, must address jointly plan beneficiary interests in receiving the benefits the beneficiaries feel they are due, as well as the sponsor's interest in achieving a low present value of future contributions.

The key constraint on return policy, of course, is that return targets must be consistent with what the capital markets will provide given the risk tolerance of the plan and how return is provided—through income, capital growth, or both. Return targets typically are set in both total return and income or yield versus capital change. The higher the total return target, the more risk the plan is agreeing to take. The higher the income target, the lower the long-term total investment return is likely to be.

Plan Constraints

Other circumstances can be of varying importance. For example, liquidity needs may be relatively more important to plans that have older employees near to retirement, a large number of people currently receiving benefits, or to hybrid plans such as cash balance plans that offer portability upon employee termination. Similarly, IRS regulations governing the deductibility of sponsor contributions and contracts between the sponsor and the plan affect policy with regard to the timing and size of contributions. Compliance with ERISA and other regulations as well as with legislative mandates that public pension funds undertake actions such as socially responsible investing also serve as constraining factors. All of these circumstances and constraints must be evaluated to determine their impact on the amount of risk the plan should take and on its return objectives.

Diversification, Market Risk, and Change

Pension investment policy should reflect principles of sound investment theory and practice. Some of the more important of these include a consideration of diversification, market risk, and how to adapt to change.

Diversification

It is commonly accepted in the investment community that diversification is a desirable goal. Diversification is achieved by allocating plan assets across asset classes (such as stocks and bonds), within asset classes (such as holding both large capitalization stocks and small capitalization stocks, or investing in several industries), and across regions and countries (such as holding international stocks and bonds). For private plans, diversification is required by ERISA at the portfolio level; for public plans, states historically provide diversification guidelines on an asset-by-asset basis, although this has changed somewhat in recent years.

The fundamental issue is that diversification is desirable because markets will not reward investors for risks that can be diversified away and because regulators require diversification. Thus, pension plan policy should specify minimum acceptable levels of diversification and permit concentrated undiversified exposures only under certain circumstances.

Market Risk

Pension plan investment policy should be specific regarding how much market risk the plan will take. In the framework of what has come to be known as *modern portfolio theory,* this consists of determining what portfolio of risky assets is appropriate given the plan's tolerance for risk and its return objectives. Modern portfolio theory is closely aligned with the concept of diversification in that market risk is risk that cannot be diversified away and therefore can be avoided only by reducing targeted expected returns. Alternatively, plans that need or wish to achieve high targeted expected returns will have to take on a relatively high amount of exposure to the market and thus to the volatility characteristic of the returns and values of risky assets.

Defining an acceptable level of market risk is the crux of the asset allocation decision. Generally, plans allocating a large proportion of total assets to stocks are taking a high amount of market risk. Correspondingly, the volatility of plan returns and asset values for these plans will be high compared with the volatility of plans with less exposure to stocks.

Adapting to Change

Among the few certainties in investing are the two truths that markets change and the factors unique to any given pension plan change over time. Thus, pension plan policy should anticipate changes that may occur and provide guidance on adapting to change when necessary.

Market change occurs simply when a market or an asset class performs unusually well or unusually poorly relative to other asset classes or relative to historical norms. The net result of this performance will be to change the plan's actual asset allocation, resulting in an overweighting in certain classes. One possible adaptation to this change is simply to do nothing—the presumption in this case is that, on average, over time, asset classes will do pretty much what we expect them to do and asset weights will correspondingly be, on average, where we wish them to be. An alternative policy is to rebalance the plan's portfolio by selling off overperforming asset classes and increasing exposure to underperforming asset classes. These and related strategies will be discussed further in Chapter 5.

Similarly, over long periods of time, the plan's and/or sponsor's circumstances are likely to change. As a result, the plan's definition of acceptable levels of risk and return targets should change to reflect the new circumstances. The nature of this change cannot be generalized; suffice it to say that policy must be dynamic, and changes to policy should be anticipated and thoughtfully considered rather than made ad hoc.

Active or Passive Management?

Another key policy decision is whether to invest actively (in an attempt to beat the market) or passively (by attempting to *be* the market). A large part of the money management community holds itself out as capable of beating the market and relies on plan sponsors, employees managing defined contribution plans, and others to provide the assets (and pay the fees) that they use in this attempt. Sponsors and employees who choose to use or not to use these managers should understand the issues involved.

Active investing essentially requires a belief that a market, sector, or asset may be mispriced and that investors will eventually recognize any underpricing (or overpricing) that exists and thereby bid up (or down) the prices of misvalued assets. In opposition to the view of active investing are the proponents of the *efficient market hypothesis* (EMH). In an efficient market, all the information available about a given asset is already reflected in the price of that asset and new information arrives randomly and, therefore, cannot be forecast. When new information arrives, prices adjust rapidly, so there is no opportunity for earning excess returns.

Passive investment strategies presume that financial markets are efficient and cannot be easily beaten. Thus, in the passive management view, money spent trying to beat the market will be money wasted and simply serve to reduce returns without providing any offsetting benefits. *Active investment* strategies, on the other hand, presume that markets—at least some markets, or some markets some of the time—are inefficient enough to provide excess returns to those who can obtain superior information or who have superior insight. To proponents of active management, these inefficiencies are exploitable opportunities that justify the expenditure of both time and money.

Passive investment strategies emphasize constructing passive portfolios that achieve exposures to asset classes that match the pension fund's risk tolerance and return objectives. In passively managed plans, the only investment decision of significance is the strategic asset allocation decision, the subject of Chapter 6. The case for passive management is supported by its low costs—passive management trades little and spends virtually no money on research—and a large number of studies that suggest that professional money managers and the active management strategies they pursue regularly fail to beat appropriate benchmarks even before their fees are taken into account.

Active investment styles are likely to start with the strategic asset allocation as a point of departure, but will not hesitate to change the asset mix or make concentrated bets within an asset class, often dramatically, in pursuit of higher returns. Active management is an information-driven philosophy that is predicated on the belief that mispriced securities can be repeatedly identified or that market trends can be successfully forecast. Thus, active management, at its extremes, uses either market-timing or security selection. In market-timing the idea is to be 100% invested in a market segment when it is going to do well and be 100% invested in some other segment of the market (perhaps Treasury bills) when the target asset class is expected to do poorly. Security selection involves shopping for mispriced assets in the hope that positions can be taken that, when the market recognizes the mispricing and corrects it, will result in positive excess returns.

There is disagreement among researchers and practitioners about which view is correct. As Blume and Siegel point out, empirical research supports the efficient market hypothesis and takes issue with it. There are practitioners who must believe in inefficiency—after all, it is their business—and there are practitioners who sincerely believe in inefficiency, who believe they can or do beat the market on a risk-adjusted basis. There also are practitioners who advocate efficient markets and thus passive management. There are also at least two new lines of scientific inquiry—market structure (see Blume and Siegel) and behavioral finance (see Wood for a good overview)—that are attempting to add to our knowledge.

We will not settle the debate in this book. In fairness to the active management constituency, the debate is not over. A small increase in basis points after fees and trading costs can add a large amount of value to a portfolio. It does seem that some markets are likely to be more efficient than others; that the efficiency with which a market processes information may wax and wane; and that investors may, for possibly rational reasons (e.g., in response to regulation), "overreact" from time to time, leaving unusually profitable opportunities around for those who may find them. That said, the question investors are left with is whether investors can identify managers (or strategies) that will beat a passive portfolio of comparable risk in the future.

The bottom line in the active/passive debate, such as it is, is that the decision maker—the plan sponsor, the trustee, the plan administrator, or the employee—must develop a clear set of beliefs about market efficiency. Based on these beliefs, the decision maker may then decide whether all, or a portion, or no plan assets should be actively managed. Investment policy should reflect the beliefs that pension boards, senior management, and other fiduciaries involved in a particular plan have about the value of active or passive management. This is not a trivial issue: many theoreticians believe active management increases investment risk. That it costs more is clear; the question is whether the added costs are more than offset by higher risk-adjusted returns. Additionally, investment policy should carefully define the investment styles to which the plan is willing to allocate money, so that managers know how they are to manage the money they are given. Policy should also specifically direct managers to follow the style they say they will follow. These policy parameters are essential if the fund is to communicate with and hold its managers accountable for investment management decisions.

Investment Style

The money management industry that serves pension funds and other investors is especially adept at product differentiation. Thus, pension plan policy might also address what are considered stylistic issues. Unfortunately, there is little agreement among practitioners as to what the phrase *investment style* means. Academics have come to define *style* as an essentially passive preference or expertise in some market sector, usually a subset of a larger investment class. For example, small capitalization stocks are a subset of the stock universe and thus investing in them rather than the stock market as a whole offers a particular investment style. We use this preference for a subset as our definition. The various styles that are offered may be pursued passively (perhaps style specialization is warranted due to information or scale economies) or actively (perhaps by pursuing security selection within a market sector).

There are at least five distinct active equity disciplines, philosophies, or styles: they are growth, income, value, market capitalization, and quality (special situations, turnarounds). International or foreign equities offer a sixth style and can, of course, be broken down into the same categories, as can developed and emerging markets. Active bond management styles can be broken down into a true trading approach, where the managers are free to select bonds that are believed to be under- or overvalued. Another style is to use a structured bond portfolio in which the manager adjusts the portfolio in response to changing market conditions (e.g., extending the portfolio's duration when interest rates are expected to fall). As with equities, with trading or structured bond portfolios, there are domestic and international versions. If we then add in special categories of investment assets such as leveraged buyout funds, real estate funds, venture capital funds, and perhaps even commodities and managed futures (not to mention market-neutral strategies), a pension sponsor faces the daunting task of evaluating not only the relatively straightforward active versus passive conundrum, but which, if any, of the many investment philosophies might be appropriate for the DBP fund or for DCP portfolios. Empirical evidence, quantitative modeling, and informed intuition are all helpful in identifying the investment styles that are likely to be appropriate in the future.

Management Fees

Active management fees typically run around 50 basis points, whereas passive fees for funds that hold portfolios that correlate highly with broad-based market indexes (such as the Standard & Poor's 500 Stock Index) may be 2 to 10 basis points. Mutual funds and other funds used in employee-directed DCPs have somewhat higher fees, with typical active equity fund expense ratios averaging around 100 basis points and index funds charging 20 to 40 basis points.

Fee differentials can be substantial over long periods of time and, as long-term investors, pension plans should be sensitive to the erosion of value that is associated with higher fees. Sensible policy requires fees that are not excessive and that are justified in terms of the benefits the plan receives. Sponsors of DBPs should care about fees because excessive fees will require higher contributions. Sponsors of DCPs should also care about fees because excessive fees will erode accumulations. Finally, sponsors should be concerned that fees that are too high will suggest the appropriate due diligence was not performed.

Derivatives

One element of policy that has become important since the 1980s is establishing guidelines for the use of derivatives. In spite of a spate of bad publicity due to the huge investment losses incurred by such diverse organizations as Orange County, Procter & Gamble, and other investors/derivatives users, derivatives have a legitimate role to play in pension fund management. On the other hand, derivatives can be misused, particularly by those who do not understand the nature of the contracts into which they are entering or the way in which positions resulting from these contracts can create exposures to unusually high or magnified levels of risk.

In general, ERISA guidelines and other regulatory constraints discourage using derivatives for speculative purposes. Thus, pension plan policy must require an understanding of the payoff structures and risk/return profiles of the contracts that are being used; the policy must also specify whether it is appropriate to use derivatives in hedging and/or return-enhancement risk-management activities. Policy should be clear on when and for what purposes derivatives may be used and how derivative exposures will be monitored (keeping in mind that for hedging strategies using derivatives, it is the net exposure that must be monitored).

Operational Policy Issues

There are a number of operational policy areas that should be addressed in the plan's written policy statement. These directly address how the plan will do certain things. They include the following:

Asset Allocation. The strategic asset allocation is the cornerstone of the operational side of investment policy. As such, it should be clearly defined in terms of broad exposures to the major asset classes as well as acceptable deviations from target weights and in terms of maximum cumulative exposures to subclasses such as small capitalization stocks, nondomestic issuers, and venture capital or special situations. Acceptable levels of asset quality and the responses required for maintaining quality levels should be defined (e.g., whether all fixed-income investments should be investment grade, and what should be done if a security's quality rating falls below the acceptable level). The allocation among active and passive management should be defined.

Rebalancing. When and under what circumstances asset rebalancing will occur or will be permitted must be specified. For example, will trading be undertaken for the sole purpose of restoring the target asset allocations if market action results in a departure from target weights outside of a ±5% range (absolute)? How often should such rebalancing occur—once a year under normal circumstances? May rebalancing be achieved through futures or options contracting? May some managers attempt tactical or insured asset allocation? If so, when and how?

Asset Management. Policy should be clear about what assets will be managed by external money managers and in what amounts within each investment category. The criteria for selecting external money managers should be explicit, and may include factors such as what assets to include under a particular manager's control, the manager's years in business, and compliance with performance reporting guidelines such as the Association for Investment Management and Research (AIMR) Performance Presentation Standards. Further, it should be clear how and how frequently the fund's money managers will be evaluated and how and for what reasons managers will be dismissed (e.g., failure to conform to policy).

Use of Soft Dollars. Should services or products required by the fund be purchased for cash or through directed commissions? Some plans have moved away from using soft dollars (i.e., credits granted in return for directing trades to a specific broker/dealer), believing they are not an efficient way to purchase research and additional services and that managers should be trying to trade at the best available price. Others have established policies to make better use of soft dollars. Still others have implemented commission recapture programs that return commission dollars to the plan. Regardless of the sponsor's preferences, the fund should articulate its position on the use of soft dollars or directed commissions. There are two issues that plan policy should address: (1) whether directed commissions are permitted, and (2) if they are permitted, who controls them and the benefits provided.

Proxy Voting. Pension funds should direct their equity money managers on how they should vote on issues brought by portfolio companies to their shareholders. This is a fiduciary obligation to the beneficiaries of the pension plans. Accordingly, funds should always direct that its proxy votes be cast in favor of those proposals that are most likely to increase the stock price of the affected companies.

Investment Policy for Defined Contribution Plans

Sponsors of defined contribution plans (DCPs) have many policy responsibilities that are conceptually similar to those of defined benefit plan (DBP) sponsors. The operational shape these responsibilities take, however, differs significantly. In part, this is because DCPs are structured as separate accounts for each beneficiary rather than large asset pools jointly claimed by all beneficiaries. In part, this is because DCPs offer sponsors the opportunity to shift investment risk to employees. Sponsors who make the plan's investment decisions, however, or who fail to meet Department of Labor (DOL) guidelines for self-directed plans face substantial risk of litigation if employees decide they are not happy with the investment results on their DCP asset pools. Thus, investment policy must recognize the impact of having many asset pools owned by each employee and must help sponsors reduce the risk that courts will shift the responsibility for adverse investment results and inadequate asset accumulations back to the sponsor.

Sponsors must first decide whether the assets of the DCP will be invested by the sponsor or the employees. To the extent that plan assets are to be invested by the sponsor, the preceding material concerning DBP policy is applicable, recognizing that the sponsor retains significant responsibility for the consequences of the investment decisions it makes. If the decision is to provide an employee-directed plan, ERISA sponsors should consider formulating policies that ensure compliance with ERISA Section 404(c) regulations. These regulations, issued in October 1992, provide a safe harbor that protects ERISA sponsors from liability if employees make poor investment decisions. The regulations require that plans offer at least three materially different investment alternatives (other than company stock), that employees be allowed to give investment instructions as often as appropriate given the volatility of the investment alternative, that employees be able to diversify adequately, and that employees be given the information necessary to make informed decisions. Public sponsors have no clear legal incentive to comply with 404(c)-like rules, but the guidelines generally are consistent with prudent management and should be carefully considered.

This section discusses what sponsors who administer employee-directed DCPs should do with regard to establishing policy to provide adequate employee education, performance information and investment choices. Additionally, we examine the policy implications of plan investment costs.

Investment Education of Employees

Policy for employee education should recognize that the vast majority of employees participating in DCPs have no formal education or training in investment decision making and, thus, will benefit significantly from educational activities. Additionally, employee education is encouraged under the DOL 404(c) regulations and is presumptive under fiduciary duty.

The DOL has issued guidelines on the type of education that 401(k) plan sponsors can provide employees without the education being interpreted as investment advice and, hence, bringing with it a fiduciary responsibility (see the articles by Rowland and Miller). In its draft interpretation bulletin, the DOL offers four safe harbors. These safe harbors are needed to reduce the likelihood that the Securities and Exchange Commission (SEC) will regulate plan sponsors under the Investment Advisors Act of 1940. The first safe harbor is providing general plan information, including a description of investment options. The second is providing financial and investment information covering basic concepts of risk and return, diversification, and so forth. The third safe harbor allows sponsors to provide asset allocation models as long as these models include a statement that employees should consider total assets rather than just retirement plan assets. The final safe harbor is that interactive investment materials—such as questionnaires, software, worksheets, and so forth—used in estimating future retirement needs must disclose what assumptions have been used in their construction.

Investor education programs must take care not to provide mistakenly what might be interpreted as investment advice (e.g., in what assets employees should invest and how they should time their investments). Rather, the basics of investor education should start with information concerning the primary asset classes and their historical risks and returns. This foundation allows the sponsor or the sponsor's designee (e.g., a consultant hired to provide investment education programs for employees) to discuss the basics of modern portfolio theory (diversification, the nature of market risk, and so forth).

Alternative investment strategies comprise the next part of an investor education program. Employees should be informed about the differences associated with various asset allocations, the actively and passively managed funds in which they might invest, and how different strategies might be expected to perform (or have performed) in various types of market conditions. Some sponsors also are now providing alternative portfolios, which are typically designed to be more conservative or more aggressive.

Other elements of investor education that sponsors should address include how to match investor circumstances and objectives to specific investment funds, how to form portfolios of funds rather than selecting individual funds, and how to integrate pension assets with other investments an employee may have. Throughout, the sponsor should be careful to avoid making—or giving the appearance of making—specific investment recommendations to avoid future liability.

Performance Information

At the time of this writing, it is common for DCP sponsors or their designees to provide woefully inadequate information on plan performance to employees. As a result, it is very difficult for employees to determine how the DCP asset pools are doing. Prudent sponsors will develop policies that will provide the information that plan participants need to make informed decisions. The four elements of communicating investment results to employees are providing comprehensive performance figures, effective asset mix information, clear and understandable descriptions of the investment strategies followed by the funds made available to employees, and showing employees the basics of interpreting actual investment results.

Performance presentation should include total returns for one-, three-, five-, and ten-year periods as well as annual returns for at least five years, preferably for ten years. Additionally, one or more standard measures of fund volatility, such as its standard deviation (calculated on the three-to-five-year record using monthly numbers) are useful information and should be provided. An informative variation on the standard deviation is a volatility index where an investment of average volatility would have an index number of 1, and higher (or lower) volatility investments would have index numbers of greater than (or less than) 1. Finally, DCP participants need appropriate benchmarks. These should include broad market indexes and averages for fund or investment-style categories. (For a discussion of constructing and/or choosing appropriate benchmarks, see Chapter 7.)

Participants also need information on the effective asset mix of each fund in which they may invest in order to maintain an asset allocation (including assets outside the pension plan) that is appropriate. Again, recent history suggests that the information typically provided is less than adequate. Specifically, funds should be described to employees in terms of asset class exposures; allocations within asset classes (e.g., large-cap versus small-cap stocks, or domestic versus international stocks differentiating emerging markets from developed markets); the interest rate sensitivity of bond funds; whether the funds are passive or index funds or actively managed funds, and so forth.

The third element of investment information is an understandable description of the investment strategy that a fund chooses to follow. Although the debate over the merits of passive versus active investing is far from over (and will probably never be settled to everyone's satisfaction), it is an important parameter in fund selection and portfolio construction. Therefore, the sponsor has a moral obligation to ensure that whatever strategy a fund pursues, it is adequately disclosed so that investors know what they are investing in.

Finally, in addition to providing reasonable numbers for employees to assess the adequacy of their investment planning and the performance of the funds in which they are invested, the sponsor should educate plan participants about the impact of a variety of factors on the performance they will achieve. For example, participants need to understand that purchasing patterns (the timing of investments) will affect the returns that they realize. Similarly, investors should know they virtually never get the index or benchmark returns that are presented unless those returns are adjusted to mimic the cash flows associated with a specific investment, trading costs, and the impact of cash holdings. Performance evaluation, of course, is difficult to do. However, giving investors performance data without informing them of how to interpret the results provides them with only part of what they need to make informed decisions about their retirement portfolios.

Investment Choice

ERISA Section 404(c) regulations defining limited relief for sponsors require that DCP sponsors provide at least three choices for plan participants, but the regulations do not define the number of choices necessary to provide a safe harbor. The upside of having more alternatives rather than fewer is potentially happier employees and evidence of meeting fiduciary responsibilities. The downside of having more alternatives is also having higher administrative costs and an increased educational burden for the sponsor. Thus, the sponsor needs to think through the elements of how many choices is enough—or too many. (Note also that employees should be allowed to make changes in their allocations among funds at least quarterly, or more often if fund volatility is high.)

A comprehensive set of investment choices will provide participants with an opportunity to gain exposure to passively or actively managed funds, small company stocks as well as large company stocks, fixed-income investments of various interest-rate sensitivities, balanced funds containing both equities and fixed-income investments, asset allocation funds (that offer different asset mixes for different risk/return objectives), international equities, money market funds, and perhaps guaranteed investment contracts (GICs). For most DCPs, these exposures can be achieved by offering six to ten alternatives.

The more important choice for the plan sponsor is that of the fund provider. The basic issue is whether to go inside or outside. Only large sponsors have the resources to consider offering internally managed funds. Even in these cases, the sponsor may not feel it has the investment expertise available in-house to manage the funds internally. Of course, for smaller organizations, the only alternative is to turn outside to an insurance company, a bank, a mutual fund, or other fund manager. Regardless, fiduciary duty requires attention to due diligence in selection.

Management and Administrative Costs

The importance of the management and administrative costs of the investment vehicles chosen for DCPs and the returns on employee portfolios is quite simple and direct—cost affects return. If all else remains the same, the higher costs are, the lower the returns will be for plan participants. The lower that net returns of costs are, the less accumulation will occur and the less adequate employee investment accounts will be upon retirement.

How will plan participants react when they reach retirement and find out that their asset accumulations are inadequate for the lifestyles they had envisioned? It is not unreasonable to suspect that suits will be brought and sponsors that cannot show appropriate due diligence with respect to pursuing the low-cost alternative—or alternatively, with respect to paying only for services that are essential—will be found liable in the courts.

Many sponsors of DCPs do not even know the total costs associated with the plans that they are offering. In one study (HR Investment

Consultants, cited by Brenner), a hypothetical $10 million plan with 500 participants might range in cost from $61,000 to $260,000. Since these costs are borne by employees, the responsibilities with which a prudent fiduciary is charged seem to make it clear that plan cost is a due diligence issue wherein fiduciary responsibility may be properly carried out—or if it is not properly carried out, significant liability may result.

Many sponsors have turned to the mutual fund industry for investment selection services, record keeping, and the like. Observers of fees recognize, however, that mutual funds charge from 20 basis points to 150 basis points for their core management and administrative activities. Compare this, if you will, to the 5 to 50 basis point fees commonly charged by professional money managers in the wholesale marketplace.

Conclusion

Pension investment policy should be articulated in a written set of guidelines designed to resolve many complex and at times contradictory issues. These written policies can serve as a guide for prudent decision making. Policy must start at the top; good policy or not, whatever investment policies are in place (as well as those that are not) will affect the financial performance of both sponsors and the pension plans they provide.

Investment policy for defined benefit pension plans originates in a philosophical choice: should the management of the plan be integrated with the management of the sponsoring organization? In general, the answer to this question is *yes* because the two are so closely entwined. However, this answer is conditional on doing what is in the best interests of plan beneficiaries. Sometimes employers and those who manage the pension plans they sponsor have an adversarial relationship. This certainly is not an optimal circumstance, but it may be unavoidable, especially in political environments. Even if this is the case, however, there is still much to be gained by using an integrated perspective to structure policies regarding factors such as diversification. Policy also requires that those who set policy understand the relationship between plan liabilities and assets as well as the impact of investment performance on the contributions the sponsor must make. Ultimately the financial health of both the sponsor and the pension fund are at stake. This interdependence is rife with potential conflicts of interest. It presents numerous opportunities for mistakes to be made. Only through forward-looking policy—policy that anticipates conflicts (e.g., between aggressive investment strategies and contribution levels) and that specifies the parameters to be used in decision making (e.g., the liability to be managed is the economic liability)—can decision makers get the guidance they need.

For defined contribution plans, the sponsor must address the issues of providing employee education, deciding the number of investment choices to which employees will have access, and ensuring that employees have adequate performance information. Investment alternatives must be provided at reasonable cost to employees, and these alternatives must in the aggregate represent a comprehensive set of investment alternatives. Sponsors must also take care to avoid crossing the line, murky as it may seem, between educating employees and offering investment advice. Overall, remember that the more control participants have, the less liability the fiduciary or sponsor is likely to have.

Whether defined benefit or contribution, the most important of the strategic policies of a pension plan to be determined is that of the plan's (or portfolio's) tolerance for risk. This cannot be overemphasized. Many asset managers get caught up in the quest for return, forgetting that the capital markets allocate return based on the exposure taken to risk. This can be catastrophic—as can be taking too little risk and over-burdening the sponsor to make up the return foregone or, in the case of the individual employee, finding that too little has been accumulated to permit the type of retirement envisioned in earlier days. Policy should guide decision makers in dealing with these matters by specifying clearly how much risk is acceptable or necessary.

Policy can be constraining; that is its nature. Policy writers should be careful not to take away the flexibility that decision makers need to do their jobs. However, the absence of sound policy leaves a void in accountability that is not consistent with prudent behavior. Those who are fiduciaries, therefore, must insist on good investment policy as a prerequisite to good investment management of plan assets.

Chapter **5**

The Asset Allocation Decision

A pension plan's investment policy is operationalized by allocating plan assets among available investment asset classes. The topic is sufficiently large and complex to warrant two chapters. In this chapter, we define what is meant by the term *asset allocation* and examine aggregate data on pension fund asset allocation. We then discuss the primary asset classes and their investment characteristics. With this background, we define the strategic asset allocation decision in terms of its role in the overall management of pension assets, and show how assets may be reallocated over time.

In Chapter 6, we present the theoretical underpinnings of the strategic asset allocation decision, and discuss the advantages and disadvantages of all-stock and all-bond portfolios and the insights these offer in setting the optimal asset mix. We then turn to what pension funds actually do. That chapter concludes by providing an analytical approach to translating investment policy into action via the strategic asset allocation decision.

Asset Classes

Broadly, the major asset classes consist of equities (foreign and domestic publicly traded stock in developed countries), bonds (foreign and domestic publicly traded bonds and private placements), cash (short-term, interest-bearing instruments), and private market equity investments such as venture capital and real estate. This list can be augmented with more exotic asset categories such as common stock investments in the firms of developing countries, equity participations in privately held leveraged buyout (LBO) funds, and commodities (including gold, farmland, commercial forest land, and managed futures pools). Each of these have been found by at least one analyst to be worthwhile additions to institutional portfolios. Although intriguing, we do not dwell on allocations to each of these asset categories for a pension portfolio; instead we consider the asset allocation decision on a broader scale.

In 1990 Sharpe suggested that the concept of an asset class is meaningful only if the asset classes used

1. Are relatively few in number

2. Explain a substantial proportion of the variance in returns

3. Have security-specific returns that are uncorrelated

4. Have beta values that are measurable

5. Have returns that are measurable

6. Have a low-cost index fund that is formable within each class

7. Represent the overall market through a combination of asset classes.

To illustrate this concept, some typical asset classes and their historical risk/return characteristics are shown in Tables 5-1 and 5-2. (The data in Table 5-2 are for a much shorter period than the data in 5-1. This is due to differences in available data.)

The historical data in Tables 5-1 and 5-2 provide some generally useful insights into the different asset classes. For example, stocks have historically outperformed bonds, which have in turn outperformed Treasury bills, but stocks are also riskier than bonds and Treasury bills. When considering these data, some cautions are appropriate, however. First, the past performance of an asset class does not necessarily predict its future performance. Note, for example, historical returns are simply averages over long periods. This means that 68.4% of the time large company stocks, for example, might be expected to provide a return next year of between −7.9% (12.5% − 20.4%) and 32.9% (12.5% + 20.4%) if the factors driving next year's returns are the same as those that drove the historical return series. Second, it is not likely that the return-generating factors, which are affected by other factors such as technology and relative price levels, will be the same in the future. Returns and risks change over time and differ from period to period. Indeed, in

Table 5-1. Asset Class Performance: 1926–1995

Asset Class	Average Annual Rate of Return (arithmetic mean)	Standard Deviation of Returns
Large-company stocks	12.5%	20.4%
Small-company stocks	17.7%	34.4%
Long-term corporate bonds	6.0%	8.7%
Long-term government bonds	5.5%	9.2%
U.S. Treasury bills	3.8%	3.3%

Source: Data from Ibbotson Associates, SBBI 1996 Yearbook, 1996.

Table 5-2. Asset Class Performance: 1976–1995

Asset Class	Average Annual Rate of Return (arithmetic mean)	Standard Deviation of Returns
Venture capital	21%	25.1%
Art (1977–1994)	10%	26%
Non-U.S. equities	15%	21.6%
Emerging markets	10%	27.9%
Commercial property	7.5%	7%
Residential housing	6%	4%
Gold	5.2%	32.6%

Source: Reproduced with permission from *The Economist* (March 23, 1996). © The Economist Newspaper Group, Inc. Further reproduction prohibited.

a sufficiently short time frame, low-risk assets could outperform high-risk assets, and in any single year, any of the asset classes in Tables 5-1 and 5-2 could be the best—or worst—in providing returns. Third, the users of this type of data must be aware of any biases or problems that are embedded in the data (e.g., valuation problems or survivorship bias). Finally, historical data may be sensitive to the period chosen. For example, the data in Table 5-1 includes the bear market in U.S. stocks that took place in 1973–1974. If the return series data had started in 1976 instead of 1926, the return on large-company stocks would be around 15%, much higher than the 12.5% for the longer period.

A more complete picture of the asset classes would include the covariance between each pair of classes and a breakdown of the income

Table 5-3. Public Pension Plan Asset Allocations[a] (Fiscal Year 1994)

	Amount (billions)	Percent of Total (dollar weighted)
Domestic stocks	$386.9	40.2%
Domestic bonds (corporate and government)	$337.0	35.0%
Real estate (equity and mortgages)[b]	$51.3	5.4%
International equities	$62.9	6.5%
International fixed-income	$23.0	2.4%
Short-term investments	$40.8	4.2%
Other	$59.9	6.2%
Total	**$793**	**100%**

[a]Large public plans tend to hold more equities, real estate, and international securities than do small public plans. Large public plans also tend to hold correspondingly fewer bonds and short-term securities (see Zorn).

[b]A study of 151 pension fund allocations to real estate in 1991 (see Bajtelsmit and Worzola) concluded that equity real estate allocations by pension plan type were: corporate plans = 4.48%, union plans = 3.78%, and public plans = 5.05%. Over the entire sample, allocations ranged from 0 to 17%.

Source: Adapted from Paul Zorn, Public Pension Coordinating Council 1995 Survey, Government Finance Officers Association Pension and Benefits Center, Chicago, IL. The survey included 310 state and local retirement systems covering 457 plans covering 13.6 million active members.

versus capital change components of the total returns shown. There are several sources of this data (e.g., Ibbotson Associates and numerous consulting firms), so we do not replicate the data here. Suffice it to say that the more familiar one is with the data, the easier it is to use it in making asset allocation decisions.

A First Look at Pension Fund Assets

In what asset classes do pension funds invest? Tables 5-3 and 5-4 offer some answers. From the data shown in the tables, it is clear that pensions invest heavily in stocks and bonds. Public plans appear to allocate somewhat less to equities than do private plans (40.2% vs. 42.9%), although multiemployer plans allocate an even smaller proportion to equities. Public plans allocate somewhat more to bonds than do private plans (35.0% vs. 26.6%).

Many plans are also using derivatives to enhance returns, reduce risk, or both. Further, as described in Appendix C at the end of this book, many pensions are increasing their allocations to international securities.

Table 5-4. Private Trusteed Pension Asset Allocations* (Year End, 1993)

Plan Type and Asset Type	Total Assets (billions)	Percent of Total
Private trusteed	$2,505	
Equity	1,075	42.9%
Bonds	666	26.6%
Cash items	271	10.8%
Other	492	19.6%
Single-employer defined benefit	$1,134	
Equity	476	42%
Bonds	311	27.4%
Cash items	107	9.4%
Other	239	21.1%
Single-employer defined contribution	$1,063	
Equity	481	45.2%
Bonds	244	23%
Cash items	135	12.7%
Other	203	19.1%
Multi-employer	$308	
Equity	119	38.6%
Bonds	111	36%
Cash items	29	9.46%
Other	50	16.2%

*Includes all assets held in trust other than assets managed by life insurance companies
Source: Data from Employee Benefit Research Institute, Quarterly Pension Investment Report, fourth quarter 1993 (Washington, DC: Employee Benefit Research Institute, 1994).

Primary Asset Classes

Why should a pension plan invest in stocks? Or in bonds? Why consider real estate? To answer these and related questions, it is necessary to understand the characteristics of the major asset classes used by pension funds.

Stocks

Common stocks represent the basic risk capital of an economy. As such, their returns are high, on average, and volatile. Some, but not all, of the volatility of individual stocks can be reduced by diversification.

Thus, the high returns characteristic of stocks take the form of a premium for bearing the remaining risk.

There are two main reasons to invest in stocks. First, expected capital appreciation is generally high, so over long periods exposure to stocks should result in the growth of plan assets. This may result in reducing future sponsor contributions or increasing payouts to beneficiaries. Second, the equity risk premium associated with stocks has historically been an effective counter to the effects of inflation. Over long periods, even modest inflation rates can destroy significant real value. The equity risk premium can offset this. This is not to say that stocks do well in times of unanticipated high or increasing inflation. They often do not. The reality is that stock returns lag behind inflation by several years. Nor can it be said that stocks are a good short-term inflation hedge; the inflation-adjusted correlation of large capitalization stock returns with inflation has been –0.22 while that of small capitalization stocks has been –0.08 (1926–95, U.S. stocks; Source: Ibbotson, 1996, p. 116). These correlations are far too low to permit short-term hedging. However, on average over long periods of time, the equity risk premium earned from exposure to stocks has been sufficient to offset the effects of inflation and still provide a real rate of return.

There is something of a puzzle regarding why the equity risk premium has been as high as it has been historically; that is, why has the return on stocks been approximately double that of the return on bonds? To some analysts, these returns seem extraordinary, especially since they far outpace the level of growth in the economy. Perhaps the expected returns on stocks are really a good bit less than appears from the historical record due to what is termed *survivorship bias*—some stocks, even some markets, do not survive and thus are not included in the return series that analysts calculate. This creates an upward bias in the numbers. Perhaps the link between economic growth and stock returns is not as direct as may intuitively seem correct. Whatever the truth, no authority suggests that the equity risk premium is simply there for the taking: the nature of equity risk is that some future periods are likely to provide handsome rewards to those who invest in stocks, but other periods will provide dismal returns.

There is a conventional wisdom that holds that stocks are not risky in the long run. This is because the dispersion of annual rates of return is lower for long time periods than for short time periods. That is, rates of return over ten-year periods are less dispersed than rates of return over three-year periods. However, some authorities have argued that it is a fallacy that stocks are less risky in the long run. For example, Bodie argues in a 1995 article that if stocks are less risky over long periods, the price of a put option on an index such as the S&P 500 (an index that can be used to insure against a loss in a long large company stock position) should be lower for a longer time to expiration. However, he suggests this is not the case. Paul Samuelson observes also that simply predicting future success based on historical success may not capture the true riskiness of stocks. Although a long time provides more time to recover from poor performance, it also provides more time to encounter poor performance. This debate is not over, and it may never be over. Furthermore, the risk preferences of the investor are clearly a key factor in how this question may be answered. Intuition suggests that high returns, however, come from exposure to high risk, so we caution against naively taking the view that time somehow eliminates the possibility of adverse outcomes.

Bonds

Bonds and other fixed-income investments are the most important alternative to stocks. A distinguishable characteristic of bonds is that they produce an income stream defined by the indenture agreement or contract. This income stream has two very attractive aspects for pension plans. First, it addresses any income or liquidity needs the plan has by producing income that can be used to meet plan spending requirements. Second, the sensitivity of bonds to interest rates and inflation can be used to match (or manage) the interest rate sensitivity of defined benefit plan liabilities and thus to reduce or eliminate the volatility of the plan surplus.

One cautionary note is appropriate for bonds. The recent performance record for bonds since the early 1980s probably overstates a reasonable long-run expectation. This is because interest rates in the United States were quite high in the early 1980s (in 1981, the long Treasury bond rate was nearly 14%) but fell steadily (with occasional spikes) through 1993 (when the long Treasury bond rate was around 6.6%). In a declining interest rate environment, bonds do especially well, producing capital gains as well as interest income. However, in periods of accelerating inflation, bond investors suffer a great deal. Furthermore, when long-term interest rates are volatile (such as from 1993 through 1996), there will be wide swings in bond returns.

Cash

Most pension funds hold some cash. More accurately, they invest in high-grade, short-term debt securities (typically with maturities of less than one year)—Treasury bills, commercial paper, and so forth. They invest this way to obtain liquidity and as a temporary parking place for funds that are destined to be invested in longer term assets.

In many respects, cash is a residual. Pension plans for companies or organizations with young workforces and few retirees need little cash and should be careful about letting cash balances build up, as cash returns generally just match inflation instead of beating it. Pension plans for organizations with older workforces and many retirees may need more liquidity, but they may be able to address this need through income-producing assets such as bonds.

Cash offers the lowest return, on average, of any of the asset classes. Thus, it creates a drag on portfolio returns that is justifiable only if there is a pressing need for liquidity that cannot be met by investment income or contributions. Managers of portions of the pension plan's assets must be monitored to make certain they are not maintaining excessive cash balances. Overall, the reduction in returns attributable to cash can be minimized by using derivatives to create effective exposures to other asset classes.

Real Estate

The case for real estate in a pension portfolio is built on improving portfolio diversification and an apparently strong track record of high-return, low-volatility performance. Evidence on the recent performance of real estate, however, paints a less appealing picture. For example, for the thirteen-year period ending June 30, 1993, the annual return on the National Council of Real Estate Investment Fiduciaries (NCREIF) Property Index (a direct real estate equity investment index) was only 6.6%. Compare this to stock, bond, and Treasury bill annual returns of 15.5%, 11.8%, and 8.0% respectively for the same period (see the chapter by Downs and Hartzell). The relatively poor returns as measured by the NCREIF Index are attributable to numerous factors— overbuilding, changes in tax laws, and so forth. Regardless of why the returns were poor, the main point is that risky investments sometimes provide poor returns: that is why they are called risky. For some investors in real estate, this was an unpleasant surprise.

Real estate differs from publicly traded stocks and bonds in that it is generally illiquid. This lack of liquidity may mean that the realizable value of real estate is substantially below its appraisal value. Further, there is a nontrivial problem in measuring and assessing real estate returns and volatilities. Since there are relatively few market transactions to use in computing returns and standard deviations, appraisals frequently are used in data series. Appraisals introduce a smoothing bias that may make it seem as though historical returns are higher and volatilities lower than they actually may have been. Moreover, real estate transaction costs are high relative to those of stocks and bonds; these costs are not incorporated into most data series that purport to measure real estate performance.

There are some other issues to consider when investing in real estate. Real estate is quite heterogeneous. Some real properties, if their leases are indexed to inflation, offer inflation-hedging possibilities. Other properties, with long-term, fixed-payment leases, look and behave a lot like bonds. Properties in some areas can be appreciating rapidly at the same time that those in other areas are depreciating. Since the market for real estate is quite segmented, diversification across region, economic exposure, and property type is especially important.

Real estate offers a variety of cash-flow and interest-rate sensitivities, degrees of equity participations, and leverage. Thus, it offers pension funds the opportunity to customize their overall asset pool to meet the structure of the liabilities of the funds better. Investments in real estate may be made through direct participations, co-mingled real estate funds (CREFs), or real estate investment trusts (REITs). The first requires an expertise few pension funds have, and CREFs can be surprisingly illiquid as investors frequently must wait a considerable time to exit positions. REITs offer a viable alternative, with the advantage of greater liquidity because they are actively traded on securities markets. REITs suffered from excessive borrowing and subsequent poor performance in the 1970s, but are now coming back into favor with many investors.

International Securities

There is evidence that adding international stocks and bonds to a basic domestic stock/bond/cash portfolio provides a better risk/return profile. Exposures to international securities also introduce an exchange rate effect, however.

International investing may offer more opportunities for excess returns through active investment management because many foreign markets may be less informationally or institutionally efficient than U.S. markets are. Managers who believe these opportunities exist may search for those markets that offer potentially higher risk-adjusted returns. But pension funds should beware of the possibility of stress events such as the peso problem. This problem often arises in foreign security and currency markets due to the occurrence of an unforeseen event that leads to changing asset valuations that are many standard deviations away from typical experience. (Appendix C offers further discussion on international investing.)

Derivatives

Financial contracts that derive their value from the value of an underlying asset, index, or formula may not be an asset class per se, but they are clearly an important and distinct part of the investment landscape. Although pension plans have not used derivatives extensively in the past, more plans are doing so, and more will do so in the future.

The most attractive aspect of calls, puts, futures, swaps, and other more exotic contracts is that these contracts offer plan sponsors a variety of ways to adjust the risk/return profiles of their portfolios in a cost-efficient manner. This is because an increased or decreased exposure to other asset classes (or other risks) can be attained fairly inexpensively through derivative contracting, while obtaining the same change in exposure through buying or selling the actual stocks and bonds themselves generally will be much more costly.

There are three unfortunate aspects of derivative securities. First, they are very difficult to understand unless one is well versed in the specifics of their payoff structures and valuation. These structures and valuation methods can require a high degree of technical expertise to properly evaluate. Second, recent large losses incurred by such diverse entities as Barings Bank, Procter & Gamble, and Orange County, California, have made derivatives politically unattractive. Third, when evaluated independently of the total portfolios of which they are a part, they can easily appear to be imprudent investments because of their high volatility. All these features make many investors reluctant to consider using derivative securities when they should. (Chapter 10 provides a more detailed examination of derivatives and how they should be used in managing pension fund assets.)

Fundamentals of Allocating Assets

How should pension fund managers, trustees, administrators, and other fiduciaries go about allocating the pension fund's assets? The starting point is to determine the optimal asset mix—the strategic asset allocation. This is the mix of equities, bonds, and cash that on average, over time, will best meet the pension fund's return needs without taking on more risk than is prudent for the fund's beneficiaries and the fund's sponsor in view of their tolerance for risk.

The fund's strategic allocation across the three primary asset classes is the single most important investment decision that pension planners can make. A widely cited study by Brinson, Hood, and Beebower suggests that as much as 93.6% of the variation in returns of pension portfolios may be attributed to their normal asset allocation weights and market index returns. Unfortunately, this decision sometimes gets shunted aside for more glamorous decisions: how much should be invested in emerging markets? How much should be invested in venture capital? The reality for most pensions is that very little will be placed in these exotic classes. However, whether to invest 70% or 30% of a fund's total assets in stocks is a decision that will have considerable impact on the long-term financial health of the pension fund.

Determining what proportion of a pension fund's assets should be invested in each type of asset class requires understanding the plan's return requirement and risk tolerance as well as expectations of the risk/return relationships offered by the capital markets. This blending of investor risk/return objectives with capital market expectations is an exercise in what is known as constrained portfolio optimization— selecting the optimal portfolio of assets subject to the joint constraints of tolerance for risk and the desire to achieve high returns.

Risk/Return-Efficient Portfolios

To select the right strategic asset allocation, the plan sponsor (perhaps aided by a pension consultant) or the plan beneficiary must quantify current expectations for asset class returns, the volatility of these returns, and the relationship (co-movement) between returns on different asset classes over time. The obvious starting point is the historical record of the asset classes, as provided earlier. A review of how the different classes have performed shows that the more volatile asset classes (e.g., stocks) have also provided the highest returns—over long periods of time. However, the analyst should be careful to avoid naively projecting the historical record into the future. Knowing that stocks have provided higher returns than bonds over long periods of time tells us little about how stocks will do next year or over the next five years. Nonetheless, the historical record is a good starting point in forming long-term expectations that will help to make a sensible allocation of the pension plan's funds.

Ambachtscheer suggested in 1988 that analysts can improve their expectations for future risks and returns by considering several factors that may cause future performance to differ from past performance. He suggested that the analyst consider replacing the historical yield curve with the actual yield curve at the time of the analysis. Further, he argued that the analyst should adjust for apparent biases and trends in history (e.g., artificially low interest rates in the 1940s and 1950s and the corresponding decline in stock dividend yields). Finally, the analyst should try to anticipate the impact of such factors as savings and trade disequilibrium, globalization, and recapitalization.

There are other approaches. Sharpe observed in 1990 that scenario analysis, correlation models, and other techniques are available to analysts. Each technique has strengths and weaknesses that should be considered when applying it. As in much that investment professionals do, subjective judgment plays an important role in deciding which factors are truly important or less so, and what they actually mean for future returns and risks.

Once a reasonable set of expectations has been determined, the analyst may compute (or estimate) what is commonly termed an *efficient frontier*. The efficient frontier is the collection of portfolios that are efficient because they have the highest expected returns for a given amount of risk. The actual computation requires some mathematical programming, but there are many software packages that help. This is not as theoretical as it sounds; it is commonly accepted in the investment profession that holding portfolios that lie beneath the efficient frontier (i.e., that offer too little return for the risk taken) is a mistake to be avoided if at all possible.

Allocation Targets

After a set of efficient portfolios has been identified, the analyst must choose from the many asset allocation portfolios represented in that set. In very general terms, sponsors or beneficiaries wishing to structure a plan with relatively little exposure to risk will favor allocations weighted toward bonds and other fixed-income assets. Where more risk is acceptable or more return is desirable, the allocation will tend to favor equities. The extreme choices range from a relatively low-risk portfolio (typically one where asset and liability durations are matched in an effort to minimize the volatility of the pension surplus for defined benefit plans, or a default-free investment such as Treasury bills for individual beneficiaries) up to a much more aggressive portfolio that pursues high total return (and attempts either to maximize pension surplus and/or to minimize the present value of sponsor contributions or maximize future real values). Various factors affect the selection of the optimal portfolio mix at or between these two extremes. For example, defined benefit plans must consider the financial strength of the sponsor, plan benefit formulas, and the demographic features of the workforce. Individuals must consider time to retirement, the expected period of retirement, retirement lifestyles, other income and investments, and target wealth levels. The asset allocation that most closely corresponds to the desired expected risk and return profile is, of course, a fundamental element of policy.

Most pension plans set asset allocation policy targets as percentages of the whole, so the policy is formulated, for example, as 30% of plan assets in long-term bonds, 60% in stocks, and 10% in cash. The sponsor/beneficiary may also set acceptable ranges for deviation from this target allocation (e.g., 30% ± 5%). Money managers, whether internal or external, are then responsible for adhering to the policy limits. Individuals are less likely to hire external managers and thus tend to serve as their own internal managers. Where external managers are being used, the sponsor/beneficiary must be prepared to adjust contributions among managers as needed to maintain the desired mix.

Strategic Asset Allocation and Reallocations Over Time

Prior to discussing the way the strategic asset allocation should be set, it is useful to consider how fluctuations in valuation in the financial markets affect initial asset allocations, and also to consider ways to reallocate assets as time passes and things change. We use as our framework a structure William Sharpe has suggested in various works (see Sharpe, 1990, and Sharpe and Perold). We begin by discussing alternative ways to maintain the strategic asset allocation once it has been established and then address in turn tactical asset allocation and insured asset allocation.

Strategic Asset Allocation

As previously mentioned, the strategic asset allocation is the stock/bond/cash mix that the pension plan's decision makers have decided is best for the plan over the long run. Secondarily, it may include other asset classes, such as real estate and international securities, but the attention of decision makers clearly needs to be focused on the stock/bond/cash mix first.

The strategic mix can best be thought of as the mix most likely to match the plan's long-term risk/return objectives over several different types of markets. This mix is generally developed on three assumptions. First, the investor cannot consistently forecast market returns. Second, riskier assets generally earn higher (non–risk-adjusted) rates of return than do less risky assets. Third, the investor can identify an acceptable long-term level of risk tolerance that is reasonably constant for the fore-seeable future. Accordingly, the strategic asset allocation decision involves optimizing across markets that are not perfectly correlated with each other, thus producing a variety of acceptable portfolios. Further, it involves trading off an aversion to investment risk today against the risk of being unable to meet plan obligations when due without having to contribute a great deal more to the plan than originally anticipated.

Once made, the strategic asset allocation is maintained in one of two ways. The first is a simple buy-and-hold strategy, in which positions in various asset classes are established according to the risk/return prefer-ences of the plan sponsor/beneficiary. In this strategy, no trades are made other than those necessary to meet plan liquidity needs (e.g., investing new contributions or selling securities to meet payment requirements). The impact of market action on plan assets and, hence, on allocations is ignored. This is an important issue as, over time, asset classes experience periods of underperformance and overperformance relative to other asset classes. These market actions translate into a change in the proportions of funds in each asset class. For example, if stocks do unusually well relative to bonds, actual bond weightings in a real portfolio go down and stock weightings increase as a percent of the whole even though no trading has taken place. The buy-and-hold strat-egy presumes that these variations in actual asset weights are acceptable because, on average over long periods of time, the average mix of assets will meet policy targets as markets reverse direction and as new contri-butions or liquidations are made in ways that will rebalance the overall portfolio. So if the target allocation for stocks is 60% and the stock mar-ket has risen so that 70% of total assets is actually invested in equities, new contributions could be directed toward bonds until the actual stock allocation falls to the target. Alternatively, if new funding is not substan-tial, the pension plan may simply wait for markets to restore the initial asset mix by reverting to the mean. As should be apparent, the buy-and-hold strategy incurs little in the way of transaction costs. On the other hand, at any given point in time, the actual asset allocation and the strategic allocation may differ from each other, and the risk/return profile of the portfolio thus may not match the target profile.

The alternative approach to maintaining strategic asset allocation is to follow a disciplined rebalancing or constant mix strategy. Rather than the no action approach characteristic of the buy-and-hold strategy, disciplined rebalancing is a dynamic strategy that requires the plan manager to rebalance the portfolio periodically, whenever actual asset allocations fall outside the targeted range or on a predetermined schedule. The general trading rule followed by disciplined rebalancing is to buy assets that perform poorly relative to other asset classes and to reduce holdings in asset classes that perform relatively well. In essence, this is a trading strategy that buys when prices fall and sells when prices rise. The objective of any set of trades is to return to the long-term strategic weights as defined by policy. That is, the disciplined rebalancing strategy attempts dynamically to restore a constant mix. Disciplined rebalancing should be done at the level of the overall pool of assets, not by individual managers. Thus, someone must be monitoring the overall asset allocation. Since disciplined rebalancing requires trading, it may incur greater transaction costs than the buy-and-hold strategy. These costs can be reduced by the use of derivatives. The advantage of this strategy over the buy-and-hold approach is that the actual portfolio weights and hence its risk/return profile will be more closely aligned with the targets specified in the policy statement.

The relative performance of these two strategies—disciplined rebalancing vs. buy-and-hold—depends on the nature of the market action. To see this, consider a simple two-asset allocation among stocks and Treasury bills. If the absolute or relative performance of stocks relative to Treasury bills makes a sustained move either up or down (i.e., if it trends), the buy-and-hold strategy will produce performance that is superior to that of disciplined rebalancing. This is because disciplined rebalancing will sell stocks into a rising stock market in which stock prices continue to rise—and vice versa. On the other hand, if an asset class such as stocks is mean reverting—that is, if reversals occur following upward or downward changes in valuation of market sectors—then the disciplined rebalancing approach will provide superior performance. This is because disciplined rebalancing will sell stocks into a rising stock market that subsequently falls—and vice versa. In either case, the sponsor should be aware that both of these strategies are primarily passive in nature, in that their intent is to maintain preselected policy target weights rather than to exploit insights or beliefs about market sectors.

In one study, Arnott showed that from 1969 to 1988, a typical manager with a 60% stock/40% bond mix would gain 16 basis points more per year using disciplined rebalancing every month, after allowing for transaction costs, versus allowing allocation drift (the buy-and-hold strategy) as market values of each sector moved apart. Thus, there is some evidence that frequent rebalancing may pay, though the frequency must be traded off against the costs of frequent trading and, as noted above, it may not work well in all markets.

Tactical Asset Allocation

An increasing number of pensions are using or exploring *tactical asset allocation (TAA)* strategies. In TAA, the strategic asset allocation targets are still considered to be valid in the sense that they provide the broad framework for the long-term investment of pension assets. However, within that framework, the pension plan sponsor intends to adjust the asset mix to exploit what the sponsor believes to be incorrect relative valuations of asset classes, sectors, or individual assets.

For instance, suppose the strategic asset allocation is 60% equities, 30% bonds, and 10% cash. Further suppose that the stock market drops suddenly and sharply. Because the dollar value of stocks has decreased relative to the dollar value of the other asset classes, adhering to the strategic asset allocation plan would require that either bonds and cash equivalents be sold and stocks bought to return to the 60/30/10% policy mix (the disciplined rebalancing approach) or simply that nothing be done (the buy-and-hold approach). The tactical asset allocation plan would not necessarily pursue either of these trading strategies. It could, instead, elect to remain heavily in bonds until more information regarding the stock decline becomes available. Alternatively, a plan manager may develop a belief that equities now are underpriced. As a result of this belief, and the corollary expectation that stocks now are likely to perform unusually well, he or she may decide to do more than merely return to the initial allocation and purchase more than the target amount of stocks necessary to restore the strategic asset allocation, so that the mix becomes 80/15/5%. The additional exposure to stocks (i.e., the 20% of the allocation that is above the strategic weight of 60%) is an active bet that stocks will do unusually well in the future.

This latter strategy is most typical of what normally is considered tactical asset allocation and is consistent with an effort to exploit the tendency of asset markets to experience reversals of movements.

Implicit in any TAA program is a theory of relative asset valuation. Reversals are responsive countermoves that occur after sharp upward or downward changes in valuation of markets, sectors, and/or individual securities. A belief in reversals generally is supported by a belief that investors overreact to new information that the market may have received and that once this overreaction is recognized, the prices of securities that rose (or fell) sharply will move in the opposite direction nearly as sharply. Note that although the tactical asset allocation trading strategy is driven by an expected reversal, it looks fundamentally the same as disciplined rebalancing—buying when prices fall and selling when prices rise. The difference is that the motivation is to exploit a perceived mispricing rather than simply to return to target policy weights.

The results of the TAA trading strategy for tactical asset allocation relative to a buy-and-hold strategy are the same as for the disciplined rebalancing in that tactical asset allocation will outperform a buy-and-hold strategy when there are reversals, but it will underperform when there are sustained moves away from normal values. The greater flexibility to take on weights outside policy guidelines, of course, permits tactical asset allocation potentially to achieve greater returns (or incur greater opportunity costs) than disciplined rebalancing permits.

Tactical asset allocation can also be applied as *sector-tilting*—overweighting and underweighting sectors of a market that are expected to do relatively well or relatively poorly—or *security selection*—the identification of over- or undervalued stocks. There are numerous models for those who wish to allocate assets tactically either by timing asset class returns or shopping for undervalued assets. They all tend to favor a contrarian approach. As one investment manager says, "Buy when there is blood in the streets." The essence of this approach is to buy when no one else seems to want the asset (or class of assets). When assets become oversold, their prices can fall below their true values and, if one simply waits long enough, their prices will recover. One must be careful in adapting this strategy—a bargain that remains a bargain is, of course, no bargain.

If a plan sponsor wants to implement a tactical asset allocation plan, there are three elements that must be very clearly specified. The first is the limitation on the percentage by which the investment and various categories can deviate from the strategic asset allocation targets. That is, the strategic asset allocation plan specifies the appropriate asset mix, but a specified range of tactical discretion is predetermined and permitted. The second element is the decision model that will be used explicitly to trigger actions to buy or sell based on relative valuations. The third element is a commitment to doing the things the selected model says ought to be done.

The last point is worth further discussion. Failures to act upon the predictions of tactical asset allocation models may lead to returns that are much worse than they should be. The advantage of any active trading strategy is that it brings to bear all the science and intuition that a decision maker can muster. The fallacy in changing one's mind about the usefulness of the output of a model and thus overriding its mechanical decision is that it effectively throws out one's best systematic thinking and substitutes an isolated component of intuition. Indeed, if an investment manager behaves differently than the manager has committed to behave, it could lead to a legal challenge on prudence grounds. The prospect of litigation alone should caution a manager against ad hoc intuitive behavior.

Does TAA work? There are studies (see, for example, the article by Arnott and Rice) that report that gains can be made if tactical asset allocation is correct as little as 51% of the time. Some experts (see, for example, Sharpe, 1990) argue that since pension plans have very long time horizons, pension plan risk tolerance can be thought of as remaining constant regardless of changes in the average risk tolerance and, hence, changes in asset class valuations. If this is true, TAA may be a sensible way to pursue excess returns because, from time to time, the average expected risk premium may be much higher than the pension plan ordinarily would require. Other authorities (see, for example, the article by MacBeth and Emanuel) suggest that traditional measures of value such as dividend yield and the price/book ratio are related to stock market returns but not in a way that can be exploited by TAA strategies that rely on mean/variance analysis. Rather, they argue that successful TAA strategies must consider the skewness—the likelihood of a large number of outcomes skewed above or below the expected outcome—of the probability distribution of equity returns if the strategy is to work.

In summary, achieving success with tactical asset allocation requires a belief in actively managing portfolios by trading on expectations of values—expectations that tend to be contrary to popular wisdom. Hence it requires considerable discipline and a model of asset valuation. If the model being used needs adjustment, by all means, make the adjustment, but do it in a long-term, strategically aware way just as strategic allocations are determined. Do not ignore the serious risks that the sponsor or manager may chicken out and not do something that should be done simply because prevailing folk wisdom is contrary to the model.

Insured Asset Allocation

In the mid-1980s, portfolio insurance became the darling of many in the institutional investor crowd. The equity market crash of October 1987 greatly reduced the attractiveness of portfolio insurance when it became apparent that the trading strategies that it relied upon could not be executed in all types of markets or in a timely enough manner to provide the insurance promised. Nonetheless, portfolio insurance may, from time to time, be appropriate for pension funds, and it can be a useful if only occasional ingredient in successful asset allocation. Additionally, insurance-like trading rules may be useful in markets that can be characterized as trending over time.

In its simplest form, insured asset allocation consists of reducing a plan's exposure to risky asset classes when those classes are performing poorly (i.e., when asset values are decreasing). As Sharpe and Perold have pointed out, the essence of portfolio insurance is to establish and then maintain a floor or minimal asset value beneath which no exposure to risky assets will be taken. Above the floor, the portfolio can invest in risky assets in proportion to the size of the cushion; that is, if a risky asset class, such as stocks, is doing well and values are going up, the portfolio will increase its exposure to stocks by purchasing more. If, however, stock prices begin to fall so that the cushion above the floor is eroding, the exposure to stocks will be reduced by selling stocks.

The trading dynamic of this strategy is just the opposite of that of the disciplined rebalancing and tactical asset allocation strategies. In fact, the performance of this strategy relative to a buy-and-hold strategy also is just the opposite. Insured portfolios will outperform buy-and-hold strategies (as well as tactical asset allocation and disciplined rebalancing strategies) when markets make sustained moves either up or down and when the trades can be executed at the proper "trigger" prices. When markets are relatively flat but volatile (e.g., when reversion to the mean is taking place), portfolio insurance strategies will underperform the buy-and-hold strategy (and also underperform the tactical asset allocation and disciplined rebalancing strategies) due to buying high and selling low. As with TAA, insured asset allocation may be implemented with derivatives (liquidity permitting).

When is portfolio insurance appropriate? One way to think about portfolio insurance is to consider it to be an occasional strategy. The primary motivation to insure should come from a sufficiently unique circumstance wherein the pension plan's risk tolerance is determined to be more sensitive to changes in market values at a specific time than is the risk tolerance of the market as a whole. When markets fall, one interpretation of the reason for the decline in market prices is that the societal or average risk premium has increased, driving asset values down. If a pension plan's sensitivity to changes in asset values is greater than the average change in risk tolerance implied by the change in asset prices, there is a case to be made for insuring the portfolio—reducing the plan's fundamental definition of an acceptable level of risk. For example, consider a sponsor who decides to terminate its defined benefit plan and use its assets to purchase annuities to affect plan liabilities. The plan now has the unusually short time horizon of perhaps one year—until the annuity contracts are arranged. In this situation, the plan might wish to insure its portfolio against loss of value.

Conclusion

The broad asset allocation decision—what portion of a pension fund's assets should be allocated to stocks, to bonds, and to cash—is the single most important investment policy parameter that senior management, trustees, and other members of the sponsor's leadership team must determine. The decision requires an understanding of what each asset class brings to the fund, knowledge of how each has performed historically, and expectations for how each might perform in the future. It requires that the decision makers understand the primary alternatives to a simple buy-and-hold implementation of whatever allocation is chosen and how these alternatives are likely to perform under various types of markets. It also requires a commitment to review the asset mix of the total asset pool regularly to see whether it still conforms to the asset weights that have been chosen.

No single one of the asset allocation techniques discussed in this chapter is exclusively the best. Rather, as Sharpe has proposed, the best approach is an integrated approach wherein full attention initially is given to establishing the correct strategic asset weights. Once this is done, the sponsor then needs to make the fundamental choice of allocating money to be actively managed or passively managed (as discussed in Chapter 4). If the sponsor/beneficiary believes that active management may lead to above average returns on a risk-adjusted basis, perhaps because one or more of the markets in which the fund intends to invest are not informationally efficient and may be subject to overreaction, then tactical asset allocation becomes a viable alternative. Presumably, there also will be times in the future, as there have been in the past, when market sectors are doing nothing special. During these times, it seems likely that the fund will benefit more if it pursues a simple buy-and-hold strategy or a disciplined rebalancing approach. From time to time there may be particular circumstances when insuring plan assets makes sense: at these times, of course, a shift in asset allocation strategies again seems warranted.

Without question, the initial strategic asset allocation decision should get the bulk of the decision maker's attention. Tactical, insured, and disciplined rebalancing are all legitimate alternatives to a simple buy-and-hold strategy. A poor strategic allocation, however, will be difficult to overcome.

Chapter **6**

Setting the Strategic Asset Allocation

Conceptually, there is nothing difficult about how the strategic asset allocation should be set. It is simply the mix of stocks, bonds, and cash (more finely parsed to other asset classes as appropriate) that, in the long run, best meets the circumstances and constraints the pension plan faces and that provides an appropriate rate of return on plan assets without exceeding the plan's ability to bear risk. Translating this simple concept into a sensible asset mix that is an operational plan that can be justified to others and is economically sound is not so easy, however.

Individuals who are responsible for allocating assets in their defined contribution plan (DCP) accounts first must be knowledgeable about investment principles and then must apply those principles to their own unique circumstances. This is no easy task. The first section of this chapter discusses the issues that apply to individuals who, as DCP participants, manage their own assets, and provides an analytical framework that demonstrates the impact of the asset allocation decision on expected risk and return.

The second section addresses the factors to consider in setting the strategic asset allocation for defined benefit plans (DBPs), as well as for employer-directed defined contribution plans. The interaction of sponsor and plan interests, of investment performance and contribution levels, and of assets and liabilities poses some difficult but not impossible to solve problems. The section concludes by providing an analytical framework for translating alternative asset allocations into results that are useful in decision making.

Readers should bear in mind that the strategic asset allocation (SAA) is the operational side of investment policy. It is the result or consequence of decisions that policymakers make. Although the SAA is the structure that positions the pension plan to obtain its long-term investment goals with an appropriate level risk, the goals themselves reflect many competing interests and diverse philosophies about what the purpose of the asset pool really is. Of course, the actual allocation chosen (whether it is 80% stocks or 40% stocks or whatever) reflects beliefs about long-term capital market returns and risks and correlations.

Strategic Asset Allocation for Employee-Directed Defined Contribution Plans

Setting the strategic asset allocation for individuals who participate in employee-directed DCPs is primarily a matter of trading off investment risk against the prospective returns necessary to achieve the individual's retirement goals. This does not mean it is easy, nor does it mean the sponsor should be completely passive. As explained in Chapter 4, sponsors that do not want to bear responsibility for the performance of DCP asset pools should give employees access to the tools necessary to the job themselves. This implies extensive education about the factors that should guide employees in making the strategic asset allocation decision. This section discusses these factors and offers sponsors insights into helping their employees make sensible decisions without giving investment advice.

Liabilities, Life Cycles, and Taxes

Several issues make individual investors different from DBPs when it comes to setting their strategic asset allocations. First, most liabilities are unique to each individual and, unlike those of many institutional investors are not fixed or specific; rather, these liabilities can be changed if circumstances change (for instance, if accumulations fail to meet certain targeted goals). Second, individuals are very exposed to inflation, since they have few fixed liabilities to hedge the inflation risk of the assets they might accumulate. Third, individuals are mortal. Their expected life spans are finite and change with the passage of time and changes in health. Finally, individuals are subject to taxes. Although earnings on qualified pension asset pools such as those of DCPs are not taxed until they are withdrawn, the impact of taxes on investments held outside of pension plans affects the choice of the assets in pension plans.

Liabilities

All of us presumably share a desire to have a prosperous retirement in which we can maintain or even improve upon current lifestyles. This is the fundamental nature of the DCP liability: an adequate retirement. Like employers, individuals must integrate their pension management and goals with the day-to-day business of living—putting the kids through school, purchasing a home, and so forth. Unlike employers, however, an individual's pension liabilities do not decrease when interest rates increase, and thus they do not offset the decline in the value of any financial assets that may also occur. Instead, individuals must adjust future plans to realign the retirement liability with the assets available to fund it.

Unlike employees covered by DBPs, the beneficiaries of DCPs have no promise from the plan's sponsor to increase funding if the accumulation of pension assets is not sufficient due to poor financial market performance or poor investment decisions or inadequate funding or some other reason. If the accumulation of assets is substantially less than anticipated, employees may sue employers, claiming the sponsor was not prudent in some way or another. Perhaps the suit will be successful, perhaps it will not be. Perhaps it will take a long time for the courts to decide. In the meantime, the individual unhappily changes his or her lifestyle.

Life Cycles

A common approach to framing the strategic asset allocation decision is to divide an individual's life into four phases (see the 1990 article by Kaiser). The *accumulation phase* is characterized by a long time horizon of perhaps 30 to 40 years to retirement and 25 years or so in retirement. Over this 50-plus-year period, an individual needs to accumulate an asset pool that will provide adequate retirement income. Accumulation comes about through employer and employee contributions and through investment performance. Contributions are constrained by regulation; investment performance is constrained by the asset allocation decision. *Adequate* usually implies achieving a wage replacement rate that will allow the desired standard of living once the individual retires. Unfortunately, over this long a time, even modest inflation can seriously erode the purchasing power of the dollar, so the growth in assets must be sufficient to offset the effect of inflation. Most authorities agree that the general allocation during the accumulation phase should favor equities in allocations as high as 100%. The rationale is that long time horizons provide sufficient time to recover from short-term adverse market actions, making the capacity to bear risk high. This high capacity for risk, coupled with the exposure to inflation that long time periods bring, makes equities appropriate for most individuals.

Following the accumulation phase is the *consolidation phase*. This is characterized by a much shorter time to retirement and the likelihood of wages and possibly contributions to the DCP being at a peak. The nearness of retirement brings a lower tolerance for risk—there is less time to recover from adverse market action—and increases the incentives to save even more. Hence, there is at least the possibility of a reallocation of assets from growth-oriented, high-volatility assets (e.g., stocks) to more conservative allocations encompassing bonds and/or cash (T-bills). Although there is some disagreement on this point, most authorities argue against allocations to long-term bonds because of the interest rate risk they pose. As noted earlier, individuals do not have interest rate–sensitive liabilities, so they cannot offset exposures to liabilities that are sensitive to interest rates with long-term bonds. Rather, if interest rates increase, bonds held by an individual will lose value but the liabilities—the retirement income goals—do not change. Consequently, individuals probably should avoid bonds or bond funds with maturities longer than 3 to 5 years unless the bonds are indexed to changes in interest rates.*

The *spending* or *retirement* phase follows employment termination. In this phase, the now former employee uses his or her retirement portfolio to provide income. Some authorities assert that this means an orientation to bonds; others assert that large equity allocations still are appropriate and that such income as is needed should come from dividend-paying stocks and disciplined sales of portfolio assets. Individuals with large portfolios may find this latter approach palatable. Those who have not been so fortunate or wise may rightly worry about the impact of a run of poor stock market performance on their portfolios. In general, those who have just entered retirement and have perhaps 20 to 30 years to live must pursue the equity risk premium in order to offset inflation. Those who

---

*The federal inflation-indexed bonds introduced in early 1997 may be attractive to some individuals, depending on their pricing, because they offer a partial offset to inflation-induced interest rate changes.

are about to die do not have to worry about inflation unless they are concerned for their heirs. One rule of thumb often used to determine the appropriate allocation to equity in this phase is to use the equation 100 − age = % in equity. We caution that this is simply a starting point. There are far too many variables for such a simple rule to be applied without further analysis.

The final phase is the *gifting* phase. Here, the objective of the portfolio is to provide for people (e.g., grandchildren) or organizations (e.g., charities) that have investment horizons well beyond that of the current owner of the assets. The bequest motive becomes the main factor at work, and there is a reorientation toward growth and a return to asset allocations that may look like those appropriate to the accumulation phase.

Note that lump sum distributions to employees upon retirement create a reinvestment problem for individuals. This problem is especially severe when the sponsor has been directing the investment decisions of the plan and then simply hands the responsibility over to the employee, who is not likely to be well versed in investing. Of course, the distribution may be annuitized, but this may not be the highest and best use of the funds, and it may not relieve fiduciaries of their duties to find creditworthy, cost-efficient providers.

Taxes

In many cases, defined contribution asset pools will not be sufficient to allow employees to retire when they wish or to live the retirement lifestyle they want. This may be the result of low contributions, poor investment performance, job switching coupled with vesting rules, or other factors. Social Security may help some although its current financial status raises serious questions. Regardless, those who want to increase the probability of living as they wish later will save more now. Once tax-exempt contribution limits to pension plans have been reached, the only alternative is to form portfolios that are subject to taxes.

There is far too much to say on this matter to cover it in a book on pension management. What must be said here, however, is that the individual must view his or her pension assets and nonpension assets as parts of a greater whole to avoid making suboptimal asset allocations. The goal should be to maximize after-tax real returns subject to the risk tolerance of the individual. For example, intermediate term tax-exempt bonds should never be held in a pension portfolio, but they may be sensible in a taxable environment. Individuals in an accumulation phase who hold stocks and intermediate term corporate bonds may want to hold some or all of the stocks in the taxable environment where capital gains are deferrable and are taxed at lower rates, and where taxable income yields are low. The bonds may be placed in the retirement portfolio where the income produced will be sheltered. Of course, as the spending phase nears, some reallocations may be appropriate, especially if postretirement tax rates are expected to be lower than preretirement tax rates.

An Approach to Setting the Strategic Asset Allocation for Individuals

How can sponsors help employees learn to define the appropriate levels of risk that can be tolerated and how investment risk should be evaluated in light of the threat of the erosion of purchasing power that inflation brings? One approach to helping individuals evaluate the tradeoff between their tolerance for risk and their accumulation goals (return objectives) is described in this section. The approach is used by the American Association of Individual Investors (AAII) in their investment seminars for individual investors.

Many individuals view risk in terms of adverse consequences. Thus, an analysis that demonstrates the impact of risk on a portfolio by examining how seriously adverse market actions can erode portfolio value in the event of a major bear market can give individuals an opportunity to assess their willingness to accept significant interim decreases in the value of their retirement assets. However, it is important not to stop here. The counterpoint to risk and adverse outcomes is the damage that even modest inflation can cause to real asset values and its resultantly adverse effect on future standards of living. For example, since the long-term returns on the least risky asset class (Treasury bills) have only matched the rate of inflation (providing no real growth before taxes and negative growth if taxed), the analysis illustrates the importance of pension accumulations in real terms and how risk becomes a necessary, if undesirable, factor.

The trade-off between risk and return requires presenting alternative model portfolios and their performances over various time periods. Consider two such portfolios. Portfolio A has 90% of its assets in aggressive equity mutual funds of one type or another and 10% in a money market fund. Portfolio B, a more conservative portfolio, has 70% of its assets invested in less aggressive equity mutual funds, 20% in fixed-income mutual funds, and 10% in money market funds. We can evaluate how these portfolios would have performed historically by simply using past performance data. (Although no one believes the historical record can naively be projected as an expectation, nonetheless it is instructive to look at the past and see what could have happened given the risk exposure brought about by alternative asset allocations. The insights gained are quite helpful in forming reasonable expectations of future performance differences among different asset allocations.)

To help individuals get a sense of their tolerance for risk, the analyst computes returns for the model portfolios by assuming that the worst one-year performance of various market sectors from the post–World War II period occurs and by assuming that this adverse performance occurs in all market segments more or less simultaneously. Although this is admittedly a very low-probability event, it has the usefulness of demonstrating that risky financial assets can and do from time to time suffer severe declines in value. During the post–World War II period, for instance, the worst that would have happened to these two portfolios is that portfolio A would have suffered a one-year loss of around 33% of its value, while the more conservative portfolio B would have lost only 22% of its value.

In counterpoint, however, the analyst then should examine the real rate of return (the actual historical return less the rate of inflation) that would have been earned on the model portfolios over a 20- or 30-year period. In our example, portfolio A would have provided an annual real rate of return of around 6.7% versus 5.2% for portfolio B. These percentages can be easily converted into dollar accumulations and retirement income. For example, if each portfolio had begun with $50,000, no additional contributions were made, and the historical record is a reasonable approximation of the expected annual returns to be earned over 20 years, portfolio A would be worth $183,000 in real terms; portfolio B would be worth only $138,000 in real terms, about 25% less than portfolio A.

With this information, individuals investing for retirement through self-directed DCPs can get some sense of their willingness to accept the low probability but nonetheless real possibility of losing a significant portion of their investment. At the same time, they can see how inflation affects portfolio values and hence retirement income. (For younger employees, it may be hoped the loss will be recouped over time as market performance improves and reversion brings markets back to some average or normal level of performance. This will not necessarily happen, however.) The strategic asset allocation decision still must be made but the central parameters—the trade-offs of investment risk and inflation—should now be more apparent.

Strategic Asset Allocation for Defined Benefit Plans

This section focuses on the decision for traditional defined benefit plans and hybrid plans where the sponsor maintains an economic interest in the investment performance of plan assets (e.g., cash balance plans). In this circumstance, the appropriate strategic asset allocation is determined in part by the preferences the sponsor has for funding the plan, in part by the interaction of plan assets with plan liabilities, and in part by a choice as to which of two philosophical views is taken with respect to whether to integrate the plan's assets with those of the sponsor. After showing how these issues affect the strategic asset allocation, we describe the theoretical arguments that favor allocations to stocks and to bonds and the circumstances under which allocations to these asset classes are sensible. Some important insights emerge from this analysis. We then present empirical evidence that shows what pension funds actually do and how sponsor circumstances may affect the allocations chosen. This section concludes with an example of how scenario analysis may be used to evaluate the trade-offs inherent in the strategic asset allocation decision.

The Funding Decision

The pension plan sponsor faces several conflicting goals with respect to funding. First, the sponsor wants to minimize the present value of expected long-term contributions. This means that the portfolio should be heavily loaded with stocks, because they have a potentially higher return. Moreover, from the sole perspective of the plan, too heavy a reliance on contributions is too much like too heavy a concentration in the securities of one company or one industry; relying too heavily on the sponsor for contributions may undo the effect of portfolio diversification.

Second, sponsors generally do not want a highly variable contribution rate—that is, they do not want to face the uncertainty of unexpectedly having to put a lot of cash into the plan, particularly if the need for this high infusion of cash occurs at a time when they themselves are experiencing cash shortfalls and cannot make all the real investments they wish, either because of lack of access to capital markets or self-imposed capital rationing. This means the portfolio should be heavily loaded with bonds because bonds have less return volatility than do stocks.

Third, most private sponsors want to meet their obligations to employees without harming shareholders by unexpected shortfalls.

Most public sponsors similarly may want to avoid the harm to tax-payers that may occur in the event of a pension shortfall. However, in both cases, the sponsor must attempt to meet the needs of plan bene-ficiaries. Beneficiaries want to maximize the value of their expected benefits and reduce the likelihood the benefits will not materialize. The conflict this presents to a goal of minimizing contributions is obvious but not easily resolved. ERISA offers some balance to this conflict for private funds; no such arbiter exists in the public sector except for public employee unions that choose to represent their members' pension interests. Although this conflict has elements that may be addressed through contracting, the dynamics of the capital markets and the expertise required suggest that good faith is a sig-nificant issue.

The Effect of Plan Liabilities, Surplus, and Integration

Defined benefit plans have explicit and implicit liabilities, the value of which may be calculated. These liabilities are determined by the benefits promised (the pension deal), the nature of the workforce covered (e.g., average age, mortality, compensation structure), and cur-rent interest rates. Changes in any of these factors change the economic value of the liability. In turn, the potential for changes in the value of the liability can have a profound impact on the way the assets of a plan should be allocated among the asset classes. Consider the following examples of how these factors interact:

1. Sponsors that increase the amount of the promised benefit also increase the present value of the pension liability and, all else the same, reduce the funding status of the plan. This creates pressure to either increase contributions to the plan or to improve investment performance. Pressure to improve investment performance affects the asset allocation by encouraging reallocation toward more risky assets (e.g., stocks).

2. Sponsors with young workforces and few current retirees ordi-narily can tolerate high levels of risk (i.e., may invest heavily in stocks) in part because the present value of the plan liabilities is relatively low and in part because the immediate liquidity needs required for benefit payments are low. Further, they probably must tolerate risk because wages are likely to grow at least at the rate of inflation and thus future benefits will grow accordingly. As the workforce ages, however, the liq-uidity needs of the plan increase and the nearer-term pension payouts increase the size of the pension liability. At this point the allocation of

plan's assets should reflect this different set of circumstances and financial claims.

3. Plan assets and plan liabilities are both exposed to changes in interest rates. When interest rates rise, option-free bond prices fall. Normally, so do the values of other assets although the relationship is not as direct. Pension liabilities are, for all practical purposes, bonds issued by the sponsor—promises to make certain payments in the future. Herein lies an important aspect of the relationship between the pension plan's asset allocation decision and the plan's liabilities. With changes in the level of interest rates affecting both assets and liabilities, asset allocation policy must anticipate the possibility of a change in interest rates disproportionately affecting one or the other—and hence affecting the financial health of the plan.

Surplus Volatility

The financial health of a pension plan typically is defined in terms of the surplus (deficit) of assets over liabilities. The surplus and hence the financial health of a pension plan is thus a function of whatever affects the values of plan assets, plan liabilities, or both. This had led an increasing number of authorities to argue that a pension plan's risk tolerance should be defined in terms of the volatility of the plan surplus (see, for example, the 1990 chapter by Haugen and the 1992 article by Elton and Gruber). Since a primary purpose of a plan's assets is to fund the plan's liabilities and since the sponsor must conceptually make up any shortfall, this view suggests that the appropriate stocks/bonds/cash mix is the one that provides sufficient return subject to an acceptable level of surplus volatility.

Managing the volatility of the pension surplus suggests a risk-minimizing pension fund should define the minimum-risk portfolio as that in which there is no volatility in the pension surplus. This may be accomplished by using cash flow–matched portfolios and immunized, duration-matched portfolios.* From this, it follows that a pension that can or chooses to bear risk in pursuit of lower funding costs

---

*Note that pension funds do not simply match the durations of assets and liabilities. Rather, they must adjust for scale differences by setting asset durations equal to liability durations multiplied by the ratio of liabilities to assets. They must also adjust for differences in the convexity—the rate of change in the assets' or liabilities' sensitivities to changes in interest rates.

or higher benefits will define its efficient frontier of possible portfolios from this riskless portfolio.

In this framework, asset or portfolio volatility is replaced by surplus volatility in analyzing alternative strategic asset allocations. Similarly, asset or portfolio return is replaced by return on plan surplus. (For a good discussion of how this may be done, see the article by Leibowitz, Kogelman, and Bader.)

The Appropriate Liability

Finally, before the appropriate asset allocation mix can be chosen, the sponsor must decide what liability is to be funded. If the sponsor takes the view that the accumulated benefit obligation (ABO) must be funded, then an all-bond strategy will be fine because it has the potential of producing a portfolio that is a perfect hedge relative to the liability. Here, the objective of the all-bond portfolio is to compose a portfolio that will rise or fall in value as the ABO rises or falls due to interest rate changes. One side effect of this, however, that it virtually ensures that contributions over time will have to be much higher than if stocks were held in the portfolio, assuming, of course, that stock returns will generally exceed bond returns over the long term.

Many practitioners and academics believe that the pension liability that should be funded is what might be termed the *total pension obligation* at least for long term strategic planning purposes. This is the best estimate as to the present value of just about all future obligations, including salary increases, a greater number of years worked, and a changing workforce due perhaps to the growth of the sponsoring organization. This number is certainly larger than the ABO. (Indeed, even the projected benefit obligation PBO, which accounts for future salary growth, generally underestimates a plan's true liability.) Because the total pension obligation may grow much more rapidly than the ABO, the timing and magnitude of future pension contributions become significant factors in setting the right strategic asset allocation.

The Integrated Approach to Managing Plan Assets

Recall that there are two views concerning the relationship between plan assets and the sponsor. One approach regards the pension plan as separate from the sponsor, as an appendage rather than an integral part of the whole organization. The integration approach considers the operating aspects of the sponsor and the pension plan as two components of the same entity. The idea that the sponsor and the pension plan are virtually independent will lead to a very different approach to deciding on the appropriate asset mix, a mix that is usually substantially different from the mix arrived at by viewing the plan as part of a whole. Thus, the interpretation one makes of this important issue will significantly affect the ultimate choice of asset weights in the plan's strategic allocation. However, the view that an optimal portfolio should be constructed without regard to the sponsor's other assets and liabilities is seriously flawed. This view ignores one of the most important assets the pension plan has: its claim on the sponsor's cash flows.

Legally, a private pension fund has a senior claim on the corporation's cash flows in the form of periodic contributions and on cash distributions from asset sales if the firm fails; thus, it has an important financial stake in the corporation. Failure to recognize that stake as a pension fund asset and take account of it when deciding the asset mix of the pension plan is wrong from an economic perspective because it can lead to misdirected diversification and hence too much risk for the return expected. For example, an auto company's pension plan has enough exposure to the economic cycles of the auto industry by virtue of its reliance on the company's ability to make timely contributions from its automobile business's operating income. It does not need more exposure by also owning shares in other automobile companies or in companies that correlate closely with the automotive industry.

Similarly, a public plan has an implicit economic claim on future taxes paid by residents and others who are part of the tax base. Tax capacity is thus a claim held by the plan—a claim that will compete with infrastructure needs and other tax-funded services. The diversification issue is similar—how much should a plan invest in local businesses when it is already dependent on the local economy?

If the operating entity and the pension plan are considered to be an economically unified body, as is appropriate, then the plan should make asset allocation decisions that consider the plan's financial exposure to the sponsor. Investments that are highly correlated with the cash flows of the sponsor should be avoided. Further, the asset allocation should not harm the sponsor's shareholders or taxpayers, since the financial health of the sponsor affects the financial health of the plan.

To underscore the notion that sponsors should integrate their defined benefit plans with their organizations, consider this rendition of the facts surrounding many private pension plans. First, assume that pension liabilities are growing by 12% per year, as they actually do seem to be growing in the aggregate due to wage increases, the increasing proximity of their workforce to retirement, and growth in the labor force. Further, suppose that the total expected return on pension assets is 9%, which is just about the average rate of return on a 60/30/10% stock/bond/cash portfolio over the period from 1925 to 1995. Finally, assume that the plan initially is adequately funded and that assets must grow at the same expected rate as liabilities. Since the sponsor must make up the difference between the growth in liabilities and the total return, the sponsor must annually contribute an amount equal to 3% of the size of the plan. (Incidentally, note also that a 1% increase in asset performance would allow a 33% reduction in contributions.) The fact that the sponsoring firm must contribute an amount equal to 3% of the fund each year is roughly equivalent to the plan having 3% of its assets in a single instrument—the sponsor. Very few plans allow that much concentration in individual assets, but here it cannot be avoided. What can be avoided is additional exposure to assets that have returns that are highly correlated with the sponsor's financial health.

Despite the seeming conflict of interest between beneficiaries and taxpayers/shareholders, potential plan beneficiaries are not necessarily detrimentally affected by an integrated approach to plan asset management: presumably they will be cared for because of their superior security status relative to shareholders/taxpayers. If private plan sponsors become financially distressed, corporations then must assign their pension liability to the Pension Benefit Guarantee Corporation (PBGC). Of course, the employee's pension benefit could be less than promised. Along with this assignment, the pension plan has a preferred status in the distribution of cash flows; pension beneficiaries are provided for prior to all nontax claims, including the claims of bondholders and shareholders, when wringing cash from the distressed corporation. Thus, the Employee Retirement Income Security Act (ERISA) prescription that the pension fund be run for the benefit of the beneficiaries is met—just not in the conventional way.

Public plans, which have no counterpart to ERISA or the PBGC, face a more ambiguous situation. The financially distressed public plan must rely on the largess of the taxpayer or turn to the courts. Any given tax base is limited in its ability to cover unfunded pension liabilities. Thus, the resolution of financial distress will depend on tax capacity and the willingness of one generation to support the former. This, in fact, is slowly becoming a matter of concern, as public plan beneficiaries and taxpayers become more aware of the significance of underfunding, sometimes exacerbated by asset allocation decisions that have political rather than economic motivations.

The decision making of participants in defined contribution plans is affected by many of the same issues. If a participant allocates a large portion of assets to his or her own firm or to the shares of similar companies, then the value of the pension portfolio will be correlated with the value of the participant's human capital, thus leading the participant to bear more risk than may be optimal.

In summary, the diversification/funding interdependence that exists between pension plans and sponsors overwhelmingly favors as least partial integration of plan asset management with the management of the sponsor's assets. This does not mean that decisions that might harm the plan but that help the sponsor should be permitted. Nor does it mean that the costs of monitoring the likely areas of conflict between the sponsor's interests and the interests of plan beneficiaries should be ignored. In fact, these conflicts of interest and the difficulty of arranging agreements to minimize them are central to any effort to manage plan assets in an integrated manner. What integrated asset management does offer is the idea that complete separation of assets is not sensible; rather, it is less than optimal for both the plan beneficiaries and the plan sponsor because it ignores the implicit investment the plan has in the sponsor and the benefit the sponsor receives from good investment performance of the plan's assets.

Lessons from All-Stock and All-Bond Portfolio

Two completely different asset allocation philosophies emerge directly from the axiom that the sponsor and its pension plan should be integrated and that the financial policies of both should complement rather than ignore each other. These competing views suggest that pension plan assets could be invested entirely in common stock or entirely in bonds, but not in a combination of the two.

The premises of each view, of course, represent extremes between which most analysts believe the optimal strategic asset allocation for a given plan actually lies. The strategic asset allocation is affected by far too many factors to be summarized as neatly as these two views suggest. Nonetheless, evaluating the merits of each helps demonstrate the trade-offs that the strategic asset allocation must somehow resolve.

In Favor of the All-Stock Portfolio

The arguments in favor of stocks are based on the high returns stocks have historically provided and the resultant lower contributions the sponsor must make if these high returns are realized. However, the structure of the argument differs somewhat for private and public plans.

Private Plans

Sharpe in 1976 and Harrison and Sharpe in 1983 were the first to persuasively argue that the shareholders of a sponsoring corporation are better off when pension plan managers invest only in common stock. As a corollary they further suggest that the level of funding be kept as low as permissible under ERISA.

The argument assumes that the price of PBGC insurance is too low—that is, it is not fairly priced in terms of the underlying risks being insured—and that its claim on the firm and its shareholders is quite limited. Even with the advent of a risk-related premium schedule, which replaced the flat, universally applied premium that each firm had to pay for each worker, PBGC insurance premiums may still be too low given the insurance provided.

The PBGC insures pension benefits up to a specified level that is indexed to the Social Security wage base. In 1996, the maximum insured benefit was nearly $32,000 per year. The corporation, in essence, holds an "in-the-money" put option by means of which it can "put" its pension liability to the PBGC in return for the pension plan assets plus some portion of its own net worth. (Of course, the firm always holds a put, except that before the PBGC, it could put the liability to its workers by reneging on its pension promise.)

If a company has an underfunded pension plan, it has a much better chance of fully funding the plan with the same contribution dollar outlays by holding stocks instead of bonds because stocks have a higher expected return. However, stocks are risky. If stock prices fall and the unfunded pension liability rises so that it exceeds the set percentage of the company's net worth that must be given to the PBGC on exercise of the pension put, the put is in-the-money and may be exercised. (Note that by holding bonds with the same dollar value as stocks, the company is less likely ever to fund its pension obligation fully. The Department of Labor, acting under ERISA, would force fuller funding. Thus, a bond strategy would thus not exploit maximizing the value of the pension put.)

There is a favorable asymmetry to the payoff for private pension sponsors that allocate all pension assets to stocks given PBGC insurance. If stocks rise (due to factors other than a decrease in interest rates), the pension plan gets funded with smaller contributions from the company than would be required if the pension plan held both stocks and bonds. On the other hand, if stocks decline by enough, the company can exercise the pension put, and its liability and subsequent loss is limited.

The conclusion that the value of the pension put is maximized by holding all stock is compelling as long as the pension put is underpriced because PBGC insurance premiums are set too low to compensate for the riskiness of the insured pension plan. The 1994 change in the premium schedule for PBGC insurance has somewhat altered the attractiveness of maintaining a portfolio that exploits the pension put, however.

Public Plans

The arguments in favor of stocks are somewhat different for public plans. First, many public plan sponsors find it politically simpler to increase employee compensation by increasing pension benefits rather than raising salaries (see the 1995 article by Weinberg). Unless funding is increased in proportion to the increase in the liability this causes, the natural result is underfunding. This underfunding provides an incentive to take on the riskiness of stocks in pursuit of higher total returns.

Consider that, in the absence of insurance such as that provided by PBGC, the ability of a public pension plan to meet its obligations depends on increased funding through higher taxes, cuts in public services, or an asset allocation that pursues high total return. Because of the political unattractiveness of the first two, there may be an incentive to reduce the use of tax dollars by taking on greater investment risk. In the long run, many analysts believe this will work; in the short run, adverse investment performance may harm the plan's funded status and increase the demand for increased contributions.

All-Stock Allocations Summary

Although the logic behind an all-stock portfolio (or at least a heavy orientation toward stocks) is compelling for sponsors because of its potential to reduce long-term future contributions, it is hard to find sponsors that have completely embraced the prescription. In the private sector, the put option scheme really works only for financially weak firms. For financially sound firms, the value of the net worth that would have to be given over to the PBGC would exceed the unfunded pension liability. Some public funds have negotiated contractual minimums for funding and thus are able to resist the pressure to invest solely for high returns. Further, when people who are not familiar with or knowledgeable about financial markets and assets are involved in setting pension investment policy parameters, too large an allocation to stocks can be politically unacceptable, and there may even be limits on the exposure a fund can take to stocks. Still, subject to whatever the acceptable level of risk is, the logic of higher long-term returns and subsequently lower (although less predictable) contributions is appealing.

In Favor of the All-Bond Portfolio

There are arguments that support large allocations to bonds as well. These generally take the form of taking advantage of the tax arbitrage opportunity provided by bonds.

Private Plans

The persuasive view that pension plans should hold all bonds was first advanced by Black and Dewhurst and by Tepper. The motivation is tax-based. Whatever stock the company, taken as the combination of the operating corporation and the pension plan, wants to hold would be held by the sponsor outside of the plan, thus facilitating tax arbitrage by the operating arm of the company because dividends received by corporate shareholders are taxed relatively lightly. The pension plan itself would hold only bonds. Bonds must yield enough to compensate for taxes paid by marginal bond holders. Thus, the untaxed pension plan investor earns excess profits in the form of the premium required to entice taxable investors to hold bonds. In short, the taxable firm should take advantage of the fact that interest on its own bonds is tax deductible, while interest on the bonds it holds in its pension portfolio is not taxed.

To exploit this insight the firm should engage in these transactions:

1. Sell all equities currently held by the pension fund.

2. Take the money from this sale and buy bonds that are as risky as any bonds the firm itself might issue.

3. Sell bonds (that is, borrow) for the firm's own account.

4. Use the proceeds of the bond sale to buy stock for the firm's own account.

The corporation is protected against the growth in the pension obligation attributable to rising wage rates and so forth by holding stocks in its general portfolio, the value of which tends to rise with productivity growth and inflation. Recall that corporate holdings of stock are tax advantaged, because only a fraction of the dividend income generated by those holdings is taxed. By arranging its investments this way, a corporation can achieve slightly higher overall post-tax investment returns without changing any of its fundamental business activities, because it pays less tax that it would otherwise pay.

A second way to think about tax arbitrage possibilities is to assume that the capital markets are in an after-tax equilibrium. That is, the expected after-tax returns are linearly related to risk, where the appropriate tax rate is that of the marginal investor.

The concept of after-tax equilibrium can be illustrated with an example. Assume the top marginal (corporate) tax rate on interest income is 34%. If corporate bonds with low default risk yield 10%, the after-tax equilibrium return is 0.10 (1.00–0.34), or 6.6%. Because all outstanding bonds must be owned, we assume the last ones sold are owned by the marginal, or most heavily taxed, investors. That is, the last investor to buy these bonds will be the one who receives the lowest after-tax yield. Dividends on common stock are tax-advantaged for corporate holders, while dividends are taxed at regular rates for individuals. Capital gains, let us assume, are taxed at nontrivial tax rates for corporate and individual holders. However, the holder of stock can decide when to sell stocks. Capital gains taxes can thus be deferred; taxes on capital gains do not have to be paid until the securities are sold. Thus investors who hold such securities have a valuable "timing option." Assume, then, the appropriate effective tax rate on common stock investments, the rate that adjusts for full taxation of dividends and the deferral of capital gains until it is advantageous to realize them, is roughly 20%. Let us also assume the expected return on stock is 15% with, say, a 5% dividend yield and a 10% expected capital gain; the expected after-tax equilibrium return on common stocks is 0.15 (1.00–0.20), or 12%. The corporation that holds the common stock receives 15% pretax, then pays a tax of 34% on only 30% of the dividend. Assuming no sales are made, so no capital gain taxes get paid, the after-tax return is

$$0.10 + 0.05 - [0.05(0.3)(1 - 0.34)] = 0.1401 \text{ or } 14.01\%$$

For after-tax equilibrium, bonds must yield 6.6% on an after-tax basis to compensate for risk, and stocks must offer total after-tax returns of 12%. In every case, the marginal investor is the most heavily taxed. By holding bonds in the tax-exempt pension fund, the tax-advantaged holder earns a "rent" of 0.100–0.066, or 3.4%. The holder gets this much (3.4%) more than should be received in view of both the investment's risk and capital market equilibrium. This difference, the gap between what this inframarginal holder gets and what those investors who produce the equilibrium get, is termed a *rent*. The rent is the difference between what can actually be realized after-tax for a particular investor less the amount the market requires on an after-tax basis. By holding stocks in the pension fund, the gross rent is only 0.15–0.12, or 3%—the difference between the pre- and post-tax equilibrium expected returns. Holding bonds yields a higher rent: 3.4% versus 3.0%. Moreover, holding stock in the corporation still leaves a rent of 0.1401–0.1200, or 2.01%. Thus, pursuing of a strategy of all bonds in the pension fund and funding the purchase of common stock through the borrowing via sale of bonds can generate earnings against the U.S. tax code, and it can all be done without increasing the risk of the combined entity. It is the tax collector that loses.

The all-bond strategy says nothing about how much stock should be held by a corporation. It indicates only that 100% of the pension fund's assets should be invested in bonds. Later we consider how much ought to be put in equities. Overall, the strategy implies that the pension plan should be as highly funded as the tax code allows since contributions to the plan are tax deductible. Thus, maximum contributions to the pension plan will minimize taxes paid.

Public Plans

Prior to the 1986 Tax Reform Act, public pension fund sponsors and plans could run a similar arbitrage operation. By issuing *tax-exempt debt* (sometimes called *pension bonds*) and investing the proceeds in higher-yielding corporate bonds of the same level of risk, sponsors were able to capture the yield differential of perhaps 2 to 3%.

Since the 1986 reforms, public plans can no longer do this, although they may issue taxable pension bonds (see the articles by Myers and Tigue). The temptation to issue taxable pension bonds is that when interest rates are low, issuing taxable debt and investing in a higher yielding portfolio of assets produces higher expected returns for the pension, thus lowering the unfunded liability. Unfortunately, this is not arbitrage; it is simply funding by borrowing—leveraging—and investing in a higher risk asset pool. Leverage can deliver the desired results if the performance of the asset pool exceeds the costs on the pension bonds. If investment returns are poor, however, the bet goes bad and the issuer—the sponsor—still must service the debt and the pension liability, a liability that could be much higher than before.

Although public entities cannot explicitly sell tax-exempt debt to fund their pensions, the commingling of proceeds from bond sales with tax collections and other revenues suggests that a partial arbitrage is possible. The steps in this process are to borrow in order to reduce the use of general revenues to fund road repairs or new buildings or whatever, so that general revenues are available to fund the pension plan.

Thus, public funds cannot benefit as private funds theoretically may from an all-bond portfolio. No complete tax arbitrage is possible for public funds. With either type of fund, public or private, it may, of course, be sensible to use bonds to immunize a portion of the pension liability—but this is another issue.

All-Bond Allocations Summary

Like the all-stock strategy, the all-bond strategy offers only partial guidance to many sponsors. To make everything work, the pension plan sponsor must be able to sell debt and get tax deductions on interest payments or favorable tax treatment (that is, tax-exempt interest) for investors. If the sponsor is in poor financial condition, it may not be able to sell enough debt at low enough interest rates to allow it to be able to meet its obligations. Further, private sponsors must have taxable income against which the tax shield on interest payments can be applied. Accordingly, the strategy is useful primarily to financially strong, taxable, pension-sponsoring companies and is useful only somewhat to strong public pension sponsors. Nonetheless, there are many of these financially strong organizations, and hence many sponsors should consider using the strategy of borrowing and buying bonds.

How Pension Plans Allocate Plan Assets (and Fund Pension Plans)

Theory aside, when attempting to arrive at the correct strategic asset allocation, it is helpful to have a sense of what pension plans are actually doing. This section reviews the most comprehensive studies that have been performed on asset allocation of pension funds and offers some interpretive comments on factors—such as profitability, taxes, the nature of the workforce, and funding—that influence the strategic asset allocation.

The Empirical Perspective

Several large empirical studies have been conducted that explore the extent to which private sponsors behave in ways suggested by the broad hypothesis that firms manage their pension plans as integrated parts of the company. In general, the studies found that few of the firms studied pursued either all-bond or all-stock allocations—virtually all pension funds in the samples had a mixture of stocks and bonds. However, several studies found that the pension plan asset allocations were tilted in ways that showed the operating corporation and the pension plan were being jointly considered when asset allocation decisions were being made. There were enough systematic connections between the corporations' overall financial conditions and their pension funding and allocation decisions that it seems clear that the decisions are treated jointly.

Friedman performed the first relevant study in 1983. He used pension plan data that firms use to report to the Internal Revenue Service on Form 5500. His sample consists of 24,426 firms that filed these forms in 1977. His principal findings are:

1. Firms with volatile earnings hold relatively less equity and more reasonably safe debt in their pension plan portfolios.

2. Firms with a great deal of outstanding debt tend to hold more debt in their pension plan portfolios and correspondingly less equity than firms with low financial leverage.

3. Firms that are highly profitable tend to hold relatively more equity in pension portfolios than firms with comparatively low profitability, as measured by return on equity and return on assets.

4. Firms with comparatively young workforces tend to invest more heavily in debt securities than firms with older workforces.

This study has not been replicated with more recent data so it is not clear that the same results would hold today. One suspects that some findings could be different. In particular, the pairing of young workforces and relatively heavy debt allocations seems counterintuitive for sponsors who desire to reduce funding pressures by pursuing higher investment returns.

The second study, by Bodie and associates in 1987, also found relationships between the asset structure of the pension plan and the oper-

ating corporation, but once again these are only tilts: they do not perfectly match all-bond or all-stock prescriptions. This study examined
939 corporate plans or subsamples thereof for the year 1980. They
learned

1. More profitable firms tend to use lower discount rates (interest
   rate assumptions) than less profitable firms in computing their
   pension liabilities. This allows them to achieve greater tax
   deductions for contributions and let them warehouse the
   funds, a sensible strategy given that excess funding could be
   recaptured in later years.

2. The greater the long-run profitability of the firm, the higher the
   degree of funding. Again, this is consistent with the idea that
   contributions are used to reduce taxes. It also is consistent with
   the idea that the pension plan is a reservoir for financial slack
   for the corporation.

3. The more highly funded a pension plan, the greater its investment in bonds; the less highly funded, the more stock it holds.
   Both are consistent with the theory of the pension put that supports the all-stock portfolio, but again very few firms conform
   exactly to the theoretical prescriptions of all of one kind of
   instrument or the other.

The third study, by Petersen in 1996, examined more than 47,000
observations drawn from the Form 5500 that firms file with the IRS.
The time frame of the study was 1988–1990. His results indicate

1. More profitable firms invest a greater portion of their assets in
   stocks.

2. Riskier firms allocate a smaller portion of their assets to stocks.

3. Overfunded plans invest a greater portion of their assets in
   stocks than do underfunded plans.

4. The less mature the plan—that is, the lower the ratio of current
   benefits to asset size—the more plan's assets are invested in
   stocks.

5. Self-directed defined contribution plans invest less in stock
   than do defined benefit plans.

Public pensions have not been studied as extensively as private
plans. In large part, this is attributable to the lack of a unified body of

regulation requiring that data be reported. What data there are suffer from the uneven investment rules imposed by various legislative bodies (e.g., legal lists and other restrictions) that may force public pensions to invest in ways they might not if they were following their economic instincts.

Although the average asset allocation of public funds tends to be less oriented to equities than is the case for private funds, public fund equity allocation has increased substantially in recent years (increasing from around 43% in 1991 to over 50% in 1995 according to Greenwich Associates [see Rehfeld]). These facts suggest that public pensions are increasingly choosing asset allocations that are more heavily weighted toward stocks. Why are they doing this? The Public Pension Coordinating Council reports that in 1992, 61% of funding for public pensions came from investments, up from 39% in 1982 (see the article by Rehfeld). Perhaps this increase is because they are under pressure to produce higher returns and reduce contributions. Perhaps it is because plans and sponsors are working more closely together to determine the optimal mix of risk, return, and contributions for both.

Interpretations

One interpretation of these findings is that pension sponsors make marginal adjustments in pension plans to compensate for the sponsors' financial policies, conditions, and preferences regarding the tradeoff between contributions and investment returns. These marginal adjustments tend to push pension plan allocation policies toward more bonds or more stocks, but very few sponsors go all the way.

An alternative interpretation is that the data show only that the theories are incomplete. Ippolito, for example, argued in 1988 that when viewed as a multiperiod tax arbitrage problem, the tax system that existed prior to the Tax Reform Act of 1986 and the Pension Protection Act of 1987 encouraged private pension plan overfunding. Taxable companies were allowed to reduce taxable income by the amount of the contribution they made to the pension plan. The allowed contribution was linked to the difference between the actuarially measured liability and a measure of asset value. Prior to the new laws, only a portion of the increase in asset value relative to liabilities needed to be considered when determining how large contributions can be. Thus significant pension overfunding was possible. Because investment returns are likely to be higher with equity than with debt, a firm could get to a highly overfunded position more quickly by using equity than by using debt. Once the level of funding relative to liabilities was sufficiently high to preclude future contributions, then it would be sensible to switch the portfolio to all (or more) bonds, as Black and Dewhurst and Tepper argue, in order to take advantage of the tax arbitrage, the gains from which would partially offset the tax shields lost due to the firm's inability to continue making contributions. If Ippolito is correct, then the reason we have not seen all-bond portfolios is not because there is no conscious coordination between the operating company and the pension plan, but rather because the interaction is dynamic, not static, and more complex than initially thought. It is also affected by the tax laws regarding the amount of funding that is legally permissible in any given year.

In Summary

Companies seem to manage their corporate financial policies more or less jointly with their pension plans. Although the connections are not so vivid as early theory suggested they might be, nonetheless they are present. Moreover, anyone designing a private plan to maximize tax benefits—that is, to minimize the present value of future tax payments, all other things being equal—would still have to develop an asset mix policy in which the pension fund would hold only bonds, and the corporation would hold equities. However, workforce demographics, volatility of operating cash flows, funding regulations, and other factors are also important. Simply maximizing tax benefits is not sufficient.

The connection between integration, funding, and asset allocation is not so clear with public sponsors and pension plans. The tax motive is much weaker. Additionally, the relationship between public sponsors and plans can be adversarial. Some public pension plans feel they must sue their sponsors to force payment of contributions. Others, however, work closely with the sponsor and presumably work toward optimal asset allocations that are integrated with the financial policies of the sponsor.

The increase in funding from investment returns noted above suggests an increased attention to asset allocations that emphasizes a higher return and hence more risk. Public funds, of course, do not have the tax incentives or ERISA mandates that private funds have. This is consistent with the low levels of funding (in essence, the pay-as-you-go approach) taken by many public fund sponsors. The implied relationship between underfunded plans pursuing the risk premium associated with stocks seems especially appropriate for public plans, as does a reallocation to bonds for well-funded plans. Accordingly, there is still a need to develop a model that embodies the pension sponsor's risk tolerance and that selects an acceptable mix of stocks/bonds/cash for the combined plan/sponsor, irrespective of where each category of investment happens to reside.

Setting the Strategic Asset Allocation: An Analytical Approach

In spite of the complexity of the decision, the strategic asset allocation must be set. The strategic asset allocation will not simply appear nor should it be merely that which the "average" pension fund has. To make the appropriate allocation of funds to stocks, bonds, and cash, the analyst must bring together the interdependency of the fund's returns and the sponsor's contributions, the interaction between the value of the plans assets and liabilities, and all the relevant financial market information that will bear on the decision. This requires a fairly comprehensive analytical approach. We present one such approach in this section.

The Approach

The approach we suggest is to use simulation analysis coupled with scenario analysis to generate reasonable data with which to examine the interplay between asset allocations, contribution rates, and likelihood of benefits. The sponsor can analyze the data produced and choose the asset mix that optimally trades off expected contributions, contribution variability, surplus volatility, and benefit assurance. Private sponsors should do this while considering the firm's shareholders as well as its pension beneficiaries. Public sponsors should do this while considering taxpayers as well as beneficiaries. Sponsors are, after all, in the unusual position of having a fiduciary responsibility to both shareholders/taxpayers and pension beneficiaries.

The first step in the process is to lay out plausible assumptions regarding the performance of various sectors of the capital markets and the other markets in which investments might be made. The decision maker may also wish to specify several different scenarios that might prevail over the relevant planning horizon (e.g., five years). Table 6-1 offers an example of a set of financial market expectations we use to illustrate how a sensitivity analysis may be conducted. (To simplify the calculations and allow the reader to follow the logic of the analysis more

Table 6-1. Alternative Financial Market Scenarios

	Stocks	Bonds	Cash
Scenario A (unexpectedly high inflation, low growth)			
Expected return	0.0	2.0	6.0
Expected standard deviation	16.0	10.0	3.0
	Stocks with Bonds	Stocks with Cash	Bonds with Cash
Correlation coefficients	0	0	0
Scenario B (normal growth and inflation)			
Expected return	12.0	5.5	3.5
Expected standard deviation	20.0	8.5	1.0
	Stocks with Bonds	Stocks with Cash	Bonds with Cash
Correlation coefficients	0	0	0

Table 6-2. Alternative Asset Allocations

Asset Allocation	Stocks	Bonds	Cash
1	85%	10%	5%
2	60%	30%	10%
3	20%	70%	10%

Initial portfolio value = $100,000
Initial liability value = $100,000
Assumed rate of liability growth = 7%

easily, we assume 0 correlations among the asset classes. Note, too, that the standard deviations differ depending upon the scenario. This is consistent with the idea that different general economic conditions produce very much different financial market behaviors.)

The second step is to identify the alternative asset allocations that the analyst wishes to examine. In Table 6-2, we look at three alternative allocations.

Now, the analyst must ask what one would expect to happen to the value of specific alternative portfolios and to the value of the pension surplus over the next five years under each of these scenarios. Although we assume a constant 7% growth in liabilities, alternative estimates of liability growth should be made under each scenario to pick up differences in salary growth and size of the labor force. Table

6-3 offers the results of the analysis. For simplicity, the analyst may wish to estimate these values first without allowing for any contributions over the period. However, the analyst will eventually have to evaluate the estimates of contributions to the plan that the sponsor must make. If full funding is assumed, the funding required is equal to the expected surplus (deficit) while a range of funding outcomes is provided by the minimum and maximum surplus (deficit) values given in Table 6-3.

The analysis will require some other fine tuning. For example, a rebalancing rule will have to be assumed. Are asset categories rebalanced annually or quarterly, or will the plan follow a pure buy-and-hold strategy? Finally, we show a single period for simplicity. Five- and even ten-year annual projections are typically more helpful.

Choosing the Right Asset Mix

With this type of data, there are several approaches the decision maker may use to choose an asset mix. The approach chosen should be consistent with the analyst's judgment about the relative importance of the competing claims made by taxpayers, shareholders, and employees. Well-written policy will serve as a guide when evaluating the alternative scenarios.

One approach is for the decision maker to choose the asset mix that requires the lowest contribution under the worst scenario—termed the *min-max strategy*. The logic for choosing this asset mix could be that, during good times, the sponsor could increase its contributions without really feeling the pinch of a cash shortage. It is only during bad economic times that the size of the contribution matters.

Another approach might focus on choosing a portfolio that would lead to the lowest average contribution or to the lowest present value of future contributions irrespective of which scenario actually comes about. Here the decision maker may need to be informed only that, should the worst occur, the asset mix chosen would not require Herculean funding efforts.

A third approach would be to choose the asset mix that, under all scenarios, results in the lowest volatility of the surplus (deficit) of asset values over expected liability values. This is appealing for pensions that want to protect an existing surplus but are not especially sensitive to funding concerns. This shift in attention to the surplus can be followed by a review of the likely funding consequences and further analysis (e.g., more asset class combinations tried) to see whether a superior joint surplus/contribution solution appears.

Table 6-3. Analysis of Alternative Asset Allocations under Different Financial Market Scenarios

Scenario	A			B		
Asset Allocation	1	2	3	1	2	3
	85% stocks	60% stocks	20% stocks	85% stocks	60% stocks	20% stocks
	10% bonds	30% bonds	70% bonds	10% bonds	30% bonds	70% bonds
	5% cash	10% cash	10% cash	5% cash	10% cash	10% cash
Expected return	0.5%	1.2%	2.0%	10.93%	9.2%	6.6%
Expected standard deviation	13.64%	10.06%	7.70%	17.02%	12.30%	7.46%
Expected portfolio value	$100,500	$101,200	$102,000	$110,925	$109,200	$106,600
Expected liability value	$107,000	$107,000	$107,000	$107,000	$107,000	$107,000
Expected surplus (deficit)	($6,500)	($5,800)	($5,000)	$3,925	$2,200	($400)
Maximum surplus [a,b,d]	$20,780	$14,320	$10,400	$37,970	$26,740	$13,940
Minimum surplus [a,c,d]	($33,780)	($25,920)	($20,400)	($30,110)	($22,340)	($14,740)

[a]Before funding.
[b]Return is 2 standard deviations above expectation.
[c]Return is 2 standard deviations below expectation.
[d]Based on the statistical data used and assuming the returns are normally distributed, the analyst may be 97.75% confident the actual surplus (deficit) will fall between the minimum and maximum values. will not be less than the minimum surplus and may be 95.5% confident the actual surplus (deficit)

Obviously, there are many alternative approaches to choosing the appropriate mix. The rules for the decision are situational and depend on the circumstances of the plan and the ability of the various parties to work together.

Just as obviously, the preceding analysis lends itself to computerization. More realistic correlations can be assumed, probabilities of alternative scenarios can be incorporated, and the effects of changes in multiple factors can be included. Long time periods can be used and alternative asset allocations can be evaluated in the context of, for example, the last 30 years of capital market performance. Additionally, the estimated contributions may be adjusted to present values to evaluate more readily the current impact of the contributions on the sponsor's economic value.

A word of caution: there are numerous simulation and optimization models available. Some are well designed; some are not. Larger plans can probably develop their own models in house, perhaps with the help of a consultant. The very process of participating in model design can be immeasurably helpful to identifying the issues relevant to a particular plan and to understanding the consequences of various actions. For plans that leave the modeling to others, care should be taken to question the model's underlying assumptions and understand the data being input.

Finally, there is an important side effect of this analysis. Although the analyst often starts with a presumably acceptable level of risk tolerance in mind, the process of making the decision will reveal the actual risk tolerance of the plan as those involved in the decision-making process see it. The numbers generated force the decision makers to explicitly confront the inter-relations that exist between various factors and to decide what is really important—that is, what they *really* believe in the presence of many possible outcomes. Given the complexity of the decision and its dependence on knowing the plan's tolerance for risk, it is hard to overstate the value of decision-makers' elimination of some alternatives in favor of others. This process of elimination ultimately leads to an informed assessment of what the plan's tolerance for risk is.

Other Allocation Issues

Once the broad asset mix is chosen, the pension plan sponsor must decide how to allocate within each category—that is, how much of the total equity pool will go toward passive investing, how much toward active management, and so forth. There is a caution here worth reiterating: the manager must remain alert to excessively high reliance on sponsor contributions, because too heavy a reliance could undo the effect of diversification.

Managers generally tend to rebalance portfolios on at least an annual basis, and many will rebalance on a quarterly basis or when a range limitation has been crossed (e.g., when the actual equity allocation exceeds the strategic allocation by 5% or more). As noted earlier (see also Chapter 5), the choice of rebalancing strategies depends on the investor's risk tolerance and willingness to exploit beliefs about the capital markets. This is more or less subjective, so there is no one right answer. However, we should note two things. In the absence of increasing supplies of securities—that is, new issues of stock or bonds or whatever—the only strategy that can be pursued simultaneously by all investors is the buy-and-hold strategy. If there are changing supplies—for instance, if corporations choose a policy of constant debt to equity, thus sell more debt when equity values rise—then investors will have to trade back toward a constant mix policy to ensure an equilibrium such that all securities that are available get held in some portfolio.

Conclusion

Asset allocation is one of the most critical investment decisions that is made. Moreover, it is never settled. It is a process in which decisions regarding the appropriate strategic mix for the long term must constantly be reviewed and occasionally revised as plan or sponsor circumstances change or if fundamental beliefs about the capital markets change.

For individuals managing DCP asset pools, the consequences of good or bad decisions are direct, but unfortunately it may be several years before they are known or understood. Sponsors need to help employees gain the knowledge they need to make sensible decisions, and employees must be willing to take the time to become their own money managers—or to hire outside advisors. In particular, employees must be aware of how poor planning, inflation, and other factors can have truly catastrophic results.

For sponsors of DBPs, the process of choosing the appropriate asset mix ultimately suggests a tremendous amount of introspection on the part of pension plan sponsors and all who are involved in the decision making or have a fiduciary relationship with the plan. It requires the sponsor to specify a risk-tolerance level in the face of competing ownership claims in recognition that, whatever level is chosen, risk taking has substantial financial implications for numerous parties as the pension plan goes forward.

There is little question the financial health and the financial policies of the sponsor should be integrated into pension fund decisions. Equally as clear, the nature of the plan liabilities—the pension plan's financial commitment to employees—must be carefully analyzed in setting the plan's strategic asset allocation. When the allocation is set, the decision-making process should be capable of withstanding the scrutiny of all parties affected by the decision, and the trade-offs made should be both evident and acceptable to those involved.

Simulation analysis seems to be the most useful (though not necessarily the most scientific) quantitative tool for asset allocation decisions for both individuals and defined benefit plans. Decision makers derive considerable insight and some comfort from having the array of possible outcomes over time laid before them. The process of specifying the data to be run and the assumptions to be made forces the analyst and those who will evaluate the results to answer some important questions before any decision is made. Experience reveals that simulation analysis is one of the most effective ways available to identify risk tolerance levels. This is well worth the effort in determining the best asset allocation for the pension plan.

Chapter **7**

Measuring the Investment Performance of Pension Funds

The fiduciary responsibilities of pension plan sponsors, administrators, managers, trustees, and others mandate that they periodically evaluate the investment performance of the fund's asset pool. To evaluate performance, it must be measured. Investment performance measurement provides information: first, about how well a fund is doing in meeting its investment goals. Second, investment performance measurement helps those involved in policy see whether the current investment policy is helping meet the goals of the pension plan or whether it is hurting. Third, performance measurement offers insights into the general competence of an investment manager and establishes whether or not the manager is following the investment policy and guidelines provided by the sponsor. Finally, performance measurement offers information as to whether the investment manager's behavior is consistent with the investment philosophy that the manager portrays as guiding decisions; that is, is the manager following the investment strategy she said she would follow?

Performance measurement should be applied to each portfolio within a pension plan and to the plan's entire asset pool as a whole as well. To see why, suppose a plan has two portfolios. Portfolio A has an unusually good historical performance relative to all benchmarks, while portfolio B has a mediocre historical performance. This does not necessarily mean that the total fund is performing well. To the senior managers of the pension plan's sponsoring organization, it matters a great deal whether it was portfolio A or B that began with $1 million or $100 million. Only by evaluating the overall plan can a sponsor determine what the results from the components mean to the total plan. Likewise, only by evaluating the whole plan can top pension managers and administrators find out whether the entire set of investment strategies and managers selected are satisfactory.

Ultimately, those who have a fiduciary relationship to the pension plan need to be able to determine whether the investment policies and managers are doing well relative to alternative policies and peers and whether they are delivering good investment performance against alternative, unmanaged, benchmark portfolios. This is equally important for defined benefit and defined contribution plans. This requires an understanding of the alternative computations used in measuring returns, the correct ways to measure and adjust for risk, how benchmarks should be chosen or constructed, and the components of investment performance—the exposure of the fund to various market segments, the quality of the selection of assets, and the timing of movements of capital among asset classes. This chapter describes how each of these issues should be handled and what each contributes to understanding performance and to decision making. Further, some recent advances in performance measurement are presented. Chapter 8, in turn, shows how the results of performance measurement can be used to evaluate and improve plan performance.

Investment Returns

Return is realized as income yield (i.e., dividends and interest), capital appreciation or depreciation (i.e., the change in the market value of the fund's assets), and currency appreciation or depreciation (e.g., if the dollar strengthens against the yen, the pension will suffer a currency loss on its Japanese investments). Income is a desirable attribute for pensions that have near-term liquidity needs such as payments to current retirees. Income not spent may be reinvested and thus can also contribute to long-term growth. The capital change component is desirable because, over long periods of time, it should help the fund grow in real (inflation adjusted) terms. The currency component is considered by some to be a source of return if a manager is skilled in selecting undervalued currencies. Others consider currency simply a cost of investing outside the United States—a risk to be hedged.

The greater the investment return on a pension fund, the lower future contributions need to be in order to achieve a specific post-retirement payment target or accumulation target. In 1993, contributions to private and public defined benefit plans (DBPs) approximated $150 billion, according to the Employee Benefits Research Institute 1995 *Databook on Employee Benefits*. If the investment performance on the asset pool of roughly $4 trillion that is controlled by these pension funds was just 1% better, $40 billion more in investment returns would have been achieved, and contributions could have been cut by 27% without reducing the financial security of the plans. The same general result applies to defined contribution plans (DCPs)—the higher the return, the higher the future benefit payments, given a fixed contribution schedule. Thus, no matter what type of pension plan, good investment returns are always beneficial.

Investment return calculations are sensitive to various choices the analyst or presenter of the data may make. One important factor is the time period chosen: annual returns may differ substantially if a calendar year return is compared to a 12-month return using other starting and ending dates. Similarly, investment managers with poor annual results may present annualized 5- or 10-year results to average in one or more good earlier years, while managers with good recent results may present only recent data. Year-by-year, multi-year annualized, and cumulative returns all have stories to tell, stories that are necessary if the full picture is to be seen. Another factor is the influence the timing of cash inflows and outflows to a portfolio or pool of assets has on actual performance. Significant cash flows (as in a sponsor's decision to allocate more funds to a specific manager) can lead to overstating or understating the returns the manager achieves, depending on subsequent market action. Finally, when investment managers present composites representing the returns on groups of portfolios they manage, whether the portfolios are equally weighted or weighted by size can matter greatly.

Measuring return correctly depends on what the analyst is trying to accomplish or evaluate. For example, time-weighted returns are useful in evaluating managers of individual portfolios that are components of the overall pension fund. Dollar-weighted returns are useful in evaluating the return on the overall asset pool and in evaluating managers who are trying to time asset allocations. The use of one when the other should be used can lead to poor decisions. For example, a poor money manager may be rewarded for the sponsor's fortuitous decision to give him or her more money just before the market went up if the dollar-weighted return is used. The time-weighted return would allow the manager's poor performance to be uncovered, however. These and some other return measures are discussed in Appendix D.

Risk-Adjusted Returns

Because expected return and anticipated risk are so intimately entwined, a careful balancing of the two is necessary when constructing a pension portfolio. For the same reason, when evaluating historical investment decisions, most investment professionals construct measures that allow risk to be considered along with return. Accordingly, when they speak of investment performance, they refer not to realized returns but to realized returns adjusted in some way for the risk borne by the portfolio.

To measure investment performance in economically sensible and managerially useful ways, therefore, estimates of return must be combined with estimates of risk. The metric must then be compared with benchmark results that could readily be achieved by naive portfolio management techniques, say by buying and holding all the stocks in the S&P 500 index in proportion to their weight in the index (i.e., a passive index fund—we return to this concept later).

Broadly speaking, two types of performance measures link up to the way the sponsor views risk. The first focuses on the investment returns achieved by a fund relative to the fund's total or absolute risk. This type of measure is particularly useful when evaluating the pension plan's total asset pool rather than simply one or another of the portfolios that may comprise it. Measures of the second type consider only the systematic risk of a portfolio rather than its total risk, part of which will likely be offset whenever the portfolio being evaluated is a portion of a much larger pool of assets. The technical aspects of both of these measurement techniques are discussed in detail in Appendix E.

Risk of the Total Pension Portfolio

William F. Sharpe developed and tested what has come to be known as the *Sharpe measure*. It compares the average portfolio "excess return"—the rate of return in excess of what could have been earned by investing in comparatively risk-free assets, such as Treasury bills—to the variability of portfolio return measured over the return period. The result is a "reward-to-variability" ratio. It captures in a single measure the excess returns earned per unit of total risk (volatility) borne. The formula is:

$$Sh_p = \frac{(R_{ap} - R_{af})}{SD_{R_p}}$$

where R_{ap} and R_{af} are respectively the arithmetic averages of the port-folio return and the average risk-free rate over the period, and SD_{R_p} is the standard deviation of the portfolio's returns over perhaps 5 years.

As an example of this, using data provided by lbbotson Associates, we know that over the period from 1926 to 1995, the average annual return on S&P 500 index stocks (i.e., relatively large company stocks) was, with dividends reinvested, 12.5%, and the standard deviation of annual equity portfolio returns was 20.4%. The average return on one-month Treasury bills over the period was 3.8%. (Interestingly, T-bills had a positive standard deviation because the strategy of rolling over one-month T-bills did not produce a perfectly risk-free constant return. However, this small standard deviation is customarily ignored in practice.) Using these data, the Sharpe measure for large company stocks was:

$$\frac{12.5 - 3.8}{20.4} = 0.426$$

Over the same period, the average annual return and standard deviation of annual returns for corporate bonds were 6.0% and 8.7%, respectively. The Sharpe measure here is:

$$\frac{6.0 - 3.8}{8.7} = 0.253$$

One inference that may be drawn from this is that corporate stocks performed substantially better than bonds on a risk-adjusted basis. The former achieved an excess return of 43 basis points for every unit of risk borne, while the latter had a reward of only 25 basis points per unit of risk borne. With the advantage of hindsight, an investor interested solely in high risk-adjusted returns would have been better off in stocks than bonds. However, this does not automatically mean that stock investments alone should be the future strategy. Rather, such a result suggests only that a future investment strategy *may* beneficially *include* stocks. Going for-ward, it is the *ex ante* risks—those to be faced—not the realized risks of the past that ought to guide good decision making. That is, *ex post* Sharpe ratios should be used as unbiased forecasts of future Sharpe ratios. Looking backward, however, it is the realized returns and risks that allow us to distinguish *ex post* what strategies worked well and which did not.

The Sharpe measure generally is used comparatively to assess the results of one investment strategy (or total portfolio) against those of another. For instance, the historical performance of a portfolio consisting of 60% stocks and 40% corporate bonds might be compared with one containing, say, 70% stocks and 30% cash equivalents (i.e., very short-term securities). The Sharpe measure will identify which strategy historically produced higher rewards for each unit of variability, thus providing insight into its likelihood of doing so in the future.

There is no absolute number against which an aggregate pension portfolio might be compared. An absolute value of 0.4 or 0.9 or 2.0 is meaningless except in that it may indicate poor absolute performance when it is negative or good absolute performance when positive. Rather, an absolute value is a ranking measure that has real meaning when it is compared with its benchmark portfolio counterpart or with other similar funds. Users should recognize that the Sharpe ratio does not address correlations between different strategies or asset allocations. Thus, its use in analyzing strategies that are not highly correlated requires further effort to incorporate the impact of correlations. Finally, note that, relative to other commonly used measures, the Sharpe measure has very few purely statistical problems. Specifically, there are no serious difficulties arising from violation of the economic and statistical assumptions necessary to compute the numbers. Of course, if the distribution of stock returns is not normal, then measuring standard deviation is only a measure of dispersion, not a perfect representation of risk.

An extension of the basic Sharpe ratio is the *differential return Sharpe ratio*. In place of the risk-free rate, the differential Sharpe ratio uses a benchmark return that can be achieved passively. A positive differential return implies that the portfolio produced an active (or selection) return that exceeds the return that is obtainable without the active management. Thus, the differential return Sharpe ratio offers insight into the value added by active management relative to a comparably risky passive strategy. (We return to measuring the success of active strategies and benchmarking later in this chapter.)

In summary, the Sharpe measure is an appropriate way to adjust a total pension fund's return for the risk taken. In general, it is not as useful for component portfolios.

Risk of Component Portfolios

A pension plan may employ many different managers, each bringing a very different investment focus and asset valuation theory to portfolio management. Frequently, these investment strategies result in component portfolios that are not well diversified. Therefore, the component funds or subportfolios of a pension plan's asset pool should be evaluated using only the systematic risk of a portfolio to avoid penal izing specialty managers for taking undiversified exposures that the plan sponsor wants. *Systematic risk* is risk that cannot be reduced by diversification. Investors may choose to take less systematic risk but, if so, theory suggests they must accept lower expected returns as well.

A measure that adjusts returns for only the systematic portion of total risk is the *Treynor measure* (see the 1965 article). The Treynor measure does not penalize a portfolio manager for investing in a narrow segment of the overall market. Rather, it considers the incremental systematic risk a manager adds to the total portfolio. Of course, use of the Treynor measure does not create any incentive for a money manager to diversify the portfolio's holdings—nor, for that matter, should it, as diversification presumably is being implemented by the manager of the entire plan.

Like the Sharpe measure, the Treynor measure is a ratio that allows interpretation as a relative reward-to-risk ratio. Additionally, a negative value reveals that the portfolio did poorly on an absolute basis. Again, however, like the Sharpe measure, the performance metric can be interpreted only in the context of a group of similar observations, a universe of other managed portfolios or some other benchmark. Apart from wanting the number to be greater than zero, at the close of any period knowing that the measure is X or Y does not alone reveal whether the portfolio manager did a good or poor job. Only when the performance is compared with that of other managers or with a benchmark portfolio can we decide whether a satisfactory investment performance was produced relative to the risk taken.

The Treynor measure is:

$$TR_p = \frac{R_{ap} - R_{af}}{\beta_p}$$

where R_{ap} and R_{af} are respectively the arithmetic averages of the subportfolio return and the average risk-free rate over the period, and β_p is the beta of the portfolio's returns over perhaps five years. To demonstrate, suppose R_{ap} was 12% over the year, R_{af} was 2.4% over the same period, and β_p was 0.9, then:

$$TR_p = \frac{12.0 - 2.4}{0.9} = 0.1067$$

This equation says that for every incremental whole unit of risk, the portfolio achieved a 10.7% return. If this measure is high when compared with the Treynor measures for other portfolios, this money manager may have achieved abnormally good investment results. (Unfortunately, the Treynor measure does not tell us if the good results are due to skill or merely luck.)

Market Risk and Active Management

Many portfolio managers pursue what are called *active management strategies* in an attempt to earn returns above those that might be obtained through passive exposures to an asset class (e.g., stocks). Measuring the success of these managers in generating excess returns requires first adjusting for the risk characteristic of their strategies and then seeing if the returns produced are higher than can be explained simply by pursuing an equally risky strategy.

Jensen developed a measure of investment performance that, like the Treynor measure, recognizes that a single portfolio may not be as fully diversified as the overall pension plan and thus focuses on the relationship between systematic or market risk and a portfolio's return. On an intuitive level, the Jensen measure is the difference between the actual return on a portfolio minus the return on a broad-based market portfolio, such as the S&P 500, adjusted for the relative riskiness of the portfolio being evaluated.

Specifically, the Jensen measure (α_p) is:

$$\alpha_p = R_{ap} - [R_{af} + \beta_p(R_{am} - R_{af})]$$

where α_p is the measure of performance and β_p is the estimate of the systematic (market) risk of the portfolio. If α_p is greater than zero, the portfolio "beat the market" on a risk-adjusted basis. If it is less than zero, the portfolio underperformed the market on a risk-adjusted basis.

To illustrate the calculation, suppose a portfolio had an average monthly return of 1.0% and the estimated β_p was 0.8 while the monthly average return on short-term Treasury bills was 0.2%. Further, suppose the average monthly return on a broad-based market portfolio was also 1.0%. Then:

$$\alpha_p = 1.0 - [(0.2) + 0.8 (1.0 - 0.2)] = 0.16\%$$

This means that this portfolio did better than might have been expected, given its systematic (market) risk: the portfolio produced excess risk-adjusted returns of 0.16% per month or 1.92% per year. In other words after allowing for risk, the portfolio did well—it beat the market—because the risk-adjusted monthly returns on the market were only 0.64% above the T-bill rate while the risk-adjusted monthly returns for the portfolio were 0.8% above the T-bill rate. Generally, the higher the α_p, the better the portfolio performance.

Users should be aware there are statistical problems with estimating β_p reliably. These include correctly choosing a market benchmark and assuming that its estimation is not contaminated by much alteration in the composition of the subject portfolio. Additionally, the measure may be misleading about how well the portfolio did absolutely. That is, following a market that dropped sharply, the α_p could be 2.0%, which would merely mean that on a risk-adjusted basis this portfolio beat the market. The absolute loss, however, could be horrendous. It is cold comfort to know one beat the market by 2% while the market itself experienced a decline of 30%. Regardless, computing a portfolio's α_p is most useful when comparing the performance of pension plan segments (portfolios) or managers of these segments to one another.

Another useful approach to evaluating risk relative to active management is the appraisal ratio developed by Treynor and Black. It adjusts excess market-adjusted portfolio return for the amount of *unsystematic* or *non-market risk*—risk that can be reduced by diversification—borne. Conceptually, this excess return is the gain from taking an exposure to diversifiable risk. Presumably, managers would take this exposure only if they believed they possessed useful special information or insight. Mathematically, the appraisal ratio is:

$$A_p = \frac{\alpha_p}{SD(\varepsilon_p)}$$

where α_p is the measure of performance (the same α_p that we saw in the Jensen measure), and $SD(\varepsilon_p)$ is the standard deviation of the error term in the market model discussed in Appendix E—the variability in the portfolio return that is not explained by the variation in the chosen market portfolio or benchmark. The more closely related the movements in the portfolio in question are to movements in the market portfolio, the smaller $SD(\varepsilon_p)$ will be, other things being equal, since it measures the risk that could be diversified away by holding a broad-based portfolio.

To illustrate the appraisal ratio, if α_p were 1.92% for the year and if $SD(\varepsilon_p)$ were 15% over the same period, then:

$$A_P = \frac{1.92}{15.0} = 0.128$$

This equation says that for every unit of risk that could be avoided with proper diversification, the manager achieved a 0.128% excess market and risk-adjusted return. Successful active managers should be able to generate consistently positive appraisal ratios. Poor active managers will produce negative appraisal ratios. Thus, this measure is most helpful when compared with corresponding measures for other actively managed portfolios and the managers who run them, as well as on an absolute basis.

Benchmarks

Woven throughout the preceding discussion is an unstated assumption that the evaluator has an appropriate benchmark or standard of comparison to answer the following two questions:

- How has the overall fund done?
- How has manager A or portfolio A done?

Too frequently, those attempting to measure performance oversimplify this issue, resorting to the use of an index such as the S&P 500 or turning to a simple manager universe. As we will see, neither of these standards is necessarily the best. Thus, in spite of some fairly sophisticated statistics, we can still reach the wrong conclusions—for example, that a manager is bad when he or she is good or vice versa—if we do not use an appropriate standard. A viable alternative to these oversimplified approaches is the normal or benchmark portfolio, a theoretical portfolio that is structurally identical to the investment strategy without whatever active management takes place. Benchmark portfolios are constructed specifically to serve as the standard against which an actual portfolio is judged. We examine the strengths and weaknesses of using indexes and manager universe and then look at how benchmark portfolios can improve performance measurement.

Comparisons Using Indexes

Sometimes a pension analyst, rather than making any technical adjustments for risk, may simply compare the return on a portfolio against the return on a broad-based index of security returns. For this purpose, most analysts would use Standard & Poor's 500 Stock Index (S&P 500). This index is a market-value-weighted index of the 500 common stocks that the Standard & Poor's Company believes are repre-

Table 7-1. S&P 500 Return as Computed by Different Organizations, 1984–1988

	Investment Return (%)					
	1984	1985	1986	1987	1988	Average
Callan	6.2	31.8	18.6	5.2	16.8	15.3
Indata	6.1	31.6	18.5	5.1	16.3	15.1
TUCS	6.3	31.8	18.7	5.3	16.6	15.3
SEI	6.1	32.0	18.6	5.2	16.8	15.3
S&P Corp.	NA	NA	NA	5.1	16.6	NA

Source: Adapted from Paul Halpern and Josef Lakonishok. "Why the Difference in Performance Measurement?" *Investing* 4, no. 1 (1990):37.

sentative of the broad market. Of course, although the pension plan sponsor would compare only the return on the equity portion of the pension portfolio with the S&P 500 return, even here the analyst is likely to be making a sizable mistake because using market indexes can create serious problems that may lead to incorrect conclusions.

One problem with using an index is that, in computing the total return, dividends must be collected and reinvested. Many consultants and money management firms compute the rate of return on the S&P 500. However, because each of these organizations makes different assumptions regarding the reinvestment of dividends, some ambiguity arises. Specifically, organizations can assume that dividends get reinvested in the same stock that paid them at the closing price on the payment day or at the next day's opening price. They can also assume reinvestment in the index rather than the dividend-paying stock at the closing or at the next day's opening.

Halpern and Lakonishok examined this issue. Table 7-1 gives some of the results of their study. S&P 500 returns as computed by various organizations are shown for the years 1984 through 1988. Although the variation seen in organizations in one year as computed by different investment monitoring organizations and Standard & Poor's itself from high to low is seemingly small—generally around 20 basis points—what is important is that there is measurable difference in something most observers would view as unambiguous. Different portfolio performance measuring organizations compute the same benchmark differently. Given the competitiveness of the money management industry and the generally very narrow dispersion of realized returns across different money managers, both among themselves and relative to benchmark portfolios, it is clear that many who might be classed as beat-the-market managers using one index measurement could move to the beat-by-the-market category using another organization's version of the index return.

Another problem with using an index for comparison is that the index may not be appropriate for the portfolio for which it is being used as a standard. There are several issues here. First is the matter of choosing an index that has a comparable level of risk to the portfolio being evaluated. For example, using the S&P 500 as the standard when evaluating a portfolio of small capitalization stocks may provide misleading results because standard risk adjustments (e.g., beta) may not completely capture the difference in risk between the index and the actual portfolio. Thus, a sponsor could conclude that a manager is successful because he or she has been "beating the market" when the reality is that the manager has been taking excessive risk. Alternatively, the sponsor might conclude that a manager has been unsuccessful when the reality is that the manager has been very successful in generating returns with very little risk.

Roll and Ross point out a related problem. Using an index as the standard presumes that the index represents a portfolio that is efficient (i.e., it offers the highest possible return for its level of risk). They demonstrate that, if the index is not efficient, the results of the evaluation may be completely different from the results of an evaluation that uses an efficient index.

Finally, indexes differ in the way they are constructed. For example, the S&P 500 is value weighted—its performance is affected more by what happens to the stocks of the larger market capitalization companies than by what happens to the smaller ones. The stocks in the Value Line index are equally weighted, however, making it an appropriate index for portfolios that hold equal dollar amounts of each security; and the Dow Jones Industrial Average is weighted by price, making it an appropriate index for portfolios that hold equal numbers of shares of each security. Further, bond indexes differ according to how bonds are priced (a very important issue, since many bonds do not trade frequently) and how maturing bonds are replaced. They differ as well by credit risk and maturity. There is a point to this delineation of index differences—a portfolio that does not share the construction attributes of a given index will of course perform differently from the index even though it may hold roughly the same assets. Yet this difference should be attributed to differing construction—it is not attributable to investment strategy per se unless the difference in construction is a strategic decision.

Are these issues important? Lehmann and Modest show that the rankings of portfolio managers are very sensitive to the choice of proxies for the market—to using the S&P 500 instead of the NYSE index, for example. In concluding that a manager has done well or poorly, the cumulative effect of the kinds of errors as described here may be quite large. And a sponsor who makes important decisions based on faulty data may be making poor decisions indeed.

The lessons for plan sponsors are these: be cautious regarding the choice of index. Choose one that is an appropriate representation of the risk to which the portfolio being evaluated is exposed. Use an index that represents the right market segment (for example, large capitalization stocks) and is constructed in a manner consistent with the way the actual portfolio is formed (for example, value weighted). Understand what assumptions are built into the index data computations that could make this proxy tougher or easier to beat. Use one organization's index consistently in order to make reasonably robust, long-term evaluations of money managers over time and among themselves.

Comparisons Using Manager Universes

Another common approach to comparative analysis is to select a set of performance numbers (return and risk measures) compiled from a sample of performance numbers from presumably comparable money managers. This method has the naive appeal of a horse race in which manager A does better (or worse) than manager B. Additionally, it is easy to get information because numerous pension consultants make manager universe data accessible so a sponsor does not have to develop its own base of comparison. However, this type of data has three serious flaws.

The first is that a manager universe is useful only if the managers represented follow similar investment styles—such as small capitalization growth stock investing, and so forth. Since managers may follow more than one stylistic discipline over time, the accurate, appropriate grouping of managers becomes problematic. Additionally, large numbers of managers are necessary to achieve reasonable statistical significance; however, the larger the universe, the more dissimilar the styles of the included managers are likely to be.

A more serious problem is that of *survivorship bias*. Any manager universe with a number of managers with reasonably long records presents the performance of managers who have been good enough to survive in a competitive business. Looked at another way, poor managers having poor performance are not likely to be proportionately included in the data presented as representative of performance standards.

Finally, the results of manager universe comparisons are difficult to interpret in a useful fashion because the rankings change from period to period. Furthermore, the return rankings generated frequently conflict with the risk rankings. It is worth noting that the risk rankings do offer some insight into whether an investment manager is complying with policy, however (see the 1995 article by Elton and Gruber for a good discussion).

Collectively, these problems make manager universes of only limited value for a sponsor evaluating performance in order to decide who to employ in the future—a decision of considerable importance.

Normal (Benchmark) Portfolios

In recent years, many analysts and researchers have criticized the risk-adjusted measures described earlier because they either assume that total risk is the relevant risk for a portfolio—which it is not when the portfolio is part of a much larger plan—or because the statistical measures, α_p and β_p, are specific to (dependent on) the proxy chosen for the return on the market portfolio (see Lehmann and Modest, and Roll and Ross). Consider a portfolio manager who is constrained to a narrowly defined strategy—for instance, purchasing stocks with high book-to-market (B/M) multiples. This manager is not likely to hold a well-diversified portfolio; hence the Sharpe measure will not be an appropriate way to measure this manager's performance. Similarly, if the index portfolio or market portfolio proxy is only imperfectly and variably correlated with the universe of high B/M stocks, then the statistical parameter estimates (the alphas and betas) will not mean very much. Thus, the Treynor-Jensen or Treynor-Black measures would not be helpful in evaluating this manager. To circumvent this problem and the problems posed by published indexes and manager universes, many analysts have suggested the use of *normal* or *benchmark portfolios*.

A benchmark portfolio constitutes the universe of all the stocks that the portfolio manager may consider. In essence this is the neutral or passive portfolio that represents the manager's style without any active decision making—that is, the benchmark portfolio should represent an available level of performance that can be achieved by randomly selecting securities from the style universe. Generally, each portfolio manager in a group of managers who are collectively responsible for the pension plan should have a well-defined, very specific investment strategy. For example, one manager may be responsible for evaluating and selecting growth stocks, while another may be searching for value stocks. With benchmark portfolios, the portfolio manager's actual investment returns may be compared with the returns on the specially constructed securities universe, allowing a meaningful comparison of an actively managed portfolio to a stylistically comparable benchmark portfolio.

For example, consider a portfolio manager who has agreed to manage a high-B/M portfolio. This manager's return should be compared with a portfolio containing all the stocks that have B/M's above a specified level and that otherwise qualify for inclusion, perhaps because they are listed on an organized exchange or are traded on the National Association of Securities Dealers Automated Quotation (NASDAQ) system; that is, they are investable. If the manager beats the customized benchmark on a pure return basis without changing styles, that would be considered superior performance attributable to the manager's skill.

Of course, this approach requires that portfolio managers and pension plan sponsors agree beforehand on what constitutes an appropriate benchmark portfolio. They must also agree on the conventions applied to dividend reinvestment, otherwise the same problem that was illustrated in Table 7-1 could arise here.

The benchmark portfolio approach to performance measurement is gaining popularity, not only because it avoids some troublesome theoretical issues (such as how many risk factors are relevant), and some thorny statistical issues (such as the optimal measurement period), but also because large computerized databases accessible by personal computers can be used to construct these customized, normal portfolios. Generally speaking, the construction of benchmark portfolios is not an easy process. It requires a very sophisticated understanding of the investment strategy that the money manager and the sponsor agree to use. The benchmark portfolio must represent the manager's style (defining and replicating this may be difficult), it must be investable, and it must be useful in differentiating between active and passive management (see the article by Bailey, Richards, and Tierney). In spite of the difficulties, construction of benchmark portfolios is not impossible. Importantly from the analyst's perspective, separating a manager's ability to select securities (or to time the market) from the plan sponsor's ability to select investment strategies to be implemented by managers is critical to evaluating how managers are doing.

Using benchmark portfolios allows plan sponsors to see how well a manager does within the parameters of the strategy that he or she was contracted to pursue by the plan sponsor. It has the added advantages of defining expectations before the fact—as such it is a useful communication tool—and of encouraging managers to stay with the style they were hired to deliver. Finally, although the Sharpe, Jensen, or Treynor measures may be satisfactory combined measures of the quality of security selection and strategy selection, they will not do for managers who are constrained to narrowly defined security markets; there are just too many nuances in markets and management behavior that these measures might miss.

Finally, a word of caution is appropriate. Benchmarks can easily be misused. This commonly occurs when an index naively is chosen as a benchmark without proper attention to what the sponsor and investment manager are really trying to accomplish. Sometimes an index may not be investable, or factors such as crossholdings (a big problem in Japan) are not taken into account. Other times, the wrong benchmark is selected—for example, the S&P 500 index is selected for a small company stock manager. Those who help select benchmarks should bear in mind that investment managers have incentives first to mimic the chosen benchmark and second not to stray too far from the benchmark. This is fine for passive strategies; in fact, it is exactly what is wanted. However, for actively managed portfolios, it can force the manager away from her area of expertise and into portfolio strategies that are different than the one for which he or she was hired. In other words, naive benchmarks can be harmful because they introduce a bias against actions that otherwise may be desirable.

Components of Investment Performance

To understand whether the decisions made have been good or poor, it is necessary to understand why actual returns are what they are. The various measures of investment performance discussed so far may indicate whether Fund A beat Fund B or beat the market, but they do not reveal why. Nor do they reveal how much of the actual performance is attributable to passive exposures to various asset classes or to active management. Generally speaking, superior or inferior returns can be attributed to one of two active management strategies. The first is security selection—unusual selections of specific stocks or bonds relative to all of those that could be bought or sold, and perhaps buying those that are thought to be underpriced. The second is market timing—being heavily invested in the stock market when it is expected to perform unusually well, or more heavily invested in bonds when they are expected to do comparatively well.

Table 7-2. Schema for Determining the Components of Investment Performance

| | | **Selectivity** | |
		Active Security Selection	Passive Security Selection
	Active Market Timing	IV Actual Return	II Policy and Timing Return
Timing			
	Passive Market Timing	III Policy and Security Selection Return	I Policy Return (Passive Benchmark)

Active returns are due to:

Action	*Squares*
Timing	II-I
Selectivity	III-I
Other	IV-III-II + I
Total	IV-I

Source: Adapted from Gary P. Brinson, L. Randolph Hood, and Gilbert L. Beebower. "Determinants of Portfolio Performance." *Financial Analysts Journal,* July-August (1986):40.

Performance Attribution

Several authors, including Fama; Brinson, Hood, and Beebower; and Bodie, Kane, and Marcus, have offered schemes designed to help analysts detect whether total plan performance is attributable to exposure to a benchmark, to market timing, or to security selection. The benchmark portfolio, in essence, represents the return attributable to passive exposures to asset classes or market segments. The purpose of performance attribution, then, is to explain why actual portfolio returns differ from a given benchmark by identifying the effect active decisions have had. Table 7-2 shows a possible framework for the components of investment performance.

To illustrate, let us suppose that a pension plan (comprised perhaps of many portfolios) experienced a total return of 25% over the evaluation period. Further, suppose that the overall portfolio was allocated so that 70% of the money was invested in stocks and 30% of the money was invested in bonds. Finally, assume that the stock portion of the total portfolio rose by 30% and the bond portion of the total portfolio rose by 13.3%.

Table 7-3. Components of Investment Performance

		Selectivity	
		Active Security Selection	Passive Security Selection
Timing	Active Market Timing	IV 25% (0.3)(0.7) + (0.133)(0.3)	II 22% (0.7)(0.25) + (0.3)(0.15)
	Passive Market Timing	III 23.3% (0.3)(0.6) + (0.133)(0.4)	I 21% (0.25)(0.6) + (0.15)(0.4)

Active returns are due to:

Timing II-I	22% – 21%	= 1%
Selectivity III-I	23.3% – 21%	= 2.3%
Other IV-III-II-I	21% – 23.3% – 22% + 21%	= 0.7%
Total	25% – 21%	= 4.0%

To determine what portion of the total return was attributable to market timing and what portion was attributable to security selection, data regarding the investment policy and the investment experience of unmanaged funds must be used. In this instance, suppose that the long-term strategic asset allocation policy (the stock-bond mix) was 60% stocks and 40% bonds. (Chapters 5 and 6 consider how this mix gets set.) Further, assume that an appropriate benchmark portfolio for stocks rose by 25% over the period and that an appropriate benchmark portfolio for bonds rose by 15% over the same period.

We can use this information to determine the components or sources of the portfolio's actual returns. We do this by filling in the matrix of Table 7-2. This can be seen in Table 7-3. In Quadrant IV, we simply put the actual total return experience of the fund, 25%. In Quadrant I, we enter the performance the fund would have had if it (a) invested exactly according to policy guidelines for the strategic asset allocation, and (b) bought the index portfolios. In Quadrant III, we enter the results that would have obtained had the fund (a) followed the strategic investment policy allocation of 60% stock and 40% bonds, but (b) selected the securities it actually held; that is, portfolio sector weights are changed from policy to actual. In doing so, Quadrant III isolates the impact of management's efforts to identify securities offering unusually high returns. Quadrant II contains the investment results that would have been achieved if (a) the fund was allocated as it actually was, that is, 70% stocks and 30% bonds, but (b) the fund simply invested in the benchmark portfolios of stocks and bonds (index funds) instead of making the specific security selections it actually made. This isolates the impact of the market-timing decisions.

In this illustration, the gain from timing is 1%, while the gain from selectivity is 2.3%. The latter is comprised of very good stock selectivity and poor bond selectivity. The overall gain attributable to active management—the collective value added by active timing and active security selection decisions—is 4.0%. Note that the actual return of 25% exceeds the benchmark return (Quadrant I) of 21% by 4%. Note also that further analysis would reveal that active bond selection appears to be poor since the actively managed bond portfolio underperformed its benchmark. However, underweighting bonds (holding 30% instead of 40%) reduced the impact of poor bond selection and magnified the impact of good stock selection.

Why Separate Performance Components?

There are several reasons why evaluating the components of performance can be worthwhile. If the pension plan sponsor is the one who makes the timing decisions by deciding whether the bond manager or the equity manager gets the next capital contribution to invest, this approach may help distinguish what portion of total performance is due to the sponsor's decisions and what is due to the decisions of money managers. Furthermore, for money managers who have latitude with respect both to selection and timing, the component approach is useful in distinguishing whether the manager is unusually good or bad at selection or timing. The plan sponsor could then write investment instructions that exploit the real skill of the manager and preclude him or her from exercising much discretion in the area of weakness. For instance, a good market timer but bad security selector may be given instructions that allow him or her to deviate from policy stock/bond allocations but that require such deviations be implemented using only passive stock and bond portfolios.

Recent Advances in Performance Measurement

There are some problems that arise when applying the preceding methodologies to real portfolios. Among the more important and difficult questions that must be addressed are:

1. How can a manager's or portfolio's investment strategy or style be defined in unequivocal terms?

2. How should a benchmark or normal portfolio be constructed?

3. What sources of return should be examined in attributing returns to specific factors?

In an attempt to improve the performance measurement and evaluation process, scholars and practitioners alike are exploring new methodologies—and they are having some success. The most promising area of advancement is the use of multi-index or multifactor models for portfolios.

Multi-Index Models

There is much to recommend the development of Jensen-type measures using multi-index models instead of the single-index model typically referred to as the *market model* (see, for example, the 1992 article by Fama and French and the article by Chen, Roll, and Ross). The primary advantage of a multifactor model with respect to assessing performance is that it allows or offers multiple factors to explain a portfolio's performance when a single market factor seems to be inadequate. Additionally, it does not rely on or require the identification of a single broad market index as the basis for comparison; instead, it allows for computing multiple risk sensitivities to multiple factors. For instance, the relationship between unanticipated real growth, inflation, and various measures of interest rate change might be thought to be the systematic factors to which a portfolio is exposed. If so, the risk premiums characteristic of these factors and the sensitivity of a portfolio to these factors may be computed and used in Jensen-type performance measures.

Multifactor models and the performance assessment results they yield still are very sensitive to the assumptions regarding construction of the underlying benchmarks. The choices of variables used to construct the multifactor models can also affect the usefulness of the model's results. Nonetheless, these models are adding to our understanding of the issues involved in defining style, constructing benchmarks, and understanding the sources of performance.

Portfolio Style

One especially promising area is the multifactor work done by Sharpe in 1992. He proposes that a portfolio's style can be identified by constructing an asset class–based (returns-based) factor model of the form:

$$R_i = \beta_{i1}F_1 + \beta_{i2}F_2 + \dots + \beta_{in}F_n + \varepsilon$$

where β_{in} is the exposure of a portfolio (and hence its sensitivity) to asset class F_n (where n may be large company stocks, small company stocks, Treasury bonds, and so forth). The primary insight this approach offers is that a portfolio's or a manager's historical performance can be analyzed and a descriptive style defined in terms of asset classes and exposures. As long as the asset classes used in the model are mutually exclusive, collectively represent the "market," and have differing return profiles, this model offers an analytical approach to determining combination of weights (betas) and asset classes that will generate returns similar to that of the portfolio being analyzed. In other words, a real portfolio's "style" may be translated into a "comparable" portfolio of major asset classes—an effective asset mix. This has important implications, among other things, for understanding what style a manager offers (or has followed in the past) and for monitoring adherence to policy.

Benchmark Construction

Benchmarks are difficult to construct properly. Sharpe's multifactor (returns-based) model offers a relatively straightforward way to construct meaningful benchmark portfolios with which to compare a manager's performance. Ideally, actual returns over 60 time periods (5 years) can be analyzed by factor analysis to identify the combination of asset classes and exposures a portfolio represents. This effective asset mix then may be used as the passive benchmark with which future performance will be compared.

Some cautions are necessary. Unconstrained factor analysis can lead to some incorrect (or highly suspect) conclusions. For example, if factor beta exposures (the percent invested in an asset class) are not constrained to realistic values, the model may come back with a conclusion that the manager is taking large short positions when this is not the case. Thus the analyst must use some judgment and evaluate what the model is saying in terms of the manager's articulated style. If the result does not conform to what seems reasonable, the factors must be constrained (e.g., if short-selling is not permitted), factor sensitivities must be greater than or equal to zero. Additionally, the manager's current style may differ from the style implied by the last few years. Thus, the analyst must be careful to consider the possibility of "style drift" when interpreting results.

Performance Attribution

Sharpe's multifactor model is also useful in examining the sources of the returns a portfolio earns. Specifically, it suggests that the difference between the returns on an actual portfolio and the returns on the style benchmark may be attributed to selection decisions made by the manager. Thus, a manager who conforms to predetermined asset class exposures and yet beats the style benchmark can be presumed to have made good selection decisions.

Another multi-index approach with potential for return attribution insights was proposed by Fama and French in 1996. The model is based on their now-famous 1992 article on the cross-sectional returns of stocks. In that study, they concluded that book-to-market and firm size seemed to explain much more of the variation in equity returns than other models, such as the capital asset pricing model (the basis for the Treynor and Jensen measures). Their current work extends their findings into a three-factor model that attempts to explain the expected return on a portfolio above the risk-free rate as attributable to the sensitivity of return to a broad-based market-risk premium, a size premium (larger for smaller stocks), and a B/M premium (larger for high book-to-market stocks). Although the model is being debated in academic circles, it seems to be useful in explaining the returns on portfolios that are formed according to size and B/M criteria. Additionally, it appears to explain other portfolio return patterns such as earnings-to-price and price/return reversals. Critics argue that problems such as survivorship bias, data mining, and irrational behavior may be creating the results the model is trying to explain. The model is promising, however, as a tool for plan sponsors to use in evaluating the plan's and component portfolios identifying the style of the manager, and monitoring the manager's conformance to that style.

Conclusion

Measuring investment performance is no simple task. There are many subtleties and pitfalls, and still much art to what looks like a science. Despite this, the prudent fiduciary must make every effort to measure performance correctly so that it can be evaluated properly.

The starting point for useful evaluation is to use the correct measure of return to answer the various questions that should be asked. Dollar weighting (for the total asset pool) and time weighting (for the multiple managers managing portions of the asset pool) are more than mathematical niceties—they can lead to profoundly different conclusions. Returns must also be adjusted for risk. The techniques for risk adjustment are not perfect, but they are much better than ignoring the relationship between risk and return. The sources of the returns produced must also be identified. It matters if a manager is successful at selection but not at timing. It matters if the active decisions add value to or subtract value from the asset pool. It matters if performance comes simply from exposure to the market but active management fees are being paid. Finally, pension funds should benchmark their performance and the performance of their investment managers and do so correctly. A major market index should not be naively selected unless this is the specific exposure that you have deemed appropriate. The benchmark should be customized to better match the portfolio being measured. The desirability and consequences of departing from the benchmark with the investment manager should be discussed before the management begins.

Sometimes, managers and consultants resist providing the data necessary to measure performance correctly. It can be costly and time consuming to do it correctly, but it is still important and must be done. Do not forget who employs whom.

The real benefit of performance measurement is that, done correctly, it provides the data necessary to understand why performance was good or bad, and thus serves as a springboard to *evaluate* performance. Performance evaluation, in turn, helps fiduciaries make the difficult decisions about who to hire, who to continue, and who to eliminate. As we will see in the next chapter, performance evaluation does improve decision making, even though it does not foretell the future. It does let others know that monitoring is occurring. It does provide an incentive for all parties to communicate about an important subject—and to look at where performance may be insufficient. In doing these things, in tying historical performance and forward-looking policy together, it opens a pathway to better future performance, a pathway that begins with the performance measurement techniques we have described.

Chapter *8*

Improving Pension Fund Investment Performance

The investment performance of pension fund asset pools is central to the attainment of virtually all beneficiary and sponsor objectives for pension plans. Improving the performance of a pension fund's asset pool or of the component portfolios that comprise the pool can increase the likelihood that the promised or expected benefits will materialize. Further, if the plan is a defined benefit plan, better performance can reduce the financial burden carried by the sponsor.

Improving plan performance begins with a careful evaluation of the performance the plan has been getting. Depending on what is found, various actions may be undertaken to improve future performance.

The obvious prerequisites to evaluation are the measurement techniques discussed in Chapter 7. In this chapter, we discuss how these techniques may be used to evaluate pension fund performance and describes some important limitations of performance measurement. Then, we review the evidence on money managers' abilities to perform and looks at the issue of using historical performance to select those managers who may have superior future performance. The chapter concludes with a discussion on why some pension funds do poorly and offers guidance on improving the investment performance of pension plan asset pools.

Using Performance Measures

Performance measurement systems that can be applied easily rely on historical data. These data are used, correctly or incorrectly, for many purposes—predicting future results, selecting managers, and evaluating the effectiveness of policy. Experience suggests that plan sponsors ought to take care to avoid reading more into performance data than is really there. What many sponsors really *should* want to know is whether current policy is being followed, whether current policy is likely to allow the pension fund to meet its goals, and whether measured good or bad performance is due to luck or skill. Sponsors can and should answer the first two questions and should use historical data to help them. No one can really answer the last question, however, but it is important to make the attempt in a systematic manner that will provide some useful insights. These insights should not be mistaken for facts, however. Otherwise, the sponsor may take inappropriate action, perhaps based on the appearance of poor or outstanding measured performance for a few quarters, that could have far worse consequences than doing nothing.

Historical and Future Performance

Does past performance predict future performance? Do active portfolio managers consistently beat passively managed portfolios or indexes on a risk-adjusted basis; that is, does superior performance exist? If it exists, does superior performance persist over time?

Although there is not a lot of comprehensive information drawn directly from the pension universe that bears on these questions, there is a considerable body of information that has been compiled on mutual fund performance. Since we are interested in the possibility of superior performance and the predictability of future returns as it pertains to managers of subportfolios, it is not unreasonable to use mutual funds as a proxy for pension subportfolios.

At best, the evidence on managers beating fair benchmarks is mixed. Virtually all of the early studies of mutual funds concluded that there are very few managers who can consistently beat the market and that, across all funds studied, returns are inferior on a risk-adjusted basis—they have negative alphas—after expenses (see the article by Jensen).

In any given period, some managers will beat their benchmarks. After all, there are many managers. An important question is whether superior performance in one period means that performance in future periods also will be superior. Does performance persist? Early studies found that successful managers in a base period are no more likely to be successful in later periods than are managers who are categorized as poor in the base period (see, for example, Dunn and Theisen). Some other studies have found hints of performance persistence (see, for example, the 1989 article by Ippolito), but other researchers find that this persistence does not appear to be statistically significant nor strong enough to be useful in forming investment strategies (see, for example, the articles by Grinblatt and Titman). Some more recent studies argue that the historical returns of mutual funds are predictive of future returns (see Goetzmann and Ibbotson). One study by Kahn and Rudd found no evidence of persistence of equity fund performance but did find persistence for fixed-income funds. However, they concluded that using past performance to find fixed income funds that could beat the median performers was not an attractive strategy because the medians had negative selection return—that is, the median manager underperformed his benchmark.

What do these contradictory conclusions mean? How should fund sponsors interpret this mixed evidence?

One way to interpret the various studies is to recall that measurement results are very sensitive to the benchmark chosen to represent the "market." For example, a study by Elton, Gruber, Das, and Hlavka reexamined a 1989 study by Ippolito and found that using a different, presumably more appropriate index for the benchmark changed the results from an alpha (excess return) of +0.4 to one of −1.59%.

Another factor to consider is that the appearance of performance persistence may be attributable to the potential survivorship bias that is problematic for all performance studies. Simply put, survivorship bias enters a data set because poor mutual funds (or poor managers) do not survive to be included in the data samples we analyze. Thus, historical statistics tend to suggest that performance was better on average than it would have been if the disappearing losers were included in the sample. Since only funds (managers) that are good enough to survive remain, an appearance of persistently good performance may arise.

The importance of this issue can be demonstrated by examining two money managers, A and B. Both may make large bets on different investment strategies. If A's bet pays off, and B's does not, A survives but B disappears. The bet may not be based on an informed judgment (which presumably would be consistent with expertise)—all it has to do is pay off. Extend this simple example over several time periods and numerous managers, and it is easy to end up with a set of managers who beat the market or persistently beat their peers when in fact they are merely the beneficiaries of a run of good luck—they survived.

Two articles (see Malkiel, and Brown and Goetzmann) analyzed different data sets in a slightly different way and concluded that survivorship bias is real—and important. Malkiel demonstrated that persistence findings are influenced by survivorship bias. He found that the average return of all equity funds in existence in a given initial year is less than the average of all surviving funds by about 150 basis points. Performance data that fail to adjust for the bias is likely to overstate the performance of the set significantly.

Brown and Goetzmann's study found that relative performance seems to persist even after survivorship bias is controlled. The effect they found is stronger for poorly performing funds than for good funds. They note, however, that a strategy of chasing winning mutual funds has a high level of total risk and that this risk may be attributable to "loading up" on a common factor.

Traditional performance measurement studies have used *unconditional* returns—returns net of a benchmark—to look at issues like performance persistence. Some very recent work on performance persistence has used *conditional* performance evaluation of returns. The main idea of a *conditional* approach is that expected returns and betas vary over time, that is they are not stationary as assumed by most measurement techniques. Consider, for example, that money managers may be motivated to trade on the basis of publicly available information such as dividend yields. If the trading activity affects expected returns and risks—that is, if the portfolios held by the managers change—what an analyst may conclude from average performance data should consider the effect of what motivated the trade.

Using this methodology, Christopherson, Ferson, and Glassman find economically significant persistence in a population of 273 institutional equity pension fund managers. Specifically they find:

- Poor conditional performance is followed by more poor performance.
- Unconditional alphas (excess returns) are not good predictors of future returns for the managers studied.
- Conditional measures seem to be more powerful in predicting future performance.

Historical Performance and Manager Selection

Few money managers would be hired if their historical records were poor. Sponsors would fear they themselves would not be perceived as prudent. However, as we have already observed, there is no compelling evidence that the historical track record helps predict future manager performance.

Further, it is extremely difficult to differentiate between luck and skill. If 10,000 money managers are flipping coins, some of them will get long runs of heads and others will get long runs of tails. Few would argue there is skill in flipping a coin, however. For each new flip of the coin, of course, the odds of getting a head or getting a tail remain the same regardless of how many flips have been made. Similarly, few would look at a run of heads and conclude that the future result will be a similar run of heads. Statistically, however, this is the problem for sponsors who select managers based on their historical performance; is the manager's record luck or is it skill?

What about the manager who already works for a fund? The same luck or skill conundrum exists. If the manager is generally close to a benchmark, say, within 10% of the target on the downside over a portion of market cycle—for example, the manager's return was 8.1% when the benchmark return was 9%—then there is only a weak case for termination. Even index funds experience as much as 10% tracking error during some periods. On the other hand, if an active manager falls below a benchmark over an *entire* market cycle by an average of, say, 50 basis points, then it may be time to place the funds with another firm. The reason is not that historical performance predicts the future particularly well. The reason is that performance this poor is most likely attributable to any of a number of factors that are not desirable. Perhaps there has been a dramatic deviation from the fund's investment guidelines or policies. Perhaps the manager has lost his or her touch or the inefficiency that existed in the past is no longer exploitable. Perhaps there is excessive trading or expenses. Of course, if the plan sponsor concludes that none of these reasons explains the excessively poor performance, then the plan sponsor must carefully consider whether it was merely bad luck or an investment strategy that is out of favor or even gross incompetence that led to the disappointing investment performance. These evaluations, of course, are subjective and require careful consideration.

There are theoretical approaches that allow quite useful distinctions between luck and skill. See, for example, the approach developed by Admati, Anat, and Ross, which uses managers' expectations of security returns and risks. Such estimates are generally unavailable, however, for prior time periods or for many managed portfolios, but some fund managers are beginning to collect sufficient data to allow for the application of some of the more advanced evaluation methods.

In summary, most of the evidence shows that historical data have very little useful predictive content, although the conditional performance measurement technique described earlier offers some promise. There is some evidence that poor managers remain poor. This suggests that these managers should be avoided.

Correct Uses of Performance Evaluation

Even though historical performance data are of limited value in forecasting future performance and hence in identifying those money managers who will outperform their benchmarks consistently, using historical performance data is prudent. In particular, performance evaluation may:

- Provide the information necessary to compensate managers if they are being paid on an incentive-fee basis. Performance evaluation, for example, can assure that incentive compensation is paid for returns that beat a fair benchmark rather than a "straw man" that may be easily beaten.
- Reveal whether actions that helped or hurt the pension plan were taken by the sponsor—for example, the strategic asset allocation decision—or by the manager—for example, security selection decisions.
- Provide information that may be helpful in altering or preventing harmful behavior in the future. For instance, a plan sponsor may discover that its method of allocating new contributions effectively got its pension plan into playing a tactical asset allocation game by unbalancing the asset mix relative to the policy mix. Performance measurement could pinpoint this as a cause for poor investment performance and suggest remedies.
- Reveal whether a manager is following or violating the agreed-upon investment instructions and policy parameters. Individual managers do not have the complete picture. Thus, it is the sponsor's responsibility to ensure that managers conform to the fund's investment policies so that the plan may accomplish what is in the best interests of the sponsor and the employees who will benefit from the plan. Sensible policy only works, of course, if the managers of the fund do what they should.
- Advise pension plan sponsors whether or not managers remained true to the policies they said they would follow. When plan sponsors hire specialty managers, they generally want them to remain with their specialty and not switch

investment strategies to chase investment fads or invest in areas in which they may not be competent (e.g., exotic derivatives). Managers who rotate among styles most likely buy yesterday's winners and sell yesterday's losers in pursuit of the last period's performance. Unfortunately for those who do this, there is evidence (see the article by Arnott and Lovell) that this is just the opposite of what they should be doing.

- Demonstrate due diligence and care. Performance evaluation, if well documented, may make pension plan fiduciaries appear to their various constituents as if they are behaving well. This, in turn, may immunize them to some extent from legal actions brought by parties interested in the behavior of their pension plans by either reducing the likelihood of such actions or providing the basis for defense if such actions are brought.

Generally speaking, the quantitative analysis of historical data should be given only equal or less weight than some important qualitative aspects of a prospective investment management relationship. Does the manager have a clearly articulated investment philosophy? Has the manager stuck with the philosophy even when it was going unrewarded by the market? Has the philosophy produced excess returns over an entire market cycle or two, say 7 to 10 years, even though any 1- or 2-year period could be dismal with respect to investment returns. Are the people honest and competent? Do they provide complete performance data? Will they explain what they do and why they do it when a plan sponsor wants to know?

In summary, even though measures of historical performance do not help very much in predicting the future investment performance, they are useful in understanding the results of the decisions in which the fiduciary participated, either explicitly or by delegation to others. This is a prerequisite to making better decisions in the future. Without question, future decisions based on the measures described in this chapter will be more informed decisions and will, on average, be better, more prudent decisions.

Performance Evaluation in Practice

There is a huge performance evaluation industry designed to help the sponsor in evaluating performance. Brokerage firms, actuarial firms, banks that serve as master trustees for pension plans, and pension fund consultants provide a variety of services. Each of these services has special features. Some will even track the performance of securities that have been sold for a month or more after the sale to see what effect those decisions had on portfolio performance so that plan sponsors can second-guess everything their portfolio managers have done. We do not recommend doing this.

A common practice of money managers is presenting historical performance data in the hope of attracting (or keeping) business—more assets to manage. This is commonly done by combining the portfolios of numerous clients at an investment firm into a single measure called a *composite*. Composites presumably represent a manager's ability to manage according to a specific strategy (e.g., growth or value), asset class (e.g., stocks or bonds), or some other factor.

The problem with composites, in addition to the limited use of historical data in identifying those who are likely to perform well in the future, is that they are subject to manipulation through factors such as the selection of time periods presented, the portfolios included, the way the portfolios are weighted in the calculations (e.g., equal weighting versus size weighting), and the way cash flows are weighted. Those who wish to look at the data provided by alternative managers must understand the data are not likely to be uniform nor comparable. Furthermore, the analyst may not have information about the way the performance composites were formed.

Of some help in this matter are the Performance Presentation Standards (PPS) developed by the Association for Investment Management and Research (AIMR). AIMR represents over 30,000 investment professionals throughout the world and grants the Chartered Financial Analyst (CFA) designation. In accordance with AIMR's mission of providing guiding investment principles for investment analysts and money managers, the PPS provide guidelines for the computation of returns, asset valuation, composite construction, and numerous other elements that affect performance presentations. Central to the PPS is the concept of presenting performance through the use of composites constructed from portfolios of similar risk and strategies. Managers who conform to the PPS must include all discretionary, fee-paying portfolios in at least one composite and must present up to 10 years of annual composite/portfolio performance that includes portfolios that may no longer be at the firm. Generally, the PPS requirements prevent firms from "buying" performance by including results that were produced by individuals at their former employers and from excluding performance when portfolios have been taken from the firm.

The PPS requirements substantially reduce the ability of a manager to present only attractive performance. They promote full disclosure and fair representation, ensure uniformity in reporting, and encourage comparability among investment performance reports. Effective as of January 1, 1993, the standards are slowly catching on as plan sponsors and other institutional investors pressure external money managers to comply.

Plan sponsors and fiduciaries should require managers to comply with the AIMR PPS. Plan staff members should be conversant with the standards so that the strengths of the standards can be applied in analyzing manager performance and the weaknesses of the standards (and there are some) can be recognized. One caution: any set of rules can be "gamed," and the PPS are no exception. If one remembers that the goal of performance evaluation is not necessarily to answer every possible question but is rather a means to the end of raising important questions, this should not be an insurmountable problem.

Actual Pension Performance

Any discussion of performance evaluation should consider how pension funds as a group have actually done. Overall, the empirical evidence on pension fund investment performance is not flattering.

Defined Benefit Plans

The data suggest that actively managed pension funds have not performed as well as unmanaged, passive portfolios or as well as actively managed mutual funds. Note that when available, data on the component portfolios of pension asset pools may not show inferior performance. When one looks at total pension plan assets or all assets of a given class such as equities, thus effectively dollar-weighting the returns on all of the individual portfolios, the poor investment performance of the total asset pools of pension plans is uncovered. Only by analyzing total assets, which include all of a sponsor's pension portfolios of a given asset class or across all asset classes, can one draw serious conclusions about collective pension plan investment performance.

One of the early substantive analyses of total pension plan performance was performed by Berkowitz, Finney, and Logue in 1988. Their study looked at the investment performance of a group of 119 ERISA (private pension) plans from 1976 to 1983 and compared this group with endowment funds, public pension plans, and a variety of mutual funds and market benchmarks over the same time period. Using raw (that is, non–risk-adjusted) returns as well as the Sharpe and Jensen performance measures, private pension plans did not compare favorably with either mutual funds or endowment plans. Public retirement plans showed especially poor investment performance relative to benchmarks, endowment funds, and mutual funds. Some examples from the study are set out in Table 8-1 with other funds' performance.

The results of the Berkowitz, Finney, and Logue study were consistent with those of Ippolito and Turner. They analyzed pension plans using a database derived from information provided by firms on the Form 5500s they filed with the IRS, and they also concluded that pension performance was poor.

In a more recent study, Lakonishok, Shleifer, and Vishny used data provided by SEI to examine the performance of the equity portfolios of pension plans. Their database included 769 all-equity portfolios managed by 341 managers. They compared the performance of the funds from 1983 to 1989 with the S&P 500 Index for the same years, reasoning that the betas of the funds clustered around 1.0 and that the stated objective of most of the funds was to beat the index. They also adjusted for the effects of holding cash. Their results are interesting:

- Using equal weighting and annual returns, the group of pension funds underperformed the index by 1.3% before management fees of around 50 basis points.
- Using value weighting and annual returns, the group of funds underperformed the index by 2.6% before management fees of around 50 basis points.
- The net result of the funds' choices of strategy were that relative performance was poor across diverse styles.
- Using overlapping periods of 3 years, the index did even better relative to the funds.

The study also looked at performance persistence and whether a manager's historical performance suggested strategies for picking winning managers. The following conclusions were reached:

- Using the simple strategy of picking from the previous year's quartile winners, there was an expected deterioration in performance of 8%, while picking from losing quartiles had an expected improvement of 13% per year.

Table 8-1.   Private Retirement Plan Performance Compared with Other Funds' Performance

	Arithmetic Average Return (%)	Geometric Average Return (%)	Mean Sharpe Measure	Mean Jensen's Alpha
ERISA Plans (n = 119)	12.05	11.67	0.132	–0.10
Public Pension Plan (n = 31)	10.25	9.90	0.056	–0.38
Endowments (n = 33)	12.96	12.50	0.160	0.05
Mutual Funds* (n = 325)	16.85	15.58	0.207	0.68

*The mutual fund group included various equity funds, bond funds, balanced funds, and so forth.

- Using a strategy of picking from triennial quartile winners, a fund can expect to beat the average manager by 100 basis points—a gain that does not cover the 130 basis points of underperformance exhibited by the average manager (nor the management fees incurred by using a manager).

The authors conclude (in their own words):

- Pension fund managers seem to subtract rather than add value relative to the performance of the S&P 500 Index.
- There is some consistency of performance, but...it is not clear that [the chosen manager] would be able to beat the market.
- [The relationship between pension funds and the money management industry appears]...to be driven by its need to provide sponsors with good excuses for poor performance, clear stories about portfolio strategies and other services that are only vaguely related to performance.

Findings such as these should concern pension fund sponsors and the parties involved in deciding who should manage assets and what they should get paid. Sponsors are "on the hook" for contributions, and fiduciaries may be held accountable if investment returns are poor.

Defined Contribution Plans

There are virtually no useful data on the investment performance of defined contribution plans. Part of the reason for this lack is the relatively recent shift in assets to DCPs. Another part of the reason is that, for self-directed plans, the asset allocation decisions of employees vary significantly, so that aggregated performance data would have little meaning.

As for the performance of defined benefit plans, the performance of DCPs depends primarily on the asset allocation choices of the overall manager of the plan's assets—the sponsor or the employee. For employee-directed plans, the asset allocation will be affected by the available alternatives, the employees' knowledge of investment fundamentals, the employees' circumstances and preferences, and the expenses and fees incurred by the investments made.

What data have been gathered indicate that employees in self-directed plans may be allocating assets too conservatively to provide adequate wage replacement upon retirement. Additionally, private sector defined contribution accounts may have far too much allocated to the employer's stock than is acceptable for diversification. A survey by the Institute of Management and Administration (IOMA) (see the article by Schultz) of 246 large employers representing 10.6 million plan participants found the following distribution of DCP assets:

Company stock	42%
Guaranteed investment contracts	24
Equity	18
Balanced	6
Bonds	4
Cash	3
Other	2

Source: IOMA (*Wall Street Journal*, September 13, 1996)

The reasons for this overallocation to the employer's stock are not clear. Perhaps it is due to participant naiveté or misplaced loyalty. Perhaps it is due to incentives such as favorable pricing provided by the employer. Perhaps it is due to employers who limit the investment options available to employees so that company stock is one of a very few alternatives—or is the *only* alternative. Regardless of the reason, the result is clear: employees who place too much of their DCP assets in employer stock are taking excessive risk and are likely to experience poor risk-adjusted returns in the future. Further, employers who encourage excessive investment of retirement funds in company stock are not behaving prudently and are running significant risk of litigation if the company's stock does not perform well.

The correct way to look at DCP performance is in terms of whether or not a given plan is likely to provide adequate retirement income—

that is, a sufficient replacement rate. There is no way to measure this in a meaningful sense, but there are some factors that correlate highly with accumulating a DCP asset pool that is sufficient for retirement.

First, employees must know enough about investing to make informed decisions. Second, the alternative investments available to employees need to provide a comprehensive enough set of risk and return possibilities that it is possible for an informed employee to achieve a reasonable accumulation of retirement assets without undue risk (e.g., excessive use of company stock). Third, contributions into the DCP asset pool have to be large enough to make a reasonable replacement possible. Finally, return inhibiting factors such as administrative costs and management fees have to be controlled so they do not erode the value of plan assets.

Even though there is not much to be said about the collective performance of DCPs, the bottom line is that poor DCP performance—whether it is attributable to lack of choice, lack of education, high costs, or simply *ex post* replacement rates that are unacceptable—may result in legal action that is potentially detrimental to sponsors and shareholders or taxpayers. Thus, plan fiduciaries should be concerned.

Factors Affecting Actual Fund Performance

Avoiding factors that are likely to lead to poor performance is a sensible first step in improving performance. There are a number of factors that may contribute to underperformance. Among the more important are attempting to market time, excessive portfolio turnover, agency problems, and regulation.

Market Timing

Can pension funds move into equities and out of bonds and vice versa at propitious times? Unfortunately, data limitations have kept this question from being asked of pension funds. However, several researchers have considered the effect of market timing on mutual fund performance, which can act as a proxy for pension fund performance in this area. Specifically, researchers have asked whether mutual funds have successfully adjusted their portfolios in anticipation of declining or rising stock markets. The answer these researchers found was a resounding *No*, despite some reasonably sophisticated tests.

Differences between mutual funds and pension plans hamper generalizing such results, however. Pension plans may consist of many portfolios; this is analogous to collections of mutual funds, not a single mutual fund. No single fund may time the market well, but investors who own more than one fund may astutely be switching back and forth between optimal market segments. Considering individual mutual funds thus may not reveal whether the markets were being timed successfully.

One 1988 study has looked directly at pension fund timing. Berkowitz, Finney, and Logue constructed a metric—the variability of portfolio allocation over time—that was designed to capture market-timing attempts by pension plans. The idea behind the metric concept is that a pension plan would attempt to maintain a constant mix of stocks and bonds if it did not follow a market-timing strategy. Allowing the actual mix to get well above or well below the target mix suggests betting on one sector or another (i.e., tactical asset allocation). The study found that the greater the variability in asset mix, the worse the investment performance of the pension plan. Accordingly, they concluded that attempts to time the market lead to higher costs and greater risks than are rewarded.

Portfolio Turnover and Trading Costs

Many scholars feel that high turnover—that is, many purchases and sales—is one reason that pension investment performance has been so poor. Every time there is a purchase and sale of securities, the brokers executing these transactions charge commissions; in addition, there are market impact costs (the difference between the price paid or received and the equilibrium price that would prevail in the absence of a large transaction).

Although intuitively appealing, inferior performance has not been definitively tied to asset turnover by researchers. In other words, there is no hard evidence that turnover has a systematic, negative effect on investment performance. Some studies have even found a positive relationship (see, for example, the article by Lakonishok, Schleifer, and Vishny). We do, however, know that at the margin the benefits of turnover, motivated by the desire to employ the most current information available regarding the relative and absolute worth of a security, must equal or exceed its cost to be acceptable.

Agency Problems

Lakonishok, Schleifer, and Vishny suggest that the poor performance of pension funds may be attributable to principal-agent problems that arise whenever a principal (e.g., the sponsor) delegates authority to an agent (e.g., a treasurer or a money manager) to act in the principal's interest. These problems arise in part because the incentives of the two parties are not the same and in part because it is costly for principals to monitor what agents are doing.

One fertile area for agency problems is the delegation of pension authority from the sponsor to the treasurer or another officer/employee. The treasurer-agent, for example, may want to build an empire and hence may be biased against economically appealing strategies that are passive in nature. Likewise, the treasurer-agent may enjoy using the services—the prestige, the free trips, the dinners, whatever—provided by money managers, consultants, and others. The treasurer-agent may also be reluctant to take full responsibility for the pension plan, so he or she may want to have plenty of partners to blame if things go wrong.

If a treasurer-agent has decided to use external money managers, another agency problem arises: the difficulty of measuring and evaluating what these managers are doing. This problem occurs in part because the external manager has better information than does the treasurer and in part because the measurement process is costly and complex.

The money management community contributes to this problem by offering a vast array of differentiated products, products that are "story-driven" and difficult to analyze and understand. Additionally, managers have incentives to "dress-up" their portfolios at the end of standard measurement periods. They do this by selling their poor investments and, if they have had some success, by shifting to index portfolios to lock-in their relative performance. Managers who are doing poorly may increase the riskiness of their strategies (e.g., by using unauthorized derivatives to leverage the portfolio) in an attempt to obtain better performance.

One other potential agency problem should be recognized: once the pension scheme has been determined, the sponsor becomes an agent for the collective employees. Thus there is the potential for a conflict between the employee/principals and the sponsor/agent. For defined benefit plans, the higher cost of contributions to make up for poor performance seems to be incentive enough for the sponsor to pursue good investment performance. It may not be sufficient incentive, however, to encourage funding beyond what is required. For defined contribution plans, the contribution level is independent of investment performance, at least in the short run. The costs of unresolved agency problems are therefore potentially very high for plan beneficiaries. These costs may take the form of inadequate attention to selecting good managers (or mutual funds), failing to control the fees charged by managers, and offering a poor selection of investment alternatives.

At their most benign level, agency problems such as these may contribute to poor performance. They may also, however, lead to catastrophic events such as the Orange County, California, municipal investment pool bankruptcy that occurred in 1994.

Sponsor fiduciary obligations, explicit and implicit, would seem to compel senior management to address the potential for agency conflicts at all levels. The cost of not doing so—possible significant underperformance leading to higher contributions for defined benefit plans, or inadequate accumulations for defined contribution plans and the possibility of legal action—would seem to warrant more monitoring and control.

Regulatory Incentives

Does regulation affect investment performance? For example, do some investors choose stocks that are likely to appear prudent even if they may not be correctly priced according to their risk?

Del Guercio offers evidence that supports the contention that the constraints imposed by prudent investor laws bias pension funds toward investing in what courts have found to be prudent investments because of fear of litigation. (She defines *prudent stocks* as those that have high S&P safety rankings and are issued by large firms.)

It seems that some portfolio managers and pension sponsors make choices that reflect their perception of how others will react. These "others" may be regulators, the courts, or the newspapers, for example. The problem this causes is that, when imprudent stocks—stocks with poor earnings histories or high book-to-market ratios or whatever—outperform prudent stocks—stocks that have strong earnings reports, stocks that are in every pension portfolio, stocks that have recent histories that make them "look good"—pension funds are likely to underperform benchmarks that contain "imprudent" stocks.

Worse, if pension funds are avoiding imprudent stocks, they may be missing a significant source of risk-adjusted returns. Several studies have suggested that the stocks of smaller firms with high book-to-market ratios may provide superior performance because the market may have overreacted to factors such as bad news (forcing prices too low) or good news (forcing prices too high [see, for example, the 1995 book by Haugen]). If these studies are correct, regulations may be discouraging pension funds from investing in potentially attractive investments. Additionally, incentives to hold "good-looking" stocks rather than stocks that may be *good investments* could be encouraging a strategy of buying last period's winners and avoiding last period's losers that may be about to turn around. Del Guercio speculates that this effect may be more pronounced for public funds than for private funds, since public funds as a group have no safe harbor regulations that recognize the portfolio effects of securities. Of course, if pension funds are assumed to be managed by rational investors who correctly evaluate the economic consequences of the regulatory environment, their performances may not be inferior when compared with a benchmark portfolio that accounts for regulatory influences on investors.

Overall, then, the portfolio manager/pension sponsor may be able to escape serious criticism because the portfolio holds prudent—that is "good-looking"—stocks: the same stocks that other pension funds hold and that regulators consider prudent. Unfortunately, although criticism may be avoided, poor performance may be the all-too-costly result of this herd-like mentality.

Other Performance Factors

It seems reasonable to expect that other factors may also affect pension fund performance. A study by McCarthy and Turner offers some insights. Using data derived from Form 5500, they computed annual raw returns and geometric mean returns over the period (not adjusted for risk). Though little can be done with the results analytically because of missing observations, they do, however, reveal that no highly visible characteristics of the pension plans themselves—collective bargaining status, defined benefit versus defined contribution type, or activity level of management—seem to influence rates of return in any profound way.

Conclusion

Better investment performance is achievable for most pension plans. Although the specific path to improvement may differ, the following are important elements to consider:

- Start by using the performance measures described in Chapter 7 to evaluate whether or not the plan's strategic asset allocation is likely to allow the plan to meet its goals. Over the long term, the strategic asset allocation will drive the plan's performance more than any other single factor.
- As a general rule, be cautious about market timing. There is no persuasive evidence that it can be done successfully.
- Give careful attention to transaction costs. A simple rule is to avoid trades unless the benefits of the trade are thought to outweigh the costs. (Trading costs are discussed in detail in Chapter 11.)
- Give very careful attention to what we have termed *agency costs*. It is here that prudent behavior often meets its greatest

challenge. Plan policy makers must anticipate the potential for conflicts of interest between boards, senior management, and employees; between the plan and external managers; and between the plan's beneficiaries and its sponsor. Failing to monitor these relationships can be detrimental to plan performance when individuals fail to act in the best interests of the plan.

- Ask whether decisions are being made in an environment that supports sensible risk taking and the application of sound investment theory, or instead focuses on avoiding responsibility and liability. If the latter is the case, change the environment by restructuring the decision-making process to be conducive to responsible decision making. Address regulatory concerns by fully documenting the decision-making process.

Note that in discussing how to improve performance we have said nothing about allocating assets to emerging markets or leveraged private equity or other secondary asset classes. There is nothing wrong with these as investments per se. However, consider that if 5% of assets are allocated to a secondary asset class that is expected to return 2% annually (200 basis points) more than a diversified portfolio of large company stocks, the potential increase in return before the probably high management fees and trading costs of this asset class may add 0.1% (10 basis points) to the portfolio's return. How much top management attention is this worth? Alternatively, consider the impact of reallocating from a stocks/bonds mix of say 40/60 to 60/40. Using the historical perspective, we might expect stocks to return 5% annually more than bonds over several years. The potential increase in returns is 1% annually (100 basis points). This is a decision that has a real impact on performance.

Finally, a key to better performance is to run the pension plan like a business. This means that those at the top must first be able to answer the question "How are we doing, given our current asset allocation, investment strategies, and organizational structures?" Once this question has been asked, the answers will suggest numerous opportunities to improve.

Chapter **9**

Managing Pension Fund Risk

Pension funds face numerous risks. In a 1995 survey, Slunt asked pension fund sponsors to identify the financial risks about which they are concerned. Their responses are provided in Table 9-1.

We may think of these risks as collectively comprising the investment risk faced by pension funds. They paint only one part of the picture, however. Pension funds are much more than simple asset pools. Thus, pensions must be concerned with the risk caused by exposures to the factors that cause the pension fund surplus to change over time. Further, pension funds must deal with the cross-exposures that arise due to the interaction between the risks faced by the sponsor on the one hand (and thus affect the sponsor's ability to fund the plan), and those faced by the pension fund on the other (which affect the extent to which the pension plan relies on funding from the sponsor). Finally, pension funds must be concerned with inflation risk whether it arises from wages and benefits that are implicitly or explicitly indexed to changes in price levels, or manifests itself through interest rate effects.

In this chapter we outline the basics of risk management, define the major risks a pension fund faces, and discuss how these risks may be managed. The principles of hedging and return enhancement (called view implementation by some) are explained and the conditions where each are sensible are examined. Throughout the chapter, various techniques for managing the three major types of risk—investment risk of various types, surplus risk, and sponsor/plan risk—are presented.

Table 9-1.   Risks of Concern for Pension Funds

Type of Risk	% of Respondents Identifying This as a Risk
Volatility risk	67
Currency risk	40
Concentration risk	40
Prepayment risk	40
Interest Rate risk	33
Liquidity risk	33
Equity risk	33
Credit risk	33
Counter-party risk	20

Some of these techniques are prescriptive: plan wisely and avoid unintended risks with no special favorable payoffs. Other techniques require choices: generally the choice is one of how much risk one should take and how much return is sensible to expect. The chapter concludes with a discussion of how pension funds can structure a comprehensive risk management program.

The Basics of Risk Management

Risk management encompasses all financial and management strategies that are designed either to reduce a certain type of risk (*to hedge*) or to increase a return of one type or another through increasing the fund's exposure to a given risk factor (*to enhance return*, typically by implementing a view on asset prices or capital market conditions). One way to think of risk management is to view it as a continuum of points along a line that represents all possible combinations of risk and return. The decision to move from one combination to another is a risk-management decision; the process by which the change is achieved is a risk management strategy. Figure 9-1 offers a graphical representation of how risk management might be conceived within the framework of investment risk.

Notice that at the hedging end of the continuum, risk is very low, and, at least conceptually, risk may be eliminated. The return one can reasonably expect is similarly low—conceptually, the return can be no more than the risk-free rate. At the other end of the continuum, expected returns may be very high, but the risk associated with these returns also is very high. This, of course, simply describes the funda-

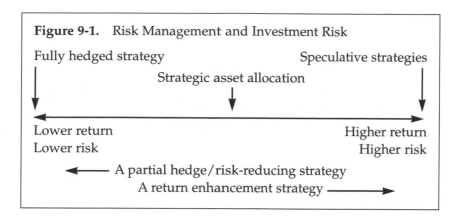

Figure 9-1.   Risk Management and Investment Risk

mental relationship between risk and return and a basic tenet of invest-ing—there are no free lunches. Every decision has consequences. Strategies that pursue higher returns almost invariably are associated with higher levels of risk and, therefore, the possibility of significant adverse outcome is greater. The reverse also is true: strategies that are designed to reduce risk also reduce expected return, perhaps by pay-ing a kind of an insurance premium or by foregoing a possibly prof-itable investment opportunity.

Thus, the true risk-management continuum itself stretches from strategies that are designed to eliminate risk of one type or another—strategies consistent with being fully hedged with respect to that risk—to strategies that involve taking on extremely high levels of risk in the pursuit of extremely high returns—strategies that might be termed *aggressive* or *speculative*. In between these two extremes are *partial hedging strategies* and *return-enhancement strategies*; these center-of-the-continuum strategies represent incremental reductions in risk or increases in return.

Note that the strategic asset allocation decision selects a specific risk/return combination—a point on the risk/return continuum—as the appropriate long-term exposure for a pension fund given its return objectives, risk tolerance, and constraints. Similarly, when market action changes a portfolio's weights, this change can be thought of as a movement from one point to another created by an external influence. Thus, a strategy such as disciplined rebalancing that is driven by a desire to maintain or implement long-term, policy-specific risk/return exposures is designed to restore the original asset allocations by mov-ing back to the original point on the risk/return continuum.

Sensible risk management begins with an understanding of the motivations that underlie the choice of a given strategy and the possible consequences of that strategy. Is a hedge being constructed because adverse outcomes are feared? Is an investment view being implemented—a view that may be right or wrong—based on the perception that an unusual opportunity for return is present? As long as pension fund fiduciaries, administrators, and managers who are hedging know that they are hedging, know why they are hedging, and are willing to incur the costs of hedging, there is nothing necessarily wrong with that hedging. Similarly, as long as those who are involved in decision making know that return-enhancement strategies must by definition be designed to implement a particular view and that there is an increased risk of adverse consequences, there is nothing wrong with any specific return-enhancement strategy per se. Not understanding the objectives of the strategy, the motivation behind it, or its possible consequences is where pension funds get into trouble.

The stakes of risk management—of choosing among the many alternative positions along the risk/return continuum—are significant. For pension funds, the low-risk solutions have a high opportunity cost—increased sponsor contributions and/or potentially large benefit shortfalls in the future. Alternatively, the high return solutions may pay off handsomely—but then again, they also may bankrupt the fund or force the sponsor to increase its contributions unexpectedly.

The Big Picture

Pension fund fiduciaries, administrators, and managers need a systematic way to think about risk and risk management. When evaluating the merits of hedging or return enhancement strategies, several kinds of questions should be asked:

General Questions
- What are the risks currently faced by the fund?
- Are these risks understood?
- Are these risks being managed and monitored correctly?

Strategic Questions
- What is the motivation of the pension fund with respect to any given strategy?
- Is the fund trying to reduce risk? Why and at what cost of opportunities foregone?

- Is the plan trying to enhance return? How and what will the impact of such enhancement activities be on the plan's overall risk?
- Are these strategies consistent with the plan's investment policy?
- How will any specific strategy affect the total risk faced by the plan?
- What is the time horizon over which the strategy will be in effect?

Management Questions

- What types of risk management strategies and tools are available?
- What are the advantages and disadvantages of each type of strategy or tool?
- How will each strategy or tool behave in a variety of market conditions?

Organizational Questions

- What expertise do the pension fund's administrators have in choosing the extent to which various risks should be hedged or exposures increased?
- How knowledgeable are the fund's money managers in the use of the available risk management strategies or tools?
- What policies exist to guide the selection and monitoring of new risk-management strategies and the managers who will implement them?

These questions must not go unasked. They must be answered carefully and as accurately as possible if the pension fund is to be successful in managing its risks.

The Risk-Risk Trade-Off

A final prefatory word is in order. It is quite possible that changing the plan's exposure to one type of risk may increase the plan's exposure to some other risk factor. Consider a pension liability fully immunized by a 100% bond portfolio. Surplus risk is virtually zero. However, what about inflation exposure? Is this risk greater than it would be if the portfolio had a significant exposure to stocks? Or consider an investment strategy that focuses on low investment risk by maintaining a very conservative asset allocation structured to keep return volatility low. Does this affect the risk the sponsor bears in providing future contributions?

Defining Risk

The way to start managing risk is by analyzing the risks faced by the fund. To do this, we need to develop some definitions of various types of risk. After these risks have been explained, we can explore the basic parameters of risk management for each type of risk.

Investment Risk

Investment risk has to do with how a given market, sector, asset, or investment strategy will perform over time. Investment risk is typically defined in terms of volatility of asset values and/or volatility of returns. Stocks, for example, have a higher investment risk than bonds in that the returns on stocks are more widely dispersed around their likely outcome. The value of stocks at any given point in time has also historically been less certain than the value of bonds.

For a defined benefit pension fund, investment risk is important but, as a risk-management concept, it can be misleading. It does not fully capture the interaction of plan assets with liabilities, nor does it directly address the risk-bearing capacity of the plan as constrained by the riskiness of the sponsor. For a defined contribution plan, however, the concept of investment risk is normally sufficient as a risk-management paradigm from the employees' perspective.

Surplus Risk

As a financial organization, the financial health of a defined benefit pension fund is sensitive to the interaction between the fund's assets and its liabilities—if liabilities increase faster than assets, the surplus (or deficit) will get smaller (or larger). The risk of changes in the surplus caused by disproportionate changes in the relative values of assets and liabilities is termed *surplus risk*. It is influenced by two factors—the relative interest-rate sensitivities of the assets and liabilities and the market risk of the assets. Consider, for example, that in spite of the strong financial performance of the U.S. equity and bond markets in 1995, pension surpluses actually decreased for many U.S. pension funds because liabilities rose more than asset values rose due to the decrease in interest rates; in 1994, however, a poor year for U.S. investments, many pension funds saw their surpluses increase due to the decrease in liabilities brought about by rising interest rates (see the article by Lowenstein).

Managing surplus volatility and the projected surplus pose a significant challenge to decision makers. Pensions with large surpluses can afford to take more risk in pursuit of higher returns (and thus they can pursue a higher assurance of benefits and/or lower sponsor contributions). Paradoxically, plans with deficits may find risky, high-return strategies appealing for their promise in reducing their deficits; however, these plans may not be able to bear the risk of short-term adverse consequences that could make their deficits worse. This possibility can be especially unappealing when the sponsor is facing financial difficulty and may not be able to make up any shortfalls.

Sponsor/Plan Joint Risk

Pension plans have a sizable stake in the fortunes of their sponsors. The sponsor is instrumental in determining the payouts to future beneficiaries and in other plan features that have a financial effect on the health of the plan. Additionally, the sponsor contributes to the pension asset pool. The performance of the investment pool in turn affects the need for contributions. The risk to which such interaction exposes a pension plan is *sponsor/plan joint risk*.

The correlation between the cash flows of the sponsor and the asset pool of the pension plan matters. Consider, for example, a pension asset pool that is sensitive to the same economic factors that affect the sponsor's profitability. When these factors result in good investment performance for the plan, the sponsor need not make large contributions, although it can. However, when the plan *needs* the sponsor to increase contributions to offset poor investment performance, the sponsor is also beset by poor performance and may be unable to deliver.

Interest Rate Risk

From our discussion of surplus risk, it is apparent that changes in interest rates affect the adequacy of a plan's funding. Interest rates also pose two very different forms of investment risk. One form of *interest rate risk* is the volatility in price associated solely with changes in interest rates. For example, when interest rates go up, the prices of assets such as "plain vanilla" bonds go down. The second form of interest rate risk is *reinvestment risk*. Consider an asset that provides, as part of its total return, a series of cash payments. If these cash flows must be reinvested as they are received, the return earned on the reinvested cash flows contributes to the overall return realized from the asset. When interest rates rise, the cash flows that this asset provides can be reinvested at a higher return, thus offsetting a portion of the decline in the asset's price.

Interest rate risk is a function of maturity (the longer the maturity, the greater the sensitivity to interest rates); cash flows (the lower the cash flows, the greater the sensitivity to interest rates); and the current level of interest rates (the higher the overall level of interest rates, the less sensitive assets are to changes in interest rates). Since these factors vary from one fixed-income investment to another and from one liability structure to another, it is helpful to aggregate them into a single measure. *Duration*, the weighted average of the time to each cash flow (using current interest rates), is a commonly used measure of overall interest rate sensitivity. We can use duration to estimate the sensitivity of a pension's asset pool to interest rate changes and to estimate the relative sensitivity of plan assets and liabilities to interest rates.

Duration, as useful as it is, is incomplete as a measure of interest-rate risk because it ignores the rate of change in price sensitivity to interest rates as interest rates change. The rate of change in price sensitivity is called *convexity*. Adjusting for convexity, a somewhat complex task, corrects for the tendency for the price change estimated by duration to be different from the actual price change as interest rates change. For small changes in interest rates, this is not a problem. For large changes it is.

Convexity can be positive (as for an option-free bond) or negative (as for most mortgage backed securities subject to prepayment risk). In terms of measuring interest rate risk, it is important because it improves our understanding of interest rate effects on assets and liabilities (and hence on pension surplus). With convexity, we form a much more robust description of how the pension fund's financial health will be affected by changes in interest rates.

Currency Risk

International investing is increasingly popular among pension funds. However, if an investor is holding securities denominated in a foreign currency, changes in the value of that currency relative to the investor's domestic currency will affect the domestic return on the investment. This is called *currency risk*.

Currency risk is first of all a function of the allocation made to assets denominated in non-U.S. currencies, although this may overstate the risk if a sponsor has employees in numerous countries. Once the initial allocation is established, currency values relative to U.S. currency may fluctuate due to interest rate and inflation differentials, economic growth and productivity, monetary policy, and the market for foreign exchange (see the article by Solnik, Boucrelle, and Le Fur for a good discussion of currency risk factors). Inflation effects on exchange rates are reasonably well documented for long periods of time, but the other factors affecting long-term rates and the causes of short-term changes in exchange rates have not been explained very well. There is much we do not know. We do know that currency exchange rates change frequently and sometimes dramatically, and we do know that these changes affect—by increasing or decreasing—realized returns on pension assets. Thus, pension investments and liabilities in other currencies pose both opportunities and problems for pension funds.

Concentration Risk

Concentration risk arises from excessive exposures to any one asset, sector, asset class, or macroeconomic factor (e.g., interest rates). The tenets of modern investment theory ordinarily would suggest that this should not be an issue—that proper attention to diversification should eliminate any such exposure. However, for pension funds this may not always be the case. Possible problems may arise from:

1. Excessive exposure to the sponsor through over-reliance on contributions from the sponsor rather than investment performance (i.e., returns generated from the plan's investments);

2. Excessive exposure to the sponsor through an Employee Stock Ownership Plan (ESOP) or a sponsor-directed defined contribution plan that invests in the sponsor's stock or in assets used by the sponsor to conduct business; and,

3. Excessive exposure to the local economy through economically targeted investments.

Concentration risk may also arise when no one is monitoring the effective asset mix of the total portfolio, or when unintended exposures to economic factors (e.g., interest rates) occur because sophisticated or complex investment vehicles or strategies are not understood well.

Inflation Risk

Inflation poses two major problems for defined benefit pension funds. One is the unanticipated changes that may occur in nominal interest rates due to changes in expectations for inflation. If, for example, the financial market changes its collective assessment of future inflation by increasing the inflation premium agreed to among buyers and sellers of financial assets, nominal interest rates will increase and the values of most financial assets (and some real assets) and pension liabilities will decline. This effect is simply the same interest rate effect discussed in the surplus risk and interest rate risk sections. There is more to *inflation risk*, however. As wages rise in response to inflation, the size of pension liabilities that are based on end-of-career wages increase, all else the same, even if pension benefits are fixed upon retirement. This in turn creates pressure for higher contributions or better investment performance or both.

For defined contribution plans, the impact of inflation is primarily felt through the potential erosion of purchasing power exerted on the beneficiary's asset pool. As is the case for defined benefit plans, this suggests that either higher contributions or stronger investment performance may be necessary to offset the effects of inflation.

Strategies for Managing Risk

Managing risk successfully depends in part on what risk is being managed and in part on the strategies and tools that are available. Strategic decisions, of course, require a goal or objective—are we trying to reduce risk or enhance return?—toward which to work. This section describes the basic strategies of managing risk exposures by category. A common theme throughout is that it is better to anticipate risks and select appropriate exposures than to react to unanticipated events.

Investment Risk

The foundation of managing investment risk is to have clear, unambiguous policy guidelines that require diversification across and within asset classes. Further, these guidelines should quantify an acceptable level of exposure to market risk (risk that cannot be diversified away). Establishing what precisely is an acceptable level of market risk for a particular plan requires extensive analysis. The level will be unique to each plan and will depend on the numerous factors that affect the plan's tolerance for risk. Ultimately it will be operationalized through the plan's asset allocation and such fundamental policy parameters as whether plan assets should be actively or passively managed.

Diversification, however, is easy to accomplish, and it is inexpensive—if there is a free lunch, this is it. With good policy and a commitment to diversification, the management of investment risk becomes a matter of occasional hedging if the value of the plan's assets needs to be temporarily protected, or occasional return enhancement if the plan is willing to take on the additional risk.

Surplus Risk

Managing surplus risk begins on the asset side (assuming that plan liabilities are more or less fixed for any reasonable planning horizon) and involves a careful analysis of relative interest rate sensitivities. Generally, surplus risk can be minimized by holding a portfolio of long-duration bonds. This probably is not desirable; however, if the plan has any exposure whatsoever to inflation through a wage-based benefit formula or through benefits that adjust to inflation. Nor is it desirable to hold a portfolio of long-duration bonds if the sponsor believes that higher investment returns are appropriate because those higher returns reduce the present value of long-term contributions.

Managing surplus risk is also a function of the size of the surplus itself. Leibowitz, Kogleman, and Bader suggest that plans with large surpluses (i.e., with healthy funding ratios) are able to take a fair amount of risk, at least in the short run, and therefore such plans should invest heavily in equities and other assets with high levels of investment risk. For these plans, the duration of plan assets relative to liabilities is not especially important. As a plan's funding ratio declines, however—that is, as its surplus erodes and perhaps changes to a deficit—it becomes less tolerant of exposure to any factor that may erode the surplus further. Thus, the asset allocation strategy for plans at this stage should focus more on duration matching and possibly lower exposures to equities. This suggests that floor-based strategies, such as contingent immunization—actively pursuing high total returns as long as the surplus is high and shifting into a progressively more immunized portfolio if the surplus decreases—and portfolio insurance (see Chapter 8), are appropriate for pension funds that are not concerned with surplus volatility when a substantial surplus exists but that become more risk averse as the surplus erodes.

Another way of thinking about managing surplus risk is to redefine the efficient frontier of acceptable portfolios by replacing the risk-free asset with a portfolio consisting of 100% bonds that immunizes the pension liability (see the 1990 chapter by Haugen). Other higher-risk (in terms of surplus risk), higher-return portfolios of varying amounts of stocks and bonds can then be evaluated against this risk-free portfolio in terms of the incremental risks and returns offered by each. A simulation Haugen performed suggests that this set of portfolios is conceptually superior to the traditional investment risk and return efficient frontier in that it will provide portfolios that are more efficient in terms of the surplus risk/return trade-off.

Some funds have gained a measure of comfort by performing a scenario analysis that allows the sponsor/investor to ask whether there is, say, a 90% or 95% probability that its plan will still be fully funded *x* years from now. This type of analysis can be helpful in examining the interactions of interest rates, asset allocation, liability structures (especially at the time when the sponsor is considering changes to the benefit scheme), and funding. Scenario analysis is also consistent with value-at-risk (VAR) analysis and stress tests (discussed later in this chapter) and with the analytical approach to strategic asset allocation (provided in Chapter 6). Larger pension funds will find it worthwhile to construct comprehensive and integrated analytical systems to help examine these issues.

In conclusion, the focus for managing surplus risk should not be to minimize it; rather the focus should be to receive adequate return for the risk to which the plan is exposed. Since the volatility of the surplus is important, exposure to this risk should be compensated. The traditional set of investment risk–efficient portfolios does not adequately address the interaction of plan assets and liabilities. Thus, pension plan decision makers should think in terms of portfolio risk defined in terms of surplus volatility as well as investment risk. Further, decision makers must explicitly consider the link between the plan's funding status and the financial strength of the sponsor; sponsors that are financially healthy are capable of smoothing the effects of high surplus volatility if need be by increased funding; financially troubled sponsors can offer no such support.

Sponsor/Plan Joint Risk

Managing the joint risks faced by the sponsor and the pension plan is closely tied to managing surplus risk. When a plan has a large economic surplus, the joint risk is likely to be unimportant. For plans with small surpluses or sizable deficits, however, the joint risk can become very important.

Because the sponsor's ability to fund is a function of the magnitude, timing, and variability of the sponsor's cash flows, it is the correlation of these cash flows with those of the pension plan's asset pool that must be managed. One sensible step is limiting or eliminating investments that are highly correlated with the sponsor's financial strength (e.g., pension funds that are already exposed to the automobile industry because the sponsor manufactures automobiles should not invest pension fund assets in automobile company securities).

Another step is gaining exposure to sectors with low correlations with the sponsor's cash flows (possibly by investing in non-U.S. securities). Direct investment in the sponsor generally is not a good idea. For private plans this discourages holding any of the firm's stock, even in an ESOP. For public plans, this discourages economically targeted investments (ETIs) if the ETI's returns are highly correlated with the sponsor's cash flows.

Interest Rate Risk

Interest rate risk is an element of both investment and surplus risk. As such, it may initially be addressed by choosing an appropriate level of exposure to interest rates. This requires evaluating the overall sensitivity of a portfolio of assets or liabilities to interest rate changes. Managing interest rate risk is similar to the process of choosing an acceptable level of market risk.

A simple approach to managing interest rate risk is the cash-flow matching strategy presented in Chapter 5. The appeal of this strategy is that the matching of cash flows significantly reduces the risk of having to liquidate assets at possibly disadvantageous times solely to meet benefit payments. A somewhat more comprehensive approach is to immunize the pension liability (partially or completely) by managing the duration of the assets relative to the duration of the plan's liabilities. As explained in the section on managing surplus risk, full immunization (i.e., no surplus volatility) probably is not an acceptable goal. It is, however, situational. Traditional approaches to calculating duration (such as assuming a flat yield curve) make duration only an approximation of actual sensitivity to interest rates. This is fairly simple to correct. Not as simple are the matters of convexity and nonparallel shifts in the yield curve. However, these more complex factors can be managed with some fairly sophisticated mathematical techniques.

Currency Risk

Currency risk can be partially diversified away by holding investments denominated in numerous currencies; since currencies are not perfectly correlated, decreases in the value of one currency relative to the pension fund's domestic currency may be offset by increases in the value of another currency. Additionally, the pension funds of multinational firms domiciled in the United States may be able to reduce significantly currency exposures brought about by benefits denominated in currencies other than the U.S. dollar simply by holding securities denominated in those same currencies.

Overall, it is not obvious that hedging currency risk is desirable (see the article by Solnik, Boucrelle, and Le Fur). Some authorities argue that currency is simply a source of risk and should be hedged; others, however, assert that currency is an asset class offering returns as well as risk. Some proponents of unhedged currency exposures argue that foreign currency offers pensions an opportunity to hedge domestic inflation and domestic monetary policy over which they otherwise have no control. Froot suggests that the need to hedge currency may be related to the investment horizon of the investor. In the short run, mean reversion is likely to reduce the need to hedge. In the long run, purchasing-power parity seems to hold and is more suggestive of the inflation/monetary policy hedging attributes of currency.

As Siegel observes, the near-term attractiveness of hedging depends on whether U.S. interest rates are higher than or lower than foreign rates. Currency hedges are equivalent to borrowing the currency to hedge (the non-U.S. currency) and buying or investing in the domestic (U.S.) currency. Thus, if U.S. interest rates are high relative to the currency hedged, the hedge will increase the dollar-denominated return on the portfolio as the borrowed foreign currency falls in value relative to the long position in U.S. dollars.

In general, currency risk is relatively high for foreign cash and bonds, but much lower for foreign stocks. Thus, given the long-term nature of investing in stocks and the ability of stocks to compensate investors for local price increases over long time periods, if hedging is desired, more attention should be given to non-U.S. cash and bond positions than to non-U.S. stock positions.

Concentration Risk

If all parties are committed to the rights of the plan participants to a reasonably secure retirement and are aware of the adverse consequences of concentration—the excessive investment risk for which the capital markets will not provide any offsetting return and the risk of liquidity problems—this problem should not arise. If it does, administrators and managers must recognize the potential breach of fiduciary duty implied.

However, with the vast array of complex financial products available today—and with our better understanding of the component or factor exposures that even simple investments such as callable bonds have—concentration risk may be incurred unintentionally. Thus, a fundamental part of managing concentration risk is to understand the investments being made, fully and completely, and to understand their role in the overall portfolio. The most powerful risk management tools that exist for managing concentration risk are (1) policy statements that set reasonable guidelines and position limits on exposures to asset classes and factor risks, and (2) a monitoring or feedback system that immediately informs senior management and others if these guidelines are being violated.

Inflation Risk

The inflation risk that manifests itself through increases or decreases in interest rates can be addressed as described in the preceding sections on surplus and interest rate risk. What about the impact of inflation on wage-based benefits? Note that some defined contribution plans are partially indexed to inflation through a contribution scheme that is a percentage of wages. As wages rise, so do the dollar amounts of the contributions. For defined benefit plans, unanticipated inflation can be offset by higher contributions, better investment performance or a combination of the two (assuming lower real benefits are not acceptable). Further, inflation risk can be managed somewhat directly by paying attention to the inflationary affects of compensation and retirement benefit schemes. Some sponsors may mistakenly believe wage increases disguised as higher pension benefits have little impact on pension plan financial health. The reality is that, with even modest wage inflation over 20 or 30 years, such schemes can dramatically impact funding ratios by increasing the size of the liability without providing more assets as an offset. The right way to think about this form of inflation risk is to directly incorporate it into the analysis of compensation and retirement planning by considering the impact on the pension liability and hence the implications for future funding and investment performance requirements.

Defined benefit plans have a built-in partial inflation offset in that inflation-induced changes in interest rates affect both assets and liabilities (although not necessarily equally). Individuals, however, do not have liabilities as such. Thus, defined contribution plans have no built-in protection. If inflation harms an individual's retirement asset pool, either by reducing the nominal value of the asset pool or by reducing purchasing power of the retirement income the assets will some day produce, the individual may have to accept a lower standard of living in retirement or make other similar adjustments.

Over long periods, both defined benefit and defined contribution asset pools can attempt to offset inflation by having relatively large exposures to common stocks. Historically, the risk premium earned on stocks has more than offset actual inflation, providing real returns of 6 to 9% annually. However, stocks are also risky, so there is a trade-off between the investment risk of stocks and the risk that inflation will inhibit real growth in asset values.

Nonfinancial Risks

There are more risks to consider than solely financial ones. Pension funds are exposed to the risks that come from not understanding investment technology and theory—those black boxes, the derivative contracts and securities and the investment strategies that the money management and banking professions may bring forth. For lack of a better term, this may be thought of as *ignorance risk*—the risk that comes from lack of knowledge. Other examples of ignorance-driven risks include the naive perception that increased exposure to international investments increases risk (a common mistake if one reads the financial press), or thinking that hedging is costless and fail-safe, or believing that the recently top performing investment strategies are riskless. Ignorance risk is best managed through trustee, administrator, manager, and staff education. The costs of not managing this risk can be high—witness the catastrophic events in Orange County, California, and elsewhere.

Most pension fund staff are well aware of what might be called *political risk*. This risk arises from the agency/principal problems and conflicts of interest that arise in any complex organization. Political risk takes many forms. It can come through pressure to undertake economically targeted investments. It may come in the form of "off balance sheet" pay raises for public employees that increase the burden on plan assets, or it may come in the form of "gaming" the accounting numbers. It may come as undue influence in the manager selection process, possibly to repay campaign contributors, or it may come in the form of not being permitted to participate in corporate governance activities that are likely to increase share values. It may come in the form of unwarranted investment restrictions (such as legal lists of stocks in which the plan is allowed to invest) with unintended consequences. It may come in the form of excessive pressure to increase investment returns in order to reduce the sponsor's contributions. It may arise when managers do not do what they promised to do and someone must be held accountable. There is no easy way to manage political risk. Education is part of the answer; some of the politics may be well intended but naive. Accountability and wide dissemination of information may be helpful; some political pressures will not stand up well to public inspection. Careful monitoring and occasionally legal remedies may be necessary to protect the rights of beneficiaries from being abused.

Hedging and Return Enhancement

Risk management strategies are intended either to hedge a given risk or to enhance returns by taking an exposure to a given return-generating factor. Hedging has the side effect of reducing expected returns that may accompany the risk being hedged. Return enhancement has the side effect of increasing the exposure taken to the risk of the return factor being pursued.

Hedging is a strategy designed to reduce or eliminate the risk of future fluctuations of an asset or portfolio's value, or of an exchange rate, or of the asset-liability surplus, or, at least conceptually, of any other risk. A basic hedge might attempt to eliminate the price volatility of an asset (or a portfolio) by taking a position in another asset—the hedge asset—that offsets any change in value the asset that is hedged experiences. For example, in a well-designed price hedge, if the price of the hedged asset declines, the asset used to hedge should increase in value by a like amount.

Why hedge? The answer may be found in determining whether hedging will make the pension fund, the sponsor, or the employees for which the pension exists better off. In general, pensions may not want to hedge the majority of their risks. Hedging sounds very attractive to risk-averse pension trustees, administrators, managers, and employees. However, the very best return a fully hedged position may earn is the risk-free rate. If the hedge is not costless—and it is not—the return to the hedged position is likely to be less than what could be obtained by simply investing in risk-free securities. So hedging may increase the sponsor's funding costs, and it may reduce the future financial health of the plan because of the low returns it provides.

Why, then, is hedging done? There are several wrong reasons. Managers and investment officers may hedge to avoid being penalized for taking certain types of risk—risk that a prudent investor should take! These penalties may take the form of loss of job, loss of bonus, public pressure, or the like. Administrators may encourage hedging because they fear legal liability. Employees may encourage hedging because they sleep better at night—not realizing that the low investment returns characteristic of hedging may adversely affect their future retirement benefits.

There are economically sound reasons to hedge, in part or in full. Pension funds require liquidity to meet current benefit obligations. Thus, a liquidity hedge that locks in the value of securities to be sold to meet near-term payments to beneficiaries may be occasionally appropriate. There are risks that should not be carried because they do not offer a reasonable amount of offsetting return. For example, concentrated investments in illiquid assets may have adverse funding, plan liquidity, and other consequences if there is unexpected market action. Thus, a hedge-like strategy designed to reduce the exposure to these assets may be appropriate. There may be a special circumstance that, for a brief period of time, makes hedging sensible. Consider for example a defined benefit plan converting to a defined contribution plan. A short-term hedge may protect the value of plan assets from the consequences of adverse short-term market action. Finally, some hedging activity may be justifiable to reduce the volatility of the combined cash flows of the sponsor and the pension fund. For example, the pension fund may wish to hedge a specific risk, such as currency risk, to ensure that the sponsor does not have to forego profitable investment opportunities simply because the plan was affected by adverse currency movements.

Note that investment risk, surplus volatility, and interest rate risk normally should be addressed through the strategic asset allocation decision. From time to time it may be tempting to "hedge" these risks because the market appears to be overpriced or interest rates appear to be ready to spike up or whatever. The problem with this form of hedging is that it begins to cross the line into active view-based strategies that are predicated on unusual capital market expectations. Thus, the hedge is really an active decision to time a market or segment.

Return enhancement or view-based strategies cover numerous strategies that, although they may appear to be different, all share the common feature of being designed to pursue higher return. With this comes higher risk. If pension funds choose to pursue higher returns through greater exposure to risk, they should recognize that higher expected returns are an "on-average-over-long-periods-of-time" concept. Risky bets that go bad early are often so costly that the gambler loses his stake and is unable to continue playing the game in order to achieve these on-average higher returns. For a pension fund, this could mean that an existing surplus may be eroded to an unacceptable level or the sponsor must increase its contributions to meet ERISA or contractual obligations or otherwise ensure the financial viability of the plan.

Are return enhancement strategies appropriate for pensions? Only if the fund's decision-makers believe the financial markets are at least partially inefficient. The caveat is to recognize the incremental risk that comes with the strategy chosen and to avoid any illusion of something for nothing. As an example of an appropriate use of return enhancement, consider a pension fund that has a belief that stocks are underpriced relative to their historical norms. If the pension fund is well funded, has a financially strong sponsor, and has policy-level authority to pursue active management, a return enhancement strategy may be a reasonable risk to take. If the fund's belief is correct, the subsequent higher-than-normal returns will increase the fund's surplus, increase the security of benefits, and reduce the sponsor's need to contribute.

Implicit in both hedging and return enhancement strategies is a sense that these are temporary or occasional strategies. If a pension fund were to hedge its investment risk fully and permanently, it would be simpler and more economically productive to buy Treasury securities. Similarly, a continual program of return enhancement strategies suggests that the fund should rethink its strategic asset allocation. Perhaps the plan should bear more long-term investment risk in pursuit of higher long-term return.

Assessing Risk Exposures

For risk management to work, risk exposures must be identified, quantified, and, if necessary, modified (see the article by Gastineau). The nature of risk and its complexity makes this a challenging task. The assessment tools available are audits, value at risk, and stress testing.

Risk Audits

One approach to assessing risk exposure is to undertake a periodic risk audit. This should, among other things, focus on the strengths of the internal control system and on the compliance of managers with investment policy and guidelines. The audit also should periodically evaluate the risk exposures of the fund on a systematic and comprehensive basis.

The audit must assess recent and prospective surplus volatility and assess the likely impact of various scenarios on funding and contribution patterns. The audit should assess the sponsor's financial strength as it relates to funding plan shortfalls. Specific attention should be given to concentrations of exposures that may be unreasonable and to identifying those that are unintended. Further, compensation and reward structures should be reviewed to see if they are adjusting for capital at risk correctly (see the article by Nederlof). Throughout, the emphasis should be on net exposures—assets should not be judged in isolation; portfolios should not be judged without reference to the overall asset pool, to plan liabilities, and to the sponsor. The results of the audit should be conveyed to senior management and the Board of Directors/Trustees.

Value at Risk

Another approach to assessing risk exposure is periodically to measure the fund's value at risk (VAR). This is commonly accomplished by asking the following questions: at a given level of statistical confidence, how large would the loss be if the financial markets repeat their worst performance from some previous historical period of time? How would this adverse performance affect the ability of the sponsor to pay current retirement beneficiaries? How would this performance affect the funding status of the plan? How would this performance affect the contributions the sponsor might have to make?

Value at risk may be calculated numerous ways and for various time periods. In 1996 Smithson described three methods: using historical data, using a Monte Carlo simulation, and using a variance/covariance analytic method that decomposes financial instruments into component cash equivalent positions. Each method has adherents and each has its own set of advantages and disadvantages. For example, the historical method is easy to program, but does not permit sensitivity analysis. The simulation method is hard to program but does permit sensitivity analysis. The analytic approach requires application of a fairly difficult "mapping" process but requires no pricing models to be applied.

Beder has shown that the outcomes of VAR analysis are sensitive to numerous factors. The most important of these factors is the length of the time horizon chosen (e.g., a one-day loss or a one-week loss?) and the data set selected (e.g., does it use intraday or end-of-day values, and are outlying events indicators of structural change?). Additionally, if the analyst is asking "how much might I lose 99% of the time?" the corollary question, "how much might I lose the other 1% of the time?" goes unanswered.

Value at risk measurement is a promising methodology for quantifying the totality of the risks an investor faces on a net basis. Its strength is that it aggregates virtually all factor risks—in option parlance, the *delta* (price), *gamma* (rate of change in price), *vega* (volatility), *theta* (time), and *rho* (interest rates) factors—as well as the correlations among factors. For pension funds to use VAR, however, the focus must be extended to how these factors affect both plan assets and plan liabilities; that is, the VAR query must be "with a confidence level of 99%, how much might the fund's *surplus* decrease in one day (or whatever)?"

An Example of VAR for a Pension Fund that Manages Surplus

Consider a pension fund asset pool that consists of a single bond. Table 9-2 uses historical data to illustrate the asset-based VAR analysis. From Table 9-2, the analyst could conclude that we are 99% confident the one-day loss on the pension portfolio will not be worse than a 2.1% loss.

Table 9-2. VAR Analysis for a Pension Asset Pool (Using the Past 100 Days of Asset Values)

Day	Percent Change in Asset Pool Value	Change in Asset Pool Value Sorted from Largest Decline to Largest Increase	
		Rank	Percent Change
-101	1.1	100	-3.2
-100	-0.2	99	-2.1 (99% confidence level)
-99	0.3	98	-0.5
-2	-0.5	2	2.3
-1	0.4	1	3.1

Table 9-3. VAR Analysis for a Pension Fund Surplus (Assets less Liabilities) (Using the Most Recent 100 Days of Asset Pool and Liability Values to Compute the Daily Change in Surplus Assuming No Funding)

Day	Asset Value	Liability Value	Surplus	Percent Change in Surplus	Change in Surplus Value (from largest decline to largest increase)	
					Rank	Percent Change
-102	$1,000	1,200	-200			
-101	1,011	1,205	-194	3	100	-2.8
-100	1,008.98	1,202	-193	0.5	99	-2.77 (99% confidence level)
-2	990	1,170	-180	-0.7	2	3.00
-1	993.96	1,175	-181.04	-0.58	1	3.32

Now, consider the same information in light of the surplus of assets over liabilities (Table 9-3). The analyst would now view VAR as "the worst change in surplus that will be experienced in a single day is a decrease of 2.77% with 99% confidence that it will not be worse."

In viewing the above examples, remember that daily changes may not be the relevant time frame. More often than not, longer time periods will be of more use to pension fund investors unless there are unusually large concentrated exposures that must be analyzed. In normal circumstances, VAR may be of more use in assessing weekly outcomes (requiring 100 weeks of data) or even quarterly. Additionally, when using historical data (as opposed to data provided by simulations or statistical analysis), it is important to recognize that the past does not predict the future.

Stress Testing

The third approach to assessing risk exposure is to conduct stress tests (see the article by Nederlof). This approach is similar to VAR, but rather than choosing a statistical confidence level, the focus of stress testing is on the consequences that a catastrophic event might cause. Stress testing assumes that the worst possible scenario occurs and then, even though it is an event with an admittedly low probability, asks how a portfolio—or a surplus—would be affected. Stress testing can be based on a single event (e.g., the peso crisis or a 200 basis point shift in yields), or multiple events (e.g., a non-parallel yield curve shift coupled with a stock market crash). Stress testing lends itself to simulation and thus offers the analyst the ability to observe numerous, albeit improbable, outcomes as the impacts of isolated events or combinations of different events are evaluated.

As with VAR, stress testing makes most sense when it jointly considers assets and liabilities and when it incorporates the impact of a stress event on the plan sponsor. Like any model, stress tests will be as good as the analyst's ability to select appropriate events and assess their consequences.

Conclusion

Risk management is an important part of pension fund management. The multitude of risks faced by pension funds; the dynamic nature of the financial markets; and the complex nature of pension fund interactions with sponsors, beneficiaries, and regulators make risk management seem daunting. Nonetheless, risk must be managed, and the activities that comprise risk management must be woven into the fabric of the pension's overall management paradigm.

A comprehensive risk management system will identify, measure, monitor, and control the risk factors to which the pension is exposed. Measurement approaches begin with the risk-adjusted performance measures discussed in Chapter 7. Beyond this, VAR and stress testing should be used to help decision makers understand the net downside exposure that exists. Audit procedures designed to review the pension fund's exposures periodically and identify significant or unintended changes in the fund's risk profile should become a part of the fund's information system.

The findings of all the measurements and assessments should be communicated to senior management and trustees and the Board of Directors on a timely basis with conformance to and appropriateness of policy foremost in the analysis.

Much of risk management is simply good investment or management practice. Diversify, consider the consequences before acting, and limit exposures through written policy. Make certain the fiduciaries, the administrators, and the managers know what they need to know to make sensible decisions and to evaluate the information provided. This, of course, implies—strongly—education about what the risks are, how they interact, how they can be managed and what the costs of the alternatives are.

Finally, carefully evaluate all policies and strategies with respect to their motivations and goals. Understanding when and what to hedge and when and what not to hedge, is important before you do decide to hedge. With hindsight, it is easy to see what should have been hedged, but of course this is of little help. Understanding the downside of a view implementation/return enhancement strategy before you undertake it is important. Making certain before acting on a decision that the decision is theoretically sound, that it is economically rational, that it has a realistic chance of working—these guidelines will take most investors far in managing their exposures. But do not forget: risk generates return. Without risk, there will be no return. Manage risk, but do not think you can or should eliminate it.

Chapter **10**

Risk Management Strategies Using Derivative Securities

Derivative securities, such as options and futures, have become immensely popular in recent years as tools for implementing risk management strategies. At the same time as this increase in popularity, widely publicized disasters have given many managers and analysts reason to pause and ask whether derivatives are prudent and to what extent they should be used—if at all. Derivatives are complex and often are not well understood by those who use them. Nonetheless, derivatives are here to stay and, in fact, are quite useful for controlling a variety of risks and lowering trading costs.

Here we describe the primary types of derivatives used by pension funds to manage risk. A review of some survey results introduces the material and provides a sense of what derivatives are being used and for what purposes. Following we discuss the advantages and disadvantages of using derivatives to carry out various risk management strategies, and then an examination of some hedging and return enhancement strategies that use derivatives. The chapter concludes with an explanation of how plan sponsors, administrators, trustees, managers, and other decision makers can decide when to use derivatives, how to choose from among the many alternatives available, and how to control their use.

The Use of Derivatives by Institutional Investors

In 1995, several surveys were released concerning the use of derivatives by institutional investors. The surveys, as compiled by Smithson and Jara, and some of their findings are presented in Table 10-1.

There are numerous derivative products available, both exchange listed and over the counter (OTC). The most popular derivatives according to the surveys (they all differ somewhat in their rankings) were foreign exchange forward contracts (used by 43–61% of respondents), exchange-traded equity options and futures (used by 41–56%), and exchange-traded interest rate options and futures (used by 26–53%). Table 10-2 presents these results.

Each survey queried different populations. Nonetheless, it is clear that derivatives *are* being used—by many investors for many different purposes. Simply knowing that other investors use derivatives, however, should not be sufficient reason to use, or to authorize the use of, derivatives. There is much more one should know to make informed and prudent choices in this area.

Basic Types of Derivatives

Derivatives derive their value from an underlying asset such as a stock, a bond, a commodity, an index (such as the S&P 500 Stock Index), an interest rate, or a formula (such as 8% − LIBOR). In the following discussion, we use the term the *underlying* to represent the asset, index, interest rate, or formula from which a derivative contract derives its value. We refer to what is known as the *payoff structure* of a derivative contract when discussing the possible values a contract can take, given a change in the value of the underlying. That is, the payoff structure represents the range of values a particular contract can take over a range of values taken by the underlying.

Derivatives come in many forms, but they may be categorized as either contracts—options (puts and calls), futures and forward contracts, and swaps—or securities such as collateralized mortgage obligations (securities issued on pools of mortgages), strips (coupon-only or principal-only securities constructed by "stripping" Treasury bonds), and inverse floaters (bonds structured to pay coupons that float inversely with changes in interest rates). Although all derivatives derive their value from changes in the value of their respective underlying, the payoff structures of different contracts on the same underlying can be considerably different. Collectively, these contracts offer a

Table 10-1. The Use of Derivatives by Institutional Investors

Institution	Samples	Date of Survey	Percentage of Respondents That Use Derivatives	Reason for Using Derivatives		
				Risk Management	Asset Allocation	Yield Enhancement
NYU Stern School of Business	Pension and endowment funds with assets ranging from $2.3 to $3 billion	Spring 1995	67	70%	60%	20%
Record Treasury Management	U.S. pension fund managers	1994–1995	92	31%	30%	28%
Institutional Investor	Quarterly surveys of corporate and public pension plan sponsors	1995	52	35%	35%[1]	33%[2]
Ernst & Young	143 investment management complexes with combined assets of more than $535 billion	1995	31			
Watson Wyatt	44 pension funds in 10 European countries with combined assets of more than $300 billion	Spring 1995	>54	54%	25%	

[1]35% reported that they use derivatives to lower transaction costs; 18% reported that they use derivatives for tactical asset allocation.
[2]33% reported that they use derivatives for "both hedging and enhancing returns"; 29% reported that they use derivatives for "enhancing returns" only.
Source: Data from Charles Smithson. *Managing Financial Risk 1996 Yearbook.* New York: CIBC Wood Gundy, 1996.

Table 10-2. Derivative Instruments Used by Institutional Investors

	Institutional Investor	Ernst & Young	Watson Wyatt
Foreign exchange forwards	43%	61%	44%
Exchange-traded futures/options on equities	52%	56%	>41%
OTC forwards/options on equities	16%		
Exchange-traded futures/options on interest rate products	26%	53%	>27%
OTC forwards/options on interest rate products	10%	36%	
Exchange traded futures/options on foreign exchange	19%	30%	>44%
OTC forwards/options on foreign exchange	34%		
Options on futures	43%		
Structured notes	12%	41%	
Interest rate swaps		16%	16%
Currency swaps		14%	6%
Equity swaps	5%	6%	3%

Source: Data from Charles Smithson. *Managing Financial Risk 1996 Yearbook*. New York: CIBC Wood Gundy, 1996.

variety of ways in which pension funds can increase or decrease the risk of their portfolios; in other words, they represent ways that pensions may achieve alternate positions on the risk/return continuum.

The most common derivative contracts are *options, forwards, and futures*. Following is a description of these contracts. *Swaps*, relatively recent forms of derivative contracting, are discussed later in this chapter.

Options

Options are the building blocks of the financial world. As such, they offer a foundation for understanding forwards and futures as well as other derivatives. Furthermore, options allow investors synthetically to replicate the payoff structures of stocks, bonds, and even various combinations of asset classes.

Options give the owner the right but not the obligation either to purchase an underlying (a *call option*) or to sell an underlying (a *put option*) at a predetermined price (the *exercise price*) for a specific period.

Users of options may go long by purchasing an option or go short by writing an option. Though owners have the right to exercise the option or not, the writer has a defined obligation—to sell the underlying at the exercise price (for a written call) or to buy the underlying at the exercise price (for a written put) if the option is exercised. That is, the option owner can tear up an option, but its writer must fulfill the contract if asked.

Users of call options first must understand what will happen to the value of the option if the underlying goes up or down in value. Second, users must also understand how the change in option value affects the long (purchase) or short (written) position taken by the user. Consider a call option on a stock market index such as the S&P 500. If the index goes up, the call option will increase in value. The percentage change in the value of the option, however, will typically be much greater than the percentage change in the value of the index. This leverage is an important attribute of derivatives that we return to later.

Now consider the position taken in the option. A long position in the call option effectively establishes a long position in the index and hence in the stocks that comprise the index. If the underlying index increases, pension funds that bought the call option (that took a long position) will see the value of their position in the option increase in value. However, pensions that wrote the option (that took a short position) will see the value of their position in the option decrease in value.

Long call positions and short put positions will increase in value when the price of the underlying increases; conversely, these positions lose value if the price of the underlying goes down. Short call positions and long put positions will increase in value if the price of the underlying falls; they will lose value if the price rises.

The payoff to an option is truncated rather than symmetrical: for example, the long position in a call can make a theoretically infinite profit but is at risk only for the premium paid for the option. Conversely, the writer of a call may lose an infinitely large amount but will profit only to the amount of the premium. (All profits, of course, are less broker fees and margin costs.)

Note that regardless of whether the value of the option position increases or decreases, this change in value should not be evaluated as an isolated event. Instead, it should be evaluated in the context of a more comprehensive picture that encompasses the total pension fund or the subportfolio using the option position. Additionally, the payoff value should be interpreted with respect to the strategic motivation for taking a position in the option in the first place. For example, if a pension fund manager anticipates funding from the sponsor in three months and intends to use the payment to buy large capitalization stocks, she may be concerned that the prices of these stocks may go up, making them more costly. To hedge this risk, she may purchase a call option such as the one described. If stocks do subsequently increase, there is a timing loss on the purchase of the stocks three months hence, but that loss is offset (completely or in part) by the gains on the call option. The joint effect is neither a gain nor loss in total. Similarly, had the index gone down in value, the option position may have become worthless. However, the loss of the premium paid to purchase the option would be offset by the gain associated with purchasing stocks later at a lower price. Again the result is neither a gain nor loss in total; the joint effect is approximately zero.

Options may be *exchange-traded*, in which case they will be defined as a series characterized by the underlying (the stock, bond, index, or other asset), a variety of exercise prices, and a sequence of terms to expiration. Exchange-traded options are normally quite liquid, but a pension fund may not be able to find a contract that meets its specific needs. *Over-the-counter (OTC) options* may be able to meet this need. These contracts have the advantage of allowing a customized structure, such as an unusual size or maturity or underlying asset or exercise feature. They are not as liquid as exchange options, however, and holders of OTC options may have to hold them until expiration. OTC contracts are available from banks and other dealers.

Futures and Forwards

Forward contracts are agreements that commit two parties to transact at a future point in time. A *forward contract* includes an agreed-upon price, an agreed-upon deferred delivery date, and either an agreed-upon underlying to be exchanged or a cash settlement formula to be applied at the future date and price. Forward contracts are available OTC and are extremely flexible because they are custom contracts between two parties—for example, between a pension fund and a bank.

Futures contracts are similar to forward contracts in that they are arrangements providing for delivery of an underlying—or, in the case of some financial futures, providing for a cash settlement—at a future date at an agreed-upon price at maturity. However, there are some important differences between futures and forward contracts. Futures contracts are traded on exchanges and therefore are standardized with respect to the underlying and the amount of the contract. In return for this standardization, users gain greater liquidity, but they give up some of the flexibility associated with customized forward contracts. Futures are guaranteed by clearing firms on exchanges; forward contracts are subject to credit risk. Futures positions are marked-to-market daily with daily cash settlement; forwards may not be marked-to-market frequently or at all. (*Marking-to-market* is the process of calculating or estimating the current value of a financial position and then posting gains or losses on the position to the account of the user.) Futures positions may be closed by taking *offsetting positions* (e.g., a short position is offset by purchasing the same contract, resulting in a net exposure of zero); forwards are not as easy to close out. The discussion in this chapter focuses primarily on futures contracts, although most of what is said, with the exceptions just noted, holds for forward contracts also.

A pension fund that buys a futures contract (goes long) will see the position in the futures contract profit if the value of the underlying goes up. Conversely, a pension fund that sells a futures contract (goes short) will lose on the futures position if the price of the underlying increases. Thus, pension funds that wish to increase their exposure to an asset class in the hope of benefiting from an increase in the price of the underlying may do so by taking a long position in futures. Alternatively, pension funds that wish to reduce their exposure to a potential decrease in the price of some underlying asset in which they are long may do so by selling futures contracts. As for options, the correct way to evaluate the gains or losses on futures/forward positions is within the broader context of the portfolio and the strategy being pursued.

Advantages of Derivatives

The most obvious advantage of derivatives for pension funds is that they reduce transaction costs. For example, a study by Goldman Sachs estimated the costs of a round-trip for U.S. stocks (this example used a $25 million trade, including commissions, market impact, and taxes and excluding settlement and custody fees) at 0.69% versus cost of 0.06% for a comparable futures contract (see the article by Hill).

Another advantage of derivatives is that they allow risk to be separated into its component parts. Consider bonds. Investors that purchase bonds are exposed to both interest rate risk and credit risk. Through interest rate and credit derivatives, portions or all of either risk may be transferred to other parties or, if desired, exposures to either may be increased.

A third attribute of derivatives is the versatility they offer investors in developing and implementing investment and risk management strategies. For example:

- Investors can use derivatives to create risk/return profiles that may not be ordinarily achievable. Customized portfolios can be created that would be impossible using only underlying assets.
- Derivatives permit currency risk to be managed without changing country exposures. Country considerations can be separated from currency considerations.
- Derivatives offer the possibility of exploiting mispricing between cash and derivatives markets if arbitrage opportunities arise.
- Derivatives offer a means of trading on a specific view regarding markets, assets, interest rates, and currencies. Derivatives allow the investor to make bets on very specific market aspects.
- Derivatives offer a means of hedging numerous risks, including market risk, interest rate risk, surplus volatility, credit risk, concentration risk, and currency risk. Derivatives allow for narrowing the range of possible outcomes.
- Pension funds wishing to establish (or terminate) an exposure to a broad market segment that is indexed may do so in a single transaction by purchasing (selling) an index derivative rather than purchasing (selling) all the securities in the index. Derivatives are low-cost ways to do large changes.
- Pension funds that are constrained from direct investment in an asset (or asset class) by regulation or other factors may be able to increase diversification by investing in these assets through derivatives. (This, of course, should be done in conformance with policy and authority limits.)
- Derivatives permit strategies to be implemented quickly. Investing (or divesting) large positions in financial assets may require a relatively long time and may result in adverse market impact results. The desired position may be achievable in a shorter time through derivatives.
- Derivatives also are well suited to specific positions that have holding periods (investment horizons) that are shorter than the overall time horizons of many pension funds.

Finally, there is a school of thought that argues that the widespread acceptance derivatives have gained in the investment community means that the use of derivatives is not only prudent but that *not* using derivatives in some instances may be imprudent (see Chapter 3 for a discussion of prudent investor obligations). Given the relatively low cost of modifying portfolio exposures with derivatives, this "prudence" argument would seem to be especially compelling for pension plans that hedge and regularly rebalance portfolios.

Disadvantages of Derivatives

The use of derivatives is not without its problems, however. To develop sensible policy governing the use of derivatives, these disadvantages should be understood and carefully weighed against the advantages offered.

Derivatives are subject to investment risk—the value of the derivatives position may decline. (In a hedge, this is not a problem since the position being hedged is increasing in value.) This problem is compounded (literally!) by leverage. Relative to the investment risk of the underlying (say, a stock or an interest rate), derivatives may exhibit much greater price and return volatility than the underlying itself exhibits. Thus, poor performance in the derivative may be much worse than a naive investor might anticipate, even though the possibility of poor performance in the underlying may have been assessed correctly.

In many cases, hedging and return enhancement strategies that use derivatives fail to live up to their promises because of tracking or correlation error. This occurs when the volatility of derivative instrument does not perfectly match the volatility of the assets being hedged or in which a position is desired. For example, if a fund attempts to hedge a position in small capitalization U.S. stocks with a contract deriving its value from an index consisting of large U.S. stocks, the tracking error could be large and the hedge therefore not very effective. This may also occur with futures when the *basis*—the difference between the spot or cash price and the futures price—changes and the futures position is terminated prior to contract expiration.

Another disadvantage is that, although many derivatives are traded on the major exchanges and are thus normally quite liquid, this liquidity can dry up in unusually turbulent markets. Witness the failure of portfolio insurance programs during the market crash of October 1987: when investors tried to hedge positions by selling futures contracts, they were not able to find speculators (or portfolio rebalancers or tactical asset allocators) to buy futures contracts.

Further, many new derivative products that may seem attractive for a specific hedge today may not generate enough trading volume to warrant continuing to make a market in them. Thus, products are often taken off the market.

For products that are not traded on exchanges, there is *credit risk*. This is the risk that the counterparty to the contract will default.

Another problem relates to the complex accounting issues associated with derivatives. Current Financial Accounting Standards Board (FASB) proposals circulating for disclosing derivatives exposure have two serious flaws. First, these proposals look backward rather than forward, where the attention of the portfolio manager should be. Second, they ignore the change in the value of assets being hedged; the result is that only the losses or gains on derivative positions are reported. Consider, for example, that the purpose of a hedge is to reduce risk. An effective hedge may be the result of a gain in the derivative position and a loss in the asset being hedged, or vice versa. Either way, it is the net value—the sum of the changes in value of the derivative position combined with the position being hedged—that matters for the pension fund, not the change in value of the individual parts.

Finally, users of derivatives should be aware that there is the potential for misrepresentation and consequently for introducing unintended risks into a portfolio. This may occur when persons selling financial products become too aggressive or greedy. Related to this is whether those purchasing the products fully understand what they are buying. Many users of derivatives rely on brokers and bankers for information about the derivative products they are selling—information such as the attributes of the specific contract being used and its performance under various market conditions. This reliance provides an opportunity for a salesperson to sell something that is not needed and that may do great harm under some circumstances. For sellers, the temptation may be too great. Instruments such as collateralized mortgage obligations (CMOs), for example, create exposures to principal repayments that very sophisticated users can only crudely estimate let alone foretell with great accuracy. CMOs are perfectly acceptable for some investors who want the risk/return exposures they offer. However, an investor that does not understand the prepayment risk and the factors that affect the prices of CMOs when interest rates fall ends up exposed to risk that may not have been envisioned. The resulting losses can be nontrivial. (Note that a knowledgeable user of derivatives is not likely to be easily misled. Further, it is not uncommon for an investor to presume he understands the contract when it is profitable and sue the dealer when there are losses, claiming he never really understood the contract.)

Derivatives and Leverage

There are numerous strategies that use derivatives. Virtually all these strategies exploit the leverage that derivatives offer to increase or decrease exposure to one or more risk factors.

Consider investing $10,000 in either the stock of company A or investing the $10,000 in at-the-money call options (an at-the-money option is an option with an exercise price equal to the stock's current price) on stock A. The stock is currently selling at a price of $50 a share, and the options may be purchased at $3 per option. Thus, one can invest $10,000 in stock A either by purchasing 200 shares of stock or by buying 3,333 call options. For the sake of analysis, assume that the price of the stock may be either $55 or $45 a share on the option's expiration date. Given these outcomes, the payoff to the stock position will be either +10% [($11,000 − 10,000)/$10,000] or −10% [($9000 − 10,000)/$10,000] ignoring trading costs. However, the payoff to the option position will be either +200% [($5 − 3) × 10,000/$10,000] or −100% [($0 − 3) × 10,000/$10,000]. The large difference between the possible payoffs to the stock position and payoffs to the option position is caused by the leverage the options provide.

The preceding example really describes two extreme positions: investing $10,000 in stocks or $10,000 in options. There are numerous combinations of stock A and call options falling between these positions. For example, if one merely wanted exposure to $10,000 worth of stock A, this could be accomplished by purchasing 200 call options for $600, thus limiting the potential loss to $600 (−100%) while providing a potential gain of $400 (+67%).

Leverage should not frighten users. However, it should be recognized that since other forms of derivatives are essentially combinations of options, leverage is endemic in all derivative products. Every derivative creates a relatively wider band of plausible outcomes.

Managing Risk with Derivatives

As explained in Chapter 9, risk management includes activities designed to reduce risk temporarily (hedging) and activities designed to increase return temporarily (return enhancement). This section introduces some common strategies and provides several examples of these strategies that may be implemented with derivatives.

Hedging with Derivatives

There are two types of hedges. A short hedge occurs when a pension fund has a long position (e.g., it owns stock) it wishes to protect by going short a derivative contract. A long hedge occurs when a pension fund intends to take a position at a future date (e.g., it intends to buy stock when the next contribution from the sponsor arrives) and to hedge the position will take a long position in a derivative contract.

To understand hedging, one must understand the concept of a hedge ratio and a delta-neutral hedge. The hedge ratio is the amount of the hedge asset needed to hedge a specific amount of an existing position in order to achieve a desired risk exposure. A delta-neutral hedge is a continuous hedge in which the effect of a price change on the underlying asset (such as a stock or a portfolio of stocks) is eliminated through an offsetting position in a hedge asset (such as a put option or a stock index futures contract). The delta hedge ratio changes as the value of the underlying asset changes; therefore, the amount of the asset held for the purpose of hedging must change also—hence the "continuous" nature of the hedge.

Note that the values and thus the hedging attributes of options and other derivatives are affected by many factors: the passage of time, the rate of change in delta, changes in the volatility of the underlying, and changes in interest rates. These factors are referred to as *theta*, *gamma*, *vega*, and *rho* respectively. Complete hedges may require attention to the influences these factors exert. (For a good treatment of these, see the articles by Arditti and Hull.)

Option Contracts in Risk Management

Options are frequently used in constructing hedging and return enhancement strategies. The following examples illustrate some basic option strategies.

Option Hedges for a Long Asset Position

Consider a pension fund with a substantial exposure to common stocks. Theoretically, if there are options on these stocks (or on an index that is very similar to the portfolio of stocks held), the fund can hedge its long stock position by either writing covered call options or buying protective put options.

Writing covered calls entitles the fund to the premium (or price) of the call option and thus generates income that cushions the impact of any decline in the price of the stocks held. The cost of this cushion, however, is that it limits the upside price potential; if the stocks go up in price, they will be "called away"—the pension fund will not participate in return beyond the exercise price of the call option because the fund will have to sell stock to the owners of the call options. Conceptually, covered call writing locks in the current risk-free rate of return as long as the number of calls written is continually adjusted as the price of the underlying changes and as long as trading costs are trivial. The continual adjustments required and actual trading costs make this strategy only partially effective as a hedge.

An alternative to writing covered calls is purchasing protective puts. In the combined position of long stock, long put option, if the price of the stock held declines, the value of the put rises. Thus, properly constructed, a protective put hedge can offset all of the loss on the long stock position. Again, this is not costless. A premium must be paid to purchase the put. This premium can be viewed as the cost of insurance. Thus, although the downside risk of holding the stock is effectively truncated, the expected return on the stock portfolio is reduced by the cost of the puts. Many investors view puts as too expensive and thus turn to other derivatives.

Pension funds may hedge the portfolio by using exchange traded options—although there may be substantial tracking or correlation risk involved with using these options, and it may be difficult to match time horizons—or by entering into an OTC market transaction. In the case of the OTC transaction there is the advantage of avoiding or reducing tracking risk through a customized hedge asset that correlates well with the portfolio, and there is also the advantage of being able to negotiate an appropriate time horizon. As noted earlier, potential disadvantages of an OTC transaction are the lack of liquidity relative to exchange-traded contracts and the credit risk of the counterparty.

Return Enhancement Through Options

Recall that hedging is fundamentally a risk-reducing strategy. From time to time, the pension fund manager may want to increase the fund's exposure to a risk in pursuit of higher total returns. The motivation for increasing the fund's exposure may be that the manager has a belief or view that an asset or sector is underpriced and thus offers unusually good expected returns. Or, the fund itself may be temporarily more tolerant of risk than it usually is and thus the manager wishes to try for higher short-term returns.

Regardless of the motivation, there are two paths to return enhancement through options. The first is to purchase calls; the second is to sell puts. If calls are purchased, the potential downside is the loss of the premium paid (a maximum loss of 100%) plus trading costs. The upside potential theoretically is limitless, although most exchange-traded options have times to expiration of only a few months and will expire at a finite time. If puts are sold, the worst that may happen is that the fund will lose an amount equal to the exercise price of the option less the net premium received. The maximum gain is the premium less trading costs. Either strategy has the potential to enhance returns; the success of both depends on an increase in value in the underlying.

Futures in Risk Management

Like options, futures contracts (and of course forward contracts as well) may be used for hedging and return enhancement. However, with futures there is no premium to pay or receive and the payoff structure is not truncated; a long futures position, roughly analogous to a long call position, increases in value when the underlying increases (as does the long call). Similarly if the underlying decreases, the long futures position declines in value, as does the long call position. However, the maximum loss on the long call is limited to the loss of the premium paid while the loss on the long future may be much greater. The following examples illustrate some uses of futures in risk management.

Changing Equity Exposures Through Futures

Consider a portfolio holding $100 million in stocks. Further assume the beta of the portfolio—its market risk—is equal to 1.0. If the pension fund manager is fearful that the stock market is ready for a precipitous drop, she may want to reduce the portfolio's level of market risk substantially by reducing the portfolio's beta to 0. The fund can hedge the risk of a price decrease by selling futures contracts on an index such as the S&P 500, resulting in a portfolio that is long the underlying stocks and short the futures contracts. Let us say that the S&P 500 contract has a current futures price of $850. The contract's face amount is 500 times the futures price. Assuming that the stocks in the equity portfolio are large capitalization U.S. stocks and that they are held more or less in quantities proportionate to their market capitalization (that is the portfolio and the futures contracts are highly correlated in that they both have betas of 1.0), the number of contracts the manager must sell in order to hedge the position is:

$$N = \frac{\$100,000,000}{(500)(850)} = 235.3$$

The fund manager should sell 235 futures contracts. If the initial beta of the portfolio differs from that of the contract, the preceding equation is adjusted by multiplying N by the relative volatility (beta) of the portfolio. For example, if the stock portfolio has a beta of 1.2 (that is, if it is estimated that the portfolio has 20% more market risk than the S&P 500), the hedge requires selling:

$$235.5 \times 1.2 = 282 \text{ contracts}$$

There are costs to this strategy. First, there are the broker fees charged to implement the transaction. These are small relative to selling or buying the underlying stocks instead of the futures contract, however. There is also the margin cost associated with taking a futures position. For an S&P 500 contract used for hedging, this may run in the neighborhood of 2 to 5% of the contract's total value. This requirement may be met by posting Treasury bills with the broker who, in turn, promises them to the clearinghouse. Since the interest earned on the Treasury bills goes to the party taking the position and in this case the purpose of the transaction is to hedge, this part of the cost is generally negligible. Finally, there is the opportunity cost of not being able to participate in a market that does unexpectedly well; that is if the stock market goes up rather than down, the pension fund will gain in the long stock position but lose in the futures position. Again, since the motivation is to hedge, this is not a matter for concern. It does serve as a reminder that there are no free lunches, however. Note that a protective put position allows participation in an up market; however, purchasing the put requires that a premium be paid by the pension fund.

Hedging is not a matter of all or none. Consider a decision to hedge 50% of the portfolio's market risk. Using beta, the volatility of the portfolio relative to the overall market, as our basic measure, we can describe a portfolio's target risk level—its target beta—as:

$$(\text{target beta})(\text{assets}) = (\text{actual beta})(\text{assets}) + N(\text{futures price})(500)$$

Using the preceding data, we can calculate the number of futures contracts needed to hedge 50% of the portfolio's market risk by:

$$0.5(\$100{,}000{,}000) = 1.0(1{,}000{,}000) + N(850)(500)$$
$$N = -117.6$$

The fund should sell 118 contracts. Note that this is half the number of futures contracts needed to construct a full hedge. The methodologies are, of course, consistent.

From the preceding example, it can be seen that a pension fund also may increase its beta (its market risk—and, hence, its exposure to stocks) by purchasing futures contracts. The margin and broker costs are fundamentally the same as they are for hedging, although margin is generally higher for strategies that are not hedging strategies. The potential cost is that, if stocks fall in value, the loss on the long stock position will be magnified by the loss on the long futures position. As noted earlier, users should carefully compare the potentially large loss of a futures position to the loss of premium on a long call option on the same index. If, for example, the stock market plummeted, the loss on the long futures position could be high, greatly magnifying the loss on the stocks also held. The loss incurred by being long call options, however, is limited to the cost of acquiring the options. Thus, the combined call options plus stock loss could be large but could be much smaller than the combined futures plus stock loss. With an option, the loss is limited to its price; with a futures position, the loss can far exceed the price of an option.

Fixed-Income (Interest Rate) Strategies Using Futures

Consider a pension fund with substantial holdings in bonds. A hedge similar to the one constructed in the preceding example can be constructed if one fears an increase in interest rates and a corresponding loss in the bond portfolio.

One of several ways to approach this type of hedge is to compute the change in value of a bond portfolio associated with a change in interest rates of one basis point. This can be done as follows:

$$\text{price change} = \frac{\text{portfolio duration}}{1 + \dfrac{\text{interest rate}}{2}} \times \text{value of portfolio} \times 0.0001$$

The next step is to compute the price change for the desired futures contract. The choice of contract is affected by factors such as the liquidity of the contract and its correlation error relative to the portfolio. The third step is to select a target duration for the portfolio and calculate the price change that will occur by using the equation above. In the case of a hedge, of course, the target duration will be well below the portfolio's current duration. Finally, the number of futures contracts needed is determined by:

$$N = \frac{\text{target price change} - \text{portfolio price change}}{\text{price change of futures contract}}$$

The hedge can be achieved by selling futures contracts using as an underlying either a bond index (for example, Treasury bonds) or interest rates (wherein the payoff to the contract is determined by an interest rate formula). This hedge creates a position that, should interest rates increase, the damage done to the bond portfolio will be offset by a gain on the short futures contracts.

Of course, real portfolios are not likely to have bonds that are all the same nor that correlate in all respects with the bonds in the futures contract. Further, there are other factors to consider—such as differences in the time to expiration of the contract versus the desired hedge period, relative volatility, and nonparallel shifts in interest rates.

Fixed-income return enhancement strategies simply increase the target portfolio duration by purchasing interest rate futures. These strategies are based on the belief or expectation that interest rates are likely to fall. The resulting position is one of long bonds, long futures. If interest rates subsequently fall, the value of the position will increase much more than if only bonds are held; whatever interest rate change occurs, the returns will be magnified relative to the straight long bond position.

Asset/Liability Interest Rate Risk Management Using Futures

Recall that, for a pension fund with a duration mismatch between its assets and liabilities, if interest rates change, the present value of the pension liability may change more than or less than the change in value of the assets. A mismatch in duration may lead to unacceptable surplus volatility.

Duration-Based Strategies. Derivatives can be useful for managing asset-liability mismatches. In the preceding example, we saw that the duration of a portfolio can be changed with futures. Consider a pension fund with an asset duration that is not equal to the duration of its liabilities. By purchasing futures contracts on bonds or using an appropriate interest rate formula, the duration of the portfolio that the pension is holding may be increased. If on the other hand the duration of plan assets needs to be lowered, the pension fund will sell futures. Thus, it is possible to construct a position in which a change in interest rates has no impact on the pension fund surplus because it affects liabilities and assets equally. If this is the desired position, the fund manager would set a duration target for the asset side as follows:

$$\text{duration of assets} = \text{duration of liabilities} \times \frac{\text{total liabilities}}{\text{total assets}}$$

and conduct an analysis similar to that already described.

Problems with Duration-Based Strategies

As in the case of delta hedging, duration and duration-based hedging strategies are sensitive to a variety of factors. Interest rate sensitivity is a function of the magnitude of the cash flows (higher interim cash flows reduce interest rate sensitivity), maturity (shorter maturities reduce interest rate exposure), and current interest rates (in general, higher interest rates are associated with lower sensitivity to changes in interest rates, although this is not always true for liabilities and assets with embedded options).

Further, duration as usually estimated assumes a linear relationship between price and yield. This ignores the fact that an asset's sensitivity to changes in interest rates is different at different levels of interest rates—the convexity or the curvilinear nature of the actual relationship. Convexity tells us how rapidly a price changes in response to an interest rate change. For example, it may reveal if a bond's price will rise if interest rates fall or if its price will remain unchanged because of the virtual certainty it will be paid off prematurely. This is especially important for large changes in interest rates. Finally, assets and liabilities with embedded options, such as a bond with a call option, may have areas of negative convexity. This is where the normally inverse relationship between price and yield is eliminated (in the case of a callable bond that is "in-the-money") or reversed (in the case of a CMO during a period of falling interest rates and rapid pre-payments of mortgages).

Collectively, this means that duration-based hedging strategies, like delta hedging strategies, are dynamic in nature and require continual monitoring and fine-tuning if they are to stay effective. Since duration based strategies rely on imperfect estimates, further analysis designed to capture the true price/yield relationship better may be necessary.

Swaps as Alternatives to Options, Forwards, and Futures

A swap contract is an agreement between two parties to exchange pre-specified cash flows at specified intervals for an agreed-upon period of time. Like options and futures, swaps are useful in hedging exposures to specific asset classes, in achieving low-cost exposures to specific asset classes, and in taking active positions consistent with one's beliefs about the performance of an asset class, interest rate, or currency. Swaps can be especially useful for pension fund managers who wish to manage a specific risk for longer time periods than most option or futures contracts permit. When a futures or option contract expires, if the investor wishes to continue the strategy that was in place, new contracts must be arranged. This results in rollover or stacking risk—the risk that the contracts may not be available or that the price required to reestablish the position may be prohibitive.

An Interest Rate Swap

Consider, for example, a plain vanilla interest rate swap from the perspective of an investor such as a pension fund. Financial institution A may currently have $50 million in fixed-rate bonds but A wishes to hold bonds that pay a variable rate of interest. The motivation may be to hedge a variable component of its liability stream, perhaps where payments to third parties are indexed to some short-term interest rate. Pension fund B, on the other hand, owns $50 million in bonds that pay a variable rate of interest, but would prefer to receive a fixed rate of interest in order to more closely match the cash flows produced by its assets with the near-term cash flows necessary to pay its current retirees. The pension fund and the financial institution may, of course, sell the bonds that they are holding and purchase new bonds that have the characteristics they desire. Alternatively, and in part to avoid the transaction costs associated with the sale and purchase of the securities, they may arrange an interest rate swap in which they essentially agree to "swap" cash flows. Thus, A agrees to pay a fixed rate of interest on a notional principal of $50 million to B in return for receiving a variable interest rate from B. The actual payments are net amounts with the party owing the larger amount paying the difference to the other party. The net result for B is that the variable rate it receives from the bonds it owns is "passed through" to A while a fixed payment stream that matches all or a portion of its payments to retirees remains.

This type of interest rate swap typically is intermediated by a dealer such as a large commercial bank or an investment bank. Thus, the two investors just described probably are not transacting with one another directly but rather are transacting with a dealer that serves as counterparty to both. The interest rate swap itself will be structured in terms of the fixed rate that A is to pay (and B receives); the variable rate that B is to pay (and A receives); the notional amount (in this case, $50 million) upon which the two payment streams are calculated; and the tenor or length of time for which the swap will be in effect. The variable rate is likely to be defined in terms of an observable short-term interest rate index such as the London Interbank Offer Rate (LIBOR). The dealer who intermediates the swap hopes to make a profit by matching swaps with other parties at a swap price spread (interest rate differential).

On the Risks of Swaps

Like other derivatives, swaps are subject to investment risk, correlation risk, currency risk, and so forth. Interest rate risk is an especially important risk for a pension fund that participates in the interest rate swap market. To understand this risk, it is necessary to understand the motivation behind a particular swap position.

Interest rate risk for swaps can be defined as changes in the market value of the swap due to unanticipated changes in interest rates. When a swap is entered into, the swap is priced off the forward rates embedded in the current yield curve. Thus the fixed-rate pay leg and the variable-rate pay leg are set to yield present values where both legs are equal in value. If, then, interest rates follow the pattern implied by the yield curve over the life of the swap (swap contracts run from 2 to 5 years as a general rule), the net result of the swap is pretty much as all parties anticipate; given an upward sloping yield curve, the variable-pay party receives positive cash flows in the early years of the swap but makes cash payments in the later years of the swap. Similarly, the fixed-pay leg pays net to the variable-pay leg early in the swap, but then receives net payments in the later years of the swap. (In the preceding example of an interest rate swap, A and B still receive income from their bond portfolios. If B makes net payments to A in the later years of the swap, this simply reduces the proceeds B receives from its variable-rate bond portfolio, which is probably paying a higher rate than it was when the swap was initiated.)

What happens, however, if interest rates suddenly and unexpectedly shift? For example, consider an interest rate shift where there is an upward parallel shift of an upward sloping yield curve. It may appear that pension fund B (paying the variable rate and receiving the fixed rate) is worse off and the fixed-pay party is better off. Is this true, however? There are two issues to consider. The first is that the floating- or variable-pay leg (pension fund B) now has the greatest incentive to default. Hence, there has been a shift in the counterparty risk of the swap. (*Counterparty risk* is the risk that the other party—or the dealer for an intermediated swap—will default.) The more important question concerns the original motivation behind the swap. If the swap was entered into to obtain a specific exposure to interest rates in order to hedge a portion of the liability structure of the pension fund—and if the swap is an appropriate hedge—any gain or a loss on the swap is being offset by a loss or a gain on the liability side of the balance sheet. Thus, the surplus of the pension is more or less unchanged and there really is no winner or loser; instead, what pension fund B is trying to accomplish with asset liability management is actually being accomplished.

*An Example of an Asset-Liability Swap**

Consider a pension fund that has one bond and one retiree. The bond has a 9% coupon and is selling at its face value of $50,000. The one retiree has an expected lifespan of 5 years. The appropriate yield for valuing the retirement annuity of $10,000 a year is 8%.

Bond	Retirement Liability
$50,000	$10,000/year for
5-year maturity, coupon of	5 years
9%, annual pay, option free	yield = 8%

The initial asset/liability position is:

	Asset	Liability
Present value	$50,000	$39,927
Duration	4.24	2.85

The suplus is $10,073 and the duration of the surplus is:

$$\text{surplus duration} = \frac{50,000\,(4.24) - 39,927\,(2.85)}{10,073} = 9.73 = D_s$$

If the pension fund wants to remove this duration mismatch and reduce the sensitivity of the surplus to changes in interest rates—to lower its duration—it can enter a swap in which it agrees to pay a fixed-interest rate on the notional or face amount of the swap, in exchange for which it will receive an amount determined by applying a variable interest rate to that notional amount. The actual payment will be a net of the two payments—that is, if the variable amount is greater than the fixed

*This example was adapted from an example in the article by McMillan.

amount, the fund will receive the difference and vice versa. Receiving a cash flow that varies with short-term interest rates reduces the duration of the fund's assets, while committing to fixed payments increases the duration of the fund's liabilities. The dollar duration of the swap is:

$$S_D = D_{FRB} - D_{FI}$$

where D_{FRB} is the duration of a fixed rate bond and D_{FI} is the duration of a floating-rate bond.

For simplicity, assume the duration of the floating-pay leg is 0 (it is actually something less than the time to the next payment) and the duration of the fixed-pay leg is 4.0.

To eliminate the volatility of the surplus the swap needs a notional amount of:

$$9.73 (10073) + (-4.0) (N) = 0$$
$$N = \$24{,}502$$

The duration of the surplus is now:

$$10{,}073 (9.73) + 24{,}502 (-4.0) \approx 0$$

Thus, the volatility of the pension surplus in this simple example has been eliminated for small changes in interest rates.

Other Swaps

A pension fund manager may also find currency swaps and equity swaps appealing at times. Currency swaps involve an initial exchange of principal, an exchange of cash flows denominated in different currencies, and a final exchange (a re-exchange) of principal. Consider, for example, a pension fund that determines it is appropriate to make investments outside of the United States but has employees only in the United States. This pension fund manager may be able to eliminate all or a portion of its currency risk in its investments by arranging currency swaps in which a pension fund that receives, for example, Swiss francs from its investments in Swiss securities can swap Swiss francs to a dealer in return for U.S. dollars. (Currency risk also may be managed through currency options, futures contracts, and forward contracts.)

Equity swaps, on the other hand, can create long (or short) exposures to both U.S. and non-U.S. stock indexes. Consider, for example, a U.S. pension fund desiring long exposure to a non-U.S. stock market. The pension fund manager may arrange a swap through a bank wherein the bank commits to pay the quarterly percentage change in an index such as the French CAC in return for payments equal to those of six-month LIBOR.

In an equity swap, the payment from the bank may be negative—that is, the pension fund may have to pay the bank if the index goes down. Additionally, equity swaps differ according to whether the notional amount on which the payments are calculated varies with changes in the index (whether gains and losses will be capitalized) or remains the same regardless of market movements. At issue here is the risk tolerance of the investor—does the risk tolerance change as markets change? An example of an equity swap is presented in Appendix F.

Specialized Uses of Derivatives

As mentioned earlier, derivatives may be used for numerous purposes besides general hedging and return enhancement strategies. For example, derivatives are also popular for rebalancing portfolios, meeting liquidity needs, and alpha separation.

Rebalancing portfolios through futures contracts is commonplace. Disciplined rebalancing and tactical asset allocation strategies, for example, commonly are carried out by purchasing equity futures contracts when stocks fall in value and selling futures when stock prices rise. Similarly, insured asset allocation strategies sell equity futures when stock prices fall and buy equity futures when stock prices rise (liquidity permitting).

Pension fund managers occasionally find themselves presented with short-term liquidity issues. As noted earlier, if a contribution is due from the sponsor in a few months and the manager fears that stock prices may increase rapidly before the contribution is available, entering a long futures position (as a hedge) until the contribution is received can establish the desired position in spite of the liquidity problem.

Finally, some pension funds that pursue active management are finding alpha separation strategies via derivatives attractive. Consider a pension fund that believes the U.S. stock market will underperform non-U.S. stock markets, and thus intends to reallocate to non-U.S. stocks.* The fund uses a manager it believes is a good stock picker, but the manager invests only in U.S. stocks. Derivatives allow the fund to:

1. Leave the current allocation of funds with the U.S. manager

2. Sell stock index futures (or enter a swap) to reduce exposure to U.S. stocks

---

*This example was adapted from an example in the article by Polsky.

3. Go long a non-U.S. stock index via a swap or futures swap contract, in order to increase exposure to non-U.S. stocks.

In steps (1) and (2), the market risk of U.S. stocks is neutralized but the manager's selection skills—her alpha—remains. Step (3) gives the immediate exposure to non-U.S. stocks desired.

Second-Generation Derivatives

As if the world of derivatives were not complex enough, a whole new wave of derivative products has emerged—and more will come. These derivative contracts are referred to as *second-generation derivatives*. A few of these are discussed in this section.

Barrier Options

Barrier options are options that come alive or are extinguished when a barrier on the underlying asset or index is crossed. For example, an up-and-out call option may be in-the-money until a barrier price is reached, at which time the call becomes worthless. This type of call has a lower premium than an ordinary call, which has no barrier; thus it may be attractive to a pension fund manager who wants to take a very short-term long hedge with calls but considers standard calls too expensive. For a pension fund manager writing calls to generate fee income, the up-and-out may be attractive because it caps the writer's potential loss.

Compound Options

Compound options are options that give the holder the right to purchase standard options. On exercise, the combined premium will be relatively high, but if the compound option expires out of the money, the loss is much smaller. Consider using a call option on a put option to protect a portfolio or asset. If the underlying falls in value and stays down, the put can be called and exercised to offset the loss. If the underlying falls but then rises again (or if the underlying stays the same or goes up in value), the call on the put is worthless but the premium lost is small.

Swaptions

A swaption is an option to enter into a swap—to take one leg or another—and it gives the holder the flexibility that a swap takes away.

If subsequent events warrant it, the holder may exercise the option and enter the swap. If not, the holder lets the option expire.

There are many more derivatives—for example, exchange-traded FLEX options, which give writers and holders the right to negotiate various terms; structured notes, which allow investors to take specific interest rate views; and credit derivatives, which allow investors to increase or decrease credit exposure and thus effectively separate interest rate risk and credit risk. This "product differentiation" is driven by the demand for better and/or more specific risk management tools. As such, it generally is an economically productive activity; however, any specific contract may have no value whatsoever for a specific pension fund.

Choosing Among the Alternatives

Options, forwards, futures, swaps—diversification, market risk, immunization—lions, and tigers and bears, oh my!—how does one choose from among the number of tools and strategies available to manage risk? The starting point is good policy: what is the pension fund trying to accomplish, and how much investment and surplus risk can the fund tolerate? The next step is to apply sound investment fundamentals—to diversify—and carefully analyze all the risks that the fund must address to avoid a knee-jerk reaction to perceived risk rather than a thoughtful assessment of the real risks that are actually present.

Pension fund sponsors and managers should view derivatives as tools that may from time to time be cost-efficient alternatives to trading primary assets in order to achieve desirable exposures. As a general rule, the longer the time period for which a given exposure is desired, the less attractive derivatives should be. Derivatives are a sensible means of rebalancing portfolios to restore target weights and constructing temporary hedges. For pension funds that pursue active management strategies with all or a portion of their assets, derivatives are useful in a number of ways—for tactical asset allocation, alpha separation, and so on.

When it is appropriate to use derivatives, pension fund managers, administrators, and other decision makers should ask the following questions:

- What is the nature of the underlying asset and/or liability? Does a matching contract exist? If not, what correlation risk exists?

- How liquid is the contract? How easy will it be to reverse the initial position?
- What are the broker costs and other fees?
- How desirable would it be to enter a customized contract and give up some liquidity?
- What is the most desirable payoff structure? For example, if a pension fund wants to reduce investment risk, a partial list of alternative strategies and payoffs includes:
  - buy puts: pay a premium but keep the upside potential
  - sell futures: pay no premium but get no upside potential; face the possibility of margin calls as the contract is marked-to-market
  - buy puts on a futures contract: pay a smaller premium and keep the upside potential
- What length of time are you concerned with? For long time periods, investing in and rebalancing directly with the under-lying is probably the best route. For shorter time periods, or in the face of restrictions that discourage direct positions, deriva-tives may be the best route. Be aware that the mismatch between a strategic time horizon and the shorter maturities of many derivative contracts introduces the risk that the deriva-tive position may not be achievable when rolling over into a new set of contracts. Consider that:
  - swaps commonly have maturities of 5 years or more and may go to 20 years
  - futures commonly have maturities up to 2 years
  - options have maturities of up to several months, although special option products such as long-term equity participa-tions (LEAPs) and FLEX options have considerably longer maturities
- How available are quotes for accurate pricing?
- How is credit risk controlled? Are the contracts marked-to-market? How often?
- What denominations are normally available?
- What is the nature of the contractual obligation? For example, option writers must perform; option buyers have the right but not the obligation to perform.

Conclusion

Pension fund managers and decision makers should be cautious of new financial technologies and derivative products. First, the risk characteristics of the product may not be relevant given the pension fund's exposures. Second, it can be very difficult to understand fully the price and risk/return profiles of new products. An overpriced derivative is no bargain, nor is a derivative with unanticipated payoffs.

Derivatives should be used when appropriate, but their use should, as with all other important variables in pension management, be governed by policy and subject to the appropriate controls and oversights. Acceptable hedging activities, instruments, goals, and times should be clearly defined in writing. Return enhancement and view-based strategies should be permitted only if the fund permits active management, and then they should be constrained to the type of strategies acceptable to the fund. Carte blanche authority should not be granted except within the confines of a leveraged vehicle such as a hedge fund or a managed futures program, limited in exposure to the assets committed. Moreover, it is critical that the top management of a pension fund advise, in writing, all the brokers and money managers with which it does business what derivative contracts and strategies are acceptable, and under what circumstances, and which are not. These parties should be required to report when these written guidelines are violated.

The presence of derivatives in a portfolio does not necessarily increase or decrease the risk of that portfolio. Remember, derivatives offer leverage, a two-edge sword. This leverage can increase risk or decrease risk. Thus, derivatives must be carefully evaluated so that an unintended shift in the fund's risk/return profile does not occur: hedges that are not monitored can quickly become speculative adventures.

Derivatives are here to stay. They are versatile, they are cost-efficient, and they offer temporal advantages that may be valuable from time to time. The proper use of derivatives is commonly accepted as sound practice and arguably is evidence of prudent behavior. The potential for misuse of derivatives, however, should not be ignored. Catastrophes have happened; more will. All in all, derivatives can add value to pension management and should be used, wisely and prudently and as part of the overall pension management strategy.

Chapter **11**

Managing Managers and the Costs of Investing

The effective management of a pension plan requires managing the people who manage the plan's assets and the costs of asset management. The former involves selecting, monitoring, compensating and, if necessary, replacing money managers. The latter involves understanding and ultimately controlling the costs of investing—the costs of trading, custody, and so forth. These issues have a significant effect on the investment performance of the plan's assets. Thus, they significantly affect the funding status and future contributions required for defined benefit plans and the accumulations for defined contribution plans. For all pension plans they are an important aspect of due diligence and the fulfillment of other fiduciary responsibilities.

The decisions discussed in this chapter are typically made by pension plan boards and/or senior management. The decisions are sufficiently similar for defined benefit plans and defined contribution plans so no distinction between plan types is made here.

Who Should Manage Plan Assets?

Of central importance is whether the sponsoring organization should manage the pension plan internally or seek external managers. Once this is decided in the abstract, the pension sponsor must implement the decision by finding the most suitable money managers, must establish appropriate control procedures to ensure that the job is being done in accordance with policy, and must develop policies for such matters as manager compensation and, if need be, the termination of money managers.

Internal versus External Management

According to Arthur Williams III in *Managing Your Investment Manager*, sponsors should answer the following questions when considering whether to use internal or external managers:

1. What are the advantages of internal versus external investment management?

2. What expertise does investment management require?

3. Does this expertise exist within the organization?

4. If not, do budgetary considerations permit hiring people with the necessary qualifications?

5. Can senior officials of the organization properly supervise the activities of an investment manager?

6. Is the organization willing to expend the time and effort that are required to manage investment funds?

7. Is the organization willing to accept the risk associated with this function?

Some authorities (see, for example, the article by Reichenstein) argue that nonfinancial organizations should stay with the nonfinancial strategies in which they have expertise rather than trying to manage investment assets directly. Anecdotal evidence from organizations designed for one purpose but actually investing as a sideline—such as the experience of Orange County, California—supports this position. However, there are consequences of going outside for expertise, in particular, higher costs of monitoring and control.

Most pension plans employ outside money managers. (Note that sponsors that hire external managers must still have competent investment personnel in-house to help formulate and implement policy and to manage the outside managers. Incidentally, it is common to manage some assets in-house and contract other assets out.) One reason for hiring external managers is that money management enjoys substantial scale economies—$1 billion in assets can be managed at little more expense than $100 million—so sponsors may often find they can buy outside management for less than it would cost to develop and use inside management. Additionally, the most skillful money managers will want to work where pay is highest. Because a lot of money can be managed with little more effort than managing a small amount of money, the very best money managers can make significantly higher incomes working in dedicated money management firms managing large pools of assets rather than working for sponsors directly. Corporate, public, or union internal salary scales also can create constraints wherein plan sponsors may be unable to pay competitive salaries to skilled money managers. Although some very large pension plan sponsors have circumvented this issue by establishing an internal money management company that is treated as an independent entity, most pension funds would generally find it more politically expedient to hire external money managers and pay them fees based on the amount of money managed (and, sometimes, on investment performance).

Note also that some plan sponsors may view the use of outside money managers as a form of legal insurance, since these managers, particularly those who manage the money of many other clients as well, would be difficult to question on grounds of fiduciary prudence. Thus, many pension plan sponsors believe they are less likely to be sued either by employees or by the Department of Labor over the investment choices a well-regarded outside manager might make than they would be to be sued over choices made by an internal manager.

One disadvantage of using external management is the question of control. It is easier to monitor and control internal managers. Similarly, it is easier to be certain that internal managers who are allocated funds on the basis of their promise to pursue a specific investment discipline or style do not end up doing something that is altogether different. Of course, as Kujaca observes, even internal managers may pursue unjust enrichment or career advancement at the expense of the pension plan. This profiteering may be as simple as empire building or as involved as collusion with outside providers of pension services through kickbacks or other schemes. Therefore internal managers must be monitored as well. It is easier to do, however, since the sponsor should have access to better and more readily available information than is the case with external managers.

The issue, then, boils down to three matters. Does the plan sponsor have the resources and inclination to manage pension assets internally? Is the sponsor willing to bear the costs of maintaining and evaluating external managers? And, is the sponsor willing to bear the responsibilities of internal management or does it prefer to shift the responsibility to outside agents?

Hiring Internal Managers

The profile of a competent senior internal manager must include extensive knowledge of and background in the money management industry as well as strong people and communication skills. The investment profession has become very quantitative in recent years and has benefited greatly from numerous scientific advances in theory, empirical studies, and computer support systems. Thus, an appropriate educational background (specialization in finance and economics) is essential. Similarly, evidence of broad-based, relevant knowledge is desirable. One way for a manager to demonstrate this is by gaining the Chartered Financial Analyst (CFA) designation, the current professional certification in the investment industry. Holders of the CFA designation have completed a self-study program; have passed three day-long examinations, each one year apart; and have demonstrated work experience in investment decision making. The examination process is rigorous (in recent years, around 50% of candidates fail to pass the Level I and Level II exams) and comprehensive (it includes ethical and professional standards, economics, analytical methods, portfolio management, derivative instruments, and so forth). Note that competency as an investment manager per se is not assured by the CFA designation; rather, mastery of a broad-based body of relevant knowledge is demonstrated. Beyond such quality signals, sponsors should look closely at relevant work experience (management of similar-sized portfolios and similar types of assets) and familiarity with the current research in investments.

The other skills required by internal investment managers have to do with the ability to manage the people who comprise the investment management team (analysts, accountants, clerical staff, and so forth) and to communicate effectively with staff and with senior management and trustees. The senior investment manager must understand the importance of hiring competent people and training them as necessary. Pension sponsors should want a management team that is not dependent solely on one or two individuals for successful investment management. Rather, the team should be a unit with several skilled people involved in decision making so that the team survives the departure of any one person. Additionally, the senior manager should appreciate the importance of complying with policy and effectively communicating with his or her superiors on an ongoing basis about the implementation of policy and results of various decisions.

Selecting External Managers

Selecting an external manager differs considerably from selecting an internal manager because the "manager" is typically a firm, and because firms frequently specialize by asset class and whether they are active or passive managers. The fundamental task of the pension plan sponsor is to choose those money managers who are best suited to manage within the framework of the asset allocation that is believed by the sponsor to be optimal for the pension plan. This can be done only after the plan sponsor has determined exactly how much risk is appropriate for the plan to bear and what the allocation of assets will be among actively managed strategies and passive or index strategies.

A related challenge is to choose managers who will actually stay within the boundaries that the sponsor sets, and, perhaps as important, continue to use the same style and/or analytical methods that they used when they were hired. Many sponsors choose managers because they are convinced of a specific investment philosophy's usefulness and the quality of the techniques applied to achieve that investment approach. Thus, sponsors do not want money managers who are hired to deliver specific approaches to change the investment techniques without notification and approval.

After a sponsor is satisfied that a particular style or strategy is a good one, the sponsor must next be confident that the money manager can provide continuity of implementation. That is, the sponsor must be assured that the money management firm can survive the loss of one or two key employees and remain faithful to its espoused analytical principles.

A host of other factors that sponsors should consider are listed in Appendix G. All potential managers should answer the general questions listed in the first part of the appendix; the second part provides specific questions for fixed-income and equity managers. Once the answers are collected, they must be analyzed. Unfortunately, as they can be weighed only subjectively, they are subject to all the biases of those doing the selection.

A common practice in virtually every investment manager search is to require potential managers to provide at least one and possibly more historical measures of investment performance for many years in the past. As indicated in Chapter 7, many serious studies show that historical performance measures have little predictive power regarding future investment performance. However, although historical performance does not predict future investment results, such data may still provide information regarding how closely the investment manager has followed the stated investment style and investment method.

An alternative to using the historical record in the selection of a manager is to evaluate what a manager will do rather than what he or she has done. Consider, for example, using an untested but appealing investment model. According to some commentators (see Gould, for example), this may result in hiring managers that produce better investment results. The basic argument for this method is that markets are efficient enough so that whatever worked in the past is unlikely to work in the future. Thus, what may work must necessarily be unproven by a prior track record—other than perhaps consistent manager performance where strategy changes according to the manager's beliefs.

Those who hire external managers should be careful to avoid the "common wisdom" that may be circulating. For example, a popular misconception is that small money management firms achieve better investment results than large investment firms. There is no substantive evidence to support this notion, however, and it is likely to be a consequence of survivorship bias. Some startup investment management firms do well; others do poorly. Those that do poorly lose accounts and leave the business very quickly, sometimes even before they have enough years of operating results to leave a measurable investment performance footprint. Accordingly, when one compares the investment records of small investment management firms with large ones, one is really comparing the historical investment results of successful startups to those of large firms. Further, some surviving smaller firms may have benefited from taking risky bets that fortunately paid off. Larger firms, by virtue of their size and prior reputation, may be better able to survive a period of poor performance than a small firm. Thus, although it may seem as if small firms do better, no findings substantiate the claim that small firms will be better investment managers in the future than their large-firm counterparts—and the future is all we care about from the vantage point of today.

Note that investment managment firms may become so large that diseconomies of scale may set in. Service may worsen. One-size-fits-all reporting may be the norm. Worse still, the desired investment strategy or style (such as investing in small company stocks or emerging market stocks) may not be implemented with the same results if the assets under management are too large.

The final step of the external manager decision is determining how many managers (firms) should be hired. The more managers, the higher will be the costs of monitoring what they do. Further, more managers means that unusually good or unusually poor performance by any one manager will be diluted and thus will not have much impact on the total asset pool. Pension funds aiming for unusually good performance may be well advised to concentrate their efforts in a very few firms (taking care to achieve adequate diversification, of course), and those seeking "normal" performance may also choose a very few firms in forming passive, index portfolios. Overall, the trend is toward hiring fewer firms and hiring firms with multiple investment products (for example, bond managers as well as stock managers). Given the difficulty and cost of monitoring, as well as the importance of monitoring the total portfolio, fewer managers is a sound approach.

Often sponsors will hire consultants to help conduct manager searches. As with hiring outside managers in general, turning to consultants is perceived by some sponsors as a form of liability insurance, a way to demonstrate to others that they made a reasonable effort in due diligence. Overall, consultants provide a useful source of benchmarking information on what other, similar pension funds are doing (for example, the number of managers that are being used) and how the various money management firms have done historically.

Monitoring and Controlling Managers

Once investment managers are chosen, the senior managers, trustees, and others who represent the sponsor and plan beneficiaries must remain active in the management of the asset managers. Because it is the performance of the total portfolio that matters, their activities must be coordinated. Also, since managers, internal or external, may or may not do what they are supposed to do, or do it as well as they are expected to, their investments and actions must be monitored. Thus, plan sponsors must develop control systems to ensure conformance to policy and to provide timely feedback for performance evaluation.

Written Controls

The first lines of control are the pension plan's investment policy statement and investment guidelines. The policy statement indicates what level of risk is acceptable for the overall plan and, operationally, it defines which asset classes the plan will hold, what the target policy asset allocations are, and the extent of deviation from the targets that is tolerable. It also explains how the relationship between money managers and the sponsor will be managed.

When using multiple managers, the sponsor needs to develop explicit guidelines for each money manager. These guidelines should spell out very clearly what investment strategy the sponsor expects each to follow, what analytical or investment techniques are to be used in implementing that strategy, and what derivative instruments (such as options or swaps) are acceptable. The guidelines should also indicate how much discretion the investment manager has to shift back and forth among asset classes and should give specific attention to allocations in cash and other short-term money market instruments. For example, if the sponsor wants to be fully invested in a specific sector at all times, that requirement should be indicated. If some percentage of cash holdings is tolerable, the maximum percentage of assets that can be held in cash should be specified. The guidelines should specify how the manager's performance will be assessed and how management and incentive fees will be computed. The frequency of communications from the manager should be defined as well as the content of those communications. The guidelines might also indicate what actions would prompt the sponsor to fire a particular investment manager.

Finally, the sponsor may want to play a role in the investment managers' trading activities. For example, the sponsor may find it advantageous to require money managers to "advertise" offers to sell and what they wish to buy to all the other money managers working for the sponsor. This could allow savings on brokerage commissions and could economize on market impact costs. Payment for order flow and related issues have become increasingly important and should be addressed so that there are no hidden costs of trading (this is discussed in detail later in this chapter).

Monitoring Managers

Once the investment policy and investment guidelines are written and investment managers have been chosen, the sponsor must remain active by monitoring the managers' behavior. Monitoring should have as its goal ascertaining compliance with policy, evaluating performance, and ensuring that managers are not misappropriating the pension's assets through poor decision making or even unethical behavior.

Getting the right information at the right time is essential to any control system. For pension fund sponsors and managers, this implies regular communication between manager and sponsor.

The sponsor must be concerned not only with the absolute perfor-mance—that is, the risk-adjusted rate of return net of costs—of each money manager, but also with his or her relative performance. Many pension plans hire consultants to help evaluate managers using tech-niques like those described in Chapter 7. These consultants have data-bases of managers and can construct customized benchmarks against which a single money manager may be compared. It may be at least lukewarm comfort to know that, although a particular manager work-ing for a pension plan sponsor lost money last year, the rate at which he or she lost money was lower than either the rates of most of the other managers who were identified as pursuing a similar investment policy or than that of the appropriate benchmark.

The primary concern for the sponsor is what one does with the data being generated. If an investment firm produces a poor record of investment performance, for example, what does that imply for the future? Perhaps the poor record was produced by a manager who failed to conform to investment policy. Perhaps the manager demon-strated gross incompetence. Perhaps also the poor performance could have been avoided if the sponsor had not committed funds to a poor or out of favor strategy. Perhaps the data show that the manager did not follow the fund's investment policies and guidelines.

It is compliance with policy that is at the heart of accountability. On a quarterly basis, the sponsor should require the manager to demonstrate that the investment portfolio conforms to previously specified policy para-meters, including allowable assets and proportions, investment strategy and style, appropriate use of derivatives, trading costs, proxy voting, and the other major elements of policy. Annually, the manager should be pre-pared to review policy and investment decision making with the sponsor.

As with the management of assets, the responsibility for monitor-ing should not be delegated away completely. Consultants can help, but the ultimate responsibility rests with the sponsor.

Audit Committee

A useful monitoring tool is a pension audit committee. This commit-tee can ensure that the overall pension investment process follows a sys-tematic, rational approach by participating in both policy formulation and monitoring compliance and the results of various decisions. An addi-tional advantage to having an audit committee formally involved in both the planning and monitoring process is that it encourages establishing performance goals *ex ante* and provides for a formal review against this prior standard. Obviously, success in market forecasting or security selection is not the goal; developing sound investment policy and adherence to that policy is. The audit committee can oversee the sponsor-manager relationship and participate in developing standards both for what needs to be communicated and for the timing of that communication.

Compensation of External Investment Managers

External managers' compensation is subject to negotiation. There are, generally speaking, three ways to structure compensation: a fixed-dollar payment, an asset-based fee (a percentage of the assets under management), and incentive fees (compensation that varies with investment performance). Fixed-dollar fees are virtually unused in the United States. Prior to November 1985, before the Securities and Exchange Commission allowed incentive fees, most investment managers of large portfolios were compensated with asset-based fees. Asset-based fees remain the norm. These fees range from 2 to 10 basis points for the major market equity index funds available to defined benefit plans, to perhaps 100 basis points or more for actively managed foreign equity portfolios, and perhaps 200 basis points for private equity such as leveraged buyout funds and venture capital funds, in addition to performance bonuses or carried interests of up to 20% of the profit above a benchmark return.

Incentive fees have become more popular; more than 20% of all plan sponsors seek incentive fee arrangements with their money managers. Incentive fees are quite complex, and hence are tough to implement. First, the sponsor and the investment manager must agree on what constitutes a suitable investment performance benchmark, and the trigger that activates the incentive fee must be determined. Second, the incentive fee formula must be specified. Specifically, it must be determined what the base fee, the bonus formula, and the fee limits are. Third, the time period must be established—the Securities and Exchange Commission has set a 1-year minimum—over which performance will be measured to determine the fee. Finally, all parties must realize that firms having incentive arrangements with some clients and not with others may find their loyalties divided. This can create serious problems.

Incentive Fees and Risk

A study by Brown, Harlow, and Starks of how managers behave when their compensation is tied to relative performance offers some insights into the effect of incentive fees on the risk-taking behavior of money managers. In looking at 334 mutual fund managers from 1976 through 1991, a picture emerges of managers who, if they are mid-year "losers," tend to increase the volatility of their portfolios during the second half of the year. This increase in risk is greater than the increase seen in a comparable group of mid-year "winners."

This evidence suggests that incentive fees may encourage excessive risk taking. The rationale is that whenever investment performance has been poor over the early portion of a measurement period, managers may try to improve overall performance by betting heavily on a few very risky assets; the gamble is worth the risk to the manager who otherwise stands to lose the race—and possible the assets taken away by angry clients—at year end. The implications of this for pension funds is that managers who are doing poorly may attempt to maximize their compensation by taking on riskier investments—a strategy that may not be in the best interests of the pension plan. If the risk pays off, the manager gets paid the incentive fee; if the risk does not pay off, the manager may be in no worse shape than would have been the case had the risk not been taken. Thus, the plan sponsor must develop methodologies to monitor investment managers to ensure that they do not alter (generally increase) portfolio risk beyond that permitted by the pension plan in order to enhance the likelihood of receiving a performance-based fee.

Managing the Total Asset Pool

All too frequently, pension funds fail to manage the overall set of managers they use—no one manages the managers or the total portfolio, according to Ellis. This can lead to paying too much for the net result obtained, inadvertent indexing, and unintended exposures to market sectors or styles.

What a pension plan pays to investment managers as compensation should be justified by the value the plan receives in investment performance. Thus, the after-fee performance of an active manager should exceed the performance of a portfolio that can be attained passively. However, it is not uncommon for a plan to pay relatively high fees to active managers but receive after-fee performance on the subportfolios managed that is substantially inferior to what could be achieved with an index fund. When these subportfolios are added together, of course, the performance of the total asset pool is poor as well. This mistake is a costly one, to be sure. The only way to avoid it is to monitor performance carefully and switch to better managers or to indexed portfolios if the after-all-costs performance fails to match or exceed a reasonable passive benchmark.

A related mistake frequently occurs when pension funds use so many different managers and styles that the total pool of actively managed assets has simply become "the market." *Closet indexing,* as this is known, is an easy trap that catches many an unwary investor. The result of getting caught in this trap is poor net of fee performance under nearly all conditions, a result that is simply unacceptable. The trap may be avoided by taking care to evaluate the total pool of pension fund assets as one portfolio from time to time rather than always focusing solely on the component portfolios run by individual managers.

Finally, pensions that use active external managers but forget to examine the overall portfolio periodically end up taking unintended style exposures so that they inadvertently become under- or over-weighted in a sector or asset class due to their choice of managers and/or their managers' choices of investments. Not surprisingly, a new money management product has appeared to remedy this problem: the *completeness fund* (see the article by Bensman). Providers of completeness funds analyze pension benchmarks and identify areas where the actual portfolio is underweighted. The manager then acquires assets in these sectors, presumably to return the overall portfolio to its intended exposure. Critics argue that these funds simply contribute to expensive closet indexing and unusual holdings in the completeness subportfolio. Advocates argue that completeness funds focus the attention of the fund on the total asset mix and take appropriate action when it gets out of line.

Replacing Managers

Greenwich Associates estimates that 25% of U.S. pensions replace one manager every year (see the article by Rohrer). What justifies this relatively high turnover? How do pension boards and senior managers make sensible decisions about terminating managers? What special problems should be anticipated in asset custody?

There are several reasons that a pension fund should terminate and possibly replace a current manager. First, the objectives and thus the needs of the fund may change. This change may lead to a change in the types of managers needed. Second, a manager may fail to conform to plan policy and investment policies provided. For example, the manager may change his or her investment style, or fail to vote proxies in the interests of the plan beneficiaries, or may use soft dollars in ways that do not benefit the plan. Or the manager may not provide timely information on performance or other matters as required. Third, the manager's investment performance may not be good enough on a risk-adjusted basis. Care should be taken to use appropriate benchmarks and reasonable evaluation periods, of course. Note that the better the design of the benchmark, the less time is needed to make a judgment. Note also that passive managers should track their benchmarks closely, and short-term deviations should be questioned. Active managers, however, are less likely to track their benchmarks in the short term so some judgment and patience may be appropriate. Fourth, the manager may be too costly. Management fees may be excessive or trading costs may be too high. Generally, performance figures reflect trading costs—but they may not reflect management fees, so the sponsor must be vigilant. Finally, the pension board or senior management may change its view on the merits of active versus passive investing or on the management of the risks the fund faces. Such a change will be likely to require a new set of managers who will deliver the new strategy.

A fundamental problem in deciding whether to terminate a manager is that there is no good way to distinguish in the short run (say, within any period of less than 3 years, or 12 quarters) whether poor investment performance is due to bad luck, or if an investment style or strategy was for a time being unrewarded, or if the managers really are implementing the strategy well. Accordingly, most pension plan sponsors establish rules of thumb. One rule is to stick with a money manager over a market cycle—bear market through bull market to the next bear market. If over the entire cycle the investment performance remains absolutely and relatively poor, the manager gets replaced. If over the cycle the investment performance is satisfactory, the manager will probably be retained. This of course presumes that the relative performance is tolerable. Significant underperformance relative to a fair benchmark can destroy value rapidly: if the manager is significantly underperforming a fair benchmark, it is a good bet that the manager is making poor decisions.

Termination and the Reinvestment Problem

When a manager is terminated, some special problems arise. If the investments of the fund are held by a trustee or custodian in the fund's name, there may be some book entry transactions but no liquidation and reinvestment problem necessarily arises. Securities purchased by the terminated manager that are to be sold may be presented to other managers to see whether they are appropriate for their portfolios. Those that are not typically will be liquidated. The terminated manager should not conduct the liquidation. If there are large blocks of securities to sell, an orderly liquidation should be planned in order to reduce market impact costs (see the next section). If large blocks of securities will be liquidated, options or other derivatives may be useful in "locking in" a price for the securities. Additionally, the fund should maintain its strategic asset allocation throughout the transition by using futures or other derivative contracts to avoid the drag on returns created by excess cash balances. Brokers can be offered commissions that allow them a share of gains realized on an orderly sale to reduce market impact and commissions.

Managing Transaction Costs

Around 75% of respondents to a March 1996 *Institutional Investor* survey reported that they monitor trading costs. Two-thirds indicate they would like to cut costs further. Seventy percent review their trading costs at least quarterly.

According to the *1996 New York Stock Exchange Fact Book*, member firms realized $18.4 billion in revenues from commissions and nearly $20.1 billion from trading in 1996. The fact that the market makers make so much shows that trading carries a large cost to regular investors.

Transaction costs erode portfolio value. Thus, a trade must be motivated by an investment idea that adds more value than is destroyed or by a constraint such as liquidity that overrides the cost of the trade. To ensure that more value is added than is destroyed, pension boards and senior management must understand the costs incurred in trading and how they may be controlled.

The Costs of Trading

The cost of buying or selling exchange-listed securities consists of the commission that must be paid plus an execution or market impact cost. Generally, over-the-counter securities are traded net of commissions, but dealers, nonetheless, make a profit from their markups or markdowns—the bid-ask spread. The magnitude of the spread compensates dealers just as commissions take care of brokers. Both of these costs are more or less observable and hence measurable at the time of the trade. Market impact costs, however, are not so easily measured. Some authorities have termed these costs the "invisible" costs of trading.

Impact Costs

At the present time, serious attempts to measure market impact costs have been made only for equity markets. This is largely because of data limitations. For bonds or real estate, data pertaining to the transaction prices obtained by other investors buying or selling nearly identical assets throughout a particular time frame, or even the transaction prices that occurred just prior to the transaction in which we are interested, are simply not available. For common stocks, however, there are plenty of data. This is fortunate because common stock trading represents most trading for most pension portfolios.

In a perfectly frictionless market, equally patient buyers and sellers would get together and trade without cost. These traders would be spirits, communicating telepathically and continually. Market impact costs for such traders would be zero. If either the buyer or the seller of a security became impatient to do the transaction, however, the other party could take advantage of this and negotiate a price concession.

Impatience can be motivated by an intense need to raise or invest cash (a liquidity motivation) or by what one believes is special but decaying knowledge about the value of the asset (an information motivation). The less patient transactor (let us say the seller) would pay an execution cost, as a consequence of impatience, while the more patient transactor (the buyer) would earn a slight benefit. The seller's market impact cost would equal the buyer's market impact benefit. Trading would be a zero-sum game between the key transactors.

In the real world, it is unusual for buyers to meet sellers without the benefit of a third party—generally a broker. Moreover, it may also be true that one side of a transaction is not around when the other side wants to act. Thus, the party that has come to do business will have to offer a concession big enough to induce a prospective trader to do the trade. Frequently it will be a securities dealer who is so induced. The dealer will take the other side in anticipation of being able to square the inventory positions (long or short) when the other party to the transaction finally does arrive. For providing liquidity to a seller or stock to a buyer, the dealer must be compensated.

With dealers included in the market, trading is still a zero-sum game for the entire community. However, dealers make money while investors pay. For buyers and sellers who are not dealers, trading is not a zero-sum game. Nondealers pay dealers for providing immediacy of exchange. Thus, dealers capture the benefits of traders' impatience, but only when they are either as well informed about the asset's value as the impatient trader or when any special information possessed by one or the other party is not really special. The charge for the immediate execution of a trade is going to depend on the inherent riskiness of the stock that is sold or bought and the time that the dealer expects to have to wait before the matching side of a transaction arrives.

Measuring Impact Costs

There is some controversy regarding how the available data might be used to estimate the market impact cost of a transaction. Although there is no consensus as to how market impact costs should be measured, there are several proposed measures of this cost for a particular transaction. Conceptually, the *market impact cost* is the difference between the price at which the transaction is done and the price that would have obtained in a perfectly frictionless market, a theoretical but never-observed ideal. One approach to estimating market impact cost is to assume total transaction costs are equal to the commission plus the difference between the price of the security at the time the decision to buy or sell was made and the price actually realized in the transaction (see, for example, the article by Perold). Unfortunately, although this is conceptually an objective standard—it includes the cost of delay along with the market impact cost—it could be subject to much self-serving manipulation. Beating this benchmark requires buying stocks that go down between decision and transactions. Moreover, its use would require substantial record keeping of a sort that is not currently in most money management institutions. Another conceptual approach to estimating market impact cost described by Leinweber is to view total transaction costs as the difference in return between the real portfolio and an identical paper portfolio. This approach is appealing for its simplicity and focus on the reason investors care about costs—their impact on performance. Finally, there is an approach used in some institutions that considers the market impact cost to be the difference between a traded block's price and the price that prevailed just before the trade, adjusted for market movements. In a sample of transactions, Wilshire estimated the market impact cost at 7.5 cents per share for buys and sells combined.

In order to use this approach, originally developed by Wilshire Associates, the investor must know which blocks, as reported on the relevant databases, are those of a given investor. That is, the transaction record must be time-stamped so that it can be matched to an explicit transaction in each stock's computerized trading record. It is often impossible, however, to obtain the information regarding time-stamped transactions for any one pension fund. Other problems exist too. Many money managers manage more than one portfolio. For instance, a money manager may manage a portion of the pension funds for sponsors X, Y, and Z. The manager may decide to sell all of each fund's holdings of a given stock. Assume total holdings are 50,000 shares, with X and Y each holding 10,000 shares and with Z holding 30,000 shares. The manager could trade one entire block of 50,000 shares. Each pension fund would then be told the price, and if time records are kept, each pension fund could compare the price it received in, say, a 1:32 PM trade of 50,000 shares with the trade that occurred immediately before it. Of course, if the prior trade was a big block of stock, then the use of the prior trade as a "frictionless market benchmark" would not be very sensible, for it too could reflect large market impact costs. But if the prior trade was not itself a large block of stock, then the measure—the difference between the block transaction price and the prior price—might at least indicate the true market impact cost—what the cost of disturbing the true equilibrium is.

Many, perhaps most, money managers would not sell all the shares at one time unless a 50,000-share order was small relative to the total trading in the stock or the money manager had special, timely information about the stock (more specifically, a reason for being impatient). If neither of these two conditions existed, many money managers would break the 50,000-share order into several smaller ones. Let us hypothesize that in this case the manager's trader, with the manager's permission, split the large order into three smaller orders: two of 15,000 shares each and one of 20,000 shares. Suppose the first 15,000-share order sold at $50, the second at $49⅞, and the 20,000-share order sold at $49¾. The price that each pension fund would be told it received for the sale would be the weighted average price of the transactions, or $49.86. This makes it impossible for the pension fund to link the price back to a specific transaction that appeared on the computerized trading record tape. (On organized exchanges in the United States, stock prices go up and down in increments of eighths or sixteenths, unless the stock price itself is very low, and decimalization is possible in the near future.)

The weighted average price obtained by this money manager and the brokers chosen to do the transactions could be higher or lower than the price other managers or other brokers might have obtained, but the simple methodologies by which market impact costs are assessed do not permit such direct comparisons. Different-size trades could have affected the transaction price relative to the prior trade's price differentially. Further, different rates of trading could also have had an effect on the price at which the transaction was done.

To overcome these problems, there is a measure of execution or market impact costs that compares the actual price achieved on a trade to the weighted average price of the security over the entire course of the trading day (see the article by Berkowitz, Logue, and Noser). The logic behind the use of the weighted average as a benchmark is this: the weighted average price is the price one would expect if one just fed orders into the system over the course of a trading day. As such, it is analogous to a passive benchmark for measuring stock performance that presumes that the trader has no special knowledge regarding when or how much to trade. Using the weighted average price, the estimated market impact cost on New York Stock Exchange stocks is about 2 cents per share, averaged over buys and sells. Sells were more costly than buys, in part because sell transactions were of larger average size than buy transactions; this also suggests that sellers may be a bit less patient than buyers.

Other approaches to the measurement of market impact costs are commercially available. The SEI Corporation compares the trade price with the stock's closing price on the trade day and for several days thereafter, adjusting, of course, for market movements. Callan Associates computes the market impact cost as the difference in the trade price relative to the average of the high and low prices for the day. Neither of these measures really captures the theoretically ideal notion of using as a benchmark the prices that would occur in a frictionless market. The closing price, SEI's benchmark price, does not seem to be representative of other daily prices, as much trading takes place at the end of a day with the intent of influencing the price. The high and low prices are themselves likely to be contaminated by large block transactions, for they are likely to occur as a result of large block trades. There is no reason to believe these two market impact costs (the buys affecting the measured high price and the sells affecting the measured low price) will cancel each other.

Commissions and Total Costs

Another important question is whether there is a trade-off between commissions and market impact costs. In other words, does paying higher commissions obtain better trade execution resulting in lower impact costs and thus lower total costs?

The Berkowitz, Logue, and Noser study found that commission charges were around 7 cents per share. For the Wilshire sample, commissions were 2.8 cents per share. Using the method of Berkowitz and associates, total costs were around 9 cents, whereas using the Wilshire method, total costs were about 10.3 cents.

Though the specific measures differ, it would not be surprising if traders who generated high total transaction costs under the Berkowitz method also incurred high measured total costs under the Wilshire measurement system, for there seems to be at least a mild, partial trade-off between commission charges and market impact costs. Most studies that asked the question discovered a trade-off between commission charges and market impact costs. Higher commission charges tended to be associated with lower market impact costs, and vice versa. Perhaps the brokers do a better job of finding the other side to a transaction when commissions are higher. Perhaps some brokers will themselves take the opposite side of a transaction for their customers by committing their own capital to a trade, thus lowering market impact costs but requiring higher commission charges to compensate for the risks they bear.

Though a trade-off exists, its quantitative significance is not firmly established. If a 1-cent increase in commission will induce broker behavior—either in the form of a more efficient search or in the form of the broker becoming a principal in the transaction—that leads to a market impact cost reduction of more than 1 cent, this should encourage the use of the more expensive brokers. On the other hand, if the market impact cost of a transaction is reduced by less than 1 cent for every 1-cent increase in commission charges, then pension plan sponsors should be pressing their money managers to search for the lowest commissions.

The Berkowitz, Logue, and Noser study found that for every 1-cent increase in commission charges, there is less than a 1-cent drop in market impact charges. Thus fund managers should seek low commissions; paying higher commissions to brokers, even those who commit their own capital to trading, seems not to produce commensurably low market impact costs.

Reducing Transaction Costs

To the extent that all measurement systems yield roughly similar results regarding which money managers or which brokerage firms are consistently high or low cost, there should be sufficient information to draw at least moderately strong inferences about the quality and cost of trading. Hence, insight can be gained into how money managers can improve performance, which brokers ought not be used at all, and what sorts of transactions should be avoided.

The lower total transaction costs are, the better the investment performance of the funds being managed, other things being equal. Consider Berkowitz and associates' measure of total transaction costs at roughly a quarter of 1% of the value of each one-way transaction or half of 1% for a round trip. If a portfolio has a beginning and ending asset value of $100 million, and has executed on its behalf trades that are worth $200 million over the year, transaction costs can easily degrade total portfolio investment performance by 50 basis points. If the money manager could figure out how to cut transaction costs in half, investment performance would improve greatly. Indeed, control of transaction costs—for instance, by dealing with less expensive brokers—could contribute much to investment performance without affecting security selection, allocation, or overall investment strategy.

Beyond selecting low-cost brokers, the obvious way to reduce transaction costs is to trade less. Trading volume and frequency are functions of liquidity (due to factors such as receipt of funding, reinvestment of income, and payments to beneficiaries) and investment strategies (passive strategies have minimal trading and active strategies may have moderate or high levels of trading). Liquidity is not amenable to much reduction in cost beyond what we have already discussed. The choice of investment strategy, however, poses some interesting issues.

There is evidence that some active investment strategies may be more cost efficient than others because, in the ordinary course of implementing the strategy, they provide liquidity to the market (see the article by Wagner). Liquidity is a service; those who provide it may charge for it. Other trading strategies, however, may ordinarily be liquidity demanding. These strategies will be, on average, higher in cost as they have to pay to acquire the liquidity to carry out their trades. For example, consider a market in which prices are falling. Both tactical asset allocation and value investing are likely to be net buyers in a market that needs liquidity on the sell side. Those who wish to sell in the face of falling prices—for example, portfolio insurers and growth or momentum investors—may have to lower their offer price to complete their desired trades. The party who buys—the tactical asset allocator or the value manager—receives the benefit of this concession.

There are a number of other ways to reduce costs. These include using crossing networks and limit orders, according to Leinweber. Additionally, trades motivated by information should try to disguise their intentions to avoid high market impact costs and may be routed through multiple brokers in an attempt to do so. A pension fund that is trading simply due to a liquidity need without immediacy, however, may want to make this known and trade patiently by advertising for the best price trade. Finally, derivatives offer a cost-efficient way to reallocate assets and change portfolio weights.

The Impact of Soft Dollars

The final question to consider is the issue of *soft dollars* and *directed commissions*. Soft dollars arise when trades are directed to a specific broker for execution. In return, the broker gives the firm that decides where the trade is executed credits that may be used to purchase research by other services. In keeping with standards of fiduciary prudence, money spent by a pension plan should be for the benefit of the pension plan. Nonetheless, many pension professionals feel that much of what gets bought with pension fund money is really not necessary or does not directly benefit the plan, the sponsor, or the participants.

According to Greenwich Associates, 45% of public funds and 32% of private funds direct commissions in return for soft dollars. They estimate that total soft dollars are around $0.8 billion of the $2.4 billion in annual commissions paid by money managers (see the article by Bergsman). Thus, this is not a trivial issue. In the best of all worlds, the buyer of the product or service would have implemented transactions that would have generated this many commission dollars anyway. Soft-dollar arrangements, however, raise two very important issues.

First, does the buyer really need what is being bought? The directed commission approach makes buying a lot of possibly useless analysis very nearly painless, because the true value of the service is masked. Indeed, it is not difficult to imagine instances where the product or service does not pass a cost-benefit standard on its own; often what gets purchased merely serves as "fiduciary insurance"—that is, something that would make it less likely for a plan sponsor or money manager to lose a lawsuit brought under the ERISA or other statutes.

Second, soft dollars can obscure the true magnitude of the transaction cost. A buyer engaging in a soft-dollar deal may receive assurances that the commissions charged by the ABC Brokerage Firm are no higher than those charged by any other firm. Thus, the buyer sees the research analysis or other service as virtually free. However, as noted earlier, market impact costs are also an important part of transaction costs. The costs of extremely poor trade executions can far exceed the cash value of the research service. Thus, in many instances it is likely to be true that paying cash for what is truly needed and systematically selecting the broker likely to produce the lowest total transaction cost may be far less costly than the soft-dollar arrangements that may push a sponsor to deal with a brokerage firm that has very high market impact costs.

The Bottom Line on Transaction Costs

Many erroneously believe that transaction costs and soft dollars are mere "nickels and dimes." Accordingly, up until a few years ago, very few pension managers or money managers, let alone top managers, worried about them. Moreover, soft dollars generated by commission expenditures were used like loose change to buy tempting little odds and ends that could come in handy while managing the pension fund, in much the same way that people buy the little things that clutter the areas around supermarket checkout counters because they never know when another disposable flashlight, or whatever, might come in handy.

But huge piles of nickels and dimes are big money. In 1996, there were 104.6 billion shares traded on the NYSE. If it cost only one dime to trade each share, that is a total cost of $10.5 billion. Add to that the cost of trading on NASDAQ (138.1 billion shares), the AMEX (6 billion shares), and regional stock exchange trading (11 billion shares), and it is easy to see how aggregate trading costs can be important. If pension staffs or the firms they hire have to pay cash for pension-related goods and services, these expenditures cannot be hidden from top management or top management's auditors. Pension fund managers will be more accountable for using the plan sponsor's funds than they are when they can hide the purchase of some services by purchasing them with directed commissions.

Maybe it was the sight of 25-year-old stock traders for the ABC Brokerage Firm buying $90,000 automobiles that got the (now-jealous) pension managers and money managers to begin to worry about transaction costs as they do now. Or maybe it was the recent attention the SEC has given to the matter. Regardless of the reasons, this is going to be an increasingly important issue for managers. Better measurement systems for the market impact cost of trading U.S. stocks will emerge; and economically meaningful measurement systems for foreign stocks and fixed-income securities may also become available. Top management, now aware that the magnitude of pension assets exceeds the net worth of many organizations, will begin to realize that the annual transaction costs on a billion-dollar pension fund might be as much as $10 million, 1% of the value of the assets; for many firms or governments with billion dollar funds this is a very large number relative to such benchmarks as corporate profits and infrastructure needs. Moreover, top management will begin to look more closely at what all their soft dollars are buying. They will begin to monitor directed-commission business much more closely, asking all the while whether paying cash for a service and shopping on Wall Street for the best execution of a transaction might not be cheaper and more effective than continuing to do business as it is done now.

Conclusion

Pension plan management requires real management. Indeed, for many sponsors, pension assets are the largest pool of assets the sponsor manages. Thus, managing these asset pools properly is imperative. Paying too little attention can be disastrous. Good management, however, can result in effective investment decision making, efficient management of resources, and better value for the resources consumed by pension funds and the pension industry.

Selecting and monitoring investment managers is a central issue. Pension plans are recognizing how costly it is to control thirty or forty external managers and are appropriately cutting the number of managers they use, often dramatically. Similarly, funds are becoming more responsible in taking the lead, supported by pension consultants, in demanding accountability and conformance with policy. These are steps in the right direction.

Monitoring investment managers is not easy. Control activities take time and consume resources. There are significant measurement and information problems. Further, as noted earlier, it is very often difficult to disentangle luck from competence. This makes it especially difficult to decide when to change money managers.

Regardless of the difficulties, control is an issue for which top pension plan managers should have well-articulated, preferably written policies in place before they are needed. Only through control can sponsors ensure that the policy they have decided on is being followed. A good investment policy out of control is, of course, no policy at all. The costs of lack of control may be high: increased liability for pension fiduciaries and higher contributions for the sponsor are the likely result.

Concern over investment manager performance must extend to the transaction costs these managers incur in managing plan assets. Without question, sponsors need to monitor closely the way securities are transacted and require managers to be cost efficient in implementing their strategies. In coming years we are likely to witness a very strong effort to reduce trading costs not only by more vigorous measuring and more detailed comparisons of the trading performance of different brokers and money managers, but also by experimenting with new ways of trading securities on more efficient securities exchanges or using new computer networks that can be set up to allow large trades among investors without relying on or paying brokers.

Pension sponsors, boards, and senior managers will have to accept the lead role in monitoring the managers who manage their plans' asset pools. Managing managers and transaction costs will be added to the list of issues that determine whether fiduciaries have in fact been prudent in carrying out their responsibilities. The bottom line is that managing investment managers is important, and managing investment costs is important. Sponsors and managers together will have to accept the fact that their actions are open to evaluation and act in ways that add rather than subtract value to the pension portfolios for which they are responsible.

Chapter 12

Decision Making and Accounting for Pensions

Accounting for pension funds has the unfortunate side effect of possibly misleading numerous people who are responsible for making decisions that affect pension funds. In part, this is because accounting uses an accrual procedure that relies on matching transactions with the time periods they presumably affect. In part, it is because some accounting rules are arbitrary and inconsistent. In part, it is because those who apply the accounting rules have considerable leeway in selecting key variables that affect the numbers produced.

Most pension decisions should be based on sound economic data. Over the very long term, accounting measures and economic measures may tend to be reasonably close. However, over the shorter term—say several years—such measures as the economic value of the pension liability, cash contributions to the plan, and cash payments to beneficiaries can be substantially different from accounting measures of the pension liability and pension costs.

This difference between measures in the short term creates a problem for decision makers. Sound decisions generally require information. If accounting data are potentially misleading, what should a pension manager or other fiduciary use? What do they need to know about pension fund accounting?

In this chapter, we provide the non-accountant sufficient background and insight to allow for effective decision making with the data typically provided. We first review the basics of pension fund accounting and then illustrate the key components of pension fund accounting data. Next, we examine some of the critical assumptions that organizations use to measure pension liabilities and pension costs and discuss how these values may differ from the economic realities with which pension plans must deal. Finally, we examine the investment and pension fund management implications of pension fund accounting and show how accounting-based decisions can be suboptimal for sponsors, plans, and beneficiaries.

Accounting Basics

Accounting for defined contribution plans is straightforward. In most cases, unless there is delayed funding, the pension plan assets and the pension plan liabilities equal each other—by definition. The only problematic issue is whether the assets are valued properly. For publicly traded securities, this is not a serious issue as valuation is comparatively simple. If, however, a defined contribution plan has investments in real estate, company stores, venture capital funds, or other illiquid assets, valuation becomes more difficult. Generally, organizations turn to appraisal firms for help in assessing the worth of these investments.

Accounting for defined benefit plans is less straightforward. Accounting and financial disclosure requirements for private defined benefit plans are governed by Financial Accounting Standards Board (FASB) Statement No. 87. Accounting guidelines for state and local governments, government-owned enterprises, and public school teachers are set forth in Government Accounting Standards Board (GASB) Statement Nos. 25, 26, and 27.* The two sets of accounting standards for defined benefit pension plans are sufficiently similar so that no further distinctions are necessary for our purposes. The two sets of standards do, however, differ in some ways, particularly in the way in which actuarial costs are amortized. These differences involve levels of detail that only CPAs need to understand, however. They are not highly relevant for pension plan managers because they deal with reports, not decisions.

Before exploring the key accounting rules, it is helpful to understand some philosophical issues. First, accounting as a discipline treats the pension fund as an entity that is separate from the sponsoring organization; that is, the balance sheets and income statements of the plan are not fully

---

*The GASB's statements are quite new and will not be fully implemented until mid-1997. See the article by Wardlow for an overview of the requirements.

integrated with the company's financial statements. This, of course, implies that decisions affecting the plan do not have to consider the impact they may have on the sponsor, a position contrary to sound pension fund management. Second, changes in the market value of plan assets and the economic value of the pension liability are not given equal treatment in the accounting approach, thus distorting the true impact of various factors on the adequacy of pension funding. Since many decisions of importance rely on a reasonable estimate of the adequacy of funding—for example, determining the risk tolerance of the plan in order to set the strategic asset allocation—this creates problems for decision makers.

Those who play a role in managing pension plans must compensate for these problems when dealing with the numbers presented. To do so requires a basic understanding of how the accounting numbers come to be and how they deviate from the underlying economic reality.

The Accounting Rules

Both private and public sector pension plan accounting requires estimates of the following values:

- Accumulated benefit obligation (ABO)
- Projected benefit obligation (PBO)
- Fair market value of pension assets
- Annual pension expense
- Actuarial interest rate
- Benefit projection interest rate
- Estimated growth of employee's salaries
- Actual plan return
- Expected plan return

The sponsoring organization is also required to report its annual service cost, the growth in its pension liabilities through the passage of time, and its annual contribution to the pension fund. A pension fund's assets must be compared with its liabilities in the footnote to the main accounting statements. Private firms are also required to reconcile the unfunded portion of the plan with liability amounts reported elsewhere in the financial statements. Governments need not do this.

Definitions

Following are definitions of some terms common to private and public pension plan accounting.

Accumulated Benefit Obligation

The accumulated benefit obligation (ABO) is the actuarial present value of benefits, both vested and nonvested, accumulated by an employee as of a specific date. Vested benefits are "owned" by the employee. Nonvested benefits are benefits that must still be earned; the employee must work additional periods to merit vesting. The ABO is based on employee service through the present and compensation as it currently stands. It is the present value of the pension plan if a fully vested employee left the firm now and began collecting benefits later. This can be viewed as a "wind-up" measure of pension obligations; it does not allow for future work or future pay increases. If a pension plan is to be terminated, this is the best initial estimate of what must be set aside for workers. Of course, if the subsequent annuity provider can produce better returns than the terminating pension plan can produce, then the cost of the pension plan termination annuity will be less than the ABO. Note, however, that selecting an appropriate annuity provider can be a challenging task. Should the provider subsequently fail, as did Executive Life, the plan's liabilities may be put back to the sponsor.

Projected Benefit Obligation

The projected benefit obligation (PBO) is the present value of pension benefits under the assumption that the amount of employee compensation will rise between the reporting time and the employee's time of retirement. The PBO will exceed the ABO only when the expected final salary or the future relevant salary history that goes into the pension benefit formula exceeds the present salary or the present relevant salary history that will be used in computing benefits. The PBO measure does not, however, incorporate the fact that more years must be worked in order to achieve the higher salary. For firms with a flat pension benefit system—for example, $1,000 for every year worked—the ABO and the PBO will be the same.

Fair Market Value of Pension Assets

The *fair market value* of pension assets is computed by determining the aggregate current amount that a pension plan reasonably could expect to receive by selling an investment to a willing buyer and itself behaving as a willing seller. That is, this assumes a price that is not a fire-sale price nor any especially concessionary price. For actively traded stocks, government bonds, and high-grade corporate bonds, estimating this is reasonably easy. Valuing real estate, venture capital investments, "junk bonds," and perhaps some other types of investments—rare coins, for instance—requires exceptional effort. Subjective appraisals are needed. Most companies have third-party appraisal experts perform this service for them periodically.

Annual Pension Expense

The *annual pension expense* is the net amount that is needed each year to keep the plan's assets abreast of its growing liabilities. This entails a complex calculation, an example of which is given later. Annual pension expense includes service cost (the growth in pension liability due to another year's work on the part of the employees), interest, any amortizations or deferrals owing to prior service, the difference between actual returns and expected investment returns, and the difference between actual mortality experience and expected mortality experience factors.

A word of caution: annual pension expense may not be the same as the cash actually contributed to the plan by the sponsor, nor is it necessarily equal to the cash needed to restore an underfunded plan. Cash contributions are calculated by using one of a number of actuarial cost methods and, for private plans, are subject to Employee Retirement Income Security Act (ERISA) and Internal Revenue Service (IRS) rules.

Actuarial Interest Rate

The *actuarial interest rate* is the interest rate the actuaries use to determine the present values required for the ABO and PBO computations. This is the discount rate that brings future payments into present value terms.

Benefit Projection Interest Rate

The *benefit projection interest rate* is the rate the actuaries use to project forward the current salaries of employees so that the PBO can be computed. It is the rate that converts current salaries into future salaries.

Estimated Salary Growth

The *estimated salary growth* is the expected nominal rate of growth of employees' salaries.

Expected Plan Return

The *expected plan return* is the return that is estimated on pension plan assets. Conceptually, it is set using the combined wisdom of the plan sponsor and the actuaries informed by historical investment per-formances and assumed future asset allocations. Although the explicit estimate is based on historical experience, it may be shaded down to reflect the inherent conservatism of actuaries.

Actual Plan Return

The *actual plan return* is the actual investment return on pension plan assets. It is comprised of both income and capital change components.

Computing Pension Expense

The most complex component of the required disclosures is the pension expense calculation. It has four components: (1) service cost (2) interest cost (3) return on plan assets, and (4) net amortization and deferral. The last component itself has four parts: asset gain or loss deferral, amortization of cumulative unrecorded net gains or losses, amortization of transition assets or liabilities, and amortization of prior service cost.

An Example

A much-simplified example can illustrate each of these compo-nents. Managers need to understand how the books are kept in order to make good management decisions. Thus, our intent is to convey the essence of the rule, not to develop sophisticated pension accountants. Bear in mind that many of the possible issues are treated in a simplified way. (Two outstanding articles dealing with the details in masterful ways are by Laurence Revsine and Clyde P. Stickney.)

Suppose there is only one employee, Harry, who expects to retire at the end of the year after the current one, which is just beginning. To this point, he has worked for the sponsor for 23 years and will have worked for the sponsor for a full 25 years at retirement in two years. His cur-rent salary is $60,000. There is no integration with Social Security ben-efits under the pension plan. The pension benefit formula of Harry's employer is:

0.015 (or 1.5%) × final year's salary × number of years worked

This formula yields the annual pension benefit that Harry anticipates receiving upon retirement.

Currently the ABO on his behalf is the present value of the annual benefit, assuming no further work. He begins to collect in 2 years and will continue to collect for an expected 20 years after retirement. Here are the computations for the ABO:

$$0.015 \times \$60,000 \times 23 \text{ years} = \$20,700$$

Assuming the actuarial interest rate applied to future benefits is 7%, the present value at time of retirement of annual retirement payments is:

$$benefit = \sum_{t=1}^{20} \frac{\$20,700}{(1.07)^t} = \$219,296$$

and the present value right now is:

$$benefit = \frac{\$219,296}{(1.07)^2} = \$191,542$$

The ABO is \$191,542.

The PBO allows for salary increases. Let us suppose that Harry's salary will rise by the benefit projection interest rate of 6% per year between now and retirement. His final salary will thus be \$67,416, or $60,000 \times (1.06)^2$. His annual pension benefit will be $0.015 \times \$67,416 \times 23$ years, or \$23,258.

The present value at time of retirement of annual retirement benefit is:

$$benefit = \sum_{t=1}^{20} \frac{\$23,258}{(1.07)^t} = \$246,395$$

The present value today is:

$$benefit = \frac{\$246,375}{(1.07)^2} = \$215,211$$

Thus, the PBO is \$215,193.

Service cost may be computed as the amount of increase due to the fact that the employee works an extra year. For the next to last year of Harry's employment, this would be the difference in the present value of the new ABO less the stepped-up-by-one-year present value of the old ABO. Service cost is thus the difference between \$191,542 stepped up by one year to reflect the fact that Harry is a year closer to retirement, or $\$191,542 \times 1.07 = \$204,950$ and the new ABO. The new ABO which takes account of the extra year and the pay increase is computed as:

Annual pension benefit = $0.015 \times \$60,000(1.06) \times 24$ years = \$22,896

Thus the present value of benefits at time of retirement is:

$$\sum_{t=1}^{20} \frac{\$22,896}{(1.07)^t} = \$242,560$$

and the present value right now is:

$$new\ ABO = \frac{\$242,560}{(1.07)} = \$226,692$$

The new ABO is $226,692 and the old ABO, merely stepped up to reflect the new proximity of Harry's retirement, is $204,950. The difference—service cost—is $21,742. It reflects a pay raise of 6 percent and an extra year of work.

The ABO-based pension cost will be more than this difference, however, as it also includes the interest cost as well as the step up in the old ABO. Interest cost is 0.07 × $191,542, or $13,408.

One way to view pension cost is the total difference between the old and the new ABO. To shortcut the calculations, just compare the new ABO, $226,692, with the old ABO, $191,542 not stepped up. However, accounting standards require this difference to be split into its two components. The first is service cost. In the example this is $21,742. The second is interest cost, which is $13,408 in our example. The total of the two is $35,150, which is the difference between the new ABO and the old ABO not stepped up.

So far our pension cost could be (taking some small liberties with the actual accounting rules) reported as:

ABO last year	$191,542
Interest cost	(13,408)
Service cost	(21,742)
Gross pension cost	$35,150

(excluding amortization for past service,
or benefit enhancements, or prior deficiencies)

One could argue that using the ABO as the basis for pension cost computation and reporting is the correct way to do it. This approach is consistent with the idea that the pension plan could terminate at any time. All the employees get is the ABO, the "wind-up" measure.*

---

*Indeed, during the 1980s, many corporate raiders carefully evaluated the magnitude of a target company's pension surplus—the difference between the value of assets and the ABO—before trying to acquire a company. After acquisition, they bought a pension plan termination annuity equal to the value of the ABO and withdrew the after-tax amount of the recoverable surplus.

Computing pension costs in this way would ratify the idea that pensions do not constitute implicit contracts. Rather, the ABO is consistent with the view that the labor market is a spot market, and there is no expectation that an employee is entitled to more than is explicitly promised. Indeed, this is what happens in pension plan terminations that are brought about in order to revert excess assets to the sponsoring organization.

As we have noted before, however, many analysts believe that the labor market is governed by implicit contracts. Accordingly, the true pension obligation of the organization is not merely the ABO, but much more. Indeed, it is even more than the PBO, because the PBO does not allow for using any more years of work in the computations. Employees may expect not only salary increases but also continued employment. Salary increases cannot occur without employment: to compute a PBO that assumes pay raises but no more years of work seems to mischaracterize the labor market. Nonetheless, the PBO as currently constructed represents a compromise value, lying between the true economic value of the pension obligation and the spot contract or ABO value in most cases.

The computation of reported pension expense for all organizations begins by taking the difference in PBOs. Last year's PBO was $215,193. This year's PBO is 0.015 × 67,416 × 24 years, adjusted for the 20-year annuity factor and discounted back to the present. It is:

$$\frac{1}{(1.07)} \times \sum_{t=1}^{20} \frac{\$24,270}{(1.07)^t} = \$240,296$$

This computation yields a pension cost of $240,296 less $215,193, or $25,103. Of this total cost, $13,828 is interest cost and $11,275 is service cost. The reason that pension cost is lower using PBO than ABO is that both the early and late PBO measures use the same future salary, whereas the early and later ABO computations use different actual salary figures that depend on the true salary computation that enters the benefit formula.

To compute net expense (once again deferring discussion of all the specific nuances of the actual accounting rules), we first compute the actual return on the pension fund assets after investment fees and expenses. This includes unrealized and realized capital gains, interest, and dividends. The actual return is then offset against the pension cost estimate. Of course, actual pension fund payments to retirees also affect the net pension expense. Benefit payments alter PBOs—those already retired are still included in the estimate of the fund's liability, and with the passage of time will get less future benefit from the pension plan because they get nearer to death. Benefit payments also alter net pension fund returns because less of the fund's assets are available for investment after benefit payments.

Suppose that at the beginning of the year (the end of the prior year) the pension fund had a value of $300,000. Further, suppose that over the course of the year it experienced a gain of $20,000, so its value at the end of the current year is $320,000. The pension cost of $25,103 would be offset against the portfolio gain. Net pension expense, again ignoring some complexities, would be $25,103 less $20,000, or $5,103. To keep the pension plan whole from an accounting perspective, and assuming that nothing else (such as pressure from ERISA, the IRS, contracts, or legislation or strategic concerns) was affecting the firm's contribution requirements, and also assuming that the sponsor followed a policy of aiming for zero reported under- or overfunding of its pension plan, the sponsor would contribute $5,103. This would be its cash payment. Of course, if the organization had underfunded in the past, the cash payment would have to be larger to close the funding gap. Similarly, if the sponsor enhanced its retirement benefits, say by changing the 0.015 multiplier to a 0.016 multiplier in the benefit formula, it would also have to contribute more in order to pay for past service costs.

Futher Differences Between Economics and Accounting

We have already seen that accounting rules may depart from economic reality by implying that employees will have no future pensionable employment. Unfortunately, this is not the only departure that FASB Statement No. 87 or GASB Statement No. 27 allows.

Actual versus Expected Return

In addition to the actual gain or loss on the pension fund, the sponsor must incorporate prior unexpected portfolio gains and unexpected portfolio losses in its pension expense. To see how this works, suppose the sponsor projected that its annual return on the pension funds would equal 6 percent. Assuming that the $300,000 it had invested at the end of last year (the beginning of this year) equaled what it expected to have invested at the time, the actuarially determined expected value of the portfolio at the end of this year was $318,000, or $300,000 × 1.06. If the actual value was $520,000, the sponsor could defer this unanticipated portfolio gain of $2,000. If it did, its books would be as follows:

Service costs	$11,275
Interest cost	$13,828
Actual return on plan assets	(20,000)
Deferred gain on plan assets	$2,000
Pension expense	$7,103

The effect of backing out the $2,000 deferred gain is to make the sponsor's pension expense appear larger than it truly is. The sponsor may wish to contribute more money now to get a bigger tax deduction and "bank" the gain. Alternatively, it may only wish to bank the gain in an accounting sense, using it—that is, drawing on it—in some year when investment performance was not good but the company nonetheless wanted to report low pension expense. Note how this moves the "pension expense" away from the cash contribution that may be necessary to make the plan whole.

For companies, if the cumulative discrepancy between actual and expected returns begins to become large, it must be reported on the company's income statement and must be dealt with explicitly. Small cumulative discrepancies may remain hidden in the footnotes. Specifically, according to Revsine,

> At the start of each reporting year, the cumulative unrecorded gain (or loss) is computed. This cumulative gain or loss will be amortized over future years if it exceeds 10 percent of the larger of (1) the present value of pension obligations based on assumed future compensation levels (termed projected benefit obligation), or (2) the market-related value of pension plan assets. If the 10 percent threshold is triggered, the cumulative gain or loss is amortized straight line over the estimated average remaining service life of active employees.

The total effect of these accounting practices is that it allows organizations to smooth their reported pension expense. However, it changes nothing fundamentally about the economics of the organization or its obligations.

Benefit Enhancement

Sometimes organizations change the formula for determining benefit amounts that affects all existing employees. Private firms may simply decide to increase the rewards for long-term employees. Many state and local governments enhance pension benefits instead of current salaries, in order to avoid raising current taxes while still increasing total compensation (see the article by Weinberg). Additionally, organizations sometimes enhance their pension benefits in response to prior unanticipated inflation. Indeed, many state and local governmental entities contractually commit themselves to provide cost of living adjustments (COLAs) that are built into their pension liability estimates. Corporations will, in contrast, typically offer ad hoc periodic adjustments.

When the benefit formula is made more generous, a larger pension obligation results. Because the change in the formula applies to years already worked, it represents not only a service cost for this year but one for all past years as well. This is termed a *past service cost*. For accounting purposes, the present value of future pension benefits attributable to the formula change is computed. This value is then amortized over the remaining working life of the employee (or the actuarially estimated lives for the current group of employees).

Transition Gains and Losses

There is also a transition asset or liability amortization. When FASB Statement No. 87 was introduced,* some companies had pension plans in which the fair market value of assets exceeded the amount of the liabilities that had to be reported under the rule. Others had underfunded plans. The amortization component allows companies to report the closing of the gap between what they had in the pension plan and what they need to indicate their pension expenses are for financial accounting reporting purposes. That is, the overfunding or underfunding gaps are amortized.

Reconciling Economics and Accounting

Amortizations and deferrals complicate the reconciliation between the economic status of the pension plan and its status in accounting terms. The Financial Accounting Standards Board (1985) itself wrote in its summary of FASB Statement No. 87:

> The Board believes that an employer with an underfunded pension obligation has a liability and an employer with an overfunded pension obligation has an asset. The most relevant and reliable information available about that liability or asset is based on the fair value of plan assets

---

*GASB Statement No. 27 had not gone into effect at the time of this writing, but state and local governments will probably face the same problem.

and a measure of the present value of the obligation using current, explicit assumptions. The Board concluded, however, that recognition in financial statements of those amounts in their entirety would be too great a change from past practice. Some Board members were also influenced by concerns about the reliability of measures of the obligation.

The FASB seems to favor an economic definition of liabilities, a definition that would allow liabilities to be computed as the ABO plus credit for expected future salary increases and for continued work. It would also disallow omitting from the computation of the pension fund surplus or deficit any reference to deferrals or amortizations. This definition was not adopted, however, because it would have caused many companies to report very substantial pension expense (though not necessarily all cash expense) soon after the rule's adoption; in turn, this would have depressed reported earnings for these companies. Those who pay for the preparation of financial statements would not accept such a cataclysmic change in reporting methods. Instead, these companies can amortize prior unfunded expenses and defer recognition of some prior gains—thus their reported income is affected gradually, rather than all at once.

Senior plan managers, administrators, and fiduciaries must adjust for the economic-accounting divergences that can have a significant impact on reported numbers and thus may obscure the true economics of the pension from decision makers. The most important of these are likely to occur in measuring plan surplus or funding status, in measuring pension expense against cash flow, and in making various assumptions in computing pension accounting numbers.

Plan Surplus

The measure of pension plan surplus or deficit that FASB Statement No. 87 and GASB Statement No. 27 require is the difference between the fair market value of the pension plan assets and its PBO. As noted earlier, even the PBO generally is less than a true economic rendering of pension obligations because it ignores potential future years of work. Also as noted, if a company terminates a pension plan, the amount it can recapture is the difference between the market value of its assets and its ABO, not its PBO, or what an annuity costs that has a present value equal to the ABO.

Decision makers must be aware that the accounting measure chosen to measure pension plan surplus or deficit lies between the alternative realities of long-term implicit contract types of labor markets and short-term spot labor markets. This is important because pension plans are fundamentally contracts between employees and employers. Managing pension plans, therefore, must reflect this reality if the strategic asset allocation is to reflect the actual risk tolerance of the parties affected by the pension plan (sponsors, employees, shareholders, and taxpayers) and to avoid "gaming" the numbers to obscure from one or more parties the economic realities of various decisions. In general, decision makers should be on the lookout for understated pension liabilities and a corresponding overstatement of the pension plan's financial health or funding status.

Pension Expense versus Cash Flow

As suggested earlier, the reported pension expense figure does not necessarily represent the cash flow to the plan from the sponsor nor the benefits paid out of the plan. Though possible, it is difficult to estimate the actual cash flow precisely by using standard financial statement analysis techniques (see the article by Stickney).

For corporations, ERISA imposes minimum standards on annual funding in order to enhance the safety of pension plans, while the IRS limits tax-deductible pension funding if a plan is economically overfunded. Even overfunded plans report pension expense; however, they are precluded by law from putting additional cash into the plan on a pretax basis. Governmental entities face no such externally imposed constraints. Many are pay-as-you-go plans; others, such as New Hampshire, impose their own minimum funding standards.

Decision makers need to consider the actual level of funding that is occurring and determine whether it is adequate in view of the plan's tolerance for risk (keeping in mind that risk tolerance is really a joint tolerance involving the sponsor as well). Decision makers must be careful not to be misled about the funding status of the plan—funding requirements and the actual funding status of the plan are interdependent.

Interpreting Pension Accounting: An Example

Tables 12-1 and 12-2 are simplified sample financial statements. Footnotes explain each entry. Table 12-1 is the pension expense table. Table 12-2 tells us how much is in the plan and how much is owed, and reconciles the gap between plan assets and plan liabilities as measured by the PBO.

Assumptions, Measurements, and Games

From the prior discussion and the simple illustrations in Tables 12-1 and 12-2, one can see how an organization can affect its reported pension

Table 12-1. Pension Expense for a Defined Benefit Plan, 200×

Expense for service during the year[1]		$300.00
Interest cost on projected benefit obligation[2]		$1,000.00
Actual return on plan assets[3]	$2,700.00	
Amount deferred to future periods[4]	(1,500.00)	
Amount reducing current year expense	$1,200.00	($1,200.00)
Amortization of excess of market value of plan assets over PBO on adoption of FASB Statement No. 87[5]		(100.00)
Net pension expense		0

[1]Present value of benefits earned this year.
[2]Interest on the PBO at 7%.
[3]This is the total earnings on the pension assets.
[4]This suggests that true investment earnings have been exceeding expected investment earnings for some time so some portion of the earnings are being deferred. In this illustration, actual earnings were $2,700 and expected earnings must have been $1,200. This leaves $1,500 of gain that can be deferred to future periods.
[5]This is transition year amortization. Prior to FASB Statement No. 87, this plan was over-funded. A portion of that historical overfunding is being used now to offset expense.

obligations. Superior investment returns will reduce pension expense. Further, in order to be able to produce a larger or smaller PBO, a sponsor can assume that salaries will grow by a higher or lower rate. Sponsors can use a higher or lower interest rate to discount future pension benefits, and this too will lower or raise the PBO. Finally, sponsors can use a higher or lower actuarial assumption regarding the expected return on pension plan assets. The use of a very high expected rate of return means that companies' actual rates of return may fall short of the expected value. Hence prior deferred profits will have to be used or a loss will be accrued; but no matter what, the company can report a low pension expense. By using a high expected return rate, the organization will report lower pension expense and will probably have to infuse less cash into the pension plan on a year-to-year basis. That is, with high enough return assumptions, the plan can move closer to a pay-as-you-go plan.

To give some sense to how variable the chief actuarial assumptions—projected return, projected salary increase, and the interest rate used to determine the present value of liabilities—we offer Table 12-3. Table 12-3 shows the assumptions used for key variables over the past 2 years for three companies and one state. The state's assumptions lag the companies' assumptions because its fiscal year ends in the middle of the calendar year, not the end.

Table 12-2. Reconciliation of Projected Benefit Obligation with
Net Pension Obligation for a Defined Benefit Plan, 200×

Accumulated benefit obligation[1]	
Vested benefits[2]	$11,000
Nonvested benefits[3]	300
Total accumulated benefit obligation	$11,300
Projected benefit obligation[4]	15,000
Less market value of plan assets[5]	(17,000)
Unrecognized transition gain (10 years remain)[6]	1,000
Other unrecognized experience gains[7]	2,500
Unrecorded pension obligation based on	$1,500
projected benefit obligations[8]	

[1]This is the present value of future benefits assuming no salary growth and no continued employment.
[2]These are benefits that are "owned" by employees.
[3]These are benefits not yet "owned" by employees.
[4]This is the present value of future pension benefits assuming salary growth.
[5]This is the fair market value of assets in the pension plan.
[6]At the time FASB Statement No. 87 was adopted, the value of its assets in the plan exceeded the PBO by some amount. This excess is amortized gradually and taken into income, by applying it to future pension costs. The legend indicates it will be amortized over 10 years.
[7]Mortality experience and employee termination dates deviate from projections. The amount on this line, which could be negative, is the net of these experiences caused by actual investment income, mortality, and termination rates differing from expectations.
[8]This is the amount by which pension liabilities are understated relative to what is expected to be given to employees. This should equal the amount of cash the company contributes to the pension.

The table shows rather vividly how widely organizations may vary in the assumptions used to estimate the ABO and PBO—projected salary increases and interest rates—and funding costs, which are heavily influenced by rate of return expectations. Moreover, small changes can have a large effect. For instance, when IBM dropped its discount rate to 7.25% in 1995 from the 8.25% it had been, this was accompanied by a nearly 20% increase in its PBO. Of course, other factors contributed, but the effect of the interest rate change was substantial. Fund American Companies' interest rate reduction was accompanied by a 35% increase in its PBO, though there was virtually no change in the number of employees covered by the plan.

Overall, then, accounting requires that judgments be made about a number of factors. Once these judgments have been rendered, the various measures—pension expense, PBO, and so on—are computed. Given the rules, these numbers are not likely to match up with reality. The nature of

Table 12-3. Comparison of Actuarial Assumptions and Other Variables

Sponsor	1994	1995
Actuarial assumptions		
IBM (U.S. Plans)	9.5%	9.25%
Fleet Financial	8.85–10.0%	10.0%
Fund American Companies	8.0%	8.0%
State of Massachusetts	8.0%	8.0%
Projected salary increases		
IBM (U.S. Plans)	5.0%	5.0%
Fleet Financial	4.5–5.0%	4.5–5.0%
Fund American Companies	6.0%	6.0%
State of Massachusetts	6.0%	6.0%
Interest rate for liabilities		
IBM (U.S. Plans)	8.25%	7.25%
Fleet Financial	8.50%	7.25%
Fund American Companies	8.0%	7.0%
State of Massachusetts	N.A.	N.A.

the process leaves the computation open to manipulation by those who may wish to understate or overstate a given factor. This "gaming" can erode the usefulness of accounting measures to those who must ultimately make important decisions about the pension and its asset pool.

Investment and Management Implications

Despite the efforts of FASB Statement No. 87 and GASB Statement No. 27 to reduce the ambiguities surrounding pension fund reporting, there are still opportunities for organizations to manage their accounting reports. Worse, some can also structure their pension fund asset portfolios in particular ways in order to affect the pattern, though not necessarily the level, of reported pension expense.

There are two broad areas in which accounting results can be aggressively managed. The first is motivated by a desire to reduce the volatility of reported pension expense or reported plan surplus—to smooth the numbers. In general, smoothing is of little consequence until, as we will see, it affects either the asset allocation decision or the rebalancing strategy that is followed. The second is motivated by the desire to manipulate or "game" the numbers—or more accurately, the assumptions that underlie the numbers—to achieve political ends such as disguising pay raises by burying them as increases in pension benefits.

Smoothing Activities

Some organizations are less worried about the magnitude of their reported investment expense or plan funding than about variability in these factors (see, for example, commentary in the articles by Arnott and Bernstein). They prize forecastability. These sponsors think it is sensible to select asset allocations for the pension asset pool that will have a true rate of return equal to the assumed discount rate on the PBO because by doing so the pool can produce very predictable pension expense reports far into the future. Unfortunately, this sometimes comes at the expense of total return on the pension portfolio, thus putting an undue financial burden on the sponsor or imperiling the financial health of the plan.

To reduce the volatility of the reported pension expense figure even more than the amortizations allow, many companies have adopted specialized pension asset allocation schemes. With these schemes, as the present value of the PBO changes, the market value of the pension plan assets changes with it. The object is generating (reported) pension expense that is never larger than anticipated. The motivation behind this is to ensure that the company does not have to report a decline in the pension plan surplus. If the value of the pension assets is perfectly correlated with the PBO and initially exceeds it, the pension plan will always be in a surplus or overfunded situation, assuming, of course, continuing contributions at the required level.

There are two broad classes of schemes that have been developed to eliminate the unpleasant surprises and sustain pension plan surpluses. These rely on dedicated bond portfolios and portfolio insurance.

Dedicated Bond Portfolios

One way to reduce the variability in reported pension expense is holding pension plan assets that move exactly as the present value of the projected benefit obligation moves. Because the PBO's present value will rise or fall as interest rates decline or increase, an asset portfolio that moves in exactly the same way will insulate reported pension expense from the effect of changing asset and liability values. This goes beyond just holding an all-bond portfolio. Here the cash flow characteristics of the structured bond portfolio are important.

Immunization of the pension expense figure from changing values can be achieved in several ways. The sponsor could hold a portfolio of bonds such that the timing of the cash throw-off from the bonds (that is, the interest payments plus maturities) matches the cash payments of the pension plan sponsor. Another way to immunize the pension expense figure is for the sponsor to use one of the various bond duration measures and select a bond portfolio the duration of which matches the duration of the pension liabilities. The idea here is taking a measure of the weighted average maturity of a bond portfolio and match it to a corresponding measure for obligations of the pension fund.* This approach offers no guarantee that the value of the liabilities will correlate perfectly with the value of the assets because duration measures generally work well only when the yield curve experiences small parallel shifts, upward or downward. (The term "parallel shift" refers to shifts in which short-term and long-term rates change by the same amount.) Nonetheless, duration matching tends to work tolerably well.

There are, however, two major drawbacks to adopting one of the dedicated bond portfolio approaches. First, equities have historically produced better investment returns than have bonds. For instance, according to Ibbotson Associates (1996), from 1926 through 1995, long-term government bonds enjoyed an average annual compound return of 5.2% whereas the compound return on common stocks over the same period was 10.5% per year. Accordingly, using all-bond portfolios to reduce fluctuations in reported pension expense may lead to significantly larger average pension expense in the economic sense—higher cash contributions, in this case—than would an investment strategy that emphasized common stock.

The second drawback to adopting a dedicated bond portfolio approach is more subtle. The PBO can be separated into two components. One is the (fixed) liability to employees who have already retired. The pension plan sponsor is under no obligation to increase those payments as time passes. The present value of this annuity, the fixed liability to retirees, will fluctuate with interest rate changes only, ignoring mortality and other demographic factors. The other component of the PBO is the projected liability to active employees. The present value of this component changes with interest rate changes and, perhaps more important, also changes with unexpected changes in

---

*This is roughly termed *duration matching*. The most common measure of duration is:

$$\sum_{t=1}^{T} \frac{(t \times CF_t)/(1 + Y/2)^t}{P}$$

where t is time, 1, 2, 3, etc.; Cf_t is the cash flow in each period t; Y is the yield on the bond; and P is the bond's price. In theory and under some very specific circumstances, two instruments with the same duration should experience nearly identical changes in value whenever Y, the yield, changes.

wage rates. Indeed, if unexpected wage changes are more significant than interest rate changes, then a dedicated bond portfolio cannot off-set variations in this component of the PBO. The bond portfolio's value will rise or fall with interest rate changes, but it may not change at all in value with wage rate changes.

Arnott and Bernstein point out that the use of bond portfolios is the result of "an inappropriate restructuring of the pension fund in terms of the true as opposed to the accounting-defined risks of the pension plan. The oversimplification arises from too much attention to the interest sensitivity of the pension surplus, a result of the FASB's emphasis on defining the surplus in terms of the interest sensitivity of the fund's liabilities."

Arnott and Bernstein argue that the value of the active workers' component of the PBO is more likely to vary with dividends than with interest rates. Thus, the asset mix (the proportions of common stock and all of the other possible asset classes in the portfolio) of the pension plan should not be determined by the way pension expense or pension liabilities are reported. Rather, it should be determined by the demo-graphics of the past and current workforce and the plan's tolerance for risk, as opposed to FASB Statement No. 87 reporting risk.

Arnott and Bernstein conclude:

> Many companies, however, are putting too much emphasis on the structures of FASB 87, and are looking to long-term bonds to save the day. Long bonds are appropriate for stabilizing the surplus in the short run where the net present value of the liabilities is the crucial consideration. Bonds are also appropriate where the liability esti-mation is highly certain, as in the case of retired lives or a pension fund for a mature work force. But there is danger in viewing all pen-sion funds in these terms....In reality, the size of pensions the corpo-ration pays in future years will have little to do with today's level of long-term interest rates.

They correctly admonish pension plan administrators not to let the tail of accounting wag the dog of investing. Emphasizing bonds at the expense of equities to keep short-run reported volatility of pension expense low can be a very costly thing to do.

Portfolio Insurance

Portfolio insurance was widely hailed as an excellent way to insulate a company's financial reports from fluctuations in interest rates and the market value of assets (see the article by Sanes and Zurack) while not eliminating the opportunity to participate in positive movements in stock prices. Under FASB Statement No. 87, fluctuations in pension expense can significantly affect earnings. Under GASB Statement No. 27, the reported government surplus or deficit can be affected. Conceptually, portfolio insurance could dampen that variability.

Portfolio insurance schemes explicitly recognize the fact that equities have historically provided higher total returns than have bonds. Recognizing this, many companies decided to pursue a different investment strategy in order to hold the promise of significantly higher returns than (safer) fixed-income portfolios. Portfolio insurance strategies typically require choosing a floor for the portfolio value. This is the value below which the portfolio will not be allowed to fall. The difference between the portfolio's current value and the floor is called the *cushion*. As the actual portfolio value approaches the floor—that is, as the cushion shrinks—risky assets are sold to reduce exposure and safe assets are bought. As the portfolio increases in value, risky assets are bought to capture more of their potential future appreciation.

The principal flaw of portfolio insurance schemes and the reason that they have fallen out of favor with the investment community is liquidity: everyone cannot sell stocks at the same time; everyone cannot move funds from risky stocks to safe bonds simultaneously without affecting market prices. Indeed, if enough investors demand portfolio insurance, a small drop in stock prices could become an avalanche, as investors sell more and more of their stocks—and have to make large price concessions to do so.

Gaming the Numbers

Gaming the numbers has two possible motivations. One motivation is simply to make the plan or some aspect of the plan's operation look better than it really is: window dressing. The other is to disguise the impact of economic decisions in order to accomplish a similar goal but this time on a grander scale—typically the scale is that of the sponsoring organization.

Window Dressing

Unfortunately, those who decide what the inputs into the accounting process should be—the interest rates, expected returns, and so forth—too often fail to ask what is economically sensible from a decision maker's perspective. Instead, they ask what numbers are needed to make the financial reports look good.

Part of the problem stems from the previously mentioned desire to achieve low variability in reported numbers. Innocuous at times, this activity can obscure important trends such as a worsening of the pension's financial condition or an increased exposure to factors such as inflation. Worse still, it may mislead decision makers into thinking that little risk is being taken—after all, the funding ratios appear stable and pension expense does not vary greatly from one period to the next—when the reality is that there are significant exposures of which decision makers should be aware.

This problem can be especially severe for public funds when a state or local entity applies pressure to change one or more of the underlying assumptions for the sole purpose of making the pension plan appear to be better off. The motivation may be to balance a budget or to reduce funding payments. Whatever the motivation, fiduciaries should resist such pressures.

Disguised Decisions

Employer/sponsors have from time to time granted employees increased pension benefits in order to avoid a pay raise that they may feel shareholders or taxpayers might find unacceptable. In a world of economic accounting, this would be seen for what it is—a substitute of one form of compensation having real economic value for another. In a world in which accounting procedures allow considerable leeway in selecting fundamental inputs in the measurement process, the impact of these decisions can be hidden from view, at least in the short run, and accountability can be avoided.

Viewed from the perspective of the pension plan, however, an increase in benefits (future or retroactive) increases the present value of the plan's liability immediately. As a result, the surplus deteriorates and pressure increases for higher returns (and risk) or increased contributions. These are the economic realities. They occur immediately upon granting increased pension rights and should be incorporated into the decision-making process. However, the leeway organizations have in computing the liability can be used to mask the real impact of the change in benefits.

Note that there does not have to be an ulterior motive to hide a pay raise from those taxpayers or shareholders who ultimately must pay it. Benefit increases may be the product of fully informed negotiations where the parties fully disclose to all affected parties what is going on. Even here, though, the consequences of the action must be correctly assessed. Unfortunately, accounting rules can get in the way.

Conclusion

If it does nothing else, this chapter should caution pension fund managers and other fiduciaries about the complexity of pension fund accounting and how it may pervert good decision making. Reporting organizations have a great deal of discretion in their choice of assumptions, and these can affect reported values rather significantly.

Trustees and others whose role is primarily that of oversight and long-run strategy must know enough about accounting for pensions to know how it can mislead and thus interfere with the decision-making process. This does not mean they need to be certified public accountants or even be able to do the calculations. It does mean they must know that funding adequacy (as measured by funding ratios), pension expense, and other decision inputs can be gamed. Even if the accounting is honest and devoid of an ulterior motivation to mask reality and make things seem better than they really are—and we believe it usually is—the rules sometimes lead to obscuring that which the decision maker needs to know.

What should pension fund decision makers do? Ask for interpretive commentary. Insist on estimates of the economic consequences of alternative courses of action or events that have already occurred. Do not accept the impact on the accounting numbers as adequate justification for a planned course of action. Make certain that the discussion, and ultimately the decisions made, turn on the economics of the matter rather than on appearances.

In closing, we also want to emphasize something every finance text you have ever read has preached: do not make what are essentially uneconomic decisions just to try to get the books to look good. Never let the way accounts are presented prevent your organization from making wealth-maximizing choices that have the short-run effect of making an accounting statement look worse than it might otherwise look. Develop investment and funding policies that are independent of the way things get reported. If some are still worried about the way results get reported, there are plenty of discretionary assumptions that can be manipulated. However, we do not advocate altering assumptions without underlying economic motivation merely in order to get the accounting "right."

Chapter **13**

The Pension Plan
as Shareholder

As reported in *The Economist* (August 1996, p. 47), the College
Retirement Equities Fund (CREF) successfully persuaded, albeit quietly, the W. R. Grace Company to cut the size of its board from 22 to 12,
impose a mandatory retirement age of 70, get rid of its chairman, and
replace half its directors. Why did CREF do this? Should other pension
plans follow suit? Should pension plans be more active in monitoring
and even working with the managements of the firms in which they
own stock? Will such intervention lead to higher risk-adjusted returns
after the costs of intervention are weighed?

A fundamental investment problem is that poor corporate performance leads to poor relative and/or absolute stock performance. This,
in turn, can contribute to poor performance for pension funds that own
stock in these corporations. Pension fund money managers of pension
plans that hold shares in corporations that are not providing acceptable
investment returns must decide what to do. According to Hirschman,
there are three alternative strategies that may be followed by pension
fund shareholders. These can be summed up in three words: exit,
voice, or loyalty. *Loyalty* occurs when the owner or shareholder takes
no actions to monitor or control management behavior, but rather
trusts company management to do what is right. *Exit* is defined as the
purchase and subsequent sale of stock. Thus, trading is a form of shareholder activism. Shareholders demonstrate approval of company man-

agement by buying the stock and disapproval by selling. In contrast, *Voice* is the use of ownership power, including voting rights, to affect the direction of the firm in which an investor holds a stake. Rather than selling, the pension plan keeps the stock and attempts to influence the direction of the firm in any of several ways.

Historically, private pension plans primarily have chosen to follow the strategies of Loyalty or Exit. There are a number of reasons why this type of behavior has been so predominant. A growing number of public plans and some private plans, however, are choosing Voice in an effort to boost returns and avoid the potentially high costs of Exit or Loyalty. In part, they feel they must exert their influence in order to be responsible fiduciaries—to protect the plan's beneficiaries and even the sponsor from poor performance that is correctable. In part, they feel they must because the costs of Exit are far too high. Today, pension funds own such a large proportion of outstanding shares that many have begun to fear that a precipitous sale would lead to exceptionally large transaction costs, principally the result of the market impact on price of a large block trade. For many pension funds, these transaction costs could be far greater than the cost of trying to correct the wealth-reducing behavior of the corporation. Even pension funds that are committed to passive investment strategies using index funds face this problem because these index funds must in turn hold stocks. If some of the companies in the index can be persuaded to perform better from a financial standpoint, the index portfolio will perform better, too. Of course, larger companies have more of an impact on the value-weighted indexes that are most commonly used, so focusing attention on smaller companies offers less potential benefit.

In this chapter, we begin by providing an overview of how U.S. corporations are governed, and then reviewing the empirical work that has tried to answer the question of whether active shareholding actually makes a difference or not. We then outline the alternative strategies that are available to pension fund managers who wish to be more active in the affairs of the companies in which they are invested, and discuss reasons why some pension funds are not active shareholders. The chapter concludes by discussing some practical issues that funds choosing to be more active shareholders should consider.

Corporate Governance

Corporate governance is the process by which decisions are made that determine the direction and performance of corporations. The participants in this decision making are the stakeholders of the company, including the customers, the suppliers, the creditors, the shareholders, the managers, and the board of directors. When discussing issues of corporate governance, particularly in the United States, the primary three participants are the board of directors, the shareholders, and the management.

According to Millstein, effective corporate governance requires "a necessary tension between the freedom of managers to make decisions and take risks yet be held accountable to shareholders, and the freedom of shareholders to buy and sell their interests in the corporation at will, yet hold managers accountable so long as the investment relationship exists." The board of directors has long been considered the intermediary between managers and shareholders. Boards and managers jointly are responsible for designing and implementing the corporate strategy. The board is responsible for representing the interests of shareholders and ensuring that management is effectively managing the implementation process.

The first regulations passed by Congress that were instrumental in defining these roles were the 1933 Securities Act and 1934 Securities and Exchange Act. The initial model of governance was intended to provide shareholders with the ability to protect their financial interests. The system was designed to operate in a way similar to the American political system, where the shareholders were each voters with one equal vote, the board members were the elected officials, and the corporate charters and by-laws were to be the governing constitutions (see the article by Monks and Minow).

In practice, the American equity market consists of a broad-based group of investors that are primarily decentralized and not able to monitor their holdings actively and effectively. The cost of a minority shareholder actively monitoring the performance of a particular management team often outweighs the benefits that are then shared by all shareholders. John Pound of Harvard University describes historical corporate governance in this country in this way:

> (The) American system of governance has never relied on a stable set of close relationships between large financial institutions and major corporations. Rather, it has relied upon no one and everyone—upon the actions of uncounted numbers of individual, corporate, and institutional investors, operating within a deep, liquid, and anonymous securities market.

In contrast, the German, French, Japanese and to some extent the British systems have relied much more heavily on the close relationships between corporations and financial institutions. This has encouraged some to speculate that, as the amount of assets managed by institutional investors, including pension plans, becomes a larger and larger percentage of the capital markets, the United States system of governance may begin to look more and more like that of other countries.

Central to effective corporate governance is the mechanism for changing the behavior of poorly performing firms, to push corporations to behave economically, to be organizations that are keenly focused upon the creation of shareholder value. Until the late 1980s, poor corporate performance was often rewarded with a hostile takeover bid. Indeed, the ease with which hostile bids could be mounted and financed probably served as a deterrent to keep otherwise errant corporations from squandering more shareholder money than might otherwise have been the case. This is corporate governance in its most extreme form—a contest for control.

That this approach to governance has declined in usage can primarily be attributed to three factors:

- Many corporations have developed new methods of defense from takeovers. Companies and their lawyers have become well skilled at designing amendments to corporate charters that would make hostile takeover bids extremely costly and risky.
- The raiders of the 1980s provoked considerable political backlash resulting in significant state regulation inhibiting takeover activity. By 1991, 40 states had enacted laws that militated against hostile takeovers of companies incorporated in their states.
- Finally, state and federal laws limiting the amount of non–investment-grade debt that banks, savings and loans, and insurance companies can hold made financing hostile takeovers much more difficult and costly.

As a consequence, the market for corporate control no longer plays the same role that it did in pushing companies to run efficiently and invest wisely.

To compensate for the decline in the efficacy of the market for corporate control, many legal and financial scholars have urged large institutional investors to exert their muscle in monitoring corporate behavior and promoting shareholder privacy (see, for instance, Pound, Sametz, and Roe). Natural players in this game are public and private pension plans.

Active Shareholding

How might pension plans try to influence corporate behavior if they choose to be active shareholders? There are a number of tactics that can be pursued. These range from those that are relatively benign to those that are aggressive and even confrontational.

First, pension funds may exert influence on the direction of a firm through their votes on corporate proxies. They can vote against specific management proposals. Even if they cast votes for the losing side, they will still have sent the message to managers that a large shareholder is unhappy with one action or another. Note that under ERISA, the Department of Labor interprets fiduciary responsibility to include proxy voting. The responsibility for this voting may be delegated to investment managers, but plan fiduciaries must periodically review voting procedures and keep adequate records (see the article by Gertner).

Second, pension funds can press to get their own proposals on the proxy ballot. For instance, they can press for eliminating provisions in the corporate charter that make takeovers more difficult, or they can push for divestitures that seem sensible.

Third, pension funds can encourage firms to structure boards in ways that maintain independence and better align board member interests with shareholder interests rather than with manager interests. For example, they can encourage companies to pay board members in stock as recommended by the National Association of Corporate Boards (see Elson for a discussion of board compensation) or lobby to get some independent directors of their choice elected to corporate boards. (Note that independence can be a subtle concept. CEOs of other firms are frequently touted as independent when, in reality, their firms may have a business relationship that can be imperiled by taking a stand against the management they are supposedly monitoring. Similarly, consultants may be sought for their expertise. The reality may be that they also do business with the firm and thus have a vested interest in the status quo.)

Fourth, pension funds can lobby and cajole from the outside. Since this form of active shareholding can be quite adversarial at times, some authorities believe active shareholding should happen through less adversarial relationship investing (as advocated by Black, Skowronski, and Pound, for instance). The argument is that large owners should develop a relationship with companies' top managements and boards, perhaps even taking a board seat, in order to influence corporate decisions quietly without the embarrassment of public shareholder proposals. The result, it is hoped, is better accountability by managers and better communication between managers and shareholders than is currently the case. Relationship investing is similar to the model successfully employed by a number of private equity funds. It may or may not, however, be a productive model for large public corporations. At this time, there is little more than anecdotal evidence to suggest that this sort of arrangement will lead to improved corporate performance.

Examples of Shareholder Activism

Perhaps the most visible proponent of shareholder activism is the California Public Employees Retirement System (CalPERS). In the early days of its activism, CalPERS identified companies that paid "green mail" (a form of bribery intended to make a hostile bidder disappear); adopted antitakeover provisions without shareholder approval; or did not use secret shareholder voting mechanisms, thereby opening the way for reprisals by companies against those institutions that voted against the wishes of management. Later, CalPERS switched to a system of simply identifying poor market performers and linking them to a single governance proposal, such as changing management compensation systems or altering the board's composition. Before pressing to get shareholder votes on its proposals, CalPERS tried to meet with the target companies in order to negotiate an agreement. If no compromise could be reached, CalPERS put the shareholder resolution, even if nonbinding, on the proxy ballot—an action facilitated by the SEC's shareholder proposal Rule 14a-8.

Another example of shareholder activism is provided by the Council of Institutional Investors (CII), a Washington-based group of public and private pension plans. The Council, dominated by large state retirement funds such as CalPERS and other noncorporate plans such as College Retirement Equities Fund (CREF), controls nearly $1 trillion in financial assets. CII provides a mechanism by which a practical barrier to activism may be circumvented. It is hard for single institutional investors to own more than 5 to 10% of a company's stock because of SEC registration requirements. However, the SEC's 1992 reforms have made it easier to communicate with other holders of large blocks of stock. This suggests that pension funds can pool their financial stakes by working with other institutional investors to encourage management to behave in desirable ways and to select minority representation on the boards of directors of companies in which they have investments (see the article by Black). This pooling, facilitated by CII, helps plans that wish to be active in corporate governance gain a louder voice.

Does Shareholder Activism Matter?

By now institutional shareholder activism has been going on long enough that some empirical work has been possible. Unfortunately however, since shareholder activism is a recent phenomenon, the studies are concerned with only relatively brief periods of time. What happens over longer periods is simply not known. For example, if a firm's share price does not respond immediately to one or more activist interventions, does this mean there will not be a long-term positive impact? Or, where a positive price reaction is observed, will the effect persist over a longer time period—that is, are changes that are induced by active intervention enduring changes? For now, these questions cannot be answered. Let us turn to questions that can.

Two studies (by Karpoff, Malatesta, and Walkling, and by Wahal) suggest that the early stages of pension intervention through the proxy process do not have much effect. There are no short-run price jumps at the time of announcement. Wahal does find a short-run price increase at the announcement of negotiations between firms and large shareholders, however.

Michael Smith studied the most active and vocal pension plan activist, CalPERS. From 1987 to 1993, 51 firms were identified by CalPERS as being unusually poor stock market performers and were targeted for action. For those companies that agreed to change their governance structures in response to CalPERS pressure, there was an increase in share price. For those that refused, the stock price declined at the time of the refusal's announcement. However, despite the stock market's reaction to announcements, Smith was not able to detect a significant change in the operating performance of the affected companies.

Another insightful study has been performed by Stuart Gillan and Laura Starks. They study the shareholder proposals put forward by a variety of investors—public pension funds, CREF, shareholder groups, union funds, individuals, and churches. In their sample period, the main proposals fell into several categories: elimination of takeover defenses, voting issues, board matters, compensation, and other issues such as divestitures.

Gillan and Starks's results show that in their early sample period, from 1986 to 1989, the announcement of shareholder proposals seemed not to have much effect on stock prices, possibly because the securities markets felt they would not affect corporate behavior very much. From 1990 to 1991, however, the authors find a significant positive stock price reaction to the announcement of public pension funds' proposals. One possible conclusion is that the market has been learning that pension plans are becoming serious about being active shareholders who are willing to use their clout to effect sensible change.

Strickland, Wiles, and Zenner evaluated the effect of a shareholders association, the United Shareholders Association (USA), on corporate governance. The evidence shows that when this group targeted a company, its stock price rose after adjusting for risk and the market. More important for our purposes, the rise was more pronounced for companies with large institutional ownership. Similarly, a study by Opler and Sokobin showed that companies targeted by the Council of Institutional Investors have responded to their urgings to change strategies, divest, and alter the composition of boards. In the year after targeting, the earlier poor performers experienced a rate of return on their stocks of 11.6% above the return on the S&P 500 Index.

Finally, Admati and Pfleiderer model large shareholder activism and monitoring technology. They conclude that monitoring by large institutional investors can have good results even though other investors may be getting a free ride.

If these results are indicative of sustained improved performance in the future, then the current shift in corporate governance toward activism could result in more efficient, better performing companies that will, in turn, produce better stock market returns. This, in turn, should lead to better pension fund performance. Although some risks of institutional abuse may exist, these risks are probably outweighed by the potential gains from the elimination of the current management abuses that already exist as a result of passive investor governance. It is really too early to say for certain, however, given the limited history of activism and data available for analysis. In general, we need solid evidence on long-term results that we do not yet have. It is one thing to observe a positive abnormal return due to a price increase attributable to shareholder activism. It is another altogether to be able to say that firms will restructure, will allocate resources more efficiently and will develop more sensible business strategies over the long term because of shareholder activism. As the current changes in governance evolve, there is the hope that the management/shareholder tension that Ira Millstein suggested is "the heart of corporate governance" will find its optimal level.

The Downside to Active Shareholding

Those pursuing or contemplating active shareholding should be aware there may be a downside to active intervention. There are two areas of concern: one concerns the judgments that may be exercised— is the pension plan right or wrong? The second is specific to the structure of the organizational, legal, and regulatory environment in which pension funds operate.

Errors in Judgment

First, and most obviously, the activist shareholder may be wrong regarding what optimal corporate behavior ought to be. Running a large pension fund does not necessarily mean that the management of the fund has the knowledge or background to judge the quality of every firm's strategic vision or the wisdom behind every proposal made. Business decisions are complex and the environment in which businesses must operate can change rapidly. There are numerous stories of CEOs who, through hubris, made disastrous decisions. Pension funds should take care to avoid the same mistake.

Second, the pension fund investor may step over the line that separates fiduciary judgment and business judgment. That is, if the activist investor pushes the corporation to do certain things, and the corporation does them, the investor may begin to bear the same sort of legal responsibility that regular board members and senior managers bear. Thus, once a pension fund decides to become active in corporate governance, this activity invites lawsuits for mistakes made (see the article by Roe). Ordinarily, the protections offered pension funds under the prudent investor standard provide some protection. However, the more active a pension plan becomes, the more likely it is the business judgment standard applied to business decision making in the boardroom will be used to decide whether liability for mistakes exists.

Structural Inhibitions

There are three factors that arise from the structure of the pension fund environment that inhibit pension plans from being active in corporate governance. The first is the nature of the managerial control structure. Corporate pension plan managers have two groups to whom they are accountable: the executives of the sponsoring corporation to whom they report and the plan beneficiaries. Many corporate executives have an unspoken golden rule that pension managers should do unto other companies as they would have those companies do unto them. The result is that pension plan managers' superiors discourage them from participating actively in corporate governance. This means that, according to Monks and Minow, the "meaningful exercise of ownership rights of private pension assets is thankless. No investment manager, in-house or outside, ever got paid extra for voting proxies well, because that would mean a number of votes against management recommendations." Public pension plan managers do not have the same broad mandate to avoid ruffling the feathers of corporate managers. From time to time, however, political pressure is applied to stop plans from pressuring managers of firms having substantial local economic impact.

Diversification requirements are the second reason that some pension plans have avoided corporate governance issues. ERISA has promoted diversification in private pension plan assets, and ERISA-like requirements are increasingly common for public pensions. Once a fund holds equity stakes in hundreds of organizations, it becomes too expensive to monitor or be active in all of them. Additionally, large portions of pension plan assets have recently been invested in index funds specifically to receive the benefits of diversification without the substantial costs of active stock selection. Index funds, narrowly construed, do not necessarily encourage shareholder activism. However, as pointed out in the earlier discussion of fiduciary responsibility in Chapter 3, index fund managers probably ought to consider some form of shareholder activism as a way to improve the performance of some of the companies held in an indexed portfolio.

The third reason is the prudent investor rules and related regulations and guidelines. These rules, particularly in the context of ERISA, have encouraged fiduciaries to imitate other fiduciaries in their investing behavior. Since pension plans have historically been passive in their corporate governance, they continue to stay passive. Additionally, the prudent investor rules as generally interpreted may discourage active involvement in corporate governance because of the liability issues that could arise in the event that the actions favored by the activist shareholder unintentionally harm shareholder value.

Practical Issues for Active Pension Funds

Private pension plans will find activism sensible only if they believe it will lead to better performance and if they can be assured that their actions will not elicit retaliatory moves by the managements or pension plans of targeted companies against the activist pension plan's sponsor.

Even if this could be accomplished in principle, it may be difficult to get top managers to believe it to the extent they must if they are to let their pension plans publicly attack or privately challenge the performance of other firms. The potential costs of lost business or reverse intervention as firms that are attacked retaliate may be perceived as too high.

So far, public pension plans have led the way as far as shareholder influence on corporate governance is concerned. They have been very active in getting takeover-impeding features of corporate charters repealed. Public pension plans—indeed, most investors—clearly feel that market forces are important in getting managers to behave as economically as possible. Unlike other institutional investors (including corporate pension plans), public pension plans are relatively free from the conflicts of interest other investors may have (see the article by Romano). "Perhaps the public pension funds' most significant contribution has been to make the world an uncomfortable place for a director of an underperforming company," wrote Monks and Minow.

Whether public pension funds can continue to play this role is a major issue. Some public pension plans may eventually be throttled by political concerns that override the interests of the plan and its beneficiaries. Politicians are no less immune to threats than anyone else. Accordingly, if a state's pension plan targets a company, and that company threatens to close a plant down in that state, the state's top politicians could put pressure on the pension plan to back away from its accusations and proposals.

Toward a More Active Role for Pension Funds

There are a number of reasons why pension funds may need to become more active than they have been in encouraging management to do economically sensible things. Without takeovers as a threat, the market is searching for new mechanisms to effect change in corporations that are deemed inefficient. Poison pills, cumulative voting for directors, a preponderance of inside directors, and directors who are not independent of management or whose compensation aligns them with the status quo simply entrench management, insulating it from the forces of efficiency and good performance. As the potential of pension funds to contribute to efficient control is recognized, and the harm of simply trusting current managers or voting with their feet becomes more apparent, the pressures to influence corporate behavior may increase. Lawrence Perlman, the chairman and chief executive officer of Ceridian Corporation, wrote

> The power of the shareholder activism movement is the simple ele-
> gance of its underlying proposition that boards and managements of
> public companies must be held accountable for improving perfor-
> mance to those who own the companies. Governance issues that sup-
> port this fundamental proposition strengthen companies.

As more and more corporate managers come to appreciate the benefits
of shareholder activism, pension funds may be forced to respond.

Another reason arises from the joint effect on pension funds that the
rapid increase in pension plan assets under management (currently, private and public pension plans together own 50% of institutionally
financed assets and a 60% stake in total institutional equity [see the article by Sametz]) and the incentives many funds face to invest in the
larger, more "prudent" stocks that constitute the S&P 500 has had. At
some point, it becomes less expensive to monitor and promote change
within a poorly performing company than it is to exit or wait patiently
for change that may never come. Sametz goes so far as to argue that any
pension fund choosing to follow active investment management strategies must implicitly accept responsibility for monitoring the performance of the companies whose stocks they own. In the face of the high
cost of exit, to do otherwise is philosophically inconsistent with the
search for superior risk-adjusted returns via active money management.

Finally, the emergence of defined contribution plans is having an
effect on the acceptance of activist roles for pension plans. As the assets
in defined contribution plans continue to grow, the natural management resistance to corporate governance has been eroded. The fund
managers that individual employees select to manage their defined
contribution pension plans are not subject to quite the pressures faced
by the corporate and public pension plan managers. These more
(although not completely) independent money managers may well
start taking a more active part in getting corporate managers to work
for shareholders, because they will be working directly for beneficiaries, not corporate managers or politicians; that is, they are not subject
to the same conflicts of interest to which defined benefit plans are subject. (Of course, if XYZ Mutual Fund has been hired by ABC
Corporation to manage ABC's defined contribution assets, they are not
likely to vote against ABC management—or for that matter, against the
management of other potential clients.)

These factors being as they are, however, Longstreth suggests that
pension funds proceed cautiously regarding the "new orthodoxies" in
corporate governance. He rightly suggests that pension funds should

be careful of unproven claims and should support the right of corporations to experiment with various business strategies.

Longstreth provides two examples of good intentions gone awry that are of special relevance here. The first is how the cry for "independent" directors has led to a proliferation of CEOs on boards. These CEOs seemingly have no difficulty approving possibly excessive pay increases for the CEOs they presumably monitor, possibly because the ripple effect on CEO salaries may be good for them as well. The second is a reminder that emerging wisdom may be wrong. In the early 1990s, some experts called for U.S. businesses to be more like their Japanese and German counterparts in order to improve competitiveness. Recent history suggests this was certainly ill-advised. So too might excessive zeal for interventionist tactics have unintended consequences.

Conclusion

We believe shareholder activism should increase beyond its current level because the pension plan, be it private or public, has a fiduciary responsibility to make its portfolio perform as well as possible within the parameters of its risk tolerance. This should not be done in an irresponsible manner, however. Corporate governance and shareholder intervention represent a continuum of possible strategies and activities. Not all should or need to be used in every case. We concur with Longstreth that it is possible to go too far or too quickly adopt a common wisdom that may not be proven true in future years.

Being an active shareholder carries a risk that the relationship between the pension fund and the management of a corporation can become too adversarial, to the detriment of the corporation and ultimately the corporation's shareholders. Further, although throughout this chapter we have encouraged pension funds to be at least somewhat active in the affairs of the companies in which they own stock, a clarification is now in order: the motivation to become involved with the activities of a company must be solely to influence the decision-making process as it relates to long-term shareholder returns. We believe it is a serious and imprudent mistake to use pension fund market power for social or political goals that are not directly tied to maximizing shareholder wealth. The ultimate purpose of the pension fund should not be put aside to serve some other agenda. To use pension assets to advance noneconomic goals could put the pension beneficiaries at risk and adversely affect the sponsor's need to fund the plan.

In general, active involvement in corporate governance in order to ensure that the interests of the beneficiaries are being considered suggests a shift toward a more balanced sharing of power between management and shareholders rather than simply implying a shift toward investor control. If this shift occurs, management will have to be more accountable to their shareholders. Activist shareholders should not forget, however, that the relationship between these two entities should be the result of a dynamic process that allows managers to manage and experiment in order to stay competitive and to adapt to an ever-changing business landscape.

With this shift will also come a new focus on corporate boards. In particular, there will be an increase in focus on the relationship between the board, the shareholders, and the managers. Increasingly, boards will be held accountable by shareholders for management behavior. Boards will be examined to see what their incentives are and to whom their members are accountable.

There do seem to be benefits to corporate governance. Specifically, better returns with possibly lower risks are at least conceptually achievable. However, these benefits are not costless. Information and solicitation have costs, and legal liability for mistakes in business judgments may prove to be nontrivial. It is not sensible to expend a lot of effort on a small investment. Corporate governance activity also invites politicians and others to become active in the pension's or sponsor's affairs. So pension plan decision makers should proceed cautiously and, as for any other strategic decision, know their goals and motivations and watch out for the sin of hubris.

Chapter *14*

The Path to Better Pension Plan Management

Pension plans and the asset pools they manage play a major role in the allocation of resources within our economy. Their active investment management helps to keep markets efficient and funds flowing to the worthiest enterprises. Possibly, they lead to higher aggregate domestic savings and thus a stronger, more rapidly growing economy than might otherwise be the case.

More important for our purposes, they are useful to employers in accomplishing a variety of goals, not the least of which is motivating employees. They are important to employees for the role they play in providing retirement income and security. They support a veritable army of investment managers, consultants, accountants, actuaries, and other service providers.

Pension plans are too important to be managed as an afterthought, to be delegated to lower level executives, or to those who cannot cut it as managers elsewhere in the organization, or to be used to correct a state's fiscal problems. The stakes are too high. The employers who sponsor pension plans should worry about the impact of plan decisions on future funding requirements and ultimately on their own long-term financial health. They should worry about whether the plan is attracting desirable types of workers and motivating proper behavior. Employees should worry about plan solvency and whether or not the promised benefit and/or the defined contribution asset pool will be sufficient to provide the type of retirement they desire. Politicians should worry about the adverse consequences, frequently unintended, that regulations or political actions of one sort or another may have on a system that, most agree, works pretty well. Plan managers, corporate board members, plan trustees, and investment managers should worry about all of these factors. Mostly, everyone involved should be concerned about how the plan can be better managed.

Pension plans will face tremendous challenges in coming years as the size of the retired population swells through retirement and increased longevity. What returns will the capital markets provide? What risks will dominate the landscape? Will federal policy change in a manner that will affect the relative desirability of one form of plan or another?

No one can answer these questions with any degree of certainty. However, those who are responsible for pension plans can ensure that their plans are prepared for whatever the future brings by thinking about their pension plans as businesses that must be organized and managed using sound economic and managerial principles. This is not to say that pension plans should be treated as either profit centers or as separate aspects of the organizations that sponsor them. Either view could lead to suboptimal results. However, pension plans are big business and they are complex organizations. Although investment management is the core competency needed, there is much more to managing plans than simply managing money.

The path to better pension plan management—and hence to better performance—is multidimensional. There are plan goals to be set and alternative plan structures to analyze. There is policy to write and procedures to develop to ensure prudent decision making. Investment activities must be integrated with management activities so that risk can be managed sensibly and so that actual returns justify the risks taken.

This chapter offers a synthesis of the key points developed earlier. We hope this final commentary will be useful in forming a complete picture of how pension plan performance can be improved. We dedicate this summary to all those who want to help their pension plans prepare for the challenges of coming years.

Plan Goals and Structure

Sensible pension management begins with a clear understanding of the purpose of the plan. What is the sponsor trying to accomplish? What do employees expect?

From the sponsor's perspective, the existence of a pension plan must be justified by its ability to attract and retain high-quality employees and to motivate behavior that the sponsor finds desirable. Different employees may find different plans attractive for a variety of reasons. The highly skilled 48-year-old worker may prefer working for an organization with a defined benefit pension plan because of the higher retirement security it generally offers. On the other hand, the 30-year-old worker may value the portability and flexibility offered by a defined contribution plan.

Who, then, is the organization trying to hire and retain? What are the costs of replacing a lost employee? What form of compensation is appropriate for managing the organization's human resources?

We believe sponsors can be too enthusiastic to adopt defined contribution plans as their sole means of providing pension benefits. There is significant uncertainty for sponsors with respect to the liability they may have in the future if these plans prove to be insufficient in providing adequate retirement benefits. Further, employers may find they cannot achieve the sort of employee turnover they want; they may not be able to get older employees with higher salaries and possibly out-of-date skills to retire. They may find younger employees leave too soon in larger numbers than is optimal. Those who jump on the defined contribution bandwagon too quickly may find that they are not attracting or retaining the types of workers they want and that employee turnover costs (retraining, hiring, and so forth) begin to soar.

No plan type—defined benefit, defined contribution, or hybrid—is dominant in all circumstances for all employers and for all employees. Each has attractive and unattractive features. Sponsors must therefore be careful in determining which plan structures they will use. If organization-specific knowledge or longevity or the option to manage the demographics of the workforce are important, the defined benefit structure is probably the best choice. If the labor force values mobility over the insurance aspects of defined benefit plans, or if turnover costs are low because there is little need for organization-specific human capital, the defined contribution structure is probably the best choice. Employers and employees would be well advised to remember that because of pooling and economies of scale, large employers have advantages over individuals in bearing mortality risk and in hiring and monitoring competent investment managers. We believe that the mismatch between employee ability to acquire the knowledge necessary to make good investment decisions versus the sponsor's ability to acquire the same knowledge and spread the costs of doing so over a large number of people represents a compelling disadvantage to defined contribution plans for large and medium-sized employers. These advantages should not be overlooked when structuring compensation packages and determining what the pension plan should be. Various forms of hybrid plans—floor plans, cash balance plans, and other types—offer employers a flexible middle ground that may better match the features of the plan to the needs of employers and employees.

Regardless of the structure and features chosen, no pension plan can be judged a success if it fails to achieve its primary purposes. First, it must fit sensibly into the overall compensation scheme of the employer. Second, it must provide a retirement benefit or asset pool that employees find attractive enough to warrant contracting their human capital to employers. In short, the pension plan must be viewed in its proper context—as a means of contracting between employers and employees.

Plan Investment Policy

The second step along the path to better performance is the policies that govern investment and management activities. Policies should be written and complete. The primary purpose of policy is to provide useful guidelines for decision making and to communicate unambiguously to all parties what the plan is trying to do and how it is going about it. Policy should not be unduly restrictive and should not discourage pension plan management from taking actions that are appropriate under whatever circumstances may be present.

Defined benefit plan policies can not be set in a vacuum. Central to sound defined benefit plan policy are two factors: the interdependency between the plan and the sponsor, and the way the asset pool and plan liabilities are entwined. To ignore these interactions is to guarantee unanticipated problems with funding and solvency.

Further, special attention must be given to resolving the conflicts of interest that exist between the various parties involved in managing the asset pool. Problems delayed are not problems solved; ignoring potential problems virtually ensures that they will occur to the detriment of the pension plan. Structuring policies that govern relationships and explicitly recognizing that the asset pool is to be managed for the exclusive benefit of employees, subject to the sponsor's interest in avoiding unreasonably high and unpredictable funding costs, may be painful to those who find their power or perquisites reduced, but it will improve the efficiency with which the plan operates and the plan's investment performance. Good policy will encourage pension decision making to be based on sound economics and financial analysis rather than on relationships and avoidance of responsibility.

Policy needs to answer questions that can be anticipated. For example, what will a plan do if there is adverse market action? Will it rebalance to predetermined strategic weights? Will it reduce its exposure to stocks? Most important, will the decision-making process be a knee-jerk reaction due to ill-conceived or inadequate policy guidelines, or will it be guided by forward-looking policy that ensures that a long-run, economically sound perspective will carry the day?

Policy for defined contribution plans is every bit as important as it is for defined benefit plans. Policy begins by deciding who will manage the pension assets—the employer or the employee? We advise the plan be employee directed, as to do otherwise removes the major potential benefit of shifting investment risk to employees. Assuming that this is the choice made, policy should clearly specify the sponsor's commitment to providing the information, education, and opportunity to manage their assets needed by employees if they are to make informed investment decisions.

Prudent Behavior

Good policy is a natural extension of prudent behavior. The concept of prudent behavior by pension plan fiduciaries has deep roots in written law and legal precedent, but it continues to evolve even as we write. For those who are fiduciaries, figuring out what it means to behave in a prudent manner is critical. This is not an easy task, as prudence and economically rational behavior can sometimes appear to be at odds. For those who are not fiduciaries, the question of what to expect out of fiduciaries is important. At issue is sound decision making supported by good analysis and theory. At issue is accepting responsibility for actions taken or not taken. At issue is good faith and trust and doing one's job well.

Fiduciaries should understand that behaving in a manner that seems to be prudent may occasionally lead to perverse consequences. For example, many fiduciaries feel there is safety in numbers, so they tend to mimic what they believe others are doing. This can lead to excessive investment in what are perceived to be high-quality, prudent securities in spite of evidence that these securities may offer inferior risk-adjusted returns or failure to use derivatives to manage undesirable risk exposures.

Prudent behavior can be especially difficult for public plan fiduciaries who do not have the guidelines and protections offered under ERISA. In many cases, these fiduciaries are uniquely vulnerable to political pressures encouraging them to go against what most authorities would consider to be prudent investment practice. Sometimes there may be no satisfactory short-run alternative other than carefully walking the tightrope between what is right for the plan and any of a number of political goals or agendas. Over the long term, however, the public pension fiduciary should quietly lobby for independence with accountability and strive to educate politicians and plan beneficiaries about the realities of sensible pension management.

To be a good fiduciary, there is no substitute for knowledge of investment strategies and alternatives. Similarly, there is no substitute for careful consideration of the relevant issues when making decisions, nor for careful documentation of what information has been used in making important decisions.

For organizations that have defined contribution plans, sponsors and those who represent the plan's beneficiaries must not act as if there are no duties to fulfill: there are. Prudent fiduciary behavior clearly implies an obligation to educate employees regarding portfolio choice and to perform adequate due diligence when selecting providers of investment services and investment alternatives. Further, sponsors should ask themselves what the consequences will be if employees decide that the asset accumulations in their pension accounts are not sufficient for retirement. Can employees be induced to retire when the sponsor determines it is time without violating age-discrimination laws if retirement accounts are inadequate? Will the organization supplement retirement accounts that prove to be inadequate?

For sponsors of defined benefit plans, prudent fiduciary behavior means achieving the optimal balance between contributions to the plan and target investment returns. This means neither the sponsor nor the asset pool should bear excessive risk; rather the joint risk of the two should be used to determine the level and timing of contributions and the strategic asset allocation. This is the hard part. The prudent hiring, monitoring, and, if necessary, replacing of managers and all the attendant tasks of managing the investment pool are hard work, but conceptually these tasks are fairly straightforward.

Those who agree to serve in a fiduciary role, either because it is part of their job or through political appointment, must take their responsibilities seriously. The consequences of not doing so include personal liability and possibly disastrous decision making. Determining the appropriate course of action as a fiduciary is not always easy. For example, recall that index investing, an increasingly popular course of action and one that many experts would argue is the most cost efficient and thus the most sensible, still has some ambiguity in that certain companies represented in an index may be judged individually to be imprudent investments. Moreover, those who follow passive index strategies still have the duty to support proxy choices that are likely to enhance shareholder value and to vote against those that may harm shareholders.

Finally, fiduciaries should accept the responsibility to make decisions and set policy based on economic factors rather than on accounting fictions. ABO, PBO, pension expense, and other accounting measures are useful in examining various aspects of defined benefit plans, but there are serious limitations to the data provided. Fiduciaries must be aware of the subjective decisions involved in selecting salary growth rates, interest rates, and expected returns as well as other factors (such as which mortality table to use) that affect the measurement process. Fiduciaries must also be aware that accounting procedures tend to have the effect of smoothing fluctuations in economic factors, thus masking the real issues that demand scrutiny.

Investing

The single most important investment management decision to be made is the long-term strategic asset allocation. In many pension plans, not enough attention is devoted to determining this allocation, while too much attention is given to "glamorous" areas such as new investment products and strategies that promise, at least to the naive investor, glorious returns at minimal risk.

In making the strategic asset allocation decision, we cannot emphasize too much how important it is for a defined benefit plan to set return goals that reflect the risk tolerance of the plan in light of the sponsor's ability to fund the plan, long-term expectations for capital market returns and risks, and the nature and magnitude of the pension liability. This is an area in which there can never be a "right" answer to many decimal places—even experts will disagree. However, the returns the pension portfolio provides and the risks that it takes in pursuing these returns will be governed primarily by the overall asset allocation of the plan and secondarily by the departures from that allocation that are the result of investment decision making. Tactical asset allocation, insured asset allocation, and the numerous asset class investment strategies are all useful, but they are merely parts of the picture. The biggest part is the overall exposures the fund takes to the major asset classes; this is where attention should be focused.

For defined contribution plans, the employee/beneficiary typically will be faced with the daunting task of setting the strategic asset allocation. Sponsors cannot simply tell employees what the allocation should be because of the liability that would create. It is not prudent to leave employees who have no special investment expertise floundering on their own, however; in fact, for ERISA-governed plans in the private sector, employers who do not assist employees by providing investment education are likely to find that the desired shift of investment risk from the sponsor to the employee is an illusion because the courts are eventually likely to assert that sponsors are responsible, in whole or in part, for the poor or ill-informed choices of employees.

The actual investment performance of pension funds has certainly been subject to criticism in recent years. Some of these criticisms are unfair, since they do not take differences in asset allocation among plans into account. Further, there are several reasons why pensions may naturally underperform seemingly reasonable benchmarks—the size of some plans makes it difficult to maneuver effectively in the short run, and some regulatory incentives inhibit sensible investment decision making. However, as a practical matter, pension plans probably should be able to do better. This does not mean simply going out and taking excessive risks in pursuit of higher returns. Frequently, performance can be improved dramatically by simply tending to the basics of investment management: keeping transaction costs low and management fees at reasonable levels.

We do believe that pension funds, especially larger ones, have an affirmative obligation to improve the performance of the asset pool by being active shareholders. We feel this is a part of their fiduciary responsibilities to plan beneficiaries, and that it is also simply good sense for sponsors given the costs of not doing so—poor performance or incurring excessive costs on exiting. However, activism must be pursued cautiously. The best way is to insist on good corporate governance at the board level; in general, we caution against getting too involved in the actual business decisions of the company, as this requires an expertise and knowledge of industry and firm-specific success factors that typically is outside the purview of most investment managers. Further, the activist pension fund must continually monitor its motives. The only good motive for shareholder activism is to maximize shareholder wealth because this will benefit plan beneficiaries and the sponsor.

Management

The fifth step to improved performance encompasses all the management activities that are not part of asset allocation or selection. Thus, good management involves managing the plan's investment managers, monitoring and evaluating performance, and controlling the costs of investing. The responsibilities of senior management and boards are clear: investment managers and trading costs directly affect the success of the plan's investment activities.

Selecting, managing, and monitoring investment managers—whether those managers are external or internal—is an important job of senior pension management. Internal managers should be competent and must be compensated appropriately. To do otherwise is either to set up a revolving door leading to high turnover costs and inconsistent investment management if pay is too low, or to put a drag on performance if it is too high. If outside investment managers are used because it is not practical to pay market wages to inside managers, plan management should anticipate an increase in monitoring costs. Those who make this decision should bear in mind how profitable the investment management industry is. Perhaps the appeal of outsourcing the investment management function would be greatly reduced if the magnitude of management fees and the costs of effective monitoring were accurately assessed by sponsors.

As a practical matter, it is highly unlikely that a sponsor really can manage and monitor as many as thirty or forty external managers. The early warning systems, communications, and accountability that are all essential elements of managing external managers become much too cumbersome. Further, the higher the number of managers that are used, the higher the probability that pension funds are at risk of paying active management fees when the combined profile of a multimanager asset pool actually mimics a broad-based market index.

Monitoring internal or external managers requires a comprehensive performance evaluation system that provides senior management and boards with timely, relevant information on how the asset pool has done and whether or not policy has been followed. Performance measurement requires the user be familiar with (1) the alternative measures of return, including knowing what return measures to use depending on what is being evaluated (for example, are we evaluating managers or the total portfolio?); (2) adjusting for risk; (3) choosing the right standards for comparison (benchmarking); and (4) breaking investment performance into its component parts for analysis. Although the measures used in these four areas are certainly not without flaws, the totality of the return/risk/benchmark/attribution approach is quite useful in helping interested parties understand how the pension plan is doing. Recent advances in performance measurement are promising, especially with regard to better benchmarking and understanding the problems with and limitations of performance measurement.

Finally, never forget that trading is costly. Investment managers trade because of the investment strategies they follow and because they need to meet liquidity needs of the pension plan. Controlling the costs of trading begins with measuring them correctly; that is, market impact costs are important. Further, costs should be monitored so that the pension plan does not incur costs that are higher than they have to be to execute the desired trade. For many plans, trading costs can be reduced simply by paying attention to what is going on and by telling investment managers they are being watched.

Soft dollars and directed commissions also are important. Many in the investment management profession have become dependent on soft dollars to pay for training, travel, and a host of services that have only tangential value for investment decision making. In some cases, the services or products that are purchased benefit the pension plan that pays for these services; in many cases this is not true, or the costs of the benefits received are excessive. The simplest way to deal with soft dollars is to avoid them by not permitting directed commissions. If soft dollar arrangements are permitted, however, their use should be governed by policy that places the burden of proving that the costs are reasonable on the firm executing the trade and that specifies that the benefits derived be used for the exclusive benefit of the plan.

Risk Management

Managing risk is not synonymous with eliminating it. Funds that simply wish to eliminate risk are committing to investment returns that are roughly comparable to those provided by Treasury bills. In virtually any reasonable scenario, these returns would not be sufficient either to meet the liability of a defined benefit plan or to provide adequate accumulation of resources in a defined contribution plan. Risks must be taken if one is to keep pace with, or better yet exceed, inflation over long periods of time. Risks must be taken if one expects to accumulate wealth and, hence, future retirement benefits. From the perspective of the defined benefit plan, risks must be taken unless the sponsor is willing to fund 100% of future retirement benefits.

There are some rules of risk management that all pension funds should keep in mind. The first is that there are no free lunches (other than diversification). Reducing risk ultimately means reducing return. The second rule is that risk management often means trading off exposure to one kind of risk against exposure to another kind. Low investment risk increases the sponsor's risk of higher future contributions. High investment risk in pursuit of high returns can result in excessive surplus volatility. The third rule is that any risk management strategy must be understood by those who use it and ultimately justified in terms of its future alternative payoffs. For example, in an effort to reduce the risk of short-term adverse market action, some managers reduce exposures to risky assets but ignore the potential cost of being out of the market if the market should go up. By failing to consider both the up-market and down-market payoffs, these managers confuse market timing strategies with risk reduction strategies. It is an easy mistake to make, but it is a mistake nonetheless. Rule number four might be that derivatives are good—and bad. It is the responsibility of the user to employ derivatives prudently. Derivatives are available, they are useful, they are generally cost efficient. Thus, in some roles, derivatives offer a prudent means of carrying out risk management strategies. However, derivatives must be used only by those who understand the actual contract involved and how the derivative is likely to behave in a variety of market conditions.

The Success Factors in Pension Management

Pension plan management requires many technical skills and at least some quantitative aptitude. It also requires common sense and an understanding of investment basics and financial market history. Sometimes, however, common sense is put aside to pursue the latest fad or some magical investment strategy. Sometimes plan administrators, managers, trustees, or board members and other fiduciaries are intimidated by the complexity and aura of the investment process and delegate far too much authority to others whose interests are not aligned to the interests of the plan, the sponsor, or the employees. Sometimes these decision makers get caught up in an irrational exuberance that somehow the future can be known and risk can be eliminated while attractive returns remain, that black boxes can somehow make sense out of the complex world in which we live. Sometimes they become so fearful of losing their jobs or being viewed as imprudent or incurring undue liability for actions taken (or not taken) that they do too little, or act too late to be effective. The results are insufficient attention to the issues that really matter, unintended risk, subpar performance, and excessive conservatism.

What, then, are the success factors in pension plan management? First, recognize that pension funds are big businesses and require talented people to run them. These people should be highly skilled and compensated accordingly.

Second, there are many complex relationships to be managed. Agency problems and conflicts of interest must be anticipated and managed in the best interests of the plan, the plan's beneficiaries, and the plan's sponsor. Be cognizant of the incentives of those who serve the plan and be careful about policies or decisions that may have unintended consequences—for example, performance incentives that can have the undesirable side effect of encouraging excessive risk taking. Interactions between plan assets and liabilities and between funding and alternative investment returns must be modeled. Decision makers must use their best judgments about what is after all, in the final analysis, a fairly subjective decision.

Third, pension plans and their sponsors as a general rule are going concerns with long time horizons. Take a systematic, long-term approach to policy development and decision making. Avoid short-term myopia. Give close attention to the seemingly small things that can erode value over long time periods—inflation and trading costs and lack of control—as well as to obviously important matters such as the strategic asset allocation.

Fourth, common sense and technical competence are equally important. Decision makers should have specific beliefs about market efficiency (or inefficiency) and how assets are priced. Inefficient markets may justify active management even with its higher costs. In efficient markets, passive investing should be the strategy of choice. The impenetrable investment strategy that ultimately unravels to the dismay of plan managers, the sponsor, and beneficiaries does so because it was not sensible in the first place—it was not based on any real theory of economic behavior. Remember that financial markets and our understanding of them change over time. Adequate training and continuing education are the cornerstones of maintaining competence at all levels—from plan trustees and corporate boards to pension staff. Even external vendors should be required to demonstrate that they stay current with new thinking and research findings.

Finally, remember that good pension performance and the changes that may be necessary to improve existing performance ultimately come about through people. Pension management requires much of those who are called to the task. Plan managers and decision makers must be part economist, part manager, part lawyer, and part politician. They must understand the history of the financial markets and yet know that today and tomorrow are not the same as yesterday. Pension fund management and hence performance, more than many areas of management, relies on the good judgment of those who have the responsibility for the plan.

Appendix A
Employee Stock Ownership Plans

Employee Stock Ownership Plans (ESOPs) are a special form of defined contribution plan available to corporate sponsors. In 1992 there were approximately 9,800 ESOP plans covering roughly 11.2 million employees in the United States, according to the Employee Benefits Research Institute *Databook on Employer Benefits*. These are plans set up to purchase stock in the employer for whom the employees work. Employees sometimes use these plans to purchase employers in entirety—complete worker ownership. In general, however, the plans are used to give employees the incentives to behave productively by providing a meaningful stake in a publicly held sponsor and to place voting rights in the hands of presumably friendly employees should a contest for control arise.

At least 51% of the assets of an ESOP must be invested in the sponsoring employer. In contrast, regular defined benefit and defined contribution plans may invest no more than 10% of their assets in the stock of sponsoring companies.

A downside of ESOPs is that they may lead to a very great concentration of an employee's projected retirement wealth in one investment; ESOPs facilitate violation of one of the principal rules of investment—diversification. This concentration makes employees with ESOPs quite vulnerable to the success (or lack of it) of one firm. On the other hand, other features of ESOPs yield substantial benefits to a sponsor's shareholders—including, of course, the beneficial owners (the employees) of claims on the ESOP itself. Employees who are shareholders gain when all shareholders gain.

ESOPs and Taxes

Generally speaking, there are two types of ESOPs: ESOPs that borrow money to buy stock in the sponsoring employer, and ESOPs that do not borrow money. Although the former are referred to as *leveraged ESOPs*, the latter can be leveraged as well. Functionally, there is virtually no difference between the two types.

There are tremendous tax advantages for both types of ESOPs. Corporate contributions to the ESOP are tax deductible. Dividends that the sponsor pays on shares held by the ESOP that flow directly to employees (whose receipts are taxable) or are used to pay down debt are also tax deductible, unlike ordinary dividends. Further, if the ESOP owns a majority of the shares outstanding, qualified lenders to the (leveraged) ESOP can exclude from tax consideration 50% of the interest received by the lender on the ESOP loan. Thus, lenders have an incentive to lend to ESOPs. Finally, shareholders in a closely held sponsor may obtain a tax-free rollover if they sell their shares to an ESOP that eventually acquires ownership of 30% of the sponsor and if the shareholders buy new qualifying securities, such as bonds.

ESOPs and Motivation

Employee motivation and productivity are often offered as prime reasons for setting up ESOPs. The argument is that employees who own a substantial share of the employer will work harder and smarter. Indeed, Congress provided the tax incentives specifically in order to encourage employee ownership; Congress must have felt that the greater productivity of employers with ESOPs would more than make up for the losses in direct tax revenues.

There is not a lot of hard evidence that ESOPs increase productivity. Rosen reports, however, on some survey evidence obtained from 2,700 workers in 37 employers. It was found that "the more stock employees owned in their sponsor, the more committed they were to the employer, the more satisfied with their work, the less likely they were to look for another job, and the more effort they said they made of the job."

Another study generally supporting the contention that ESOPs are employee motivators is one by Chang. He found that the stock prices of publicly held companies generally rose around the time they announced the formation of ESOPs. Indeed, for those companies that adopted ESOPs as wage concessions, average stock prices rose by nearly 4.2% after adjusting for risk and market movements on the day prior to and the day of the announcement. For those employers announcing the establishment of ESOPs as pure employee benefit plans, the average two-day excess return was nearly 2.5%. Clearly, shareholders tend to respond positively to the creation of ESOPs. It is unlikely that their entire response is attributable to the impoundment of future tax savings into current share prices. Thus, it is reasonable to conclude that some of the benefit is attributable to shareholder anticipation of improved employee motivation.

Park and Song confirm that ESOPs provide positive incentives, but find that this is true only for firms with large independent outside shareholders. They hypothesize that these "blockholders" are good enough at monitoring their holdings that they will not permit management to expropriate the ESOP's voting rights for their own interest. Thus, in this circumstance, ESOPs tie together shareholder and employee interests without entrenching management.

ESOPs and Corporate Governance

Many employers adopted ESOPs either in anticipation of a control battle or in response to a contest for corporate control. ESOPs associated with publicly controlled employers are required to pass all their voting rights through to the employees owning claims against the ESOP. However, many issues—such as tender offers—do not have to lead to shareholder voting. Moreover, when asked to vote their ESOP interests, employees generally tend to vote with management because, in most corporate restructurings, the great fear of employees is the loss of jobs, and current management is perceived as more likely than outside raiders to do what can be done to preserve existing jobs. ESOPs associated with employers that are not publicly held do not have to pass voting rights through to beneficiaries. In these cases, ESOP trustees, generally managers and their appointees, control the votes.

Scholes and Wolfson contend that the major reason for ESOPs is found in their anti-takeover characteristics. They argue that the tax incentives of ESOPs are overstated; some of the same tax incentives can be obtained through other devices, and existing ESOPs seem not to exploit the incentives as fully as they might. They also believe employee motivational advantages are overstated; these can be closely approximated through alternative means. However, with ESOPs, managements can generally count on more shares voting to sustain them than might occur otherwise.

When management is supported by ESOP votes, shareholders suffer. Chang's work shows that, for the 32 employers in his sample, the average two-day abnormal return on the announcement of ESOPs for takeover defense purposes was roughly –2.3%. Clearly, shareholders, presumably including ESOP holders, lose when ESOPs are used to protect entrenched, possibly inefficient managers. Park and Song confirm this by demonstrating that, without monitoring by large, independent outside blockholders, performance losses and the proportion of ESOP ownership are positively related.

Apart from takeover defense, management also generally "controls" votes on other issues. This creates a dilemma for management. It must honor its fiduciary responsibility to do what is best for the plan beneficiaries, but it also knows where its own interests lie. There is clearly much rationalization in these circumstances, with, we fear, management frequently "rising above principle."

Conclusion

There is little to suggest that companies should not establish ESOPs in addition to other kinds of retirement plans and compensation plans. These plans allow for tax advantages, and under almost no circumstances can they be viewed as detrimental to employee motivation. However, as many (including Blasi), advise, ESOPs must be used with care.

One of the chief pitfalls of ESOPs seems to be their use as the exclusive pension plan of a sponsoring organization. This subverts the principle of asset diversification and subjects the pension beneficiary to substantially more risk than is necessary to achieve the same expected return. A second major pitfall is the use of ESOPs as a takeover defense tactic. In this case, it can be charged, management cynically plays on employees' fears of job insecurity while getting employees themselves to pay for sheltering management from the sometimes harsh discipline of the market for corporate control.

There is no simple solution to the conflict between managers as management and managers as fiduciaries for ESOP funds. The issue is becoming considerably more prominent, however, as more and more ESOPs are established and as each becomes an increasingly important shareholder relative to other shareholders, gaining increasing voting power. Farsighted organizations should examine ways in which they can insulate their top managers from the need for casting votes on behalf of ESOPs. Otherwise they will almost inevitably face serious and possibly devastating charges of conflict of interest regarding their control over ESOP votes.

Appendix B

An Example of a Multi-Employer Hybrid Pension Plan

The Operating Engineers Central Pension Fund (CPF) provides an example of how a hybrid plan can be used to meet a variety of needs. The CPF provides benefits to members of the International Union of Operating Engineers (IUOE). The IUOE represents over 350,000 members.

As a multi-employer pension plan, the CPF is regulated under the Taft-Hartley Act and is overseen by an equal number of union and management trustees. Over 8,000 employers contribute to the plan. In 1993, it was the sixth largest multi-employer plan and 148th largest among all U.S. pension plans.

The CPF demonstrates how a pension plan may be structured to meet not only the needs of employers and employees but also the needs of an industry with a homogeneous but mobile workforce. The CPF is a defined benefit plan. The monthly benefits paid to beneficiaries under the terms of the plan, however, are based on a percentage of the contributions made to the plan on the beneficiaries' behalf. The 1993 monthly benefit was 3.3%.

Like backloaded plans designed to tie employees to a firm or government organization, CPF benefits are higher for people who remain operating engineers for a long time; this same attribute encourages skill development. Vesting (a 5-year schedule is used even though multi-employer plans may use 10-year schedules) and break-in service requirements help eliminate poor workers. As a defined benefit plan, the employers bear the risk of adverse investment.

Like a defined contribution plan, the CPF is easy for participants to understand. Additionally, it is easy to calculate the benefit to be paid. Although the employee is tied to his trade, he is not tied to one employer and thus may move from job to job. Unlike defined contribution plans, the account on which benefits are calculated does not deplete so beneficiaries do not outlive their resources.

The material in this appendix relies on Teresa Ghilarducci, Garth Mangum, Jeffrey S. Peterson, and Peter Phillips. *Portable Pension Plans for Casual Labor Markets: Lessons from the Operating Engineers Central Pension Fund*. Westport, CT: Quorum Books, 1995.

Appendix C

Global Investing for Pension Funds

U.S. pension funds in 1995 had nearly $366 billion invested overseas (compared with $151 billion at the end of 1992) (see the article by Bensman). A Greenwich Associates survey of nearly 1,600 large pension funds reveals that the average allocation of these funds to non-U.S. securities is over 10% of their total assets, with funds of over $1 billion averaging 18% (see Bensman). Thus, it is clear that global investing—or investing worldwide—has arrived.

One reason for this increased exposure to international investment is quite simple: in 1969, the U.S. equity market accounted for approximately 31% of the value of all investable capital assets worldwide, but, by 1994, this had fallen to around 16%. Although U.S. dollar-denominated bonds kept a somewhat constant share at about 22% of all investable capital assets (due in part to an increase of foreign issuers issuing dollar-denominated bonds), non-U.S. bonds rose from around 16% to over 29% of the total of all capital investable assets, according to Fritz. Thus, pension funds needing a place to invest are virtually forced to look overseas for additional investment opportunities. Other reasons for the increase in international investment include the potential benefits of international diversification and the overall trend toward deregulation and integration of the global markets. Additionally, some analysts also argue that some overseas markets may not be as efficient as the U.S. marketplace. Thus, there may be occasions for earning positive risk-adjusted excess returns from active global management.

Investing in foreign securities is not the same as investing in U.S. securities. There are at least two questions pension funds should ask when investing outside the U.S.: Does the country of interest have a mature economy that should grow at a modest but relatively stable rate, or is it an emerging economy that could grow explosively but erratically? Are the local markets governed by competitive forces or are they subject to government regulation and intervention? The answers to these questions are important in selecting exposures and investment strategies.

International investing also has a risk/return profile that is different from investing solely in domestic markets. For example, currency exposure can be an important determinant of realized total return. The effect of currency has given birth to a new investment strategy, the *currency overlay*. The risks and returns of foreign equities and bonds are also different from those of their U.S. counterparts—or at least they have been. Significant differences also may exist in the market structure of foreign markets as well as information availability and regulation. Of course, the fundamentals of the economy of a specific country or region may vary widely.

Currency, Risk, Return, and Diversification

Currency return is without doubt an important factor in year-to-year returns and the variability of those returns. Consider, for example, the following examples of decomposed returns from the unhedged Europe, Australia, and Far East (EAFE) index of equities for U.S. investors (in U.S. $s):

Year	1988	1990	1992	1994
Total return	34.00%	−29.6%	−5.83%	−1.83%
Currency effect	−5.41%	6.41%	−6.02%	9.86%

Source: Bruce Russell, Paribas Asset Management. Dealing with the Pesky Currency Problem. Presentation at the Market Makers Seminar, Institute of Fiduciary Education, Carmel, CA, June 1996.

Clearly, the impact of changes in currency valuations can be substantial to a U.S. investor. Also as clearly, changes in currency values affect the volatility of a U.S. investor's portfolio.

According to some analysts, foreign-exchange risk offers opportunities to forecast currency valuations and thus pursue active (and, it is hoped, profitable) currency management. According to others, currency risk is simply an unsystematic risk to be avoided and thus hedged. Currency risk may be partially diversified away by holding investments denominated in numerous currencies simultaneously as long as these currencies are not strongly correlated. Derivatives, too, offer the opportunity to hedge currency risk fully at low cost, if such a hedge is desired. Whether to hedge at all is an issue, however, that becomes more and more important as more pension assets are invested overseas. We discuss this in some detail in Chapter 9.

Foreign Equities

Non-U.S. equities may be divided into the same categories used for U.S. equities: large and small company equities, value and growth equities, and so forth. There is much more to the story, however.

The common wisdom is that non-U.S. equities have historically offered higher returns at lower risk than have U.S. equities, and that the inclusion of non-U.S. securities increases a portfolio's diversification—that is, risk may be reduced and/or return increased through exposure to international equities. There are numerous studies that suggest that correlations between markets remain low enough so that, at a similar level of risk, returns can be raised substantively by diversifying internationally (for example, see Odier and Solnik, 1993). There is some debate, however. Other research suggests that the apparently good performance of indexes such as the EAFE relative to the S&P 500 can be attributed solely to the currency component of return (see the article by Sinquefield. From 1970 to 1994, in terms of local currency, EAFE had average annual compound returns of 10.52% versus 10.97% for the S&P 500—and also had a higher annual standard deviation. Additionally, after analyzing a number of alternative portfolios, Sinquefield's study is unable to demonstrate that simply adding international equity market segments (i.e., indexes) to a traditional 60% stocks, 40% bonds U.S. portfolio adds substantially to diversification. Interestingly, Sinquefield finds a value effect and size effect, as have been found in the United States. This finding supports those of Capaul, Rowley, and Sharpe that value stocks outperform growth stocks in six major markets and those produced by Fama and French for 12 of 13 countries studied. Finally, Solnik, Boucrelle, and Le Fur have found that, during periods of high volatility, the correlations among markets increase. That is, just when low correlations are needed for diversification, they disappear!

Foreign Bonds

Currency risk is, of course, a central issue when investing in foreign bonds. It accounts for as much as half of total bond market risk.

The historical record for unhedged foreign bonds in U.S. dollar terms suggests that the returns are (or have been) more volatile than U.S. returns are. Although there seems to be a modest diversification benefit to be gained by adding unhedged foreign bonds to portfolios of U.S. bonds, authorities disagree on the desirability of doing so.

Hedged foreign bonds have performed very well when compared with unhedged foreign bonds and with U.S. bonds. However, as Rosenburg points out, the periods studied are characterized by financial markets that are now less regulated and more integrated than they were in the past. Additionally, U.S. monetary policy could have affected the historical results. In other words, the seemingly superior historical performance of hedged foreign bond portfolios should be viewed with caution: the environment can change and as more investors globalize their portfolios, free lunches are not likely to persist (indeed, they may not have been really free in the first place).

Overall, the evidence on the performance of foreign bonds shows neither overwhelmingly good nor bad results. For pension funds that have currency exposures due to benefits payable in non-U.S. currencies, foreign bonds offer a natural hedge. Foreign bonds may also offer the potential to exploit interest rate or currency views and security selection opportunities for those pension funds that believe in active management.

Currency Overlays

A *currency overlay* is a portfolio management activity that assigns the authority to manage currency risks and returns to an overlay manager. The overlay manager may attempt to enhance portfolio returns by taking positions in currencies based on a particular view of how a given currency will do relative to other currencies. The overlay manager may attempt instead to reduce the portfolio's exposure to currency risk by hedging all or a portion of the portfolio's net currency exposure.

The appeal of a currency overlay is twofold. First, there is a specialist who presumably understands currencies and currency management. Second, there is someone who "sees the big picture" and has the authority to make decisions according to the net exposure a pension fund may face or want.

Although currency overlays are relatively new, some research on their efficacy has been done. Jorion used simulation to compare currency overlays to portfolios that were formed by jointly selecting currency and asset class weights. He concluded that currency overlays are inefficient relative to portfolios that integrate the asset class/currency decisions, reasoning that the interaction between assets and currencies is not fully considered in the overlay approach. He does suggest that overlay managers may be able to add value through active management, but cautions that this again appears to be suboptimal compared to a fully integrated approach.

The Regulatory and Information Environment

Structural issues should be of special interest to pension funds as they globalize their investment portfolios. Deregulation and integration of markets throughout the world have led to generally lower costs of international investing, better information, and more efficient trading mechanisms through computers and electronic communications. However, it is still more costly to trade in most markets outside of the United States—as much as 25 to 75 basis points more costly.

Another factor that must be considered is that taxes—ordinarily not a problem for U.S. pensions—can be an issue when investing in foreign securities. Withholding taxes on dividends and interest may come into play and may or may not be fully recoverable, depending on the tax treaties in effect with the relevant countries.

Securities regulation may also differ substantially among the different countries. There is no SEC outside of the United States, although there may be roughly analogous counterparts to the SEC. Accounting standards vary from country to country making it difficult to interpret whatever financial statements *are* presented. There may also be restrictions on foreign investment that make certain investment positions unobtainable. For example, in some countries, foreign investors (i.e., U.S. investors) may be prohibited from taking positions in certain securities.

An appreciation of the diversity and dynamics of structural issues in international investing may be gained by examining the changes in the European markets in recent years, as described by Benos and Crouhy. The fifteen members of the European Community alone have 35 stock exchanges and 23 futures and options exchanges. The merits of dealer markets versus auction systems are being debated as the exchanges compete for business. With the European Monetary Union of 1999 a distinct possibility, European nations are adopting new information technology systems, and automated trading is the new wave. Changes in currency risk and other risks can be expected as Europe moves to a unified currency, a convergence of accounting and regulatory standards, and improved trade execution. However, these are only possibilities—as in other regions of the world, the European financial markets are changing, but the final outcome is not known.

The bottom line for pension funds, then, is that international investing poses new challenges with respect to information, regulation, and structural issues. As a consequence, pension funds and their managers must recognize that the rules for international investing are not the same as those for domestic investing. Investment strategies that rely on timely, high-quality information, speedy trade execution, or low transaction or custody costs may not work in some markets. Thus, international strategies that will achieve the goals of the pension fund are likely to differ from traditional U.S. strategies: they will have to adapt to the countries to which they are being applied.

Management Issues

There are also other issues for pension funds that choose to invest internationally. Not the least of these is finding experienced managers. For pensions that prefer passive investing—and there are many funds that favor passive investing abroad in order to keep transaction costs low—experienced management simply means being conversant with the trading mechanisms and exchange characteristic of the countries or regions to which the pension wishes to achieve exposure. For pensions that pursue active management strategies with all or a portion of their assets, managerial expertise becomes even more important, because countries differ greatly by accounting standards, quality of information provided, and so forth. Traditional security analysis is also likely to be substantially different in different countries due to the difficulty of properly analyzing the effects of demographic, social, and political factors on asset values, and also due to the difficulty of getting high-quality price data for use in technical analysis.

Pension fund decision makers who believe in active management have, in the international market, a larger set of strategies from which to chose than is available in the United States. Pensions can attempt country selection strategies (how countries are expected to perform economically relative to other countries) and currency selection strategies (which currencies are expected to do well relative to other currencies). Even proponents of efficient markets may be attracted to emerging markets, based on the possibility of inefficiencies due to information problems or trading frictions. Of course, information is costly and inefficient trading systems may interfere with otherwise profitable trades. Moreover, some emerging markets may never emerge, failing to survive long enough and to provide reasonable return for the risk taken. It is worth noting that emerging markets account for only 1 to 2% of the total capital markets. Pension fund managers should think carefully about where they are focusing their time and resources. A lot of return on 1 to 2% of a portfolio's assets will not offset a poor strategic asset allocation.

Conclusion

Overall, it seems that large and medium-sized pension funds should be thinking along the lines of developing and implementing optimal global investment strategies as opposed to domestic-only strategies. Sponsors of employee-directed plans should include one or more non-U.S. alternatives to employees as well. However, the track record of risk/return data for non-U.S. investing is not as long as it is for U.S. securities. The world has changed rapidly, and, given the probable impact of currency on the historical data, we have to be careful not to infer too much from the historical record. The U.S. companies in which pensions invest are increasingly exposed to currency and country risk through their normal operations, however. Sponsors have more multinational workforces than ever before, and U.S. securities markets, relative to those of the rest of the world, are smaller and less capable of meeting the investment needs of pension funds than they were several years ago. Thus, foreign markets seem to offer reasonable and fertile investment alternatives for U.S. pension funds.

With what we know now (and remembering that there is much we do not know), pension funds should be willing to invest outside the United States. Domestic-only portfolios are likely to be inefficient, providing too little return for the risk taken. But in order to globalize, the sponsor needs to take a broader perspective in terms of many of the topics considered in this book. For example, the strategic asset allocation decision now becomes one of choosing not only asset classes but exposures to regions, countries, and possibly sectors within those countries. Additionally, the strategic asset allocation now must address a currency component. Performance measurement also takes on additional complexity. For example, returns will normally be stated in terms of the investor's base currency and will be a function both of local investment returns as well as relative currency movements. Benchmarking must become more robust, as the scope of the benchmark must expand to include countries as well as asset classes. These country exposures make determining the appropriate set of benchmark weights a more difficult task because appropriate weightings can be determined by amount of assets held, the total market capitalization for a given country, or the gross domestic product for a given country.

We offer the following caveats. Remember that the risk/return characteristics of non-U.S. markets are not as well documented as they are for U.S. securities. In the international marketplace, trading is more costly, and information is more uneven in quality and is more costly. The magnitude of the benefits of diversification is open to debate and the impact of currency risk is both real and somewhat confusing. Go cautiously, pay attention, do not forget about the bigger issues such as strategic asset allocation, and, as always, do not expect a free lunch.

Appendix D

Measuring Returns

The basics of measuring return are fairly straightforward. However, there are subtleties that become very important when trying to use a return measure to say something about performance. This appendix addresses the essentials of calculating and correctly using measures of return.

Total Return

The first metric convention necessary to assess investment performance is the measure of investment return over a single time period. Here there is no disagreement among analysts. The simple measure of single-period investment return for an asset is:

Total Return (TR) = Income Yield + Percentage Price (Value) Change

or

$$\text{Total Return} = \frac{\text{Portfolio Value at End of Period } (Pv_t)}{\text{Portfolio Value at Beginning of Period } (Pv_o)} - 1$$

This assumes no contributions. If there are contributions (C_t) or distributions (D_t) over the period,

$$TR = \frac{Pv_t - C_t + D_c}{Pv_o} - 1$$

This equation states that the return on an asset over the first period equals its income yield (the cash flow—that is, dividends, interest, royalties, or net rent—paid during the period divided by the price of the asset at the beginning of the period) plus the change in price (or value) of the same asset during the period. This yields a total return that appropriately includes the income and capital change components of investment return performance.

As an example, consider a fund that invested $100 in a single stock two years ago. One year later, a dividend of $10 was received (and reinvested) and the price of the stock had increased to $105. Two years later, another $10 dividend is received (and reinvested), but the price of the stock has fallen to $90. The *Total Return* (TR) in each year is:

Year 1 $10/100 + ($105 − 100)/100 = 0.1 + 0.05 = 0.15 or 15%

Year 2 $10/115 + ($90 − 115)/115 = 0.087 + (−0.217) = −0.13 or −13%

As this example shows, neither the income nor capital change components are sufficient to describe investment performance; both are necessary to present an accurate picture.

For simplicity, we ignore the complication that arises when the dividend flow occurs in the middle rather than near the end of a period. (Note that an earlier receipt of cash enables the investor to earn more on the reinvested amount.) Similarly, the above ignores an issue of vital importance for real-world pension funds—the cash flows that occur due to payments to beneficiaries and new contributions during the course of the measurement period (this period is generally a year, a quarter, or a month).

Intraperiod flows must be accommodated in the calculations if the return component of the conventional performance measures are to be computed in ways that would ultimately allow for the assessment of quality of investment management. In the following sections on time weighting and dollar weighting, we address the technical aspects of these adjustments.

Evaluating Managers: The Time-Weighted Rate of Return

A significant factor in return performance can be the sponsor's decision to allocate more (or less) money to an asset class or manager. This timing decision can come about for a variety of reasons. Perhaps it is simply the result of additional funding contributions, or perhaps it is due to the sponsor's belief that a given manager is doing well and should manage more of the plan's assets. Regardless of motivation, the decision to invest more with a particular manager—or less—coupled with subsequent market action, may affect the return calculated for a given time period. As a result, the sponsor who uses the wrong measure of return could end up deciding to reward a poor manager or fire a good one.

To achieve insulation from such sponsor decisions, the Bank Administration Institute recommends, and the investment profession agrees, that using the Time-Weighted Rate of Return (TWRR) generally is appropriate when evaluating manager performance. For a particular evaluation period, the TWRR for a portfolio is calculated exactly as the total return measure is calculated in the previous section. The unique aspect of TWRR is in how per period returns are linked together to get an annualized return. The use of this measure requires additional information about the value of the portfolio at the time of cash infusion and/or cash withdrawal.

The annualized *TWRR* for any n periods within a year given the total return (TR) in each period is:

$$TWRR = [(1 + TR_1) (1 + TR_2)...(1 + TR_n)] - 1$$

For example, consider an investment in a stock of $100. At the end of six months, the investment is worth $125 and there are no dividends. At the end of the second six-month period, the investment is worth $100 and again no dividends are paid. The total returns in each period are:

$$TR_1 = 25\% \text{ and } TR_2 = -20\%$$

The annualized *TWRR* may be computed as:

$$TWRR = [(1 + 0.25)(1 - 0.2)] - 1 = [(1.25)(0.8)] - 1 = 0.0, \text{ or } 0\%$$

Thus, the annualized total return for the one year period is 0%—an intuitively appealing result, since the value at the end of one year is the same as originally invested.

The characteristic of the *TWRR* in which we are most interested is that, for it to be useful, total return must be calculated every time there is a significant cash flow into or out of the portfolio being measured. By performing this calculation when cash flows occur, TRWW takes the impact of the cash flow out of the evaluation.

Evaluating the Total Portfolio: The Dollar-Weighted Rate of Return

The correct way to accommodate and evaluate the performance impact of cash inflows or cash outflows is to use a Dollar-Weighted Rate of Return (*DWRR*). This is obtained by solving for the internal rate of return of a set of cash flows and end-of-period values, as shown below:

$$V_0 (1 + DWRR)^N + \sum_{t=1}^{n} C_t (1 + DWRR)^{(n-t)} = V_N$$

where V_0 is the starting value of the portfolio, C_t is the cash inflow or outflow in period t, and V_N is the ending value of the portfolio.

Assume the initial portfolio value is $100, and two years later it is worth $150. Also assume $10 was contributed at the end of the first year.

$$\$100 \ (1 + DWRR)^2 + \$10 \ (1 + DWRR) = \$150$$

Solving for *DWRR* we find:

$$DWRR = 17.58\%$$

The *DWRR* is certainly adequate as long as one is comfortable about estimating the cash-flow timing and as long as one is comfortable about who has control of the inflows and outflows of cash. It usually is satisfactory for individual managers or funds that do not have large inflows or outflows over a period. However, this computation can be tricky when performed over many time periods because, as inflows, outflows, inflows and outflows occur, there are many changes in algebraic signs (+ or −). For every change, there is a value of *DWRR* that solves the mathematical problem. With, say, three sign changes, there will be three answers, so interpretation is often not as simple as it may seem.

Apart from this technical consideration, note that using a DWRR to evaluate a single manager implies that the fund manager being evaluated controls the timing of inflows and outflows. The computed DWRR would be higher or lower if all the dollar values remained the same, but the timing of the intermediate cash flow occurred sooner or later. If managers do not control this cash-flow timing, then equally talented managers could have different DWRRs, depending on when funds were contributed or withdrawn by the sponsor. Because plan sponsors generally make the decisions about fund contribution and withdrawal, the manager loses some degree of control over the performance measure relative to the plan sponsor. Thus, the DWRR can produce a somewhat distorted view of investment return for managers. It is, however, generally an appropriate measure for the total pension asset pool—that is, the entire amount under the control of the plan sponsor—or for the entire portion invested in equities, for example. This last observation is conditional, however, on being able to filter out the impact of cash contributions and liquidations used to pay beneficiaries.

Comparing the TWRR and DWRR

To illustrate the difference between the TWRR and the DWRR better, we return to our first example. Suppose that the plan sponsor gives a manager $100. Subsequently, the sponsor observes that a 25% return is produced by the manager in the first period and decides to invest $50 more with the manager at the beginning of period two. Thus, during the second period, \$175 has been invested (\$125 + 50). The manager then loses 20% of the total so at the end of the period the value is \$175 (1 − 0.2), or \$140. Recall, the TWRR is 0% per period. However, the DWRR is now calculated as:

$$\$100 \, (1 + DWRR)^2 + (\$50) \, (1 + DWRR)^1 = \$140$$
$$DWRR = -4.066\% \text{ per period}$$

Note especially that, because the contribution to the portfolio was made after the period of better investment return (the 25% return that occurred in the first period) and before the period of poorer performance, the DWRR is less than the TWRR. In other words, since the sponsor elected to increase the exposure of the portfolio just before a period of bad performance, the DWRR is lower than the TWRR. If we are trying to evaluate the manager, therefore, the manager should not be penalized for the unfortunate (in this case) timing of the cash inflow.

The primary reason for this difference between the DWRR and the TWRR is that the DWRR implicitly assumes a constant rate of return over the entire evaluation period, and the TWRR does not. Thus, intraperiod cash flows affect the DWRR but are excluded as part of the measurement process when using TWRR. Of course, the DWRR is appropriate when the objective is to evaluate how well the entire investment portfolio has performed, and to decide whether to invest more (or less)—a decision that presumably is controlled directly by the plan sponsor. The assumption that the plan sponsor had control over the magnitude and timing of inflows and outflows may not always be accurate.

The only drawback to the TWRR is the need to develop intermediate portfolio values; this can be done precisely by frequently generating a complete portfolio valuation. If this is nearly costless, it should be done. For instance, public mutual funds must report portfolio values daily. Thus an active mutual fund investor can easily compute the TWRR. When there are noticeable costs to valuation, such as the cost of appraisals for non-traded stock or real estate, evaluators will sometimes use a proxy to estimate portfolio value. This might be necessary for funds that do not normally compute their values daily. If actual returns are computed only monthly, for example, then a midmonth valuation necessitated by a mid-month cash inflow or outflow might be approximated by using a broad market index as a proxy for the return on the portfolio being evaluated. Thus if the index rose by $S\%$ from the beginning to the time of the month in which the cash flow occurred, the portfolio value might be treated as if it too rose by (a hypothetical) $S\%$. The computation would then proceed as shown earlier. For example, if the starting value was \$100, \$25 was infused during the period, the ending value was $150, and the market rose by 5% between the period's start and the cash flow, the return would be:

$$[(105 - 100)/100] + [(150 - 130)/130] = 21.4\%$$

over the period.

Generally speaking, the shorter the measurement interval is—for example, months versus years—and the smaller the cash inflows and outflows are relative to the portfolio's starting size, the closer the DWRR and the TWRR will be. Indeed, with monthly measurement periods and with contributions or outflows that are, say, equal to 10% or less of the starting value, generally there will be only very small differences between the two measures, which may not be large enough to warrant the data collection effort necessary to compute TWRR. Nonetheless, it is generally more precise to use the TWRR to evaluate the manager of a fund.

In reality, most pension plans that compute returns periodically use consultants to do this. The consultants obtain the basic data from the pension plan's master trustee, the trust company that is responsible for keeping track of the holdings, dividends, interest, receipts, and cash flows, once a quarter. They then use approximation techniques to estimate the TWRR. Because consultants presumably do all evaluations in the same way, all interested parties hope and pray—given the data limitations they may be unable to do much more—that what biases exist, are systematic, affecting all evaluated portfolios in the same way. Note that with the trend among money management firms and consultants to comply with the Association for Investment Management and Research (AIMR) Performance Presentation Standards, the data gathering and computational issues that once were barriers to the correct way of dealing with these issues are rapidly disappearing.

Returns Over Many Periods

Once a single-period measure of returns is computed (for example, once annualized returns have been computed), the question arises of how to combine single-period returns to make up a multiple-period measure. There are two alternatives. The first approach is using an arithmetic average. The second is to use a geometric average. The arithmetic average is:

$$TRa_{it} = \Sigma TR_{it}/T$$

where TRa_{it} is the arithmetic average of the returns on the ith portfolio over the periods 1 through T, R_{it} is the return in each period t, and T is the number of periods. In this formulation, the average will be given in the same time dimension as each period's return is computed. If the periods are months, for instance, the average will be in terms of months. To put the average of monthly returns into annual terms, multiply by 12.

If portfolio returns were 5%, 10%, 15%, and –10% in each of four quarters, the average quarterly return would be:

$$(5 + 10 + 15 - 10)/4 = 5\%$$

per quarter. To calculate the annual return, simply add the quarterly returns, or multiply the average quarterly return by 4—either way, the annual return is 20%.

Note that while the computed annual return is 20%, the true return is not. Suppose that at the beginning of the first quarter, the portfolio value was $100. A 20% return would suggest that the portfolio's value at the end of the year would be $120, but this is not so. The portfolio rises by 5% in the first quarter; its dollar value increases by 5%. If the starting value was $100, its value would be $105 at the end of the first quarter. The portfolio rises by 10% in the second quarter; its new dollar value is $105 (1 + 0.10) = $115.50. In the third quarter it rises by 15%, so its dollar value rises to $115 (1 + 0.15) = $132.25. In the final quarter it falls by 10%, so its ending dollar value is only $132.25 (1 – 0.10) = $119.02. This is less than the $120 suggested by the arithmetically determined annual return. Thus, the arithmetic mean computation can lead to the overstatement of the dollar value that is truly there.

To remedy this problem, use the geometric mean return. The geometric average is:

$$Rg_{it} = (\frac{V_T}{V_O}) - 1$$

where Rg_{it} is the geometric average return for the ith portfolio, T is the number of measurement periods, and k is the time dimension divisor. If returns are computed quarterly and there are four quarterly observations, then to get a geometric average annual return, the exponent is ¼, or 0.25. Thus, the annual geometric mean is:

$$Rg = (\frac{\$119.02}{100})^{0.25} - 1 = .0445 \text{ or } 4.45\%$$

As long as all the returns are the same for each measurement interval, the arithmetic mean will equal the geometric mean. When the returns differ, the geometric mean will be less than the arithmetic mean. Indeed, the higher the period-to-period variability, the lower the geometric mean relative to the arithmetic mean. When assessing historical investment performance, the geometric mean is more useful because it will not allow for an implied overstatement of the dollar values at the end of the evaluation period. When projecting historical investment performance into the future, the arithmetic mean coupled with the standard deviation is generally more useful to avoid understating the per period return.

To illustrate, suppose Portfolio A experienced a return of 10% in each of two years, and suppose Portfolio B had a 20% return in year 1 and a 0% return in the second year. To confirm the appropriateness of the geometric mean in this example, consider a dollar investment. If $100 were invested in Portfolio A, it would be worth $110 after one year and $121 after two years. If the same $100 were invested in Portfolio B, it would be worth only $120 after two years. The arithmetic mean does not reveal this difference in terms of dollar amounts, but the geometric mean does. Thus the geometric mean return reflects changes in dollar values better than the arithmetic mean does. The arithmetic mean return for Portfolio A is $(0.10 + 0.10)/2$, or 10% per year; the arithmetic mean for Portfolio B is also 10%. The geometric mean return for Portfolio A is:

$$(\frac{121}{100})^{0.5} - 1 = 10\%$$

while the geometric mean return for Portfolio B is lower:

$$(\frac{120}{100})^{0.5} - 1 = 9.5\%$$

As noted, when a return estimate is combined with an independent risk measure, as in forming expectations of future performance, the arithmetic mean return is generally used. This is so partly by convention and partly because the geometric mean itself changes with the variability of outcomes, and hence it is not truly independent of customarily used measures of risk. For instance, suppose Portfolio C has a 30% return in one year and –10% return in the next. It is much more volatile than Portfolio A and somewhat more volatile than Portfolio B, although it has the same arithmetic mean return. Its geometric mean return is only 8.2%, however. Using a geometric mean return in conjunction with a risk measure is, in some sense, double-counting, since the geometric mean return declines with volatility, other things being equal.

Appendix E

Adjusting for Risk

Two conceptually different measures of risk typically are used to evaluate portfolio performance. The first of these is the time-series variance of total portfolio returns. The second is a measure related to systematic or market risk rather than to total portfolio risk.

Total Risk

The measure of total risk most commonly used for portfolio evaluation purposes is the time series variance or the standard deviation of returns. This measures the dispersion around the arithmetic mean of the time series returns. In doing so, it captures the volatility of returns over time relative to the average per period return. The variance is:

$$\text{Var}(TR_p) = \sum_{t=1}^{T} (TR_{pt} - TRa_{pt})^2 / T$$

where TR_{pt} is the total return on portfolio p during period t, TRa_{pt} is the arithmetic mean total return, and T is the number of observations. The standard deviation $SD\ (TRp)$ is merely the square root of the above quantity. Nearly every statistics textbook describes this measure.

Market Risk

Rather than measuring total risk, many authorities advocate measuring only the systematic or market risk to which a portfolio is exposed. This is the portion of the total risk that cannot be eliminated by holding a diversified portfolio. Conceptually, the total risk of an asset is comprised of both systematic risk and unsystematic or diversifiable risk. The advocates of using market risk argue that a portfolio manager should not be penalized by attributing total risk to the portfolio manager because unsystematic risk, a component of total risk, can generally be eliminated only by broad investment strategy decisions that are customarily made by the plan sponsor, not the money manager.

A common approach to estimating systematic or market risk is to use what is known as the market model. The *market model* is a regression estimate of the relationship between the periodic return on a portfolio and the return on a broad-based market index, such as the S&P 500. The regression equation takes the following form:

$$R_{pt} - R_{ft} = \alpha_p + \beta_p(R_{mt} - R_{ft}) + \varepsilon_{pt}$$

where R_{ft} is the tth-period return on the risk-free asset, R_{pt} is the tth-period return on the market portfolio, α_p is the regression intercept, β_p is the estimate of systematic risk of the portfolio (formally this is $[\text{Cov}[(R_{pt} - R_{ft}), (R_{mt} - R_{tt})]/\text{Var}(R_{mt})]$), and ε_{pt} is a random-error term with a mean of zero and a finite variance. In equations such as this, the β estimate indicates the volatility of the portfolio relative to the market portfolio. If the β_p were estimated as 2.0, then with a risk-free rate of 10% and a market increase of 18%, you would expect the portfolio to rise by

$$0.10 + 2.0\,(0.18 - 0.10) = 0.26, \text{ or } 26\%$$

The expected risk premium of a portfolio with a β_p of 2.0 is twice the expected risk premium of the market portfolio.

For performance measurement, of chief concern are the statistically estimated parameters α_p, β_p, and Var(*ep*), the variance of the portfolio's return variance not explained by the variable R_{mt}. Generally, these can be well measured when such a model is estimated over five years or so of monthly data, thus yielding sixty observations. Twenty observations at least are necessary for this to have any serious economic content. There is a trade-off, however. The more observations, the stronger the statistical inference. But the longer the time period, the more probable that the current investment policies are unlike those that prevailed at the start of the time period. There is no easy resolution to this trade-off; common sense, however, helps. If there have been no policy changes, go for length. If there have been investment policy changes, use only data available since the last change and accept the fact that the statistics will, because of few observations, be a bit suspect. Finally, the market parameters used will change over time. Thus, the risk-free rate (R_{ft}) is likely to vary over time, and α_p and β_p will be slightly biased measures of the true variables. The result is that the analyst must use judgment regarding the likelihood of changes in any fundamental market parameters.

Note there is an explicit link between total risk and its systematic and unsystematic components.

> *Total Risk = Systematic Risk + Unsystematic* or *Diversifiable Risk*
> *= Market Risk + Diversifiable Risk*

More formally:

$$\text{Var}(TR_p) = \beta^2\,\text{Var}(TR_m) + \text{Var}(\varepsilon_p).$$

This equation says that the total risk of a portfolio is comprised of the total risk of a market portfolio adjusted for the relationship between it and the managed portfolio, β^2, *plus* the variance of the amount of portfolio return that is unexplained by the market's movements.

Appendix F

Example of an Equity Swap Hedge

Consider a pension fund that holds DM 4,000,000 in large capitalization German stocks. Although the fund manager has no concern or view about the value of the German Mark, she is worried about the performance of the German stock market over the next two years, but is generally good over a longer time horizon. To hedge for two years, she may enter into an equity swap.

The swap will commit the pension fund to pay the change in the German DAX equity index to a counterparty (effectively "passing through" the change in value from the DAX index). In return, the investor will receive a money market–based return tied to the London Interbank Offer Rate (LIBOR).

The terms of the swap are:

Currency	DM
Notional amount	Variable
Initial notional amount	DM 40,000,000
Stock index	DAX
Spread to dealer	0
Index interest rate	6-month LIBOR
Payment frequency	Semi-annual
Maturity	2 years

After the swap is established, assume the following pattern of interest rates and changes in the DAX occurs:

Time (months)	DAX	% Change	LIBOR
0	2500	—	6%
6	2750	10%	5.5%
12	2650	–3.64%	5.25%
18	2600	–1.9%	6%
24	2400	–7.69%	6.5%

Cash Flows (from pension fund's perspective)

Time (months)	% Change from Index	Index Receipt (Pay)	Interest Receipt	Net Receipt (payment)	Notional Amount
0					40,000,000
6	+10%	(4,000,000)	1,200,000	(2,800,000)	44,000,000
12	–3.6%	1,584,000	1,210,000	2,794,000	42,416,000
18	–1.9%	805,904	1,113,420	1,919,324	41,610,096
24	–7.7%	3,203,977	1,248,303	4,452,280	38,406,119

The "Net Receipt" column shows the proceeds the pension fund will receive (or pay) as a consequence of the swap. In this example the pension fund may appear to have made a profitable swap in the second through fourth periods (and an unprofitable one in the first period), because the falling DAX results in payments to the fund from the equity side of the swap in addition to the LIBOR-linked payments. Remember that the portfolio of German stocks held by the pension fund is losing value in these periods (assuming it correlates with the DAX index), as well, however. Thus, the swap per se is not profitable— it simply is offsetting the losses in the portfolio in these periods; the hedge is working. Note that, as it is structured, the swap exposes the investor to currency risk. If desired, this risk may be hedged with a currency swap or with other derivatives.

Manager Selection

I. General Provisions of Manager Selection Request for Proposal
    1. *Summary Cover Sheet*
        - Name of the firm
        - Address of the firm
        - Name, telephone number, and title of individual with authority to commit the firm
        - Name, telephone number, and title of proposed account manager, if different from above
        - Year of SEC registration
        - Product type
            - Equity
            - Fixed Income
            - Cash
            - Real Estate
            - Other
        - Date of Submission
        - Time-Stamped Date of Receipt
    2. *Description of Organization*
        - Submit an organization chart indicating the reporting relationships of the entity responsible for this proposed relationship and the most senior management of the organization.
        - Indicate the location of your firm's offices and indicate the staff size in the following categories:
            - Professionals
            - Portfolio managers
            - Research analysts
            - Economists
            - Traders
            - Client service
            - Marketing

Reprinted, by permission, from Stephen A. Berkowitz and Louis D. Finney (1989), "The Selection and Management of Investment Managers for Public Pension Plans," Report to the Government Finance Research Center.

- Administration (including accounting and record keeping)
- Non-professionals
- Describe joint ventures or other affiliations of your firm requiring a commitment of capital, a commitment of personnel or the acceptance of liability.
- Provide copies of the most current SEC filings and audited financial statements. Please note material changes since the preparation of these documents.

3. *Qualifications and Experience of Key Personnel*
   - List the key personnel for whom no substitutions will be made without prior written consent. Provide biographies of key personnel that include:
     - Education
     - Complete professional history including duration of term in present position
     - Current position and responsibilities
     - Current client responsibilities where relevant number of accounts and total size of accounts by class of assets being managed (e.g., equity, fixed, cash, balanced)
   - Provide a list of investment management clients indicating the clients for whom more than $25 million is being managed.
   - List clients obtained within the last three years and client contacts.
   - List clients who have terminated in the last three years and client contact where available. List significant new hires and terminations within the last three years for the entity responding to this proposal.

4. *Business Arrangements*
   - Provide proposed management fee schedule including:
     - Start-up fees
     - Annual fees and method of computation and payment schedule
     - Quarterly presentations before Investment Committee
   - Provide performance-based fee alternative.
   - Proposed arrangement for brokerage services.
     - Provide total commission costs over the last 12 months.

- List brokers executing at least 10% of dollar volume over the last 12 months.
- List total value of "soft dollar" services purchased over the last 12 months.
- Specify procedures for handling transfer of assets.
- Provide sample reports for accounting and auditing purposes.
- Provide a specimen contract.

II. Technical Requirements: Fixed Income Management

1. Please submit the holdings of a representative $25 million portfolio assuming investment in the most recent quarter. If respondent is proposing a commingled fund, please submit the holding of the fund as of the most recent quarter end. List representative buys and sells or, if a commingled fund is proposed, list all transactions. Calculate the following summary statistics for the portfolio:
   - Market-weighted duration
   - Market-weighted average maturity
   - Market-weighted average quality rating
   - Cash and cash equivalents as a percent of portfolio assets
   - Number of issues and proportion of market value represented by the largest 10 holdings
   - Holding period return in most recent quarter
   - Income yield over the period
   - Capital appreciation over the period

2. Please submit performance of fixed-income holdings for each of the last 20 quarters and annual time-weighted rates of return net of all fees and management costs. Calculate the following summary statistics:
   - Market-weighted duration
   - Market-weighted average maturity
   - Market-weighted average quality rating
   - Cash and cash equivalents as a percent of portfolio assets
   - Number of issues and proportion of market value represented by the largest 10 holdings. Standard deviation of returns in excess of the risk-free rate over the last 20 quarters.
   - The ratio of the arithmetic mean return in excess of the risk rate (20 quarters) divided by the standard deviation of returns (20 quarters). Level of portfolio turnover

measured as the lesser of purchases and sales each quarter as a percent of average assets over the period.
- Income yield over the holding period. Capital appreciation over the holding period.
- Level of turnover over the period measured as the lesser of purchases and sales divided by the average market value of assets over the period.

3. For each of the last 20 quarters provide detailed proportional asset allocations quality rating with the duration computed for the portion of the portfolio assigned each quality rating.
4. Provide a detailed description of management style:
   - Specify decision rules for making buys.
   - Specify decision rules for making sells.
   - Specify screens or filter rules to subset the universe of securities considered.
   - Provide technical and summary descriptions of portfolio optimization algorithms.
5. Provide a detailed description of resources:
   - Is software used to implement decision rules owned or leased? If leased, name the vendor.
   - What provisions are in place to ensure the maintenance of the software?
   - What electronic databases are used to support portfolio management?
   - What is the source of bond pricing used by your firm? Under what conditions can bond pricing be overridden by dealer quotes?
6. Provide samples of client reports and indicate the frequency of these reports:
   - List reports and other research routinely provided clients without additional charge.
   - Who will represent your firm at quarterly client meetings?

III. Technical Requirements: Equity Management
1. Please submit the holdings of a representative $25 million portfolio assuming investment in the most recent quarter. If respondent is proposing a commingled fund, please submit the holding of the fund as of the most recent quarter end. List representative buys and sells. If a commingled fund is proposed, list all transactions. Calculate the following summary statistics for the portfolio:

- Market price/earnings ratio and portfolio beta
- Proportional investment by broad industry grouping
- Proportional investment by exchange or security market
- Average market capitalization
- Number of issues and proportion of market value represented by the largest holdings
- Holding period return in most recent quarter

2. Please submit performance of equity holdings for each of the last 20 quarters and annual time-weighted rates of return, net of all fees and management costs.
   - Calculate summary statistics as in 1 above.
   - Market price/earnings
   - Portfolio beta
   - Proportional investment by industry group and market
   - Average market capitalization
   - Holding period income yield
   - Holding period capital appreciation
   - Cash and cash equivalents as a percent of portfolio assets
   - Number of issues and proportion of market value represented by the largest 10 holdings
   - Standard deviation of returns in excess of the risk-free rate over the last 20 quarters
   - The ratio of the arithmetic mean return in excess of the risk-free rate (20 quarters) divided by the standard deviation of returns (20 quarters)
   - Level of portfolio turnover measured as the lesser of purchases and sales each quarter as a percent of average assets over the period

3. Provide a detailed description of management style.
   - Specify decision rules for making buys.
   - Specify decision rules for making sells.
   - Screen filters to subset the universe of securities considered.
   - Technical and summary description of optimization algorithms.

4. Provide a detailed description of resources.
   - Is software used to implement decision rules owned or leased? If leased, name the vendor.
   - What provisions are in place to ensure the maintenance of the software?

- What electronic databases are used to support portfolio management?
- What is the source of equity pricing for thinly traded issues used by your firm? Under what conditions can equity pricing be overriden by dealer quotes?

5. Provide samples of client reports and indicate the frequency of these reports.
   - List reports and other research routinely provided clients without additional charge.
   - Who will represent your firm at quarterly client meetings?

Appendix H

Issues for Corporations with Multinational Pension Obligations

The multinational firm that sponsors pension plans in countries other than the United States faces a number of issues that domestic firms do not. Sponsors must adapt their pension plans to differential tax treatment, regulatory environments, and cultural effects. Additionally, sponsors need to consolidate asset management activities and information systems where feasible to avoid a fragmented, inefficient system. Overall, managing multinational pension plans is much more complex than it is for domestic plans.

The Multinational Environment

Taxes, regulation, and culture must be understood by those who manage multinational pension plans. Some observations on these factors follow.

Tax and Regulatory Factors

We have already seen that tax regulations provide an incentive for employers to contribute to pension plans because those contributions are tax deductible and can be invested tax free, and for employees to demand pension plans because taxable payouts of pension assets can be deferred until retirement. Differential tax rates obviously play a role in the desirability of any given pension scheme, however. For example, in countries with high marginal tax rates, employers and employees both may prefer compensation packages that heavily weight the pension scheme (relative to direct wages) since deferred pension income may be taxed at a lower rate in the future. On the other hand, if differential tax rates are low, pension schemes may lose some of their appeal for both employers and employees.

Much of the material in this appendix relies on Debbie Harrison, *Pension Fund Investment in Europe*. London: FT Financial Publishing, Pearson Professional Limited, 1995.

Regulatory treatment comes in a variety of forms. A common issue is that of investment restrictions, particularly with respect to allocations among the alternative asset classes. According to the *Wall Street Journal* (27 January 1995), Japan, for example, is subject to Ministry of Finance guidelines that limit asset allocations of Japanese companies to maximums of 50% in Japanese bonds, 30% in Japanese stocks, 30% in foreign securities, and 20% in real estate. On the other hand, U.K. pension funds, other than being subject to a 5% limit on self-investment, face few explicit investment restrictions. Regulation, however well intended, may lead to suboptimal asset allocations, potentially higher contributions, and potentially less diversification for pension funds. Fortunately, a multinational sponsor may be able to manage the total asset pool in a way that offsets or counters the effects of country-specific regulation, such as those imposed on the portion of the asset pool subject to Japanese regulation. For example, perhaps the U.S. component of the asset pool will not hold Japanese securities when it otherwise would. Of course this depends on a firm's ability to integrate its view of the funding/investment performance interaction across plans in multiple countries, since assets per se typically may not be moved from one plan to another.

Additionally, prudent investor rules can be considerably different, depending on the country in which the pension scheme is chartered. This is really a matter of more or less rather than the absence of any prudent investor rules whatsoever. There is also a country-specific cultural influence as to what type of behavior is deemed prudent (for example, the degree to which investing in nondomestic securities is appropriate varies from country to country).

Finally, solvency requirements vary from country to country. Consider some of the differences between the U.K. and Germany. In the U.K., the 1995 Pensions Act established minimum funding requirements as well as provided a compensation plan for beneficiaries when pension plans become insolvent. In contrast, private German pensions historically have operated on a book-reserve basis in which the employer is the guarantor of pension liabilities. Funds were not put into asset pools as such but were retained within the company through a system of balance sheet reserves. In general, solvency requirements may have the effect of encouraging plans to change their asset allocations from what they otherwise might be. For example, more mature, well-funded pension plans subject to strict solvency requirements may find it sensible to reduce their exposure to equities while increasing their investment in bonds. Similarly, limits on contributions for tax purposes may affect funding decisions and hence, plan security.

Cultural Factors

Country-specific cultural factors can have a significant influence on pension management in many subtle ways.

One way is in how pension assets are managed. Pension funds in some countries use mainly internal asset managers, while those in other countries use external asset managers. For example, the larger pension funds in the U.K. tend to use in-house management while the smaller ones tend to favor external management. In Switzerland, the preferred managers tend to be the banks located in Switzerland. In France, supplemental occupational pension funds tend to use insurance companies while the pooled/mutual fund market relies on banks and investment management firms. It should be noted, however, that there seems to be a trend among European countries towards more performance-oriented investing, regardless of historical preferences.

Another way is how culture may affect the structure of pension plans. Consider, for example, that defined contribution plans have not been as popular in Europe as they have been in the United States. (However, there are indications that these plans are becoming more popular in European countries and may even follow adoption trends similar to those in the United States.)

Finally, culture is entwined with demographics and politics. France, for example, has a compulsory second-tier pension system that is pay-as-you-go. The system is strained by factors such as high unemployment and an aging workforce. This puts pressure on asset managers to perform better. Additionally, the French government is attempting to increase plan contributions and hence improve funding levels.

Consolidation of Pension Management

A chronic problem multinationals face is that subsidiary pensions tend to be managed independently. This is due in part to regulatory factors and to using many different managers who may be more knowledgeable of the financial markets in certain regions than others. In part, too, this may simply be due to inertia. No matter the reason, the result, however, can be inefficiencies, unintended risk exposures, too little return, and higher than necessary contributions.

As a general rule, pension asset pools and countries where such pools are part of the overall system must be segregated for multinational firms. This presents a challenge for sponsors who wish to realize economies of scale through consolidation. Nonetheless, consolidation is on the minds of many. One survey by Hawthorne indicates that 26% of large corporate sponsors have already consolidated some of their investment management activities and another 48% are considering it.

Consolidation has three distinct elements. The first is *asset custody*. Custody arrangements affect both pension management costs and the ability to compile meaningful information. Typically, custody arrangements are restrained by local regulation. The second element is *asset management*. Asset management has implications for the fulfillment of fiduciary responsibility (the definition of which differs from country to country), for the aggregate amount of management fees, and for performance. Part of this decision is the internal versus external management issue discussed in Chapter 11. Part of this issue, however, may be subject to both regulatory restrictions and/or cultural norms within the country where the pension liability exists. Finally, consolidation has a *strategic element* in that the sponsor must ultimately be concerned with overall funding costs, the management of the entire pension portfolio, the magnitude of the multinational pension liability, the effectiveness of the entire multicountry compensation scheme, and so forth—at least on a conceptual basis.

The benefits of at least partial consolidation should not be ignored: the costs of individually managing each pension scheme in each country may be exorbitant. Redundant organizational structures, incomplete information for decision making, ineffective compensation schemes and investment strategies, and excessive custody and management costs are likely consequences for multinational firms that do not address these issues.

Conclusion

Since pension schemes are part of the total compensation package, and since the desirability of pension plans depends on factors such as tax levels and regulations, companies should carefully evaluate their pension plans on a country-by-country basis. What makes sense in one country may not be sensible in another. Thus, using firms that manage assets in several countries and are knowledgeable of these country-specific factors is a good first step to dealing with country issues without setting up barriers to consolidation.

Overall, consolidation makes sense. Consolidation offers multinational sponsors several potential benefits. First, there are the economies of scale that can potentially reduce transaction, custody, and even management costs. Second, consolidation may be necessary to prevent suboptimal asset allocations across the entire spectrum of countries in which a multinational has pension liabilities, and to avoid country-specific problems with diversification. Third, the consolidation of pension assets, at least in bookkeeping form (since it may not be achievable on an asset pooling basis, due to regulation), has implications for managing currency risk. Finally, consolidation should result in more accurate and complete information on pension asset allocations, investment performance, and risk exposures for top management and trustees/board members. This bigger, more complete picture is essential for sound decision making.

Remember, even though there are numerous barriers to consolidated management, investment strategies still should address the total pension liability and the relationship between the totality of the pension fund and the sponsor. The pension plan should be managed cost-effectively. Performance must be evaluated for the entire plan in a timely manner. Monitoring must also take place. The pension plan is both one of the largest assets and one of the largest liabilities for many firms. No multinational firm would argue that it is sensible to ignore regulatory or tax or cultural effects on marketing or personnel or whatever; similarly, it is also unwise to ignore these effects on multinational pension plans.

Appendix I

A Guide for the Prudent Fiduciary

Broadly speaking, the responsibilities of a pension plan fiduciary are to exercise care and loyalty. With these two responsibilities in mind, we present what we believe to be the minimum requirements fiduciaries must meet to fulfill their legal, and perhaps ethical, obligations in planning, staffing, and monitoring the plans that they serve.

Duty of Care

1. Participate in and oversee the development of the pension investment policy statement. This statement should include broad guidelines regarding strategic asset allocation, acceptable investment strategies, and permissible types of transactions, or alternatively, the types of transactions that are prohibited (for instance, writing uncovered call options). This statement should also indicate whether the chief investment officer (CIO) is allowed or expected to overlay decisions made by portfolio managers. For example, the statement should address whether or not the CIO is allowed to take positions in futures that increase or reduce the equities exposure of individual managers.

2. Establish a risk tolerance for the pension plan that reflects the circumstances and preferences of both sponsors and beneficiaries. The pension plan fiduciary should actively participate in assessing risk, in setting limits on the total acceptable dollar loss (value at risk), and in developing policies that will keep the plan invested in a way that is consistent with the risk tolerance.

3. Hire a CIO with the appropriate educational credentials and experience to serve as a competent administrator.

4. Decide whether internal or external management of the pension plan will produce the highest risk-adjusted, cost-adjusted investment returns that are consistent with the risk tolerance set for the fund.

5. Select investment managers based on clearly defined, rational criteria, such as historical performance (i.e., performance that yields insight into predictable future behavior), anticipated future investment

strategies, ability to handle administrative tasks, willingness to participate in the monitoring process, compensation, trading style and activity, and use of soft dollars.

6.   Establish investment guidelines for each manager. These guidelines should specify the minimum and maximum exposure to each relevant asset. For example, this might limit a manager to owning less than 5% of a company and investing no more than 10% of the managed portfolio in a company.

7.   Monitor the performance of investment managers for investment returns as well as for their level of adherence to the previously agreed upon investment guidelines.

8.   Assure that all administrative and clerical functions are performed accurately and in a timely manner.

9.   In the case of fiduciaries of defined contribution plans, develop policies regarding investment alternatives and make these available to employees. Fiduciaries should select a preferred list of money managers, monitor the performance of these investment organizations, and educate employees so that they are able to make responsible investment decisions. Fiduciaries of defined contribution plans should also provide investment and performance measurements, and assist employees in interpreting these measurements. Fiduciaries should also facilitate portfolio rebalancing at reasonable intervals.

Duty of Loyalty

1.   Develop methods for resolving conflicts of interest between the sponsoring organization and the pension plan, as well as between the plan and its vendors (e.g., external investment managers), in ways that are not disadvantageous to the pension plan from an *ex ante* perspective.

2.   Develop an approach to exercising shareholder rights. An example of this is proxy voting that works to the advantage of the pension plan from the shareholder's perspective rather than the manager's, regardless of the manager's connection to the sponsoring organization or the pension plan.

3.   Learn as much as possible about pension plan governance and investment management to maintain a high level of competence, and be as faithful as possible to the interests of pension plan beneficiaries.

Glossary of Pension and Related Terms

Compiled by Judith O. Mayers

Accrual of Benefits

In the case of a defined benefit pension plan, the process of accumulating pension credits for years of credit service. In the case of a defined contribution plan, the process of accumulating funds in the individual employee's pension account.

Accumulated Funding Deficiency

A deficit balance in a pension plan's funding standard account that means that the required minimum funding requirement has not been met by the plan.

Active Participant

Includes (1) any individuals who are currently in employment covered by a plan and who are earning or retaining credited service under a plan; (2) any nonvested individuals who are earning or retaining credited service under a plan, even if not employed.

Actuarial Assumption

Factors that actuaries use in estimating the cost of funding a defined benefit pension plan.

Actuarial Cost Methods

Methods used for accounting and tax purposes to allocate the expected cost of a defined benefit pension plan for a group of participants to their years of service. There are several allowable cost methods, and each produces a different flow of contributions. Some produce increasing contributions, others level contributions, and others declining contributions.

Actuarial Equivalent

Benefit having the same present value as the benefit it replaces. Also, the amount of annuity that can be provided at the same present value cost as a specified annuity of a different type or a specified annuity payable from a different age. For example, a lifetime monthly benefit of $67.50 beginning at age 60 (on a given set of actuarial assumptions) may be said to be the actuarial equivalent of $100 per month beginning at age 65.

Actuarial Gain

Where the actual experience under the plan is more favorable than the actuary's estimate.

Actuarial Loss

Where the actual experience under the plan is less favorable than the actuary's estimate.

Actuarially Reduced Annuity

Annuity payable to an employee who retires before normal retirement age in an amount less than would have been payable at normal retirement age. See "Actuarial Equivalent."

Actuarial Valuation

An examination of a pension plan conducted by applying an actuarial cost method to determine whether contributions are being made at a rate sufficient to provide the funds out of which the promised pensions can be paid when due.

Actuary

A person professionally trained in the technical and mathematical aspects of insurance, pensions, and related fields. The actuary estimates how much money must be contributed to a pension fund each year in order to provide the benefits that will become payable in the future.

Amortization

Paying off an interest-bearing liability by gradual reduction through a series of installments, as opposed to paying it off by one lump-sum payment.

Annuity

An arrangement to provide an income for a specified number of years, or for the remaining lifetime of an individual, or the remaining lifetime of more than one individual.

Asset Allocation

The division of the pension assets among various investment media, such as stocks, bonds, and real estate.

Assignment of Benefits

Assigning to an alternate payee the right to receive all or a portion of a benefit payable. Assignment of all or a part of a participant's benefits under a pension plan frequently occurs in divorce or separation settlements.

Backloading

Providing a higher or faster rate of benefit accrual for later years of service in the pension plan than for earlier years.

Basic Benefits

Retirement benefits that are nonforfeitable because the employee has met all the pension plan's requirements. These are insured by the Pension Benefit Guaranty Corporation up to statutorily set limits.

Beneficiary

The person designated to receive benefits under an employee benefit plan in the event of death of the person covered by the plan. (*Author's note: we use this term to include those persons who receive benefits from pension rights earned as employees, including the covered employee.*)

Break in Service

A calendar year, plan year, or other 12-consecutive-month period designated by the plan during which the plan participant does not complete more than 499 hours of service.

Buy-Back Provision

A plan provision affecting terminating employees. If a terminating employee withdraws his or her own contributions when he or she is 50% or less vested, a pension plan that cancels the rest of his or her benefits must allow the employee to buy back the forfeited benefits by repaying the withdrawn amounts plus interest.

Cafeteria Plan

Also called a "flexible benefit plan," this program permits employees to select from employer-provided nontaxable benefits. Nontaxable benefits include pensions, group term life insurance (up to certain amounts), health, disability, prepaid legal, and accident benefits.

Cash or Deferred Profit Sharing Plan

Also known as 401(k) plans. Under plans with cash or deferred arrangements, a participant can elect to receive direct cash payments from his or her employer or can direct such payments to be contributions to a trust. Taxes on the contributions, as well as investment earnings on the contributions, are deferred until the participant receives a distribution.

Cash-Out

A lump sum payment of the employee's nonforfeitable interest prior to retirement.

Class Year Plan

A defined contribution plan in which each year's contributions vest separately.

Cliff Vesting

A vesting schedule under which an employee becomes 100% vested after a specified number of years of service, with no vesting prior to that number of years.

Contributory Plan

A plan to which participants contribute as well as the employer. Under certain contributory plans participants may be required to contribute as a condition of eligibility.

Credited Service

A period of employment that is recognized as service for plan purposes to determine eligibility to receive pension payments and/or to determine the amount of such payments.

Defined Benefit Plan
A pension plan providing a definite benefit formula for calculating benefit amounts, such as a flat amount per year of service or a percentage of salary or a percentage of salary times years of service.

Defined Contribution Plan
A pension plan in which the contributions are made to an individual account for each employee. The retirement benefit depends on the account balance at retirement. The balance depends on amounts contributed, investment experience, and, in the case of profit-sharing plans, amounts that may be allocated to the account due to forfeitures by terminating employees.

Early Retirement Age
An age defined by the terms of a defined benefit pension plan, which is earlier than normal retirement age, and at which a participant may receive an immediate although possibly reduced pension under the plan.

Elapsed-Time Method
Determining credited service of an employee from the date of employment to the date of severance rather than on the basis of hours worked in a 12-month period.

Eligibility Requirements
(1) Conditions that an employee must satisfy to participate in a plan; (2) conditions that an employee must satisfy to obtain a benefit.

Employee Benefit Plan
A plan established to provide welfare and/or retirement benefits to employees, which is maintained by an employer and/or employee organization.

Employee Stock Ownership Plan (ESOP)
A qualified stock bonus, or qualified money purchase pension plan that is designed to invest primarily in employer securities.

Enrolled Actuary

A person authorized by the Joint Board for the Enrollment of Actuaries to prepare actuarial reports required by government agencies.

Equivalencies

Methods for measuring hours of service of an employee that credit employees with 1,000 hours of service when they have worked an equivalent amount of time. An equivalency system may use time periods such as days, weeks, shifts, or payroll periods. See "Elapsed-Time Method."

Fiduciary

(1) Indicates the relationship of trust and confidence where one person (the fiduciary) holds or controls property for the benefit of another person; (2) anyone who exercises power and control, management or disposition with regard to a fund's assets, or who has authority to do so, or who has authority or responsibility in the plan's administration. Under ERISA, fiduciaries must discharge their duties solely in the interest of the participants and their beneficiaries, and are accountable for any actions that may be construed by the courts as breaching that trust.

Flexible Benefit Plan

See "Cafeteria Plan."

Forfeiture

Amounts lost by nonvested participants due to termination of employment. In a defined benefit plan, such amounts reduce future employer contributions. In a profit-sharing plan, such amounts are allocated to the accounts of remaining participants.

Full Vesting

The point in a vesting schedule at which all accrued benefits of a participant become vested benefits.

Funding

A systematic program under which contributions are made to a pension plan in amounts and at times approximately concurrent with the accruing of benefit rights under a retirement system.

Funding Standard Account	An account that every tax-qualified pension plan must maintain to determine whether the plan is meeting the minimum funding standards imposed by the law.
Futures	Contracts that require an investor to deliver or purchase a basket of commodities or securities at an agreed upon price for future delivery. In contrast, an option gives the purchaser the right, but not the obligation, to buy or sell at an agreed-upon price for future delivery. Both options and futures involving market baskets of stocks or fixed-income securities are used as hedging devices by many managers.
Governmental Plan	A plan established or maintained for its employees by the government of the United States, by the government of any state or political subdivision thereof, or by an agency or instrumentality of the foregoing. The term also includes any plan to which the Railroad Retirement Act of 1935 or 1937 applies and that is financed by contributions required under that Act and any plan of an international organization that is exempt from taxation under the provisions of the International Organizations Immunities Act.
Graded Vesting	A vesting schedule under which an employee is partially vested, typically 25%, after a certain number of years of service, with the vesting schedule increasing until full vesting is achieved.
Guaranteed Benefits	Vested accrued pension benefits insured by the Pension Benefit Guaranty Corporation in the event of the termination of a pension plan.
Guaranteed Investment Contracts	Contracts offered by insurance companies that guarantee a rate of return on an investment for a given period and payment of principal and accumulated interest at the

end of that period. These are similar to certificates of deposit offered by banks.

Hedging
Using one kind of security to protect against unfavorable movements in the price of another kind of security. Usually hedging is accomplished by the use of options or futures.

Hour of Service
An hour for which an employee is paid, or entitled to payment, for the performance of duties for the employer. This concept is used to determine employee eligibility for participation, vesting, and benefit accrual under a pension plan.

Index Funds
Stock or bond portfolios structured so that their risk levels and expected returns closely approximate those of stock or bond market indexes.

Individual Account Plan
See "Defined Contribution Plan."

Individual Retirement Account (IRA)
A retirement account to which a worker can make annual tax-deductible contributions for him- or herself up to $2,000 or 100% of compensation, whichever is less, and up to $2,250 for him- or herself and a nonworking spouse. (*Author's note: this has changed somewhat due to 1997 tax legislation.*)

Insured Plan
A plan funded solely by means of level premium contracts with an insurance sponsor.

Integration with Social Security
Defined benefit plans often provide, in order for private pension benefits not to be duplicative with Social Security, that part of the Social Security pension be subtracted from the private annuity. Defined benefit or defined contribution plans can provide that lower pension accruals be applied to employee's earnings below a specified level (generally, this level is the Social Security taxable wage base).

Joint and Survivor Option	A provision that enables a plan participant to take annuity payments with continuing payments of all or part of the benefits after his or her death going to a designated beneficiary. The survivor annuity will automatically be provided to a married participant if he or she does not choose against it. The annual pension benefits of the participant electing to have such a survivor annuity are generally reduced to provide for the survivor.
Keogh Plan	Also known as an H.R. 10 plan, these plans allow a self-employed individual to establish a qualified pension or profit-sharing plan, but with certain restrictions and limitations. The amount a self-employed individual can contribute for his or her own benefits is limited to 15% of earned income, not to exceed $30,000 per year.
Lump-Sum Payment	Payment within one taxable year to the recipient of the entire balance payable to the participant from a trust that forms part of a qualified pension or employee annuity plan.
Money Purchase Plan	A defined contribution pension plan in which the employer's contributions are determined for, and allocated with respect to, each participant, usually as a percentage of compensation.
Multiemployer Plan	A collectively bargained pension plan to which more than one nonrelated employer contributes.
Noncontributory Pension Plan	A plan in which the employer pays the entire cost of the pension.
Normal Costs	Annual cost to a pension plan for the benefits accrued that year by employees.
Normal Retirement Age	The age, as established by a plan, when unreduced benefits can be received. ERISA

defines "normal retirement age" as the earlier of: (1) the time a plan participant attains normal retirement age under the plan or (2) the later of: (a) the time a plan participant attains age 65, or (b) the 10th anniversary of the time a plan participant commenced participation in the plan.

Participant
An employee participating in, receiving benefits from, or eligible to receive benefits from an employee pension plan.

Participation
The term used to describe the status of an employee who is covered by an employee benefit plan after having satisfied any plan age and/or service eligibility requirements.

Party-in-Interest
Under ERISA, generally any individual with an interest in an employee benefit plan, such as an administrator, contributing employer, officer, fiduciary, trustee, custodian, counsel or employee. Also, a person providing services to a plan or an employee organization whose members are covered by the plan.

Past-Service Liability
The liability of a pension plan for the benefits credited for service before the establishment of the plan.

Pension Benefit Guaranty Corporation
The nonprofit independent government employer established to insure defined benefit plan pension benefits in the event of plan terminations (PBGC).

Pension Plan
An employee benefit plan established and maintained by an employer that provides retirement benefits over a period of years by the purchase of insurance or annuity contracts, or the establishment of a trust fund, or a combination of both.

Plan Sponsor
(1) The employer, in the case of a plan established or maintained by a single employer;

(2) the employee organization, in the case of a plan established by an employee organization; (3) the association, committee, joint board of trustees, etc., in the case of a plan established or maintained by two or more employers or jointly by one or more employees and one or more employee organizations.

Plan Termination

Describes the ending of a pension program, when benefit accruals cease.

Plan Termination Insurance

Insurance to protect defined benefit pension plan participants from loss of pension benefits due to failure of employer to fund properly. This insurance is administered by the Pension Benefit Guaranty Corporation (PBGC).

Plan Year

The 12-month period for which the records of the plan are kept.

Portability

The right of an employee at termination of employment to take vested benefits in cash and transfer the funds to an individual retirement account or another pension plan.

Portfolio Insurance

An investment strategy that attempts to guarantee a fund a minimum level of return while allowing the fund to achieve most of any market appreciation.

Preemption

The superseding of state law by provisions of ERISA covering reporting, disclosure, fiduciary responsibility, participation and vesting, funding, and plan termination insurance.

Private Pension Plans

Pension plans established by private (in contrast to governmental) agencies, including commercial, industrial, labor, and service organizations, nonprofit organizations, and nonprofit religious, educational, and charitable institutions.

Profit-Sharing Retirement Plan	A program where the employee's retirement benefit is based on the employer's contributions to a fund and the earnings of the fund. The employer's contributions are made from profits and may be based either on a formula or on a discretionary basis.
Prohibited Group	Shareholders, officers, and highly paid employees, on behalf of whom pension plans seeking tax-favored status must not discriminate.
Prohibited Transaction	Activities in which plan fiduciaries are prohibited by ERISA from engaging, such as the lending, purchasing, or selling of plan securities or other properties without adequate consideration, or the sale or exchange of property between the plan and a party-interest.
Prudent Investor Rule	A requirement imposed by ERISA that plan fiduciaries carry out their duties with the care, skill, prudence and diligence that a prudent investor acting in a like capacity and familiar with such matters would use under the conditions prevailing at the time.
Qualified Plan	A pension, deferred profit sharing, or stock bonus plan that meets the requirements of Section 401(a) of the Internal Revenue Code of 1954 and the applicable regulations. Such IRS approval qualifies the plan for favorable tax treatment.
Reportable Events	Certain events that may indicate possible termination of a pension plan which must be reported by a plan administrator to the Pension Benefit Guaranty Corporation, such as a failure to meet minimum funding standards.
Rollover	See "Tax-Free Rollover."

Savings Plan	A plan requiring the participants as well as the employer to contribute. Employee contributions are generally based on a percentage of compensation, and with the employee usually being able to pick that percentage within a range, with the employer fully or partially matching a portion of each employee's contributions. Savings plans are also known as *thrift plans*.
Service	Employment taken into consideration under a pension plan, including paid leave and periods for which back pay are due.
Simplified Employee Pension (SEP)	A pension plan under which the employer makes contributions to individual retirement accounts for employees in amounts up to a certain maximum amount per year or certain maximum percent of compensation, whichever is less.
Stock Bonus Plan	A defined contribution plan with contributions either fixed or based on profits and with benefits distributable in employer stock that may be shared among employees or their beneficiaries. Such a plan is subject to the same requirements as a profit-sharing plan.
Stock Purchase Plan	A deferred profit-sharing plan that provides that an employee's share of the fund may be invested at his or her option in the employer's securities, insurance contracts, or governmental obligations.
Summary Plan Description	A description of the major features of an employee benefit plan written primarily for the employees covered by the plan.
Survivor Annuity	See "Joint and Survivor Option."
Target Benefit Plan	A defined contribution plan for which contributions are based upon an actuarial valu-

ation designed to provide a "target" benefit to each participant upon retirement.

Tax-Free Rollover A provision under ERISA permitting employees to safeguard distributions to and from qualified plans and IRAs from taxation at present. Rollovers can occur from: (1) a qualified plan to an IRA; (2) an IRA to a qualified plan; or (3) an IRA to an IRA.

Tax-Qualified Plan See "Qualified Plan."

Termination See "Plan Termination."

Thrift Plan See "Savings Plan."

Top-Heavy Plan A pension plan under which the value of benefits for key employees (officers and owners) exceeds 60% of the value of benefits for ordinary employees.

Unfunded Liabilities Liabilities of the pension fund for which there are not sufficient assets to pay.

Vesting The right of an employee to the benefits he or she has accrued, or to some portion of them, even if employment under the plan terminates. An employee who has met the vesting requirements of a pension plan is said to have a *vested right*. Voluntary and mandatory employee contributions are always fully vested.

Welfare Plan A plan which provides medical, surgical, or hospital care or benefits in the case of sickness, accident, disability, death or unemployment; it may also include other benefits such as vacation or scholarship plans.

Withdrawal Liability The responsibility of an employer leaving a multiemployer pension plan for its share of the plan's unfunded vested liabilities.

Year of Service A 12-month period during which the employee works at a specified number of hours or equivalent designated by the plan. Used to determine eligibility for participation in a pension plan and the satisfaction of requirements for vesting as well as the determination of accrued benefits.

Yield

The income stream of an investment divided by the price of the security (i.e., the yield of a common stock is the annualized dividend payment divided by the current price of the stock).

Yield to Maturity

The rate of return yielded by a bond held to maturity when both interest payments and the investor's capital gain or loss on the security are taken into account.

References

Admati, Anat R., and Stephen A. Ross. "Measuring Investment Performance in a Rational Expectations Equilibrium Model." *Journal of Business* 58, no. 1 (1985):1–26.

Admati, Anat R., Paul Pfleiderer, and Josef Zechner. "Large Shareholder Activism, Risk Sharing and Financial Market Equilibrium." *Journal of Political Economy* 102, no. 6 (1994):1097–1130.

Albert, Rory Judd, and Neal Schelberg. "Debate on ETI's Continues; Exemption for InHams." *Pension Management* 31, no. 9 (1995):44–45.

Allen, Everett T. Jr., Joseph J. Melone, Jerry S. Rosenbloom, and Jack L. Van Derhei. *Pension Planning.* 6th ed. Burr Ridge, IL: Irwin Professional Publishers, 1988.

Altman, Edward. *Corporate Financial Distress.* New York: Wiley, 1983.

Ambachtscheer, Keith P. "Total Quality Management." *Investment Policy, Seminar Proceedings.* Charlottesville, VA: AIMR (1995):41–53.

Ambachtsheer, Keith P. "Employee Benefits as Corporate Debt: What Investment Professionals Should Know." *Financial Analysts Journal* 45, no. 2 (1989):5–6.

Ambachtsteer, Keith P. *Telling the Prospective Returns' Story. The Ambachtsteer Letter.* Toronto: Keith P. Ambachtsteer and Associates, 1988.

American Association of Individual Investors. *Mutual Funds Seminar Workbook.* Chicago: American Association of Individual Investors, 1996.

Arditti, Fred D. *Derivatives*. Boston: Harvard Business School Press, 1996.

Arnott, Robert D. "Managing the Asset Mix: Decisions and Consequences." Paper presented at the Fourth Annual Allocation Congress, Boca Raton, FL, February 1990.

Arnott, Robert D., and Peter L. Bernstein. "The Right Way to Manage Your Pension Fund." *Harvard Business Review* 67, no. 1 (1988):95–102.

Arnott, Robert D., and Robert M. Lovell, Jr. "Monitoring and Rebalancing the Portfolio." In *Managing Investment Portfolios*, edited by John L. Maginn and Donald L. Tuttle, 13-1–13-41. Charlottesville, VA: AIMR, 1990.

Arnott, Robert D., and David L. Rice. "Asset Allocation Risks, Rumors, Responses." *Investment Management Review* 3, no. 2 (1989):7–15.

Bank Administration Institute. *Measuring the Investment Performance of Pension Funds*. Park Ridge, IL: Bank Administration Institute, 1968.

Baliga, Wayne. "States Enact Prudent Investor Regulations." *Journal of Accountancy* 179, no. 1 (1995):11–12.

Bagehot, Walter. "Risk and Reward in Corporate Pension Funds." *Financial Analysts Journal* 28, no. 1 (1972):80–84.

Bailey, Jeffrey V. "Are Managers Universes Acceptable Performance Benchmarks?" *Journal of Portfolio Management* 18, no. 3 (1992):9–13.

Bailey, Jeffrey V., Thomas M. Richards, and David E. Tierney. "Benchmark Portfolios and the Manager/Plan Sponsor Relationship." In *Current Topics in Investment Management*, edited by Frank J. Fabozzi and T. Dessa Fabozzi. New York: HarperCollins, 1990.

Bajtelsmit, Vickie L., and Elaine M. Worzala. "Real Estate Allocation in Pension Fund Portfolios." *Journal of Real Estate Portfolio Management* 1, no. 1 (1995):25–38.

Barrett, W. Brian. "Term Structure Modeling for Pension Liability Discounting." *Financial Analysts Journal* 44, no. 6 (1988):63–67.

Beck, Barbara. "The Luxury of Longer Life: The World is Growing Older." *The Economist* 338, no. 7950 (1996):S3–S5.

Beder, Tanya Styblo. "VAR: Seductive but Dangerous." *Financial Analysts Journal* 51, no. 5 (1995):12–24.

Benos, Alexandros, and Michel Crouhy. "Changes in the Structure and Dynamics of European Securities Markets." *Financial Analysts Journal* 52, no. 3 (1996):37–50.

Bensman, Miriam. "Doing Without Style." *Institutional Investor* 30, no. 2 (1996);79–85.

Bensman, Miriam. "Far From Home." *Institutional Investor* 30, no. 4 (1996):77–82.

Bensman, Miriam. "Hedging on Hedges." *Institutional Investor* 30, no. 6 (1996):73–79.

Bergsman, Steve. "Soft Dollars: Where Do We Go From Here?" *Pension Management* 32, no. 5 (May 1996):24–26, 53.

Berkowitz, Stephen A. and Douglas L. Rowe. "Pension Plans." In *Handbook of Modern Finance* 2d ed., edited by Dennis E. Logue, 33-1–33-27. New York: Warren, Gorham and Lamont, 1990.

Berkowitz, Stephen A., Louis D. Finney, and Dennis E. Logue. *The Investment Performance of Corporate Pension Plans.* Westport, CT: Greenwood Press, 1988.

Berkowitz, Stephen A., Louis D. Finney, and Dennis E. Logue. "Pension Plans vs. Mutual Funds: Is the Client Victim or Culprit?" *California Management Review* 30, no. 3 (1988):74–91.

Berkowitz, Stephen A., Dennis E. Logue, and Eugene A. Noser. "The Total Cost of Transactions on the NYSE." *Journal of Finance* 43, no. 1 (1988):97–112.

Bhagat, Sanjai, and Bernard Black. "Do Independent Directors Matter?" Paper presented at The Power and Influence of Pension and Mutual Funds Conference, New York University, Stern School of Business, New York, NY, February 1997.

Black, Bernard S. "Institutional Investors and Corporate Governance: The Case for Institutional Voice." *Journal of Applied Corporate Finance* 5, no. 3 (1992):19–32.

Black, Fischer, and Moray P. Dewhurst. "A New Investment Strategy for Pension Funds." *Journal of Portfolio Management* 7, no. 4 (1981):26–34.

Blasi, J.R. *Employee Ownership: Revolution or Ripoff?* New York: Harper & Row, 1988.

Blume, Marshall E., and Jeremy J. Siegel. "The Theory of Security Pricing and Market Structure." *Financial Markets, Institutions and Instruments* 1, no. 3 (1992).

Bodie, Zvi, Alan J. Marcus, and Robert C. Merton. "Defined Benefit Versus Defined Contribution Benefit Plans: What Are the Real Trade Offs?" *Pensions in U.S. Economy*, edited by Zvi Bodie, John B. Shoven, and David A. Wise, 139–160. Chicago: University of Chicago Press, 1988.

Bodie, Zvi, Alex Kane, and Alan J. Marcus. *Essentials of Investments.* 2d ed. Burr Ridge, IL: Irwin Professional Publishing, 1995.

Bodie, Zvi, Jay O. Light, Randall Morck, and Robert A. Taggart, Jr. "Funding and Capital Allocation in Corporate Pension Plans: An Empirical Investigation." *Issues of Pension Economics*, edited by Zvi Bodie, John B. Shoven, and David A. Wise, 15–44. Chicago: University of Chicago Press, 1987.

Bodie, Zvi. "Managing Pension and Retirement Assets: An International Perspective." *Journal of Financial Services Research* 4, no. 4 (1990):419–460.

Bodie, Zvi. "On the Risk of Stock in the Long Run." *Financial Analysts Journal* 51, no. 3 (1995):18–22.

Brenner, Lynn. "Have Pension Will Travel." *CFO* 11, no. 9 (1995):85–87.

Brenner, Lynn. "Facing Up to Total Plan Costs." *CFO* 12, no. 4 (1996):51–56.

Brinson, Gary P., CFA, L. Randolph Hood, CFA, and Gilbert L. Beebower. "Determinants of Portfolio Performance." *Financial Analysts Journal* 45, no. 2 (1986):39–44.

Brown, Keith C., W.V. Harlow, and Laura T. Starks. "Of Tournaments and Temptations: An Analysis of Managerial Incentives in the Mutual Fund Industry." *Journal of Finance* 51, no. 1 (1996):85–110.

Brown, Stephen J., and William Goetzmann. "Performance Persistence." *Journal of Finance* 50, no. 2 (1995):679–698.

Bulow, Jeremy I. "What are Corporate Pension Liabilities?" *Quarterly Journal of Economics* 97, no. 3 (1982):435–452.

Bulow, Jeremy L., and Myron Scholes. "Who Owns the Assets in a Defined Benefit Pension Plan?" *Financial Aspects of the United States Pension System*, edited by Zvi Bodie and John B. Shoven, 17–32. Chicago: University of Chicago Press, 1983.

Bulow, Jeremy L., Randall Morck, and Laurence Summers. "How Does the Market Value Unfunded Pension Liabilities?" *Issues in Pension Economics*, edited by Zvi Bodie, John B. Shoven, and David A. Wise, 81–103. Chicago: University of Chicago Press, 1987.

Burchill, Andrew. "The Virtual Reality Global Pension Fund." *Institutional Investor* 29, no. 12 (December 1995):205.

Byrne, Harlan S. "Mad as Hell: Institutional Investors Turn Activist." *Barron's* 70, no. 7 (1990):28.

Capaul, Carlo, Ian Rowley, and William F. Sharpe. "International Value and Growth Stock Returns." *Financial Analysts Journal* 49, no. 1 (1993):27–36.

Chang, Eric C., and Wilbur G. Lewellyn. "Market Timing and Mutual Fund Investment Performance." *Journal of Business* 57, no. 1 (1984):57–72.

Chang, Saeyoung. "Employee Stock Ownership Plans and Shareholder Wealth: An Empirical Investigation." *Financial Management* 19, no. 1 (1990):48–58.

Chen, Nai-Fu, Richard Roll, and Stephen A. Ross. "Economic Forces and the Stock Market." *Journal of Business* 59, no. 3 (1986):383–404.

Christopherson, Jon A., Wayne E. Ferson, and Debra A. Glassman. "Conditioning Manager Alphas on Economic Information: Another Look at the Persistence of Performance." Working paper 5830, National Bureau of Economic Research, Inc., 1996.

Copeland, Thomas E. "An Economic Approach to Pension Fund Management." In *The Revolution in Corporate Finance.* 2d ed., edited by J. Stern and Don Chew, 411–426. Cambridge, MA: Blackwell, 1992.

Copeland, Thomas E., and J. Fred Weston. *Financial Theory and Corporate Policy.* Reading, MA: Addison-Wesley, 1988.

Crawford, George. "Case Study: A Fiduciary Duty to Use Derivatives?" *Stanford Journal of Law, Business and Finance* 1, no. 1 (Spring 1995):332.

DeAngelo, Harry, Linda DeAngelo, and Stuart G. Gelson. "The Collapse of First Executive Corporation, Junk Bonds, Adverse Publicity, and the 'Run on the Bank' Phenomenon." *Journal of Financial Economics* 36, no. 3 (1994):287–336.

Del Guercio, Diane. "The Distorting Effects of the Prudent-Man Laws on Institutional Equity Investments." *Journal of Financial Economics* 40, no. 1 (1996):31–62.

Divecha, Arjun, and Richard C. Grinold. "Normal Portfolios: Issues for Sponsors, Managers and Consultants." *Financial Analysts Journal* 45, no. 2 (1989):7–13.

Downs, David H., and David J. Hartzell. "Real Estate Investment Trusts." In *The Handbook of Real Estate Portfolio Management*, 801–826. Burr Ridge, IL: Irwin Professional Publishing, 1995.

Droms, William G. "Fiduciary Responsibilities of Investment Managers and Trustees." *Financial Analysts Journal* 48, no. 4 (1992):58–64.

Dunn, Patricia C., and Rolf D. Theisen. "How Consistently Do Active Managers Win?" *Journal of Portfolio Management* 9, no. 4 (1983):47–50.

Dyer, Jack. "Fiduciaries Less Rigorous with 401(k) Plans." *Pensions and Investments* 23, no. 11 (1995):10.

"The Economics of Aging." *The Economist* 378, no. 7950 (1996):S5–S16.

Ellis, Charles D. *Investment Policy: How to Win the Loser's Game.* 2d ed. Burr Ridge, IL: Irwin Professional Publishing, 1993.

Elson, Charles M. "Director Compensation and the Management-Captured Board—The History of a Symptom and a Cure." *Southern Methodist University Law Review* 50, no. 1 (1996):127–174.

Elton, Edwin J., and Martin J. Gruber. "Optimal Investment Strategies with Investor Liabilities." *Journal of Banking and Finance* 16, no. 5 (1992):869–890.

Elton, Edwin J., and Martin J. Gruber. "Evaluation of Portfolio Performance." In *Modern Portfolio Theory and Investment Analysis*, 630–671. New York: Wiley, 1995.

Elton, Edwin J., Martin J. Gruber, Sanjiv Das, and Matthew Hlavka. "Efficiency with Costly Information: A Reinterpretation of the Evidence from Manager Portfolios." *Review of Financial Studies* 6, no. 1 (1993):1–23.

Employee Benefits Research Institute. *Pension Funding & Taxation: Implications for Tomorrow*, edited by Dallas L. Salisbury and Nora Super Jones. Washington, D.C: Employee Benefits Research Institute, 1994.

Employee Benefits Research Institute. *EBRI Databook on Employee Benefits*. 3d ed. Washington, D.C: Employee Benefits Research Institute, 1995.

Employee Benefits Research Institute. *EBRI Databook on Employer Benefits*. 4th ed. Washington, D.C.: Employee Benefits Research Institute, 1997.

Ezra, D. Don. "How Actuaries Determine the Unfunded Pension Liability." *Financial Analysts Journal* 36, no. 4 (1980):43–50.

Ezra, D. Don. "Economic Values: A Pension Pentateuch." *Financial Analysts Journal*, 44, no. 2 (1988):58–67.

"Fair Trading." *Institutional Investor* 30, no. 3 (1996):177.

Fama, Eugene F. "Components of Investment Performance." *Journal of Finance*. 27, no. 3 (1972):551–567.

Fama, Eugene F., and Kenneth R. French. "The Cross-Section of Expected Stock Returns." *Journal of Finance* 47, no. 2 (1992):427–466.

Fama, Eugene F., and Kenneth R. French. "Multifactor Explanations of Asset Pricing Anomalies." *Journal of Finance* 51, no. 1 (1996):55–84.

Fama, Eugene F., and Kenneth R. French. "Value versus Growth: The International Evidence." Working paper no. 449, University of Chicago Graduate School of Business.

Feldstein, Martin, and Randall Morck. "Pension Funds and the Value of Equities." *Financial Analysts Journal* 39, no. 5 (1983):29–39.

Fischel, Daniel, and John H. Langbein. "ERISA's Fundamental Contradiction: The Exclusive Benefit Rule." *University of Chicago Law Review* 55, no. 4 (1988):1105–1160.

Friedman, Benjamin M. "Pension Funding, Pension Asset Allocation and Corporate Finance: Evidence from Individual Company Data." In *Financial Aspects of the United States Pension System*, edited by Zvi Bodie and John B. Shoven, 107–152. Chicago: University of Chicago Press, 1983.

Fritz, M. Dale. "Developing Asset Allocation Strategies." In *Global Portfolio Management: Seminar Proceedings*, edited by Jan R. Squires, 26–33. Charlottesville, VA: AIMR, 1996.

Froot, K.A. "Currency Hedging Over Long Horizons." Working Paper 4355, National Bureau of Economic Research, Cambridge, MA, 1993.

Fuller, Russell J., and G. Wenchi Wong. "Traditional Versus Theoretical Risk Measures." *Financial Analysts Journal* 44, no. 2 (1988):52–57.

Gastineau, Gary L., and Sanjiv Bhatia. "Risk Management: An Overview." In *Risk Management Proceedings*, 1–4. Charlottesville, VA: AIMR, 1996.

Gertner, Marc. "DOL Enhances Enforcement of Pension Investments." *Pension World* 26, no. 12 (1990):18–20.

Ghilarducci, Teresa, Garth Mangum, Jeffrey S. Petersen, and Peter Philips. *Portable Pension Plans For Casual Labor Markets: Lessons from the Operating Engineers Central Pension Fund*. Westport, CT: Quorum Books, 1995.

Gillan, Stuart L., and Laura T. Starks. "Shareholder Activism and Institutional Investors: The Effects of Corporate-Governance Related Proposals." Working paper, University of Texas, 1996.

Goetzmann, William N., and Roger Ibbotson. "Do Winners Repeat? Patterns in Mutual Fund Behavior." *Journal of Portfolio Management* 20, no. 2 (1994):9–18.

Good, Walter R. "Measuring Performance." *Financial Analysts Journal* 39, no. 3 (1983):19–23.

Gould, Floyd J. "Efficient Markets, Investment Management Selection and the Loser's Game." In *Current Topics in Investment Management*, edited by Frank J. Fabozzi and T. Dessa. New York: HarperCollins, 1990.

Greenwich Associates. *Institutional Investment Management: Grace Under Pressure*. Greenwich, CT: Greenwich Reports, 1989

Grinblatt, Mark, and Sheridan Titman. "Mutual Fund Performance: An Analysis of Quarterly Holdings." *Journal of Business* 62, no. 3 (1989):393–416.

Grinblatt, Mark, and Sheridan Titman. "Portfolio Performance Evaluation: Old Issues and New Insights." *Review of Financial Studies* 2, no. 3 (1989):393–421.

Gustman, Alan L., and Thomas L. Steinmeier. "Pensions, Efficiency Wages and Job Mobility." Working paper 2426, National Bureau of Economic Research, 1987.

Halpern, Paul, and Josef Lakonishok. "Why the Difference in Performance Measurement?" *Investing* 4, no. 1 (1990):36–43.

Hamilton, Sally, Hoje Ho, and Meir Statman. "Doing Well While Doing Good? The Investment Performance of Socially Responsible Mutual Funds." *Financial Analysts Journal* 49, no. 6 (1993):62–66.

Harrison, Debbie. *Pension Fund Investment in Europe*. London: FT Financial Publishing, 1995.

Harrison, J. Michael, and William F. Sharpe. "Optimal Funding and Asset Allocation Risks for Defined Benefit Pension Plans." In *Financial Aspects of the United States Pension System*, edited by Zvi Bodie and John B. Shoven, 91–103. Chicago: University of Chicago Press, 1983.

Hartzel, Jerry. "ESOP Investments, Fiduciary Conflicts of Interest, and ERISA Liability." *Journal of Employee Ownership Law and Finance* (Summer 1996):125–146.

Haugen, Robert. "Pension Investing and Corporate Risk Management." In *Managing Institutional Assets*, edited by Frank J. Fabozzi. New York: Harper & Row, 1990.

Haugen, Robert. *The New Finance: The Case Against Efficient Markets*. Englewood Cliffs, NJ: Prentice-Hall, 1995.

Hawthorne, Fran. "Getting a Grip on Foreign Pension Plans." *Institutional Investor* 29, no. 12 (1995):211–213.

Hay/Huggins Company, Inc. "Pension Plan Expense Study for the Pension Benefit Guaranty Corporation." September 1990.

"Heavily Discounted Rates." *Institutional Investor* 30, no. 7 (1996):149.

Henricksson, Roy D. "Market Timing and Mutual Fund Performance: An Empirical Investigation." *Journal of Business* 57, no. 1 (1984):73–96.

Hewitt Associates. "Employee Retirement Systems: How It All Began." *Pension World* July 1976:6–11.

Hill, Joanne M. "Adding Value with Equity Derivatives: Part II." In *Derivative Strategies for Managing Portfolio Risk*, 62–73. Charlottesville, VA: AIMR, 1993.

Hirschman, Albert. *Exit, Voice and Loyalty*. Cambridge, MA: Harvard University Press, 1970

Hull, John C. *Options, Futures and Other Derivatives*. 3d ed. Englewood Cliffs, N.J.: Prentice-Hall, 1997.

Ibbotson Associates. *Stocks, Bonds, Bills, and Inflation: 1996 Yearbook*. Chicago: Ibbotson Associates, 1996.

Ippolito, Richard A. "The Economic Function of Underfunded Pension Plans." *Journal of Law and Economics* 28, no. 3 (1985):611–651.

Ippolito, Richard A. "The Labor Contract and True Economic Pension Liabilities." *American Economic Review* 75, no. 6 (1985):1031–1043.

Ippolito, Richard A. *Pension, Economics and Public Policy*. Homewood, IL: Dow Jones/Irwin, 1986.

Ippolito, Richard A. "The Role of Risk in a Tax Arbitrage Pension Portfolio." Working paper, Pension Benefit Guaranty Corporation, 1988.

Ippolito, Richard A. "Efficiency with Costly Information: A Study of Mutual Fund Performance." *Quarterly Journal of Economics* 104, no. 1 (1989):4–23.

Ippolito, Richard A. *The Economics of Pension Insurance*. Homewood, IL: Irwin, 1989.

Ippolito, Richard A. "Toward Explaining the Growth of Defined Contribution Plans." *Industrial Relations* 34, no. 1 (1995):1–20.

Ippolito, Richard A. "Low Discounters as Higher Quality Workers: A Sorting Theory of Pensions." Working paper, Pension Benefit Guaranty Corporation, 1996.

Ippolito, Richard A., and John Turner. "Turnover Fees and Pension Plan Performance." *Financial Analysts Journal* 43, no. 6 (1987):16–26.

Jensen, Michael C. "Risk, the Pricing of Capital Assets, and the Evaluation of Investment Portfolios." *Journal of Business* 42, no. 2 (1969):167–247.

Jobson, J.D., and Bob M. Korkie. "Performance Hypothesis Testing with the Sharpe and Treynor Measures." *Journal of Finance* 36, no. 4 (1981):889–907.

Jobson, J.D., and Robert M. Korkie. "The Trouble with Performance Measurement." *Journal of Portfolio Management* 14, no. 2 (1988):74–76.

Jorion, Phillippe. "Mean/Variance Analysis of Currency Overlays." *Financial Analysts Journal* 50, no. 3 (1994):48–56.

Kahn, Ronald N., and Andrew Rudd. "Does Historical Performance Predict Future Performance?" *Financial Analysts Journal* 51, no. 6 (1995):43–52.

Kaiser, Ronald W. "Individual Investor." In *Managing Investment Portfolios: A Dynamic Process.* 2d ed., edited by John L. Magin and Donald L. Tuttle, 3-1-45. New York: Warren, Gorham and Lamont, 1990.

Karpoff, Jonathan M., Paul H. Malatesta, and Ralph A. Walkling. "Corporate Governance and Shareholder Initiatives: Empirical Evidence." *Journal of Financial Economics* 42, no. 3 (1996):365–395.

Koppes, Richard H., and Maureen L. Reilly. "An Ounce of Prevention: Meeting Fiduciary to Monitor an Index Fund Through Relationship Investing." *Journal of Corporation Law* 20, Spring (1995):413–449.

Kotlikoff, Lawrence J., and David A. Wise. "Labor Compensation and the Structure of Private Pension Plans: Evidence for Contractual Versus Spot Labor Market." In *Pensions, Labor, and Individual Choice*, edited by Zvi Bodie, John B. Shoven and David A. Wise, 57–85. Chicago: University of Chicago Press, 1987.

Kujaca, James A. *The Trillion Dollar Promise.* Burr Ridge, IL: Irwin Professional Publishing, 1996.

Lakonishok, Joseph, Andrei Schleifer, and Robert W. Vishny. "The Structure and Performance of the Money Management Industry." In *Brookings Papers on Economic Activity: Macroeconomics*, 339–391. Washington, D.C.: Brookings Institution, 1992.

Lazear, Edward P. "Pensions as Severance Pay." In *Financial Aspects of the United States Pension System*, edited by Zvi Bodie, John B. Shoven, and David A. Wise, 283–336. Chicago: University of Chicago Press, 1983.

Lehmann, Bruce, and David M. Modest. "Mutual Fund Performance Evaluation: A Comparison of Benchmarks and Benchmark Comparisons." *Journal of Finance* 42, no. 2 (1987):223–265.

Leibowitz, Martin L., Stanley Kogelman, Lawrence N. Bader. "Funding Ratio Return." *Journal of Portfolio Management* 21, no. 1 (1994):39–47.

Leinweber, David J. "Using Information from Trading in Trading and Portfolio Management." In *Execution Techniques, True Trading Costs and the Microstructure of Markets*, 24–34. Charlottesville, VA: AIMR, 1993.

Light, Larry. "The Power of the Pension Funds: The Top 200; Who's Who Among Corporate Pension Plans." *Business Week* (6 November 1989):154–158, 173–174.

Logue, Dennis E. *Legislative Influences on Corporate Pension Plans*. Washington, D.C.: American Enterprise Institute, 1979.

Longstreth, Bevis. *Modern Investment Management and the Prudent Man Rule*. New York: Oxford University Press, 1987.

Longstreth, Bevis. "Takeovers, Corporate Governance and Stock Ownership: Some Disquieting Trends." *Journal of Portfolio Management* 16, no. 3 (1990):54–59.

Longstreth, Bevis. "Corporate Governance: There's Danger in New Orthodoxies." *Journal of Portfolio Management* 21, no. 3 (1995):47–52.

Lowenstein, Roger. "How Pension Funds Lost in the Market Boom." *Wall Street Journal* 1 February 1996, C1.

MacBeth, James D., and David C. Emanuel. "Tactical Asset Allocation: Pros and Cons." *Financial Analysts Journal* 49, no. 6 (1993.):30–43.

Malkiel, Burton G. "Returns from Investing in Equity Mutual Funds: 1971–1991." *Journal of Finance* 50, no. 2 (1995):549–572.

Marr, M. Wayne, John R. Nofsinger, and John L. Trimble. "Economically Targeted Investments." *Financial Analysts Journal* 50, no. 2 (1994):7–8.

Marr, M. Wayne, John R. Nofsinger, and John L. Trimble. "Economically Targeted Investments: A New Threat to Private Pension Plans." *Journal of Applied Corporate Finance* 6, no. 2 (1993):91–95.

Matthews, Gregory E. "The Cinderella of Qualified Plans—Target Benefits." *Trust & Estates* 129, no. 11 (1990):23–30.

McCarthy, David D., and John A. Turner. "Pension Rates of Return in Large and Small Plans." In *Trends in Pensions*, edited by John A. Turner and Daniel J. Beller, 235–285. Washington, D.C.: U.S. Government Printing Office, 1989.

McMillan, Henry M. "Asset/Liability Management: Implications for Derivative Strategies." In *Derivative Strategies for Managing Portfolio Risk*, 35–44. Charlottesville, VA: AIMR, 1993.

Merton, Robert C. "On Market Timing and Investment Performance: An Equilibrium Theory of Value for Market Forecasts." *Journal of Business* 54, no. 3 (1981):363–406.

Miller, Jeffrey. "DOL Clarifies 'Advice' vs. 'Education.'" *Pension Management* 32, no. 2 (1996):26–28.

Millstein, Ira M. "Distinguishing 'Ownership' and 'Control' in the 1990s." Paper presented at Institutional Shareholder Services Conference, 1994.

Monks, Robert A.G., and Nell Minow. *Corporate Governance.* Cambridge, MA: Basil Blackwell, 1995.

Moore, Cassandra Chrones. "Whose Pension Is It Anyway? Economically Targeted Investments and the Pension Funds." *Policy Analysis* no. 236. Washington, D.C.: Cato Institute, 1995.

Myers, Randy. "Pension Bonds?" *Institutional Investor* 28, no. 8 (August 1994):73–74.

Nam, Joong-soo, and Ben Branch. "Tactical Asset Allocation: Can It Work?" *Journal of Financial Research* 17, no. 4 (1994):465–479.

Nederlof, Maarten. "Risk Management Programs." In *Risk Management Proceedings*, 15–23. Charlottesville, VA: AIMR, 1996.

New York Stock Exchange. *1995 New York Stock Exchange Fact Book.* New York: New York Stock Exchange, 1996.

"Not Awakening the Dead." *The Economist* 340, no. 7978 (August 1996):47.

Ochs, Joyce. "Staying Out of Trouble." *Pension Management* 31, no. 9 (September 1995):16–19.

Odier, Patrick, and Bruno Solnik. "Lessons for International Asset Allocation." *Financial Analysts Journal* 49, no. 2 (1993):63–77.

Opler, Tim C., and Jonathan Sokobin. "Does Coordinated Institutional Activism Work? An Analysis of the Activities of the Council of Institutional Investors." Working paper,. Columbus, OH: Charles A. Dice Center for Research in Financial Economics, Ohio State University, 1995.

Park, Sangsoo, and Moon H. Song. "Employee Stock Ownership Plans, Firm Performance and Monitoring by Outside Blockholders." *Financial Management* 24, no. 4 (1995):52–65.

Patterson, D. Jeanne. *The Use of Public Employee Retirement System Resources for Economic Development in the Great Lakes States.* Bloomington, IN: Indiana University Institute for Development Strategies, 1992.

Peltz, Michael. "Not-For-Profit Derivatives." *Institutional Investor* 28, no. 8 (1990):35–39.

Perlman, Lawrence. "A Perspective on Shareholder Activism." *Journal of Applied Corporate Finance* 6, no. 2 (1993):35–38.

Perold, Andre F. "The Implementation Shortfall: Paper versus Reality. *Journal of Portfolio Management* 14, no. 3 (1988):4–9.

Petersen, Mitchell A. "Cash Flow Variability and Firm's Pension Choice: A Role for Operating Leverage." *Journal of Financial Economics* 36, no. 3 (1994):361–383.

Petersen, Mitchell A. "Allocating Assets and Discounting Cash Flows: Pension Plan Finance." *Pensions, Savings and Capital Markets*, edited by P.A. Fernandez et al., 1–26. Washington, D.C.: U.S. Department of Labor, 1996.

Phillips, Don, and Joan Lee. "Differentiating Tactical Asset Allocation from Market Timing." *Financial Analysts Journal* 45, no. 2 (1989):14–16.

Polsky, Lisa K. "Integrating Risk Management and Strategy." In *Risk Management: Seminar Proceedings*, 8–14. Charlottesville, VA: AIMR, 1996.

Poterba, James, and Lawrence Summers. "Mean Reversion in Stock Prices: Evidence and Implications." *Journal of Financial Economics* 22, no. 1 (1988):27–59.

Pound, John. "Raiders, Targets and Politics: The History and Future of American Corporate Control." *Journal of Applied Corporate Finance* 5, no. 3 (1992):6–18.

Ramirez, Carlos D. "Did J.P. Morgan's Men Add Liquidity? Corporate Investment, Cash Flow and Financial Structure at the Turn of the Century." *Journal of Finance* 50, no. 2 (1995):661–678.

Rappaport, Anna. "A Fresh Look at Defined Benefit Pensions: A Consultant's Perspective." Working paper 95-2, Pension Research Council, 1995.

Reichenstein, William. "Why the Corporate Pension Fund is not Just Another SBU." *Journal of Applied Corporate Finance* 6, no. 4 (1994):103–108.

Rehfeld, Barry. "Not Just Covering Their Assets." *Institutional Investor* 30, no. 7 (1996):51–54.

Revsine, Laurence. "Understanding Financial Accounting Standard 87." *Financial Analysts Journal* 45, no. 1 (1989):61–68.

Roe, Mark J. "The Modern Corporation and Private Pensions: Strong Managers, Weak Owners." *Journal of Applied Corporate Finance* 8, no. 2 (1995):111–119.

Rohrer, Julie. "Cash and Carry." *Institutional Investor* 29, no. 4 (1995):139–140.

Rohrer, Julie. "Rediscovering Defined Benefit Plans." *Institutional Investor* 30, no. 6 (June 1996):51–59.

Roll, Richard, and Stephen A. Ross. "On the Cross-Sectional Relation Between Expected Returns and Betas." *Journal of Finance* 49, no. 1 (1994):101–122.

Romano, Roberta. "The Politics of Public Pension Funds." *The Public Interest* no. 119 (Spring 1995):42–53.

Rosen, Corey. "The Record of Employee Ownership." *Financial Management* 19, no. 1 (1990):39–48.

Rosenberg, Barr, Kenneth Reid, and Ronald Lanstein. "Persuasive Evidence of Market Inefficiency." *Journal of Portfolio Management* 11:3 (1985):9–16.

Rosenberg, Michael R. "International Fixed Income Investing: Theory and Practice." *The Handbook of Fixed Income Securities.* 4th ed., edited by Frank J. Fabozzi and T. Dessa Fabozzi, 1045–1076. Burr Ridge, IL: Irwin, 1995.

Rowland, Mary. "Lower Education." *Institutional Investor* 30, no. 4 (1996):139.

Russell, Bruce. "Dealing with the Pesky Currency Problem." In Paper Presented at the Market Makers Seminar, Institute for Fiduciary Education, Carmel, CA, June 1996.

Sametz, Arnold W. "An Expanded Role for Private Pensions in U.S. Corporate Governance." *Journal of Applied Corporate Finance* 8, no. 2 (1995):97–110.

Samuelson, Paul A. "Asset Allocation Can Be Dangerous to Your Wealth." *Journal of Portfolio Management* 16, no. 3 (1990):5–8.

Sanes, Steven P., and Mark A. Zurack. "Pension Plans, Portfolio Insurance and FASB Statement No. 87: 'An Old Risk in a New Light.'" *Financial Analysts Journal* 43, no. 1 (1987):10–13.

Schanes, Steve. "Ratios Improve Benefits." *Pension Management* 32, no. 1 (January 1996):5–7.

Scholes, Myron S. "Commentary: Managing Pension and Retirement Assets: An International Perspective," *Journal of Financial Services Research* 4, no. 4 (1990):465–470.

Scholes, Myron S., and Mark A. Wolfson. "Employee Ownership Plans and Corporate Restructuring: Myths and Realities." *Financial Management* 19, no. 1 (1990):12–28.

Schultz, Ellen E. "Workers Put Too Much in Their Employee's Stock." *Wall Street Journal*, Sept. 13, 1996, New York.

Sharpe, William F. "Mutual Fund Performance." *Journal of Business* 39, no. 1 (1966):119–138.

Sharpe, William F. "Corporate Pension Funding Policy." *Journal of Financial Economics* 4, no. 2 (1976):183–193.

Sharpe, William F. "Integrated Asset Allocation." *Financial Analysts Journal* 43, no. 5 (1987):25–32.

Sharpe, William F. "The Sharpe Ratio." *Journal of Portfolio Management* 20, no. 1 (1994):49–58.

Sharpe, William F. "Asset Allocation." In *Managing Investment Portfolios: A Dynamic Process.* 2d ed., edited by John L. Magin and Donald L. Tuttle, 7-1–7-70. New York: Warren, Gorham and Lamont, 1990.

Sharpe, William F. "Asset Allocation: Management Style and Performance Measurement." *Journal of Portfolio Management* 18, no. 2 (1992):7–19.

Sharpe, William F., and Andre F. Perold. "Dynamic Strategies for Asset Allocation." *Financial Analysts Journal* 44, no. 1 (1988):16–27.

Siegel, Jeremy J. *Stocks for the Long Run.* Burr Ridge, IL: Irwin Professional Publishing, 1994.

Sinquefield, Rex A. "Where Are the Gains From International Diversification." *Financial Analysts Journal* 52, no. 1 (1996):8–14.

Skowranski, Walter, and John Pound. "Building Relationships with Major Shareholders: A Case Study of Lockheed." *Journal of Applied Corporate Finance* 6, no. 2 (1993):39–47.

Slunt, Joseph. "Survey of Risk Management Practices for Pension Funds." New York University Stern School of Business. Unpublished. Spring, 1995.

Smith, Michael P. "Shareholder Activism by Institutional Investors: Evidence from CalPERS." *Journal of Finance* 51, no. 1 (1996):227–252.

Smith, Roger F., and Thomas M. Richards. "Asset Mix and Investment Strategy." *Financial Analysts Journal* 32, no. 2 (1976):67–71.

Smithson, Charles. "Calculating and Using VAR." *Risk Magazine* 9, nos. 1 and 2 (1996).

Smithson, Charles. *Managing Financial Risk 1996 Yearbook.* New York: CIBC Wood Gundy, 1996.

Solnik, Bruno. *International Investments.* 3d ed. Reading, MA: Addison-Wesley, 1996.

Solnik, Bruno, Cyril Boucrelle, and Yann Le Fur. "International Market Correlation and Volatility." *Financial Analysts Journal* 52, no. 5 (1996):17–34.

Steiner, Robert. "Pension Problems May Curb Japan Stocks." *Wall Street Journal* (27 December 1995), p. 19.

Stickney, Clyde P. "Analyzing Post Retirement Benefit Disclosures." *Journal of Financial Statement Analysis* 1, no. 1 (1995):15–25.

Strickland, Dean, Kenneth Wiles, and Mark Zenner. "A Requiem for the USA: Is Small Shareholder Monitoring Effective?" *Journal of Financial Economics* 40, no. 2 (1996):319–338.

Tepper, Irwin. "Taxation and Corporate Pension Policy." *Journal of Finance* 36, no. 1 (1981):1–13.

"The Rise of Public Pension Funds." *Wall Street Journal* (April 16, 1995):A-15.

Thomas, Jacob K. "Corporate Taxes and Defined Benefit Pension Plans." *Journal of Accounting and Economics* 10, no. 3 (1988):199–237.

Thomas, James M. "Target Benefit Plans Blend Best of Both Worlds." *Pension World* 27, no. 5 (1991):16–17.

Tigue, Patricia. "Pension Obligation Bonds: Benefits and Risks." *Government Finance Review* 10, no. 2 (1994):30–32.

Treynor, Jack L. "How to Rate Management of Investment Funds." *Harvard Business Review* 43, no. 1 (1965):63–75.

Treynor, Jack L. "The Principles of Corporate Pension Finance." *Journal of Finance* 32, no. 2 (1977):627–638.

Treynor, Jack L., and Fischer Black. "How to Use Security Analysis to Improve Portfolio Selection." *Journal of Business* 46, no. 1 (1973):66–86.

Tversky, Amos. "The Psychology of Decision Making." In *Behavioral Finance and Decision Theory in Investment Management*, 2–6. Charlottesville, VA: AIMR, 1995.

U.S. General Accounting Office. "Leveraged Buy-Out Funds: Investments by Selected Pension Funds." Report to Congressional Requesters, 1989.

Venti, Steven, and David A. Wise. In *The Savings Effect of Tax Deferred Retirement Accounts: Evidence From SIPP*, edited by B.D. Bernheim and J.B. Shoven. Chicago: University of Chicago Press, 1991.

Wagner, Wayne H. "Defining and Measuring Trading Costs." *Execution Techniques, True Trading Costs and the Microstructure of Markets*, 15–23. Charlottesville, VA: AIMR, 1993.

Wahal, Sunil. "Pension Fund Activism and Firm Performance." *Journal of Financial and Quantitative Analysis* 31, no. 1 (1996):1–23.

Wardlow, Penelope S. "GASB's New Pensions Package." *Journal of Accountancy* 180, no. 1 (1995):56–58.

Watson, Ronald. "Does Targeting Investment Make Sense?" *Financial Management* 23, no. 4 (1994):69–74.

Watt, Lindsay. "Hybrid Plans Fit Evolving Workforce." *Pension Management* 32, no. 3 (1996):12–19.

Wayne, Leslie. "Where Playing the Stock Market is Really Risky." *New York Times* (1 May 1995).

Weinberg, Neil. "Votes Today, Taxes Tomorrow." *Forbes* 5 June 5 1995, 88–98.

White, Gerald I., Ashwinpaul C. Sondhi, and Dov Fried. *The Analysis and Use of Financial Statements*. New York: Wiley, 1994.

Williams, Gordon. "The Trouble with T-Bills." *Financial World* 164, no. 16 (1995):80–82.

Williams, Arthur III. *Managing Your Investment Manager*. 3d ed. Homewood, IL: Business One Irwin, 1992.

Wood, Arnold S. "Behavioral Finance and Decision Theory in Investment Management: An Overview." In *Behavioral Finance and Decision Theory in Investment Management*, 1. Charlottesville, VA: AIMR, 1995.

Zorn, Paul. *Public Pension Coordinating Council 1995 Survey*. Chicago: Government Finance Officers Association Pension and Benefits Center, 1995.

Index

About the Authors

Dennis E. Logue is the Steven Roth Professor of Management at the Amos Tuck School of Business Administration at Dartmouth College, where his current research topics include corporate finance, governance, and international finance. Dennis holds an M.B.A. from Rutgers University and Ph.D. in managerial accounting from Cornell University. He is the editor and author of many books and monographs, including *Managing Corporate Pension Plans* (1991), *The Investment Performance of Corporate Pension Plans* (1988), and *Managing Corporate Pension Plans: The Impacts of Inflation* (1984).

Jack S. Rader is the executive director of the Financial Management Association (FMA), the largest academic finance institution in the world, as well as an adjunct professor in the finance department of the University of South Florida, where he teaches courses on security analysis, portfolio management, strategic and financial planning, and valuation and risk management. Jack holds a B.S. in management science from the University of Tennessee and an M.B.A. from the University of South Florida. He is the editor of *Careers in Finance* (1990), a contributing author to the *AMA Management Handbook* (3d ed.), and the editor of the FMA's *Financial Management Collection*.